# AARON COPLAND
*in Latin America*

**MUSIC IN AMERICAN LIFE**

*A list of books in the series appears at the end of this book.*

# AARON COPLAND
## *in Latin America*

## MUSIC AND CULTURAL POLITICS

CAROL A. HESS

UNIVERSITY OF
ILLINOIS PRESS
Urbana, Chicago, and Springfield

Supplemental material can be found at the University of Illinois Press website and accessed through the webpage for the book.

Publication of this book was supported by grants from the Iberian and Latin American Music Fund and the General Publications Fund of the American Musicological Society, supported in part by the National Endowment for the Humanities and the Andrew W. Mellon Foundation, and from the Henry and Edna Binkele Classical Music Fund.

Published with support from the UCD Office of Research and Letters & Science Dean's Office.

Some of the material in this book has been previously published: portions of "Copland in Argentina: Pan Americanist Politics, Folklore, and the Crisis of Modern Music," *Journal of the American Musicological Society*, 66 no. 1 (2013): 191–25 appear in chapters 5, 9, and 11 and portions of *Representing the Good Neighbor: Music, Difference, and the Pan American Dream* (New York: Oxford University Press, 2013) in chapters 3 and 10.

© 2023 by the Board of Trustees
of the University of Illinois
All rights reserved
1 2 3 4 5 C P 5 4 3 2 1
♾ This book is printed on acid-free paper.

Library of Congress Cataloging-in-Publication Data
Names: Hess, Carol A, author.
Title: Aaron Copland in Latin America : music and cultural politics / Carol A Hess.
Description: Urbana : University of Illinois Press, 2022. | Series: Music in American life | Includes bibliographical references and index.
Identifiers: LCCN 2022034822 (print) | LCCN 2022034823 (ebook) | ISBN 9780252044854 (hardback) | ISBN 9780252086953 (paperback) | ISBN 9780252054006 (ebook)
Subjects: LCSH: Copland, Aaron, 1900–1990—Travel—Latin America. | Music and diplomacy—Latin America—History—20th century. | Cultural diplomacy—Latin America—History—20th century. | Pan-Americanism—History—20th century.
| BISAC: MUSIC / Genres & Styles / Classical | BIOGRAPHY & AUTOBIOGRAPHY / Music
Classification: LCC ML410.C756 H47 2022 (print) | LCC ML410.C756 (ebook) | DDC 780.92—dc23/eng/20220725
LC record available at https://lccn.loc.gov/2022034822
LC ebook record available at https://lccn.loc.gov/2022034823

To Richard Taruskin (1945–2022)
In memoriam

# Contents

Acknowledgments  ix

Editorial Note  xiii

### PART I. A CITIZEN DIPLOMAT PREPARES

1  Introduction  3

2  Copland and the Beginnings of U.S. Cultural Diplomacy  13

3  Copland as Good Neighbor  32

### PART II. COPLAND, LATIN AMERICA, AND WORLD WAR II

4  Diplomat "in the Field"  57

5  Copland in Argentina  76

6  Copland in Brazil  92

7  Copland in Chile  107

8  The Americas at War  121

### PART III. COPLAND, LATIN AMERICA, AND THE POSTWAR

9  The Early Cold War  153

10  Shifting Ground and the Crisis of Modernism  187

11  The Sixties   207
12  Latin American Classical Music and Memory   238

Notes   255
Recommended Reading   301
Index   305

# Acknowledgments

One of the best parts of working on a long-term writing project is thanking the many people who helped make it possible. First, I am grateful to Laurie Mattheson of the University of Illinois Press for her diplomacy, good humor, and practical suggestions. I also thank the two anonymous readers of the manuscript. Similarly willing to share their insights were several colleagues and friends: Kevin Bartig, Howard Pollack, Jennifer DeLapp-Birkett, Danielle Fosler-Lussier, Emily Abrams Ansari, Eric Chasalow, Annegret Fauser, Mather Pfeiffenberger, Ricardo Lorenz, Lydia Hammesley, and Alyssa Cottle. I am equally grateful for informal conversations with Mark Katz on cultural diplomacy, an area in which he has accumulated so much real-world experience. I also thank the leaders in Latin American musical scholarship, an area of study that seemed precarious only a few decades ago but which is now thriving thanks to the vision and tenacity of Walter Aaron Clark, Grayson Wagstaff, William J. Summers, John Koegel, Craig Russell, Drew Edward Davies, Leonora Saavedra, Rogerio Budasz, Eduardo Herrera, Alejandro Madrid, Jacqueline Ávila, Susan Thomas, Ana Alonso-Minutti, Deborah Schwartz-Kates, Cristina Magaldi, Edgardo Raúl Salinas, and many others, including several newly minted PhDs who are putting their own stamp on the field.

At the University of California, Davis, where I have the great satisfaction of being employed, colleagues and friends have been as encouraging as anyone could wish. Leo Bernucci answered my many questions on Portuguese translation; Juan Diego Díaz has been similarly helpful with Spanish. Milton

Azevedo of the University of California, Berkeley, gave valuable translation advice. Also at Davis, Christopher A. Reynolds, Jessie Ann Owens, Pierpaolo Polzonetti, Esther Delozier, Gail Finney, Naomi Janowitz, and Molly McCarthy shed light on various iterations of this project. Others less involved with the manuscript but who have patiently listened to me rattle on about Copland in recent years include Kurt Rohde, Beth E. Levy, D. Kern Holoman, Pablo Ortiz, Phebe Craig, Amelia Triest, Rhio Barnhart, Laurie San Martin, Sam Nichols, Mika Pelo, Henry Spiller, Chris Castro, and Rebecca Plack. Of course, any errors are my own.

The University of California, Davis has also been generous with funding. In 2018 I received a New Research Initiatives and Interdisciplinary Research Grant, which, in combination with a summer stipend from the National Endowment for the Humanities, enabled me to visit several archives. My main base of operation was the Aaron Copland Collection of the Library of Congress, where the staff of the Performing Arts Reading Room proved helpful in every way, especially Paul Sommerfeld. So, too, were George Boziwick, Jonathan Hiam, and Danielle Cordovez of the Library for the Performing Arts of the New York Public Library. Gary Galván of the Free Library of Philadelphia offered his firsthand knowledge of the collection of Latin American orchestral scores housed in that institution. Geoffrey Stark and Misha McQuillen of the Special Collections Reading Room at the University of Arkansas, Fayetteville, were similarly attentive, as was the staff of the National Archives and Records Administration in College Park, Maryland. I am also grateful to Julie McMaster of the Archives of the Toledo (Ohio) Museum of Art and Stephen Howes of the Cummington Historical Commission (Cummington, Massachusetts). Thanks to Marie Labonville, who kindly provided me with copies of clippings from the Archivo Juan Bautista Plaza (Caracas), I was able to delve into the Venezuelan press of the 1950s.

I am blessed with warm and generous colleagues in Latin America. In Buenos Aires, Argentina, Valería Cancer of the Instituto Torcuato Di Tella archives made available to me correspondence between Copland and Alberto Ginastera. Historians Andrea Matallana and Romina Dezillio suggested fascinating angles to explore, just as Argentine musicologists Omar Corrado, Hernán Vázquez, and Laura Novoa have shared with me their knowledge of Argentine music in Copland's era. As always, Silvia Glocer of the Biblioteca Nacional (Buenos Aires) accessed sources in ways not necessarily self-evident to the foreign traveler. In Bogotá, Colombia, Gisela Cramer and Egberto Bermúdez gave me much food for thought. In Santiago, Chile, Cecilia Astudillo Rojas of the

Biblioteca Nacional helped with documentation, and I especially treasure my experience at the Universidad Alberto Hurtado (Santiago), where I taught a graduate seminar, "Música y diplomacia cultural," in 2019. There I was able to try out many of the ideas in this book, thanks to a lively group of students and to faculty members Daniela Fugielle Videla, Juan Carlos Poveda, and especially Juan Pablo González, who coordinated my visit. I met many of these remarkable people thanks to the Fulbright program, one of U.S. cultural diplomacy's primary achievements and of which I have twice been a beneficiary.

Meeting composers who remembered Copland (or his Latin American colleagues) has been especially stimulating: Mario Davidovsky, Graciela Paraskevaídis, Mesías Maiguashca, León Schidlowsky, and alcides lanza all offered their experiences. I especially enjoyed conversing with Henry Raymont of Washington, DC, a journalist who covered Latin America but had previously studied music at the Juilliard School and Indiana University. (He would later remark that he was the first to report on the Cuban missile crisis and the last to believe it had actually happened.) In 1947 a young Mr. Raymont attended Copland's rehearsals at the Teatro Colón in Buenos Aires. He also took long walks along the Calle Florida with the composer, who confided to Raymont his worries over increasing restrictions of civil liberties in the United States. For Copland, these came to a head in 1953 when he confronted U.S. Senator Joseph McCarthy in a congressional hearing.

During my Copland-related travels I have greatly appreciated the hospitality of many friends. David and Betsy Hawkings (Washington, DC), Cristina Magaldi (Potomac, Maryland), Silvia Glocer (Buenos Aires), Lynn Carter (New York City), Laurinel Owen (Bellport, New York), and my cousin Nancy Meneses Hess (Bogotá) all opened their homes to me. Local friends are just as important: every Tuesday, our little group gets together for supper, either live or, during the pandemic, via Zoom. In whatever medium, I am deeply gratified to know Xiaomei Chen, Gail Finney, Juliana Schiesari, Maureen King, Linda Mattheson, Jim Adams, and Bill Corliss. Milton Azevedo, whom I have known for four decades, is a steady source of friendship and good humor. I am especially grateful to Dorothy Weicker, who encouraged me at the beginning of my career and whose friendship I cherish these many years later.

As always, my family—lively, loving, eccentric, and fun—has always been my principal support system. I can never thank them enough for all that they do for me each day, directly and indirectly.

# Editorial Note

All translations are mine unless otherwise indicated. For endnotes from sources that might prove difficult to track down in a good research library, I provide the original language on the website for the appendixes and other support material of this book.

In recent years, scholars and the general public have debated the use of "American" versus "U.S." This debate centers on the fact that many inhabitants of the Americas are citizens of countries other than the United States, some of whom identify as Americans and resent the appropriation of that term by the United States. In English, we lack an adjective that denotes "of the United States," as in *"estadounidense"* (Spanish) or *"estadunidense"* (Portuguese). Further complicating the matter is the prevalence of the term *"norteamericano"* (North American) in the Latin American press of the period covered in this book. It is almost always used to mean "of the United States"; indeed, one sees it only rarely in reference to other parts of North America, such as Canada or Mexico. For all these reasons, I use "U.S" to refer to "of the United States" and translate *"norteamericano/a"* as "U.S."

Names of institutions, ensembles, and compositions are given in the original language. When necessary, I translate titles, as in *Del Terruño* (From the Homeland) by Guillermo Uribe-Holguín.

In proper names I use diacriticals except when the individual in question does not.

# AARON COPLAND
*in Latin America*

# PART I
# A Citizen Diplomat Prepares

# 1
# Introduction

"I was very tired, and not reacting very fast." So observed Aaron Copland in his travel diary on 29 October 1947. He had just attended an especially grueling reception at the American Embassy in Montevideo, Uruguay, part of his second U.S. State Department–sponsored tour of Latin America. Copland's host, ambassador O. Ellis Briggs, was pleasant enough company. (Copland described him as "a better Groucho Marx.") But the composer's innate good humor was sometimes tested at such events. Exhausted from making small talk with people he would likely never see again, he confided to his diary, "Standing up for three hours and shaking hands with eighty people is not much fun."[1]

Why was the Brooklyn-born composer of *Music for the Theatre* and *Appalachian Spring* exerting himself so far from home? The short answer is that Copland was serving his country as a cultural diplomat, one of a phalanx of citizen or "amateur" diplomats.[2] Such individuals lend their talents to their governments to enhance international relations, despite lack of training in government or diplomacy. In other words, they practice cultural diplomacy: the exchange of art, research, and ideas across national boundaries.[3] In the United States, cultural diplomacy was in private hands until the administration of Franklin D. Roosevelt, when the government took it on.[4]

The more complete explanation for Copland's presence in Latin America involves Pan Americanism, a loose assortment of economic, political, and cultural objectives that rests on the premise that the Americas have much in common. For example, Americans (residents of the Americas) toppled

European colonial power and sustained democracy through constitutional governments.[5] Presumably the Americas share a common sensibility, giving rise to what one of Copland's contemporaries called "the Western Hemisphere idea."[6] In Copland's day, this sensibility—of dynamism, vitality, and what many called "freshness"—suggested the enticing metaphor of a tabula rasa on which new histories would be written and new cultures would take root.[7]

Nowadays we recognized that the mere notion of "newness" is profoundly Eurocentric, like the label "New World": as the musicologist Gary Tomlinson pointedly asks, "new to whom?"[8] Further, Pan Americanism began not as an exercise in spiritual bonding but in commerce, with the founding of the Bureau of American Republics in 1890 (later the Pan American Union) in Washington, DC. Whatever the shared optimism over a common commercial zone, memories of the U.S.-Mexican War (1846–48) were still vivid, as were other incursions by the "Colossus of the North." Subsequent conflicts, including the Spanish-American War (1898), interventions in Colombia (1903), Nicaragua (1912–33), Haiti (1915–34), Mexico (1914), and the Dominican Republic (1916–24), all eroded Pan Americanist ideals, as did dollar diplomacy and exploitation of cheap Latin American labor by U.S. business.[9]

Yet even in the face of these tensions, the Pan American Union increasingly reached beyond commerce. Cultural events included concerts, presented from the 1920s on and often by Latin American artists.[10] Also, a series of Inter-American Conferences promoted scientific and educational exchange.[11] At the sixth such conference, in Havana in 1928, the Coolidge administration felt obliged to counter the United States' reputation as a "ruthless giant, without conscience and with unrestrained lust."[12] On a more positive note, President Herbert Hoover signed into law Pan American Day, first celebrated on 14 April 1931 and still observed.[13] Hoover also hinted at cultural diplomacy, declaring in Rio de Janeiro that "the development of literature, art, music, and the drama . . . make for increasing satisfaction, and nobility amongst men."[14] But the stock market crash of 1929 and the ravages of the Great Depression left little appetite for such objectives and by March 1933, with Hitler now in power, the sense of calamity had grown. This was the backdrop for Copland's debut as a cultural diplomat in Latin America.

## Pan Americanism and U.S. Cultural Diplomacy

Axis propagandists now spread their message to citizens of the Americas through radio, the press, and person-to-person contact.[15] As European fascism threatened the hemisphere, the Roosevelt administration swiftly repackaged

Pan Americanism as the Good Neighbor Policy. In his first inaugural address, the president famously asserted, "We have nothing to fear but fear itself." But he also outlined his concept of the good neighbor: one "who resolutely respects himself . . . who respects his obligations and respects the sanctity of his agreements in and with a world of neighbors."[16] A few weeks later, at the Pan American Union, Roosevelt elaborated, declaring that "true Pan Americanism" depended on the very qualities of "a good neighbor, namely, mutual understanding . . . of the other's point of view."[17] Concrete policy changes followed. In December 1933, at the seventh Inter-American Conference, in Montevideo, U.S. Secretary of State Cordell Hull announced that the United States would renounce military interventionism in the region. In 1936 Roosevelt himself, who proposed and then attended the Pan American Conference for the Maintenance of Peace, was cheered on the streets of Buenos Aires, and images of enthusiastic crowds circulated in the media.[18]

Cultural diplomacy would be a weapon against the Axis. At the 1936 conference, for example, the Buenos Aires Convention for the Promotion of Inter-American Cultural Relations was crafted, initially a university exchange program.[19] Back home (and in tandem with the New Deal) the idea of government-sponsored cultural diplomacy also gained ground, with Latin America as a testing ground. By 1938, when the Division of Cultural Relations was established under the State Department, the foundations had been laid. Its ideals—of a Western Hemisphere cultural identity—seemed to blend perfectly with Copland's own artistic goals. Since returning from study in France in the mid-1920s, he had been seeking a musical voice distinct from that of Europe. Such music, he believed, would evince dynamism, energy, and that ineffable "freshness." In 1941, when war had overtaken Europe, Copland made his first official visit to Latin America.

But Copland was also called upon after the Allied victory. During the Cold War, U.S. cultural diplomacy expanded dramatically, now with the Soviet Union and its satellites the main targets. Latin America no longer enjoyed a special relationship with the United States but was subsumed into a global scheme, relegated to the status of "underdeveloped" with Asia and Africa, all susceptible to communism. Worse, the United States both resumed interventionism in Latin America (Guatemala, 1953; the Dominican Republic, 1965; Chile, 1973) and supported anticommunist military regimes. Not surprisingly, many Latin Americans concluded that the entire Good Neighbor project had been insincere. U.S. cultural diplomacy in the region soldiered on, however, just as a variety of new musical approaches were taking hold worldwide. During his final tours in Latin America, in 1962 and 1963, Copland faced these realities.

During the Cold War, Copland also practiced cultural diplomacy in many other countries, reflecting his commitment to global peace.[20] Various musicologists have researched Copland's travels in Europe, the Soviet Union, and Asia, complementing the spate of studies completed since the centenary of his birth, in 2000, in which scholars investigated his homosexuality, Jewishness, stylistic eclecticism, conflict-ridden negotiation of modernist and populist aesthetics, and his politics, including his confrontation with U.S. Senator Joseph McCarthy and the House Un-American Activities Committee (HUAC).[21] As discussed below, however, little has been written on Copland's government-sponsored tours to Latin America, which took place in 1941, 1947, 1962, and 1963, spanning the critical period just outlined.

## Copland's Cultural Diplomacy in Latin America: Overview

In 1976, at the height of the Cold War, the historian J. Manuel Espinosa lamented that the origins of U.S.–Latin American cultural diplomacy were "almost a forgotten aspect in the history of U.S. foreign relations."[22] By now, several scholars have explored this "forgotten" phenomenon.[23] But the fact that a distinguished expert such as Espinosa would gently hint at collective amnesia with respect to Latin America is well worth examining, including in musical terms. For the past twenty-five years or so, musicologists have been analyzing the role of music in cultural diplomacy, focusing mainly on the Cold War and the East-West divide.[24] Latin America has commanded less attention.[25]

Most scholars who address Copland's cultural diplomacy in Latin America have concentrated on Mexico.[26] Thanks to Robert L. Parker and Leonora Saavedra, we know a great deal about his friendship with the Mexican composer Carlos Chávez.[27] Other scholars consider *El salón México*, a fruit of his 1932 (unofficial) visit to Mexico in which Copland quotes fragments of Mexican folk tunes, a format he described as a "modified potpourri" and which also heralded his rejection of aggressive modernism.[28] Yet Copland's Latin American experience took him to eight other countries besides Mexico. In addition to Chávez, he befriended Domingo Santa Cruz (Chile); Mozart Camargo Guarnieri (Brazil); Alberto Ginastera, Juan José Castro, José María Castro, and Mario Davidovsky (Argentina), all of whom shared with him their own perspectives on Latin American music. Also, Copland's music was reviewed by several distinguished Latin American critics (some of whom were also composers): Juan Carlos Paz, Albert Ginastera, Carlos Suffern, Leopoldo Hurtado, Daniel Devoto,

Jorge D'Urbano, Adolfo Salazar, Juan Orrego-Salas, Federico Heinlein, Alejo Carpentier, Francisco Curt Lange, Pablo Mañé Garzón, and Eurico Nogueira França.

It is also important to address certain misconceptions. One is the notion that musical Pan Americanism was fundamentally isolationist.[29] It is undeniable that the United States retreated from the world stage during the 1920s and 1930s.[30] Pan Americanism itself, musical or otherwise, was anything but isolationist, however. One goal of the Good Neighbor Policy was to persuade U.S. Americans to *broaden* their worldview by giving the occasional thought to Latin America, the history and culture of which are habitually overlooked even today. As a prominent U.S. historian once observed, many of his colleagues "couldn't be sure of spelling Ecuador correctly or be quite sound on the question of whether Chihuahua is north or south of Tierra del Fuego."[31] Similarly, few U.S. Americans *listen* to Latin America, at least to its classical music. However attractive the "Latin" ballroom dances of the 1920s and 1930s or recent popular genres, such as salsa and *hip hop en español*, Latin American classical music is largely marginalized by the recording industry, concert life, and postsecondary music programs in the United States.[32] Part of Copland's assignment as a cultural diplomat was to familiarize himself with this repertory, or "serious music," as he called it. At home, he alerted his compatriots to the mere fact that it existed. In Latin America, he introduced works by U.S. composers, including his own, to the publics of Rio de Janeiro, Bogotá, or Lima.

## Methodology, Sources, and Orientation

This book covers Copland's four government-sponsored trips to Latin America. (I also refer briefly to two privately funded visits to Venezuela during the 1950s, which exemplify some of the issues just mentioned.) It grew out of my 2013 study, *Representing the Good Neighbor: Music, Difference, and the Pan American Dream*, in which I analyzed discourse on Latin American classical music by U.S. critics from the 1920s to the height of the Cold War. Initially, I planned to counteract this decidedly U.S. perspective by including a chapter on Copland in Latin America and interpreting Latin American reactions to his music. After encountering hundreds of Spanish- and Portuguese-language press reports, either at the Aaron Copland Collection at the Library of Congress or in Latin American archives, I realized that a separate study was in order.

Many of these press reports are reviews of Copland's music, although others are interviews with the composer or reports on his activities, including his numerous lectures. Since his visits took place in some charged political circumstances—U.S. interventionism and cultural imperialism but also genuine attempts at righting wrongs—I have striven to contextualize readerships, that is, to identify a paper as Nazi-funded, left-leaning, Catholic, U.S.-friendly, middle-of-the-road, or blatantly anti-Semitic. I also try to weigh the background, training, and aesthetic or political leanings of Copland's critics, all with the goal of including Latin Americans in the reception of Copland's music as much as possible. To be sure, fluency in Spanish and Portuguese hardly entitles me to represent Latin Americans. Throughout, I have endeavored to let these critics to speak for themselves as much as possible.

I am well aware of the problems posed by press analysis, in which a quotation or a headline (equivalent to the sound bite), is saddled with distilling complex ideas. But at least for the present, these press sources are what we have. Moreover, they lend credence to the idea that cultural diplomacy is invariably a performance, whether in brash assertions by propagandist George Creel during World War I or in the meticulously staged television appearances of later years.[33] The question becomes an epistemological one: is it better to know imperfectly or not at all? I have opted to "see through a glass darkly." Other sources on which I draw include Copland's correspondence with Latin American musicians, his lecture notes, and scripts for his radio broadcasts. In addition, I have had the good fortune to interview (or correspond with) a handful of Latin American composers who either knew or worked with Copland: Graciela Paraskevaídis, Mario Davidovsky, alcides lanza (who lowercases his name), Mesías Maiguashca, and León Schidlowsky.

I also rely on Copland's travel diaries. Well-known diarists, such as Anaïs Nin, Anne Frank, Franz Kafka, or Virginia Woolf, kept diaries for any number of reasons. More often than not, Copland's served as the basis for his future writings, whether articles, essays, or reports for the State Department. Mainly, the diaries enumerate his activities, verifying the passage of time while leaving behind a bare-bones record of his experience. As such, they exude an antinarrative quality that one scholar calls "dailiness, the act of writing *in* the days rather than *of* the days."[34] This "dailiness" affords new insight into Copland's biography, shedding light on the routine that lies behind cultural diplomacy's lofty goals and on the extent to which the composer coordinated the pace and nature of his activities. For a backdrop to these activities, I also consulted government documents on cultural diplomacy housed at the National Records and Archives Administration in College Park, Maryland, and at the Library of the University of Arkansas, Fayetteville (Special Collections). Besides outlining broad intentions, these documents reveal fissures in policy, expose bureaucratic headaches, and offer glimpses of some of the big-picture societal issues cultural diplomats confronted, such as racism.

Throughout this book, I ask, "Who was Copland?" Despite the abundance of recent scholarship—not to mention our sheer familiarity with his music, whether heard in concert halls or television commercials—Copland continues to mystify. In Latin America, he tenaciously promoted folkloric "Western hemisphere" music and with few exceptions, criticized Latin American composers he believed were too indebted to Europe. Yet he resisted the label "nationalist" and inched only slowly toward "universalism," a concept he never satisfactorily defined.[35] At least initially, he was opposed to serialism in Latin America, believing it was incompatible with what he termed "the Latin American temperament." This conclusion was one of Copland's lapses into essentialism, that is, the notion that certain groups of people are biologically predisposed to specific behaviors, perhaps surprising to those who have uncritically accepted Copland's status as the affable face of musical Pan Americanism.[36] Yet by 1954, buffeted by political and aesthetic headwinds at home and having ventured into serialism himself, Copland complained that the Latin American works he heard at a festival in Caracas sounded "too Latin American!" and urged composers of the region to try twelve-tone composition. Ultimately, he determined that the musical public was divided: back in Venezuela in 1957, he compared a violin concerto (or "Ballad Concerto," as he called it) he was then sketching out to the complex Piano Fantasy, completed that year, quietly observing in his travel diary, "The works are likely to appeal to two different publics."[37] Whether such a position reflects aesthetic waffling or innate flexibility was a subject of debate among both U.S. and Latin American critics. It is not too much to say that Copland's cultural diplomacy tells us more about him than about an "Othered" Latin America.

## On the Job in Latin America

Was Copland expected to exercise what Joseph Nye Jr. has described as "soft power," that is, to achieve a desired goal without arm-twisting?[38] The composer would likely have bristled at the term "power," which presupposes manipulation if not outright domination. Yet challenges arise when music is the means of persuasion. An ostensibly nonrepresentational art lacking in explicit meaning, music might seem a "safe" or at least neutral vehicle for cultural exchange. Copland's experience confirms, however, that listeners are perfectly willing to attach meaning to musical works, meanings that can vary widely from one constituency or nation to another. In relationships of unequal political and economic power, such as that between the United States and Latin America, political fault lines can surface. Further, like "winning friends and influencing people," music could be seen as strategy oriented rather than sincere, or even as an offshoot of U.S. consumerism.[39] As Copland discovered, the adage "music is the universal language" is tested whenever musicians take up the day-to-day duties of cultural diplomacy.

Those duties are considerable. Copland's advance work consisted of confirming schedules, negotiating compensation, and arranging travel, sometimes with secretarial help. For some trips, he received study materials from the State Department, which, to judge from his annotations, he read. He also corresponded with CAOs (cultural affairs officers) and other embassy personnel who would inquire as to his availability for social gatherings at embassies, consulates, government centers, or local musical and civic institutions. Sometimes agents, orchestra directors, or others in the musical community failed to communicate promptly on rehearsal schedules or on the holdings in Latin American orchestra libraries. When this happened, he worried that too many details were being left to the last minute and that his performances would suffer. Occasionally they did.

There were also Copland's lectures. He presented most of them in Spanish, which he spoke reasonably well in 1941 but did not practice much thereafter. (He could pronounce Portuguese but did not speak it unless scripted.) He always tried to complete his lectures before leaving home, often recycling his own writings. When he fell behind, however, he had to isolate himself in his hotel room and forego the attractions of Rio de Janeiro or Buenos Aires. Also, anyone who has lectured in Latin America, especially in universities, knows that the speaker may be expected to perorate for hours and that the specter of the question-and-answer session looms throughout: invariably an attendee will ask a question utterly incomprehensible to the speaker, leaving them to flounder or await rescue by a true bilingual. When Edward Purcell, the cultural affairs officer of the American Embassy in Montevideo asked Copland in 1962, "Can you tell me something of your ability to answer questions from the floor in Spanish?" Purcell undoubtedly had this situation in mind.[40] Copland's radio broadcasts were only slightly less labor intensive. It was his good fortune that they took place before the advent of call-in programs.

Travel itself could be stressful, especially in the 1940s, when a flight from New York to Mexico City involved a layover in Texas. In that era before luggage wheels, Copland often transported books, scores, and records, either for local musicians or for his own use in his lectures and broadcasts. Unfamiliar food and the time difference between various countries sometimes took their toll. He also had to reserve a certain amount of energy for performing, either at the podium or at the piano. As noted, social events could be tiring. In Rio de Janeiro in 1947 he wrote in his diary, "A diplomatic party such as one might expect—DULL." On other occasions, Copland had to attend concerts by local amateurs, such as one in Fortaleza, Brazil, that he described as "god-awful." Upon returning home, he was expected to spend several days in Washington for "debriefing" with State Department officials.

## A Diplomat's Background: Character and Experience

Copland possessed several personal qualities fundamental to his success as a citizen diplomat: receptivity to other cultures, tact, and curiosity about the world. As the youngest of five children of Jewish-Russian immigrants, he was raised in a multiethnic community in Brooklyn. Although he made his bar mitzvah, and his family was observant, a sense of community mattered to him far more than religious dogma.[41] Copland neither drew particular attention to his Jewish background nor played it down; at one point, he became interested in Eastern religions and sometimes would enjoy a special meal with friends on Christmas Day. As a gay man in an era when homosexuality was illegal, he accepted—and even celebrated—himself and his various companions while behaving with the necessary discretion.[42] As for tact, Copland generally knew when to keep quiet. Able to take a balanced view of both positive and negative aspects of a given situation, he resisted simplistic, either-or thinking. Circumspect in public and encouraging to young Latin American composers, he nonetheless registered in his diary any number of complaints about the music he heard, often rather stridently.[43] Likely he did so with the expectation of privacy. If these expectations seem to be violated in this book, it would not be for the first time, since occasionally Copland himself went public with some of his reservations. In fact, we learn a great deal from comparing his judgments with those of others involved in musical Pan Americanism, many of whom arrived at very different conclusions about Latin American classical music than he.

Copland's curiosity about the world took him to France in 1921, when he began studying at the newly founded Conservatoire Américain in Fontainebleau. The school itself was essentially a cultural diplomacy project: in 1918 U.S. General John Pershing sought to improve the performance of military bands through French methods of musical instruction, and by 1921 the school had expanded beyond band training to offer talented men and women, many from the United States, the solid training they had once automatically sought in Germany.[44] Copland's composition teacher there, Nadia Boulanger, was still largely unknown in that male-dominated field.[45] Another landmark of that period was the American Library, established in Paris and the first of its kind.[46] As detailed below, libraries would come to mean a great deal to Copland the citizen diplomat.

Once home from France, Copland recommended travel, urging his compatriots to seek out new "people to meet, customs and morals so different from our own to be observed."[47] Copland may have entered cultural diplomacy for practical reasons as well. Early on, he likely believed it would advance his career. In 1941 he may have appreciated the financial compensation, although by the 1950s, when he was making a comfortable $25,000 a year, he had no such needs.[48] As one who feared entrapment in the ivory tower, Copland often expressed hope that his music might do some social good, a goal cultural diplomacy could fulfill.[49] In his later years, cultural diplomacy filled a different need. As is well known, from around 1960, Copland began composing less. Ideas came to him only haltingly: he once made the chilling confession that it was "as if someone had simply turned off a faucet."[50] During the 1960s and 1970s Copland continued traveling, conducting, teaching, and engaging in the person-to-person interactions to which he was so naturally suited.[51] As is also well known, by the 1980s dementia began to dull his once-lively mind.

Throughout his career, Copland was motivated by sheer faith in cultural diplomacy's aims, especially the idea that peaceful relations in the arts could serve as a model for world peace. Having launched his citizen diplomacy in Latin America, he returned there even in times of political strife, forging ties with Latin American musicians and helping them in their careers. Not for nothing did the Chilean composer Juan Orrego-Salas declare that Copland's interest in Latin America went beyond "just a Good Neighbor policy."[52] Despite some missteps, Copland's efforts in Latin America are a tribute both to his psychological resilience and his commitment to world peace. They also serve as an example for the present, when the role of the U.S. State Department—and indeed, the place of the United States in the world—spark heated and often partisan debate. For these reasons, I hope that this book sheds new light on Copland's biography and the reception of his music worldwide. I also hope it will awaken interest in Latin American classical music, a repertory for which Copland's experiences are an ideal means of engagement.

# 2
# Copland and the Beginnings of U.S. Cultural Diplomacy

In October 1935 the New School for Social Research initiated a series of "one-man" concerts to showcase music by U.S. composers.[1] Copland, who had lectured intermittently at the school since 1927, was the first to test the idea. The audience listened to his *Symphonic Ode*, arranged for two pianos; *Vitebsk (Study on a Jewish Theme)*, for piano trio; the Piano Variations; and *As It Fell upon a Day* for soprano, flute, and clarinet, all familiar to the public.[2] Also featured was a new work, *El salón México*, arranged for two pianos by John Kirkpatrick, who performed with Copland that evening.[3] The press barely covered the event. An unidentified critic for the *New York Times* took note of several details, however.[4] One was "the modernist circles in which Mr. Copland's music chiefly has its being." Another was the notion that "Mr. Copland has not been a musician of the weathercock variety," an opinion that effectively bypasses charges of the composer's eclecticism then circulating. The same critic also observed that despite a "brief dalliance with jazz [Copland] . . . had a logical development along lines of his own choosing." As for *El salón México*, it seemed prudent to withhold judgment and await the orchestral version. The anonymous critic did, however, suggest that the folkloric work might well portend a quest for "full-blooded musical appeal for the broader public."[5]

These pithy reactions all relate to Copland's cultural diplomacy in Latin America. Most obvious is his attraction to Mexico, which he first visited in 1932. In Latin America, Copland would also be obliged to explain his "dalliance" with jazz and to withstand charges of "weathercock" eclecticism. At various points, he would also offer "full-blooded musical appeal" to a broad public. This chapter details ways in which these issues played out at this critical stage of Copland's career, laying the groundwork for his experiences in Latin America. It also surveys the initial stages of U.S. cultural diplomacy as Copland encountered it during the Good Neighbor period.

## Looking South: "A new world with its own new music"

When Copland returned from France in 1924, the United States was a different country from the one he had left three years earlier. Restrictive immigration acts ensured that his native land was open only to those deemed "true Americans" (Anglo-Saxons), who would safeguard cultural homogeneity in the United States.[6] Surely aware of this shift, Copland set about establishing himself in New York where he taught a bit, published articles, and assumed leadership roles in various organizations, especially the League of Composers.[7] These efforts paid off. In 1925 Copland became the first composer to receive a Guggenheim Fellowship. The same year also saw the premiere of his Organ Symphony, which Boulanger performed. During her visit, she speculated about a U.S. school of composition, a project she deemed entirely within reach.[8] Copland, increasingly well situated to help realize this objective, committed himself to defining a musical voice that distinguished itself from its European roots. Decades later, he recalled his goal: to "speak of universal things in a vernacular of American speech rhythms."[9]

Copland was all for promoting musical identity. But as Martin Brody points out, he never fully resolved the "dialectical opposition" between the national ("American vernacular") and the universal.[10] Over history, nationalism and universalism were not necessarily incompatible: in the nineteenth century, for example, it was perfectly possible that music by a nationalist composer could be so compelling as to achieve universality.[11] Copland, however, was bent on modernism, not hewing to some romantic-era model. He also struggled with the fact that in the Americas, universalism was often pegged to the European canon, with elites upholding a body of received masterworks as culturally legitimizing. Especially in Latin America, this repertory could help counter the taint of parochialism or backwardness, such that the concept could be fraught with tensions over identity, power, and geopolitics.[12] As Copland's compatriots narrowed their sights as to who "true Americans" were, many in artistic and intellectual circles were uncertain about identity. One music critic, for example, expressed horror at "greaser ditties."[13] Others, however, rejected the very notion of Anglo-Saxon roots: in 1922 the author Harold Stearns asserted, "Whatever else [U.S.] civilization is, it is not Anglo-Saxon."[14] Still others looked southward. Waldo Frank, Copland's left-leaning colleague at the New School, excoriated the Anglo-Saxon, Protestant, materialistic United States and rhapsodized over the "wholeness" to be achieved through a spiritual union of the Americas.[15]

Copland too began to discover Latin America. In Paris he had visited the Brazilian composer Heitor Villa-Lobos, who showed him his collection of percussion instruments.[16] Chávez, whom Copland probably met in New York in late 1926, was more of a kindred spirit, and both composers promoted one another's music. On 22 April 1928 Chávez's third piano sonata and his three sonatinas (for solo piano, cello and piano, violin and piano) figured in the Copland-Sessions Concerts, the series Copland founded with his colleague Roger Sessions.[17] Chávez's timing was perfect: New York was in the midst of what one journalist called an "enormous vogue of things Mexican," thanks to which interest in Mexican culture was running high, especially in artistic circles.[18] Due in part to Abby Aldrich Rockefeller, who declared Mexico "the most paintable country" she had ever seen, exhibits of ancient Mexican art or recent works by Diego Rivera drew crowds in various U.S. cities during the 1920s and early 1930s, as Aztec-themed fundraisers united various constituencies.[19] Several critics covered the all-Chávez concert, among them the effusive Paul Rosenfeld. In a breathless paean to the "authentic expressive values" inherent in Chávez's music, Rosenfeld averred that Chávez's works "make us feel America."[20] Clearly "America" now extended below the Rio Grande.

Copland also reviewed the concert. Less extravagantly than Rosenfeld, he explained that Chávez had studied the European masters but eventually divested himself of their influence to compose "fresh, vital music [with] roots . . . firmly in an ancient culture."[21] Nonetheless, Chávez had managed to resist the exotic, channeling the music of Mexican Indians such that "only its essence remained."[22] Chávez's "refreshing, original music" thus "present[ed] itself as one of the first authentic signs of a new world with its own new music." Copland also called forth universalism, observing that "Chávez is essentially of our own day because he uses his composer's gift for the expression of objective beauty of universal significance. . . . [His music] is extraordinarily healthy; it is clear and clean-sounding."[23] Thus, Copland saw musical Pan Americanism as capable of distillation to a perceptible essence, of achieving "universal significance" while retaining its identity as "new world music," all by virtue of vitality, health, and freshness. Copland evaluated the music of Chávez's compatriot Silvestre Revueltas similarly. Despite some shortcomings in form, Copland found that Revueltas composed "almost organically" such that his music "leaves one with a sense of the abundance and vitality of life."[24]

Promoting "a new world with its own new music" from another perspective was the Pan American Association of Composers (PAAC), founded in 1928 by Edgard Varèse, Henry Cowell, and Chávez.[25] Despite funding from the avant-garde composer Charles Ives and some international tours, the PAAC attracted little notice in New York, its home base. Meetings were infrequent, partly due to the geographical distances separating its constituents and perhaps to administrative ennui. (As one member complained, "There wasn't even any stationery.")[26] In repertory, the PAAC focused on the avant-garde: more than once, its unofficial conductor Nicolas Slonimsky incurred complaints of "pandemonium" or "cacophonous tumult."[27] Copland did not participate in the PAAC, possibly because some of its members were avowedly anti-Semitic.[28] The PAAC survived only six years. Yet it succeeded in one respect: of the six composers most frequently performed on its concerts—Chávez, Ives, Villa-Lobos, Wallingford Riegger, Amadeo Roldán, and Alejandro García Caturla—four were Latin Americans, a level of attention unprecedented in the United States.

## A "brief dalliance with jazz"

Some music lovers of Copland's day considered jazz the only sui generis music the United States had ever produced.[29] The polemics surrounding jazz are well known. It bespoke speakeasies and houses of ill-repute: when Roy Harris heard the "Burlesque" of Copland's *Music for the Theatre* of 1925, with its "solo grotesco" blues theme, he apparently exclaimed, "It's whorehouse music! It's whorehouse music!"[30] Jazz could also represent the primitive, an untamed quality presumably inherent in its rhythmic structures that, moreover, encouraged lewd behavior, as the twittering editorial "Does Jazz Put the Sin in Syncopation?" proposed.[31] Some of its detractors were frankly racist, insisting that jazz amounted to little more than "the antics of uncultured Negroes with their endless, senseless, improvisations."[32] Others, such as Rosenfeld, sought refuge in aesthetics, insisting on music's dialectic with the environment and arguing that in jazz, there existed "no union of the man and the matter."[33]

Copland too wrote about jazz. But first he composed a handful of jazz-inflected works, nearly all of which would be heard in Latin America. His first published composition, *Humoristic Scherzo: The Cat and the Mouse*, is based on the fable by Jean de la Fontaine in which a young mouse seeks escape from an old cat only to be eaten, confirming the dire punchline, "Youth deludes itself into believing that it can obtain everything; old age is merciless."[34] The work's Gershwin-esque opening gesture, variety of scales (pentatonic, whole-tone scale, octatonic), and harmonic structures foretold Copland's approach to jazz in subsequent works.[35] The piano piece "Jazzy," the third of the series *Three Moods*, contains stride piano, "swung eights," and a tonal language that combines the blues scale and whole-tone clusters.[36] In 1926 Copland finished Blues no. 1 and Blues no. 2, the former published separately as *Sentimental Melody: Slow Dance* in 1929.[37] Another blues-based work from this period was "Nocturne," one of *Two Pieces* for violin and piano.[38] If *Music for the Theatre* is Copland's best-known jazz work, his Piano Concerto, which he premiered in January 1927 with the Boston Symphony under his great champion Serge Koussevitzky, is the most substantive. Its opening orchestral fanfare heralds the meditative entry of the piano followed by a blues melody passed back and forth between soloist and orchestra. Copland then launches the second movement with wild, improvisatory-sounding dissonances after which bustling Charleston rhythms take over.

In a 1927 article "Jazz Structure and Influence," Copland eschews vague references to the "spirit" of jazz music, analyzing instead its structure and discussing ragtime bass lines, fox trot notation, and mixed meters. (Polyrhythm, he believed, was jazz's "real contribution.")[39] He also hints that jazz might be a passing fancy. Of the several European composers drawn to it, only Darius Milhaud, with his *La création du monde*, struck Copland as noteworthy. Was the composer of *Music for the Theatre* and the Piano Concerto suddenly rejecting jazz? On that point, Copland had no shortage of advice. Harris cautioned him that "the Jazz idiom is too easily assumed" and that "as a serious expression it has nearly burned out." Sessions issued similar warnings.[40]

## "Modernist circles in which Mr. Copland's music chiefly has its being"

An important nonjazz work from the twenties was Copland's Organ Symphony, which proved something of a modernist banner. In reviewing the premiere in January 1925, for example, Rosenfeld applauded "obsessive rhythm as advanced as anything in Stravinsky."[41] Conductor Walter Damrosch was more direct. "Ladies and gentlemen," he announced at the premiere, "I am sure you will agree that if a gifted young man can write a symphony like this at twenty-three, within five years he will be ready to commit murder!" Copland's modernist compositions from this period that found their way to Latin America included *Two Pieces* for string quartet, the first movement of which Boulanger particularly admired.[42] *Symphonic Ode*, which Copland began in 1928, had a convoluted history: because the players in the Boston Symphony Orchestra were stymied by its rhythms, Copland had to rebar many passages, and the premiere was delayed. When the work was finally heard, critic Warren Storey Smith called it a "gray and sodden mass," although H. T. Parker was somewhat more responsive, hearing "hard-edged, stripped-surface modernist speech."[43] A few months later, however, Chávez conducted *Symphonic Ode* with his Orquesta Sinfónica de México (OSM) in Mexico City, thus challenging the notion that Latin America was backward.[44] In 1933 he performed Copland's *Short Symphony*, with its ostinati, jagged melodic lines, and mixed meters, eleven years before it was heard in the United States.[45] Having essayed the "modernist speech" of the *Ode*, Chávez found the logic of the *Short Symphony* "simply unprecedented in the whole history of music."[46]

Copland's Piano Variations, which date from 1930, were also known in Latin America. Scholars have called attention to the four-note motivic cell of the theme and to the structural integrity of the twenty variations that follow.[47] In the United States, a few performances were necessary to establish the importance of this abstruse, dissonant work. But accolades flew when Copland played the Variations at the Yaddo Festival in 1932, thanks in part to critics such as Arthur Mendel.[48] A favorite trope was "austerity": as the composer and author Arthur Berger once remarked, references to the Piano Variations seldom went "unaccompanied by the epithet 'austere.'"[49] In 1934 the composer and musicologist Charles Seeger heard Copland play the work at the Pierre Degeyter Club, a communist organization, and pronounced the work "one of the most undeniably revolutionary pieces of music ever produced here."[50]

## Political Engagement

Well might Seeger see things this way. As the Great Depression exposed capitalism's flaws, a sharp leftward turn took hold under the ample embrace of the Popular Front, a worldwide coalition of constituencies with many adherents in the United States. Artists, intellectuals, and ordinary people took a stand on the economy, political systems, and world events. Copland began attending meetings of the Composers Collective (a subset of the Pierre Degeyter Club), bent on making music a "weapon in the class struggle," to use the parlance of the day.[51] Their main preoccupation was "proletarian music," that is, music rooted in contemporary techniques but nonetheless accessible to untrained listeners. It was vigorously debated. Seeger, one of its main defenders, insisted that workers were perfectly capable of performing musically complex works.[52] The communist critic Mike Gold, on the other hand, condemned the "use of Arnold Schoenberg or Stravinsky as a yardstick [for musical creation]" as "utopian."[53] Initially, the Composers Collective considered folk music incompatible with proletarian music.

Some members of the collective addressed racial justice. In 1931, when nine African American men were falsely accused of raping two White women near Scottsboro, Alabama, the so-called Scottsboro Boys became a cause célèbre. Elie Siegmeister composed the song "The Scottsboro Boys Shall Not Die," and Copland began setting "The Ballad of Ozie Powell," a poem about one of the young men by the African American poet, journalist, and activist Langston Hughes.[54] Copland never finished it but traces of the work surface in *Music for Radio: Saga of the Prairie*, written on commission for the Columbia Broadcasting Service (CBS).[55] In *The Second Hurricane*, an opera for schoolchildren, Copland stages the effects of racism via the character of Jefferson Brown, a Black child.[56] Copland never joined the Communist Party, but he signed plenty of petitions and supported various leftist causes. (Somewhat to his surprise, in summer 1934 he found himself spontaneously delivering a political speech to Minnesota farmers.)[57] He also took a stand on the Spanish Civil War, defying the official neutrality of the Roosevelt administration by joining the Musicians' Committee to Aid Spanish Democracy and participating in fundraising to help defeat the forces of Francisco Franco.[58]

Copland also displayed his fluency with leftist political rhetoric. In the essay "Workers Sing!" he reviewed the *Workers Song Book 1934* for the leftist magazine *New Masses*.[59] In the songbook's foreword, composers are instructed "not only to teach the masses *but also to learn from them*," as noted, a matter of debate.[60] Copland took a middle ground, advising composers to "raise the musical level of the masses but . . . also learn from them what species of song is most apposite to the revolutionary task."[61] Copland's most explicitly political composition was a mass song, a genre intended to inspire political action. "Into the Streets May First!" on a text by Alfred Hayes, contains some modal inflections and harmonic wandering. Perhaps for these reasons, Seeger doubted it would "ever be sung on the picket line."[62] Yet it was performed at the Second Workers Music Olympiad in April 1934 and known in Latin America. Also known there was *Statements*, which Copland began in 1932. That work is seen as both a valedictory to Copland's modernist period (the theme of the Piano Variations appears in "Dogmatic," reh. 3 + 1) and a reflection of his political beliefs, in part because of the evocative titles for its six compact movements, such as "Militant" and "Jingo." (For the latter, he initially considered the title "Petty Bourgeois.") Parts of it were premiered in 1936, although a full premiere of *Statements* was still years away.

## "A legacy he could not inherit"

Another work from this period was *Quiet City*, incidental music for the eponymous play by Irwin Shaw of the Group Theatre, the New York–based company that took on political themes during the Depression years. Copland later refashioned *Quiet City* for string orchestra, solo trumpet, and English horn (the version heard in Latin America) to depict an urban landscape fraught with the anxieties of contemporary life.[63] A nonpolitical work was *An Outdoor Overture*, frequently performed in Latin America, and originally intended for young performers.[64] Reviewing its 1938 premiere, Elliott Carter called it "lofty and beautiful" whereas Rosenfeld dwelt on its pictorial associations, finding *An Outdoor Overture* "full of fresh air and blue sky" and evocative of a "holiday excursion."[65] Two film scores from this period proved successful in Latin America as well: *Of Mice and Men*, Copland's Hollywood film debut based on John Steinbeck's eponymous novella, and *Our Town*, on Thornton Wilder's play.[66]

But Copland was also under attack. However much Harold Stearns had insisted that "whatever else [U.S.] civilization is, it is not Anglo-Saxon," several of the composer's colleagues thought otherwise. For Daniel Gregory Mason, "the poignant beauty of Anglo-Saxon restraint" was lacking in Copland's music by virtue of his being "a cosmopolitan Jew."[67] Cowell conflated the "oriental" (often a code word for "Jew") and the Black, remarking, "Jazz is Negro music, seen through the eyes of these Jews."[68] Rosenfeld, who clearly admired Copland, nonetheless speculated that the composer's taste for "garish jazziness" had to do with his "oriental-American psyche" and blamed Copland's limitations on "jazzing," which reflected "more of a racial past than of a present."[69] None of this stopped Copland from delving into his "racial past" in the piano trio *Vitebsk* of 1928, which draws on the Hassidic melody "Mipnei Mah" ("Wherefore, O Wherefore"), treated as a canon; elsewhere in *Vitebsk*, he employs quarter-tones and parlando style, all suggestive of "the harshness and drama of Jewish life in White Russia," as he put it.[70] *Vitebsk*, which premiered in February 1929 at New York's Town Hall, was performed in Latin America.

As noted, Copland was also accused of eclecticism. In early 1932 Virgil Thomson declared "Aaron Copland's music is American in rhythm, Jewish in melody, and eclectic in all the rest."[71] Consciously or not, Thomson was reinforcing yet another anti-Semitic trope, that of the assimilating Jew who, lacking in originality, fashions non-Jewish elements into "bricabrac" for display in an oriental "art-bazaar."[72] Lazare Saminsky took aim at Copland on similar grounds. A composer, author, and director of music at a New York synagogue (and himself Jewish), Saminsky registered Copland's "observing, absorbing nature, rather than a creative one," a point the Latin American press would take up.[73] To be sure, in his 1932 essay Thomson also accused non-Jewish U.S. composers of eclecticism, shrugging that "Copland's best recommendation is that he is less eclectic than his confrères."

True to form, Copland wrote Thomson a polite letter thanking him for his insights while still continuing his search for an authentic "new world" music. Now, however, Copland called on folk music to achieve that end, an idea he had been developing for some time. In 1925 he told an audience in Rochester, New York, of hearing jazz in Vienna two years earlier, remarking, "It was like hearing it for the first time."[74] The experience also confirmed an essential element of folk music. As he confided to his public, "I began by thinking—what is a folk-song after all? And I came to the conclusion that in my case it was the songs I heard when I was a child—rather commonplace jazz tunes and music of the 'Old Black Joe' variety.... If we have only these elements as essentially American, our music must make the best of it and do the work so well that something worthwhile will come from the effort."[75]

"Folk-music is the music that people commonly know," Copland asserted. He also dismissed the idea of its mysterious, primeval origins, arguing that folk music was being written in the present and thus "becomes a part of current life."[76] Other U.S. composers now began taking folk expression more seriously, including some members of the collective who were becoming aware of the limitations of proletarian music.[77] Like Copland, Gold observed no particular distinction between folk and commercial music. He also cites "Old Black Joe" as emblematic: "What songs do the masses of Americans now sing? They sing 'Old Black Joe' and the semi-jazz things concocted by Tin Pan Alley. This is the reality."[78]

In sum, Copland faced several challenges. Not only was he beginning to doubt the aesthetic potential of jazz but he grappled with the failure of modern music to communicate with a broad public. Anti-Semitic rhetoric and the taint of eclecticism also hung over him. Folk music, if hardly a guarantee of "Anglo-Saxon restraint," nonetheless seemed a reasonable path. All portended a turning point, which Beth E. Levy eloquently describes: "Had Copland chosen to portray himself as the natural conduit for some instinctive folk spirit, he could have been sure that his words would fall on more than a few disbelieving ears. Instead he invoked a more compatible story line: he was working to earn a legacy that he could not inherit."[79] All led to Copland's most celebrated works.

## Mexico: "Something fresh and pure and wholesome"

Of course, neither was Copland qualified to "inherit" a Mexican persona. But by the time he visited Mexico in August 1932, he and Chávez were good friends. (Chávez was one of few Latin American colleagues with whom Copland used the pronoun *tú*, the second-person singular intimate form of address.) Besides conducting Copland's modernist *Symphonic Ode* and *Short Symphony*, Chávez had introduced *Music for the Theatre* to Mexico City in 1929, probably at some risk since much of his public was either hostile to or unfamiliar with jazz.[80] Copland and Chávez also saw themselves as allies in the quest for a music of the Americas, one capable of standing up to Europe; indeed, in 1931 (perhaps in an unguarded moment) Copland wrote, "Carlos, I've had it with Europe."[81] For Copland's 1932 visit, Chávez organized the first all-Copland concert in history. Copland's stylistic versatility—or eclecticism, as his detractors would have it—was on full display, with young musicians from the Conservatorio Nacional playing the *Two Pieces* for string quartet and the choral works "An Immortality" and "The House on the Hill," both from 1925. Copland himself conducted *Music for the Theatre* and played his Piano Variations.[82]

While in Mexico, Copland relied on the guidebook *Your Mexican Holiday: A Modern Guide*, one of several books by Anita Brenner.[83] Born in Aguascalientes, Brenner moved with her family to the United States in 1910, dividing her time between Mexico and New York, where she studied anthropology at Columbia University with Franz Boas.[84] In New York, she, Chávez, and Copland socialized together, once sitting up all night to argue the finer points of Stravinsky's *Oedipus Rex*.[85] *Your Mexican Holiday*, in whose pages Copland first learned of the dance hall El Salón México, is hardly the typical guidebook. The high-spirited Brenner harangues U.S. tourists by pointing out the hypocrisy of the puritanical visitor put off by the small-scale, recreational gambling of the Mexican lottery but who thrills to the vicissitudes of Wall Street; she also makes fun of monolingual tourists struggling to understand the Mexican comic actor Cantinflas.[86] Copland needed no such scolding. He idealized Mexico even as he accepted his own tourist status, reveling in an ineffable quality, "something fresh and pure and wholesome," he found there.[87] In composing *El salón México*, he sought to communicate a Pan American "essence" that did not detract from universalism. He also wanted to respect his raw materials while bringing the folk tunes to life in accordance with his own aesthetic. Finally, he had to reconcile modern musical vocabulary with the dubious requirements of "travel music" or "picture-postcard music," epithets critics often bandied about to suggest commodification or mass production. In fact, Copland made no pretense of capturing the grandeur of indigenous monuments or post-revolutionary fervor. Rather, he openly acknowledged that with *El salón México*, he sought only "to reflect the Mexico of the tourists."[88]

He was not entirely successful. When the communist composer Marc Blitzstein heard the two-piano version of *El salón México*, he made short work of it. "A good chance for musical reportage wasted in up-to-the-minute travel-slumming music," he scoffed.[89] In other words, *El salón México* failed both as music and message—in both form and in content, to use the political-aesthetic jargon of the day.[90] As for the orchestral version, Mexico City heard *El salón México* before New York, again thanks to Chávez, who performed it in August 1937.[91] In May of the following year, Adrian Boult conducted it with the NBC Symphony in a radio broadcast and that fall, the Boston Symphony Orchestra performed *El salón México*, first in Boston and then in New York. Critics noticed Copland's new style, finding it more welcoming than his previous forays into modernism. Pitts Sanborn called the score "surprisingly decorous" and Oscar Thompson observed that the Mexican folk tunes interspersed throughout the score "fairly drip molasses."[92] Olin Downes, writing in the *New York Times*, praised Copland's "facile orchestration" and harmony that did "not seek for strangeness" whereas others focused on the "brilliant life" Copland had given his materials.[93] Indeed, the folk melodies were seen as so compatible with Copland's evolving ideals that a later critic believed that they seemed "much more true to themselves than in their songbook versions."[94] It would seem that Copland's musical persona had solidified.

## Good-Neighbor Cultural Diplomacy and Latin America

Meanwhile, the U.S. government was establishing a program in cultural diplomacy. Here the Roosevelt administration confronted several obstacles. In at least some quarters, no large-scale government project was to be trusted. Also, many U.S. Americans were skeptical of ideas from abroad, long considered a malady "imported by our returning diplomats and by the foreign ambassadors sent here by monarchs and despots to corrupt and destroy our American ideals," as one nineteenth-century congressman complained.[95] Some seasoned diplomats were skeptical about targeting Latin America. O. Ellis Briggs (the "better Groucho Marx" we met in chapter 1, then employed by the Division of the American Republics) believed that with some exceptions, Latin American intellectuals were "rather a seedy lot."[96] Even Undersecretary of State Sumner Welles, Roosevelt's adviser on Latin America and a Good Neighbor enthusiast, compared "the Anglo-Saxon type," endowed with a centuries-long tradition of education, science, and government, to the limited experience of most Latin Americans, a view as condescending as it is ahistorical.[97] Other U.S. government employees were unconvinced that their *own* culture was worthy of export.[98]

Racism could sabotage cultural exchange. U.S. historians and politicians were wont to describe Latin America as a continent of "half-breeds," as one widely used textbook maintained.[99] A survey by the Office of Public Opinion Research asked respondents to choose from a list the most apt descriptors of Latin Americans. The word most often selected—at 80 percent—was "dark-skinned." ("Backward" came in at 44 percent, "lazy" at 41, "dirty" at 28, and "honest" at 13.)[100] These prejudices reflect conflicting notions of race. In the United States, where intense fear of miscegenation prevailed, phenotype has historically determined race. By contrast, in Latin America race is likelier to be a social construction, according to which class and other factors are given considerable play such that a person may be "born 'brown' but become 'white' through upward mobility."[101] Still, few Latin Americans behave as if race did not exist, and plenty of hierarchies and debilitating prejudices are based on phenotype.[102] In Chile, for example, considered one of the "white republics" in Copland's day, *mestizaje* (miscegenation) between the descendants of Europeans and the "noble (indigenous) savage" was accepted while Black people were marginalized.[103] Brazil, with its far larger Afro-descended population, a legacy of slavery, undertook the practice of whitening (*branqueamento*) after abolition in 1888, to gradually eliminate "black blood" through intermarriage with Whites, whose "superior" blood would prevail, a practice that lasted through World War I.[104] In the United States, however, the "one-drop" rule could cause a light-skinned person with a Black ancestor to be classified as Black.[105] Red Cross offices in the United States distinguished White from Black donors on the premise that White U.S. Americans—not just those in the south—would object to receiving blood from Black people.[106] Scientific racism supported these legal mechanisms while literature reified the mixed-race individual, sometimes through the trope of the "tragic mulatto."[107] In the early years of the Roosevelt administration, moreover, southern segregationists in the U.S. Congress wielded power over the president who, amid a grim uptick in lynchings, depended on their votes to enact New Deal legislation.[108]

Cultural diplomacy projects affected by racism included a proposal by the director Pare Lorentz for a series of films on Latin America. It was reviewed by an anonymous diplomat who, in an unsigned letter of August 1938, balked at a proposal containing "the appalling suggestion" that a mestizo embody "the manhood of South America."[109] The 1933 film *Flying Down to Rio*, an early Good Neighbor movie musical in which Hollywood, government, and business collaborated, contains a splashy production number in which Brazil's multiracial society was on full display.[110] Criticized on similar grounds, *Flying Down to Rio* was hardly welcome in the southern United States.[111] Other projects, including Orson Welles's exploration of samba, are discussed below.

Consequently, when Laurence Duggan, chief of the Latin American Division of the State Department, faced the Seventy-Fifth Congress in December 1937 to promote the founding of a Division of Cultural Relations, he expounded not on cultural diplomacy's idealistic objectives but emphasized national security, warning against Axis infiltration in the Americas.[112] The new division would justify its existence by disseminating propoganda-free information about the United States, pursuing "a diplomacy of truth," as Richard T. Arndt comments.[113] Richard Pattee, of the Division of the American Republics, supported these ideas, arguing that although private efforts had yielded some cultural understanding in Latin America, governments could lend cohesion and heft as they "legitimately aspire to make known the best of their civilizations."[114] Naturally, what counted as "the best" would be a matter of debate.

In July 1938 the Division of Cultural Relations was established, with Ben Cherrington, a professor from the University of Colorado, serving as its first chief. Moving deliberately—one diplomat proposed "making haste slowly"— the division was ultimately convinced to promote "universal" culture, believing that it, not some rough-hewn U.S. sensibility, would be a selling point.[115] This strategy was at odds with that of the Good Neighbor policy, which was regional. But universal culture would appeal to university-educated Latin America cultural elites, the 5 percent of the population invested with the power and influence to set cultural agendas and "the point of departure for any contact with public opinion in the American Republics," as Pattee observed.[116] Many such elites were also convinced of a "Latin" sensibility, one that distinguished them from their northern neighbors.[117] Victoria Ocampo of Argentina, for example, founded the widely read journal *Sur* (South), which articulated a modernizing, universalist aesthetic that resisted mass culture and popularization. Although *Sur* would frequently report on culture from the United States, Ocampo's own essay in the inaugural issue made the journal's orientation clear. "Turn our backs on Europe?" she queried. "Does one sense the infinite ridiculousness in this phrase?"[118]

Musical sensibilities fit naturally into this panorama. In Montevideo, Bogotá, Santiago, and Lima, concert halls in neoclassical style served as shrines to High Art, often with a French-"Latin" orientation; the Municipal Theater in Rio de Janeiro hints at Charles Garnier's Paris Opéra. In Buenos Aires in 1936 the acoustically perfect Teatro Colón welcomed Stravinsky. His *Perséphone*, which Richard Taruskin has described as a "neoclassical extravaganza," was performed there with Ocampo as the reader, delivering Gide's text in the original French in her *porteño* (Buenos Aires) accent.[119] *Sur* praised the work, along with *Apollo* and *Oedipus Rex*, for its "formal aspect, within the classic design."[120] Indeed, whereas many composers in the United States rejected neoclassicism for its ties to Europe, their Latin American counterparts admired many of its presumably Latin traits, such as refinement, wit, clarity, and order.[121] At the same time, popular culture from the United States, whether in the form of Hollywood movies, jazz, or comic books, fascinated many Latin Americans. A government program in cultural diplomacy could justify itself only by reaching beyond the mass media. Still, promoting elite culture—"the best"—risked canceling out the questions Copland himself was beginning to ask, namely, what does a democratic culture look like, and how is it realized musically?

## Music and U.S. Cultural Diplomacy

In December 1938, weeks after the rampage known as *Kristallnacht* destroyed Jewish homes, businesses, and institutions in Germany, Austria, and the Sudentenland, killing over ninety Jews, the Eighth Annual Conference of American States met in Lima. The Declaration of Lima, finalized there, stipulated that all twenty-one American republics would engage in common defense in the event of an "attack on any one of the American family," as Espinosa reported.[122] Delegates at Lima also discussed culture. They decided to establish a music center in the Pan American Union to disseminate scores and recordings and coordinate activities of musical organizations and individual musicians throughout the Americas.[123] Music thus became part of cultural diplomacy's mission. In September 1939, days after Hitler invaded Poland and World War II became a reality, a contingent of musicians from Latin America showed up at a meeting of the fledgling American Musicological Society in New York. One session, devoted to "Hispanic Music," was written up in the magazine *Musical America* by the young critic and future musicologist Gilbert Chase.[124] Among the presenters was the musicologist Francisco Curt Lange, a native of Germany who had earned his doctorate at the University of Bonn in 1929 with a dissertation on fifteenth-century polyphony. He then emigrated to Montevideo and became a Uruguayan citizen—Francisco Curt rather than Franz Kurt—and founded the Instituto Interamericano de Musicología, which Copland would visit. Like Copland, Lange sought to cultivate a musical voice of the Western hemisphere, which he called "americanismo musical."[125] Also present were Cuban composer and author Eduardo Sánchez de Fuentes; his compatriot, composer, violinist, and pianist Gonzalo Roig; Panamanian violinist Alfredo de Saint Maló; pianist and composer Joaquín Nin-Culmell; and Brazilian conductor Burle Marx, who had recently conducted two programs of Brazilian music at the 1939 World's Fair.[126]

On 18 October the first Conference on Inter-American Relations in the Field of Music convened at the Library of Congress, sponsored by the Division of Cultural Relations. Representatives from government, academia, music librarianship, media, and music education, along with professional musicians, attended, all paying their own way. Robert Woods Bliss and his wife, Mildred Barnes Bliss, (later the dedicatees of Stravinsky's *Dumbarton Oaks* Concerto) hosted a concert for the delegates at their home, featuring the Latin American art song specialist Elsie Houston. That very day, W. H. Auden's poem, *September 1, 1939*, appeared in the *New Republic*, a bleak meditation that not only marked the exact beginning of the war but lamented "the whole offence . . . that has driven a culture mad." It was an anxious assemblage of delegates that Archibald MacLeish, the newly minted Librarian of Congress, welcomed. Copland was not among them. But because he later served on the division's Music Advisory Committee (along with a rival committee formed in 1940), it is worth meeting some of attendees, several of whom would collaborate with Copland in the pursuit of cultural diplomacy.[127]

One of Copland's future colleagues was Carleton Sprague Smith, musicologist, flutist, and chief of the music division of the New York Public Library. Fluent in Portuguese and Spanish, Smith was soon to be dispatched by the Division of Cultural Relations on a four-month, fact-finding mission in Latin

America.[128] Another eventual collaborator was Marshall Bartholomew, chair of the music department at Yale University and director of the Yale Glee Club. There was also William Berrien, a professor of literature at Northwestern University with strong opinions on Latin American music. Also present were Davidson Taylor of CBS and Philip L. Barbour of the international division of the National Broadcasting Company (NBC), who would join forces with Copland. So too would another attendee, Evans Clark, director of the Twentieth Century Fund (now the Century Foundation) and a strong-minded polemicist: among Clark's publications was *Facts and Fabrications about Soviet Russia*, a blistering attack on the conservative press in the United States. Also in attendance was Seeger, now in his capacity as director of the music program of the Works Progress Administration and soon to become chief of the music division of the Pan American Union.

At the conference, Seeger argued that folk music was best suited to uniting the hemisphere, disparaging as "unhealthy" Latin America's attraction to European classical music.[129] Others saw things differently. Howard Hanson, composer and director of the Eastman School of Music, countered that many Latin American listeners cared deeply about "serious symphonic music."[130] Lange, who didn't so much as mention folk music, complained of general ignorance in the United States about Latin America.[131] Conductor George Hoyen, recently returned from three years in Latin America, remarked that such ignorance was mutual: Latin American audiences "did not have any idea whatsoever that North America had serious composers."[132] Berrien was also concerned with "serious" music and expostulated at some length on modern music and its virtues. For him, that eliminated compositions by Alberto Williams of Argentina or Antônio Francisco Braga of Brazil. Their rather conventional music, Berrien argued, would "not appeal particularly to groups keeping to the highest standards."[133] He aimed to emphasize "the best music of the Americas appearing alongside the best music of all the world," a strategy likely to succeed with Latin American elites.[134] Smith, however, pointed out that libraries make no such elitist distinctions and that suitable materials for export to Latin America should include classical music but also spirituals, fiddle tunes, and marches. In comparison with Latin Americans, Smith observed, U.S. Americans "have certain peculiar habits." "We chew gum, for example," he noted. In short, there was no point in U.S. cultural diplomats presenting themselves as "sophisticated Europeans."[135]

Delegates to the conference were a diverse lot, at least for the era. Most were White males from the United States, but several Latin Americans and women attended, as did three African Americans: opera singer Lilian Evanti, composer and choral conductor William L. Dawson, and composer R. Nathaniel Dett.[136] Evanti and Dawson said relatively little, but Dett, an advocate for "Negro music," posed an urgent question: how could "the other Americas" fully grasp the richness of U.S. culture unless Black music was understood?[137] He was not timid about pointing the finger. "Americans do not know the Negro folk songs," he declared. "You do not know our music, our music which has been the basis of *your* music."[138] Like Smith, Dett offered some advice to prospective cultural diplomats. As he told the attendees, "When you go to Latin American countries, carry along all of the advancements which have contributed to the advancement of [U.S.] culture. The small republics are interested to know what the minority is doing and how the minority fares. They are themselves minorities and the minority question is one of the world's great questions today."[139] Dett's impassioned plea made little impression. In minutes of future meetings of the Division of Cultural Relations, any discussion of "Negro music" is conspicuously absent.

Music was nonetheless considered capable of winning hearts and minds. Addressing the delegates, Adolph Berle, assistant secretary of state for Latin American affairs, declared that nations are better off knowing "something about each other's art, and music, and books."[140] Still, in 1938, the same year the U.S. government embraced the ennobling goals of cultural diplomacy, U.S. Representative Martin Dies became the first chair of the House Committee Investigating Un-American Activities, later called the House Un-American Activities Committee (HUAC). In routing out communists and their sympathizers from the federal government, the HUAC would become obsessed with State Department personnel such as Duggan, who evinced interest in Soviet culture.[141] Others, including those tagged as homosexuals, would be affected as well.

## "In danger of working in a vacuum"

That dark period still lay years ahead. Also in 1938 Copland undertook his next big project. Like *El salón México*, the ballet *Billy the Kid* quotes preexisting melodies. A tale of villainy, identity, and death in the U.S. West, it came about through the arts entrepreneur Lincoln Kirstein, with whom Copland would join forces in Latin America. The bare, open fifths of the ballet's opening measures have come to emblematize the vast expanses of the U.S. West, just as the dramatic gunshots of the ending suggest adventure and daring.[142] To be sure, reaction among Latin American critics was mixed: one would complain of "United States music critics accept[ing] with applause . . . the nationalism of Copland's *Billy the Kid*—gunshots and all—while sneering at the 'maracas and drums' gestures they themselves had attached as a label to every Latin American concert music piece."[143]

Copland continued defining himself. In the 1939 essay "Composer from Brooklyn: An Autobiographical Sketch," he establishes his status as a nonelitist who grew up in an inauspicious environment but who, by dint of perseverance and initiative, achieved a musical version of the "American dream."[144] In the same essay, Copland renounced jazz, given what he calls its "limited emotional scope."[145] Most significant, he concluded that in writing exclusively for a coterie of new music aficionados, he was "in danger of working in a vacuum." Instead, he would approach the mass public that radio and the phonograph had suddenly created. "It made no sense to ignore them and to continue writing as if they did not exist," he reasoned. "I felt it was worth the effort to see if I couldn't say what I had to say in the simplest possible terms."[146]

This expansion of the musical public coincided with "middlebrow" culture.[147] That ambivalent concept, derided by some for intellectual laziness and welcomed by others for inclusiveness, appealed to Copland on at least a practical level, as he began teaching music appreciation, a middlebrow pursuit that Thomson dubbed the "appreciation racket."[148] Between 1927 and 1939 Copland offered "appreciation" at the New School, first a survey of contemporary music but eventually covering the Western canon, the staple of the music appreciation curriculum.[149] His *What to Listen for in Music* of 1939, a handbook for the layperson, resulted from this experience. *Our New Music*, a series of essays on contemporary topics (including a reprint of "Composer from Brooklyn"), followed in 1941. In neither does Copland refer to the "class struggle," "the masses," or the "revolutionary task." But his vision of a participatory public is undiminished, including the listener who randomly turns on the radio, knowing nothing about the music being played but nonetheless competent to judge it without prejudice. "For the first time," Copland declares rather grandly, "democracy has entered the realm of serious music."[150]

Also in *Our New Music*, Copland addresses nationalism and universalism, although rarely arriving at clarity. Thanks to nationalism, he argues, "one small country after another" established its own national style, ensuring little more than provincialism.[151] Truly modern composers, on the other hand, sought "a more universal idea." Copland fails to specify any musical procedures such an orientation might involve. He does, however, touch on identity vis-à-vis universalism, noting a "kind of universality of feeling in a Russian folk tune," again, without specifics. Also, whatever his interest in modernism, Copland heartily disliked twelve-tone music.[152] (Elsewhere he condemned Schoenberg's Woodwind Quintet op. 26 as "an outstanding failure" for its empty theoretical grounding.)[153] In reviewing *Our New Music*, the composer Theodor Chanler allowed that Copland was well aware of the difficulty of writing for the broad public. Yet Chanler takes aim at Copland's lack of precision, insisting that merely urging composers to write "simple and direct" music that is also "great" scarcely constitutes an argument.[154] Part of Copland's failure to convince was that despite his "keen sensibility" and receptivity to many styles, he was "too modest to claim the last word when a point of doubt" arises. Instead, Chanler notes, Copland took refuge in "half-diffident charitableness," revealing "softness of critical fibre."[155]

Such rhetorical conundrums would accompany Copland on his Latin American trips, the first of which was approaching. By now, he was established as a composer, author, and teacher. He was a leader in musical circles, whether at the festivals for contemporary music he founded at Yaddo (the artists' colony in Saratoga Springs, New York), serving on the board of directors of the League of Composers, or cofounding and serving as president of the American Composers Alliance. In summer 1940, in the company of Serge Koussevitzky and Leonard Bernstein, he began his long association with the Berkshire Music Center at Tanglewood (Lenox, Massachusetts). It was from there that he left for his State Department–sponsored tour the following year.

# 3
# Copland as Good Neighbor

In late July 1941, when Copland was already at the Berkshire Music Center, he received a note from one of the government committees he was serving on behalf of musical Pan Americanism. It was sent by Conchita Rexach, one of the bilingual secretarial staff. She reported that yet one more Latin American composer was interested in the Piano Variations. Juan Carlos Paz of Argentina, the first twelve-tone composer in Latin America, had already received a copy from Copland. Now his younger compatriot Alberto Ginastera was hoping for the same. "My, isn't it getting popular in South America!" Rexach quipped.[1]

In fact, Copland did not perform the Piano Variations during the 1941 tour, either in Argentina or elsewhere. Mainly, he promoted a different aesthetic, one that complemented the values of the Office of Inter-American Affairs (OIAA) on whose music committee he now sat.[2] Created in August 1940 to accelerate the Good Neighbor Policy, the OIAA sought to counteract the pokiness of the Division of Cultural Relations. In contrast to the universal culture the division favored, moreover, the OIAA was unabashedly regionalist. For Copland, its most powerful selling point was likely the mere *idea* of a Western hemisphere music. This chapter considers the OIAA's objectives by tracking Copland's work with the music committee prior to his departure.

## "The United States is way behind"

Fear was growing in the hemisphere. By late June 1940, after tottering for months, France had fallen to the Nazis, as had Poland, Czechoslovakia, Austria,

Denmark, Norway, Luxembourg, Belgium, and the Netherlands. Officials of the Americas met in Havana, and Latin American governments discussed whether to cast in their lot with the United States. Secretary of State Cordell Hull's Tennessee accent and folksy expressions—he told a Central American foreign minister that one German official was "tryin' to treat you like a houn' dawg chasin' a rabbit"—evidently resisted translation.[3]

That fall, Carleton Sprague Smith returned from his four-month tour of Latin America. In a three-hundred-page report, he described the vast reach of Axis cultural diplomacy, of which music was part. Smith ridiculed prior efforts by the United States. "During the past few years, scores and parts have been sent by the Pan American Union to a thousand bands in the Southern hemisphere," he observed. But Smith could not say if "the music is actually played, or is used for lighting cigarettes or is just lying on the library shelves." The German government, on the other hand, had invited the Brazilian composer Francisco Mignone to conduct the Berlin Philharmonic in 1937, with additional appearances in Hamburg and Munich. The Italians were no less assiduous. From its office in Buenos Aires, the music publisher Ricordi circulated the *Noticiario Ricordi*, a magazine Smith described as "frankly full of Fascist Propaganda." Nor did the Axis overlook less powerful Latin American countries. In 1938 the Bolivian composer José María Velasco Maidana spent nine months in Berlin as a guest of the German government, preparing programs for shortwave radio broadcasts to South America and overseeing rehearsals of his ballet *Amerindia*. "The United States is way behind in extending such courtesies to South American musicians," Smith chided his colleagues.[4]

Similarly impatient was Nelson A. Rockefeller, scion of the Standard Oil family. Despite having voted for Hoover in 1932, Rockefeller, imbued with what Darlene Rivas has called "evangelistic" goals of U.S. world leadership, offered his talents to the Democratic administration.[5] From 1940 he worked closely with Roosevelt to establish the OIAA, initially intending to impede Latin American trade with the Axis.[6] But on one of his trips to Venezuela, where Rockefeller's family had founded Creole Petroleum, he conversed with President Eleazar López Contreras, an advocate of Pan Americanism who also feared intellectual imperialism.[7] Rockefeller came away convinced that culture could be a weapon in the OIAA's arsenal. To be sure, he had little direct experience with diplomacy. But he was well connected in philanthropic and artistic circles. He also took the trouble to learn Spanish and, like his mother, Abby Aldrich Rockefeller, appreciated Mexican art.[8] Known as the "coordinator," Rockefeller had no compunctions about blending government funds and private monies, resulting in a complex mix of transactions. Of government funds he had aplenty: in its first year alone, the upstart OIAA received $3.5 million from Roosevelt's emergency fund.[9] Like the Division of Cultural Relations, the OIAA styled itself as a national security entity. Even the music committee was instructed to use National Defense letterhead.[10]

Immediately, Rockefeller antagonized the State Department. Career diplomats gagged over his budget: as one ruefully noted, the OIAA would have at its disposal "more than *fifty times* the amount [the Division of American Republics] had so painstakingly budgeted for the first cooperative program with Latin America."[11] Other differences were ideological. For Rockefeller, "a diplomacy of truth" amounted to empty words. So too did muddle-headed notions about "universal" culture, which in any case smacked of Europe. Instead, Rockefeller offered the United States as a cultural model for Latin Americans, which his critics attacked as "force feeding of [U.S.] culture."[12] Such was Rockefeller's zeal that he was accused of fashioning what amounted to propaganda, the very activity Welles, Duggan, and the Division of Cultural Relations had decried.[13] Yet the urgency of the cause, coupled with the immense popularity of the Good Neighbor Policy—it spawned clubs, contests, school activities, institutes, and many activities—seemed to justify this heavy-handedness.[14] Besides, many U.S. citizens shrugged off notions of propaganda. In 1942, when Walt Disney released the animated Good Neighbor cartoon feature *Saludos Amigos!* (commissioned by the OIAA Motion Picture Division), one educator asserted, "If this is the type of propaganda film that Disney is going to put out let's have more and many of them."[15]

Many OIAA personnel and associates shared Rockefeller's distrust of Old World values. It was not so much a matter of being for or against Nazism; rather, were you for the Americas or for Europe? After France fell, for example, Henry Allen Moe, a Rockefeller ally and the secretary of the Guggenheim Foundation, expressed disillusionment with "the whole Paris gang," bemoaning its "spiritual and mental bankruptcy."[16] Prodding Latin Americans to look northward for artistic stimulation rather than to Paris or Vienna was no small challenge, however. A case in point was Domingo Santa Cruz, composer and dean of the faculty of music at the University of Chile. In 1941 he spent four months in the United States as a guest of the Pan American Union. Having written symphonies and string quartets, Santa Cruz took every opportunity to promote Chile as an "occidental" country rooted in European tradition.[17]

U.S. cultural diplomats nonetheless supposed that Latin American elites could be persuaded that U.S. culture amounted to more than jazz and Hollywood. But would these elites conclude that their culture had something in common with that of the United States? Might "freshness," that elusive quality Copland so admired and that presumably distinguished the Americas from Europe, unify artists North and South? Certainly Copland avoided "force feeding." But for anyone as eager as he to advance "serious" music of the United States—cultivated but communicative, modern but accessible, identifiably of the Americas yet as fine as anything Europe might produce—the OIAA afforded the ideal opportunity.

## A "Lofty Composer" and the OIAA

The OIAA Music Committee met in New York, convening for the first time on 6 November 1940 with Smith as chair.[18] Its charge was ambitious: "to increase solidarity and understanding between the peoples of the United States and of Latin American countries through the medium of music."[19] By then a handful of Copland's works had been performed in various Latin American countries. Among them was Chile, where long-strained relations were now aggravated by pockets of Nazism.[20] During the 1938 presidential elections, a pro-Nazi Chilean congressman instigated an armed coup that was thwarted only with considerable loss of life.[21] Career diplomat Edward G. Trueblood, then posted in Santiago, had joined forces with the Chilean-born, Berkeley-educated historian and music lover Eugenio Pereira Salas to establish the U.S.-Chilean Institute. Its one-year anniversary coincided with the Fourth of July 1939. As acting head of the embassy, Trueblood wanted to mark the event with something other than "a merely social kind of cocktail party which usually turned into a mass alcoholic and gastronomic orgy," as he vividly described such proceedings. He took the following steps:

> We engaged the services of about thirty members of the Santiago Symphony Orchestra to perform a concert in the Embassy and warned persons who would be attending the reception that the first hour would be given over to the concert, which would be directed by the young American conductor George Hoyen. ... The program opened with a classical composition and was then followed by one work by a Chilean composer and another by Aaron Copeland [sic]. ... Many persons, both American and Chilean, told me later that they thought our experiment had been a good one and one that might well be emulated.[22]

We do not know which Copland work was performed that Fourth of July in Santiago but the fact that it was applauded as part of a diplomatic function augured well. So did a concert in Rio de Janeiro, then the capital of Brazil, at the Escola Nacional de Musica in July 1940. Before an audience of about a thousand, Smith played works by Copland, Harris, Quincy Porter, Francisco Mignone, Oscar Lorenzo Fernândez, Radames Gnattali, Guarnieri, and Villa-Lobos. "Critics seemed to be favorably impressed with the idea generally and the American compositions particularly," Smith reported, adding, "Aaron Copland's piece was the most applauded."[23] The work in question was *As It Fell upon a Day* for flute, clarinet, and soprano, the bright timbres, tripping contrapuntal lines, and pastoral poetry of which defied the tensions of the moment.

Objections to the OIAA Music Committee immediately arose. In the New York–based *Sunday Mirror*, an editorial titled "Only Human" and signed by one "Candide" expostulated,

> *The Mirror* has expressed nothing but praise and applause for the work of Nelson Rockefeller and the other able men co-ordinating the Commercial and Cultural Relations between the American Republics. And we have had nothing but praise for Mr. Rockefeller's appointments. Today, the first criticism: We refer to the Music Committee. It is composed of one "musicologist"; one chairman of the music department at Yale; one executive director of the Twentieth Century Fund; one lofty composer, and one gentleman from the "American Council of Learned Societies." The fault we find is simply this: "Get down to earth." You can't lick Only-Human nature, Mr. Rockefeller. We wish you had appointed to your Music Committee *only* leaders of America's dance orchestras and perhaps made Bing Crosby and Ethel Merman co-chairmen.[24]

Who were these clueless snobs? The "lofty composer" was of course Copland. Smith earned the scare quotes around his dubious profession because musicology was then struggling to gain traction in U.S. universities, with the pseudo-scientific suffix "-ology" making fine joke fodder.[25] Similarly tainted by academia was the "gentleman from the 'American Council of Learned Societies,'" William Berrien, the tireless advocate of quality control and avant-garde music. The "chairman of the music department at Yale" was Marshall Bartholomew, who traveled by train from New Haven for meetings. The lone OIAA Music Committee member who was not classically oriented was Evans Clark, the "executive director of the Twentieth Century Fund." His main qualifications were his enthusiasm for popular music and zest for lengthy reports. All but Copland had attended the 1939 conference on music sponsored by the Division of Cultural Relations.

Smith chuckled over the *Mirror* editorial and sent it around to the rest of the committee with the attached note, referencing the gossip columnist Walter Winchell:

Dear Boys:

Even if we didn't make Walter Winchell's column, we are on the editorial page of the *Sunday Mirror*! Mr.—or should I say Madame? Candide seems to think we are lacking in enthusiasm for the popular jazz for which this country is rightly known. Should we invite said columnist up for a drink or ignore the article in high and lofty tones?[26]

"Candide" was not so far off the mark. An aura of gray-suited elitism hung over the music committee's proceedings. Meetings were often held at New York's Harvard or Yale Clubs, and a whiff of old-boy camaraderie occasionally emerges in correspondence. (Bartholomew, for example, referred to the U.S. Ambassador Spruille Braden, then based in Bogotá, as "a good Yale man.")[27] Still, to the feisty Clark, the piece in the *Mirror* hit home. He argued in one of his numerous reports that "concert, classical or 'art' music is far less useful both for mass entertainment or for an understanding of the life of other countries" than popular music. "Except in so far as composers of concert music make use of local themes and rhythms," Clark observed, "their music tends to be an entirely individual expression in a sort of international—usually European—musical language."[28]

As such debates continued, additional hands were brought on. In early January 1941, Philip Barbour of NBC joined as executive secretary to take up the committee's considerable paperwork. (NBC made him "available to the Council of National Defense.")[29] Also pressed into service was Davidson Taylor of CBS, who believed that broadcasting companies were "the Brandenburgs, the Haffners, and the Esterhazys of today." (Taylor and Copland were already acquainted thanks to Copland's *Music for Radio*.)[30] The Spanish expatriate Gustavo Durán, a pianist, folklorist, and sometime composer, showed up intermittently at OIAA meetings. Having served as a lieutenant colonel in the Republican army during the Spanish Civil War (readers of Hemingway's *For Whom the Bell Tolls* can catch a glimpse of him in chapter 30), Durán was now working for the very administration that had turned its back on his native land.[31] Handling the music committee's voluminous correspondence was the bilingual secretarial staff of Rexach and María de Freitas.

## "South American rhythms are swell"

In recommending funding for exchange visits, subsidies, and other proposed activities, the OIAA Music Committee confronted the question of musical identity. Early on, the minutes note that Latin American musicians chosen to perform in the United States should represent "the land from which the artist comes."[32] Artists specializing in the "universal" music of the European canon would likely not receive OIAA support: in principle, the noted Chopin specialist Guiomar Novaes of Brazil would not be funded.[33] One of Copland's several ideas for the committee sparked discussion on this point. At a meeting of 8 January 1941, by which time his tour was already being planned, he suggested that Latin American composers be commissioned to write for U.S. orchestras "and vice-versa."[34] Smith consulted the pianist and future author Arthur Loesser, then teaching at the Cleveland Institute of Music. On 14 April (Pan American Day) Loesser wrote Smith to suggest pooling money from several orchestras. He also offered some advice to prospective Latin American composers:

> Do not interpret the commission as an opportunity to show off the extreme limits of your imaginative horizons. South American rhythms are swell, and Indian percussion instruments are fine, provided they are not too hard for our boys to learn how to play. But webs of atonal dissonant counterpoint are definitely *out*. Nothing remotely resembling Hindemith, Schoenberg, post-*Sacre* Stravinsky, or Bartók will do. Here I am not speaking as myself but as a representative citizen of a fairly progressive middle-western large city.[35]

Loesser urged composers to distinguish their music from "universal" models:

> The titles of the compositions are important. *Variations on an Original Theme* is not particularly calculated to arouse an interest in South America. But a title like *Anaconda* or *Commodore Rivadavia* is intriguing and will start a burgeoning of program notes, with consequent fixation of attention.[36]

Of course, Loesser was not a member of the OIAA committee. (He was the brother of the musical theater composer Frank Loesser. Whereas Arthur was witty and charming, Frank had a sharp tongue and was known as "the evil of two Loessers.") Yet Arthur's advice was informally heeded. Throughout its brief existence, the music committee favored "the moderate mainstream" rather than the avant-garde music for which the PAAC had gained notoriety.[37] In cautioning composers to avoid "extreme limits," Arthur echoed Copland's own ideas about expressing himself "in the simplest possible terms." Also, by rejecting generic (universal) titles in favor of identity-conscious suggestion—the giant anacondas of the Amazon rain forest or Latin American statesmen, such as Bernardino Rivadavia—Loesser affirmed *El salón México*'s tourist gaze.

Although the committee resoundingly supported Copland's plan, orchestra directors expressed only guarded interest. Artur Rodziński, music director of the Cleveland Orchestra, doubted his board would supply the proposed $500 for a work that might survive only one performance whereas Eugene Goossens, conductor of the Cincinnati Symphony Orchestra, saw a "problem" in "finding sufficient first-class Latin American composers to provide fourteen major orchestras with first-class works!" as he emphatically put it.[38] (In other words, Goossens was not unlike those State Department officials who considered Latin American intellectuals "rather a seedy lot.") Copland's project lay dormant until late July 1941, when Smith reported that Cleveland had "crashed through" with $250.00.[39] Yet whether due to administrative overload or ennui, the project never saw the light. Still, U.S. orchestras would eventually perform works by some Latin American composers, including several that Copland would meet.

## "Goodwilling" and Music for Export

It was one thing to sell the U.S. public on music by their southern neighbors but another to decide which music to export from the United States. Among the music committee's duties was reviewing proposals for visits to Latin America, known as "goodwill tours." According to this ritual, famous individuals shared their talents with Latin Americans, encouraging friendly feelings about the United States. Thornton Wilder, Douglas Fairbanks Jr., and Walt Disney all made goodwill tours.[40] Playing to other publics but equally interested in goodwill (and in burnishing their careers) were Arturo Toscanini and Leopold Stokowski. Each performed in several major Latin American cities during 1940, and each attracted plenty of publicity at home. U.S. Americans who supported Toscanini believed that the mere of fact of sending a European-born cultural symbol who had chosen to reside in the United States spoke volumes.[41] Stokowski champions, however, protested that Toscanini "stands for no part of the culture of this country.... In all his thirty-odd years here he has played no more than three pieces of [U.S.] symphonic music," as a Mrs. Samuel Lyle Conner complained.[42] Neither programmed more than a handful of compositions from the Americas on their respective tours, although Stokowski, the media genius, assembled a special All-American Youth Orchestra, embodying the "freshness" of the Americas. Public intellectuals also visited Latin America. Waldo Frank made headlines by opening a talk in Mexico City with the words "I have come ... to learn," an utterance deemed so comment-worthy that it was repeated in the Latin American press.[43] On another occasion, he dazzled his public by declaring, "I have not come to preach."[44] These simple declarative sentences were no mere rhetorical ploys. Rather, they reflected Frank's distaste for a "subject-object hierarchy" while affirming that Latin America had something to teach the United States, a rare position even during the Good Neighbor period.[45]

Goodwill tours had to be approached with care. The 1940 movie *Argentine Nights*, which revolves around a goodwill tour, is filled with slow-witted Latins and geographical inaccuracies; its main musical number, the "Rhumbaboogie," features the Andrews Sisters frolicking in Caribbean ruffles to a bizarre amalgamation of pseudo-Cuban rhythms and boogie-woogie, neither related even remotely to Argentine music.[46] The term "goodwill" could also smack of amateurism. In summer 1941, the Yale Glee Club toured six Latin American countries, one of the music committee's most successful projects.[47] Yet Smith worried that since performances were free, some Brazilians suspected that they were put "in a goodwill class" and speculated that "the expression 'goodwill' will come to be an insult before long."[48]

Copland weighed in on U.S. music suitable for export by the OIAA. He fashioned two repertory lists, one for record libraries of Latin American radio stations and the other for a projected tour. (The latter he divided into music for either "big, sophisticated towns" or "less sophisticated publics.") As Jennifer L. Campbell points out, these lists constitute a veritable "Who's Who" of U.S. composers.[49] They included works with elements of jazz (George Gershwin's *An American in Paris*), references to U.S. traditions (Ives's "Barn Dance" from the *Holidays Symphony*), or evocations of emblematic figures (*Billy the Kid*, Robert Russell Bennett's *Abraham Lincoln Symphony*), all furnishing a carefully cultivated image of the United States. So that Latin Americans could appreciate broad historical trends, Copland added "older-generation" pieces, such Henry F. Gilbert's *Comedy Overture on Negro Themes* and Edward MacDowell's "Dirge" from *Indian Suite*; he also recommended the more-current William Grant Still's *Afro-American Symphony*. In addition to *El salón México*, Copland included Robert McBride's *Mexican Rhapsody*, confirming that U.S. composers were now looking southward for inspiration instead of to Europe. To be sure, Copland suggested a few abstract works: violin concertos by Walter Piston and Samuel Barber and symphonies by Randall Thompson and Harris (nos. 2 and 3, respectively). In only one instance, however, did he venture into the avant-garde, suggesting *Amériques* by Edgard Varèse, hardly a U.S. composer but practically embraced as such given his long residency in the United States.[50] Once "in the field," as diplomats of the era were wont to say, Copland offered only a few abstract or avant-garde pieces to his Latin American public.

Still, the OIAA Music Committee recognized the need to "work" Latin American elites, those listeners receptive to "webs of atonal dissonant counterpoint." Chamber music, with its aura of connoisseurship, fit the bill. The newly formed League of Composers Woodwind Quintet comprised David Van Vactor, flute; Alvin Etler, oboe; Robert McBride, clarinet; Adolph Weiss, bassoon; and John Barrows, horn, each of whom also composed. They would perform in Latin America but also "study local rhythms and melodies with an idea to harmonizing them or composing new works based on Latin American themes."[51] In promoting them, the music committee argued that despite lacking popular appeal, the group would "interest the musical elite," adding that "the importance of the small, well-educated music circles in Latin American [could not] be over-estimated."[52] Likely the project was approved for this reason. The tour included cities such as Bahia Blanca (Argentina) and Recife (Brazil) in addition to Central America (Guatemala, Costa Rica, and Panama). Audiences were indeed small, and the repertory, of Bach, Mozart, Hindemith, Villa-Lobos, Mignone, and some of the players' works (none specified), departed from the OIAA's informal criteria.

The music committee also weighed possibilities other than classical music. Several proposals for folk music, enthusiastically embraced at the 1939 conference, reached the committee. When Sarah Gertrude Knott, director of the National Folk Festival, submitted a proposal for research in Brazil, she was advised to consult folk music scholars George Herzog or Alan Lomax since her project was "a little bit out of [the committee's] scope."[53] Undaunted by the committee's ostensible indifference to nonclassical music, Clark began compiling lists of folk and popular music, which he planned to offer Hollywood to ensure that the musical misunderstandings so richly exhibited in *Argentine Nights* would be avoided in future. To that end, Clark enlisted Durán and Chase, who published bibliographies under his stern editorial eye.[54]

## Jazz as Export?

Another possibility was jazz. However much "Candide" complained, it cannot be said that the OIAA Music Committee ignored jazz.[55] Members studied, for example, an anonymous memo on radio programming in Latin America whose author held that "one of the most insistent criticisms [by Latin Americans] of American stations is the over-emphasis on jazz music." Swing bands are "completely unintelligible to most Latin American listeners," the memo read, such that "any considerable playing of jazz would gain more enemies than friends";

likewise, Smith reported only lukewarm feelings for jazz in Latin America.[56] These accounts were far from complete, however. For decades, lively jazz communities had thrived in any number of Latin American countries. Some jazz fans were musically sophisticated. Chávez, for example, admired Art Tatum and visited jazz clubs in Harlem with his compatriot the painter Miguel Covarrubias.[57] Like many of his generation, Chávez composed modernist, jazz-inspired works, such as *Foxtrot* (1925), *Fox* (1928), and *Blues* (1928), all for piano.[58] He also programmed jazz-based works: besides Copland's *Music for the Theatre*, in 1928 he conducted John Alden Carpenter's *Skyscraper Suite*. When Victoria Ocampo heard Duke Ellington at Harlem's Cotton Club in 1931, she took in the music's "fury," along with the "intensity of its rhythms and hardnosed insistence." Her conclusion? That "a public used to explosions such as these will . . . find itself perfectly capable of listening to the *Rite of Spring*."[59] Juan Carlos Paz never lingered at the Cotton Club. But from Buenos Aires (prior to adopting twelve-tone writing), he wrote the piano piece *Tres movimientos de jazz*, a wry work with strategically placed syncopations, growls in the low register of the piano, and ironic titles (the first two movements are called "De profundis" and "Spleen").

Jazz was more than an intellectual pursuit in Latin America. Chileans had been dancing the shimmy since around 1920, and jazz thrived in Santiago and Valparaíso.[60] In 1920s Mexico the México Jazz Band and the Jazz Band León entertained the public.[61] In Cuba, the traditional Afrocuban rumba risked transformation as elements of jazz were added to its essential framework.[62] Certainly jazz had its detractors. From Uruguay, Lange observed that it distracted the modern Latin American man from "his mystic energies."[63] As elsewhere, jazz was likened to a disease: in 1927, one critic wrote that "the epilepsy of jazz . . . galvanizes our bodies," reflecting "anxieties and worries that previously passed by unnoticed."[64] All fingers pointed to the United States for having unleashed the jazz "invasion" in the first place. (In Haiti, where Creole-speaking musicians referred to *djaz*, an actual invasion had taken place in 1915, with the growth of Haitian jazz bands one result.)[65] Some Latin American critics racialized jazz and attacked the United States in one fell swoop. The Mexican journalist Luis G. Urbina observed that "black music has invaded . . . like a wave of mud," for which "Yanquilandia" was solely to blame.[66] In the end, the OIAA Music Committee sent no jazz musicians to Latin America, seriously considering only one possibility: a "whitened" form of jazz in the person of the pianist Oscar Levant.[67] It is safe to say that when Copland went to Latin America, he was unaware of the jazz culture that had taken root.

## "Part of a slave race"

Reports on Axis infiltration continued to mount. In April 1941, President Roosevelt told the governing board of the Pan American Union that war was "approaching the very brink of the Western hemisphere."[68] When Seeger visited a music committee meeting, he scolded it for failing to send scores and publications to Latin American conservatories and orchestras, that is, "the type of cultural propaganda which the Italians and Germans have carried out for some time," he remonstrated.[69] According to an unsigned report, the United States "must point out to each [Latin American] what German domination would mean to his way of living.... It must warn him that he would be part of a slave race."[70]

The OIAA Music Committee also confronted the "slave race" in the United States. In July 1941 Mary Winslow of the coordinator's office proposed a Latin American tour for William Grant Still.[71] By then, Still had composed chamber works, over a dozen orchestral pieces, and many smaller-scale compositions. His *Song of a City*, for chorus and orchestra, was used as ambient music for the 1939 World's Fair, an honor that gave Still great satisfaction even if he could only attend the fair without police protection on "Negro Day."[72] Stokowski and his All-Americans had essayed the Scherzo of the *Afro-American Symphony* in Argentina and the Orquesta Sinfónica de Yucatán programmed Still's blues-tinged *From the Black Belt*.[73]

By the time the committee considered Still's proposal, all seemed to be in place for presenting the United States as a land where Black artists received their due. He would not have been the first: in 1940 Lillian Evanti, one of the three Black delegates to the 1939 Conference on Inter-American Relations in the Field of Music, visited Rio de Janeiro. She became involved with the Sociedade de Cultura Artistica, whose president was the medical doctor and music lover Rodolpho Josetti, seen by some as a fascist sympathizer. Yet, Smith noted, Josetti was "sufficiently broadminded to invite Lillian Evanti to sing at his house ... hardly what Hitler would have done."[74] The light-skinned Evanti, who sometimes "passed" for White and who mainly performed the Western European canon, was clearly a safe choice for U.S. diplomacy. The music committee recommended other similarly qualified Black artists for Latin American tours: Dorothy Maynor, Marian Anderson, Paul Robeson, and Roland Hayes, representing in microcosm W. E. B. Du Bois's "Talented Tenth," the gifted few that would uplift the race.[75] (One "unsafe" exception was Robeson, by then an avowed leftist.)[76] All figure only in this initial list, however, and do not appear to have been subsequently discussed.

Cultural diplomats brought home their impressions of Brazil's mixed-race society. In 1941 the Pan American Union sent a music education team of John W. Beattie, dean of the School of Music, Northwestern University, and Louis Woodson Curtis, past president of the National Association for Music Education, to visit Latin American schools and meet music teachers. In the *Music Educators Journal*, Beattie and Curtis described "the seeming ease with which [Brazil] has solved its race problem," noting that although complete racial justice still eluded Brazil, Black and White Brazilians were "gradually approaching amalgamation," including in the education system.[77] If this rosy scenario were true, several episodes in cultural exchange would have turned out quite differently. The experience of Orson Welles is telling: in 1942 he traveled to Brazil to make a movie about Carnaval in Rio but encountered resistance from the Brazilian government because the project emphasized samba's African roots and life in the favelas (hillside shantytowns) at the edge of Rio de Janeiro, where impoverished Afro-Brazilians lived.[78] Further, some Latin Americans were unwilling that their countries be presented as anything but White. The Brazilian historian Pedro Calmon, for example, cautioned against representing Brazil as filled with "negroes" and "predominantly African" dances.[79]

On 10 July 1941 Smith, Taylor, and Durán discussed the possibility of a Latin American tour for Still. (Copland, already at the Berkshire Music Center, was not present.) All that remains of their conversation is a cryptic reference in the minutes to Still's choral ballad, *And They Lynched Him on a Tree*. With a text by Katherine Chapin and scored for contralto soloist (the *mater dolorosa* of the lynched man), male narrator, double chorus (one White and one Black), and orchestra, the work had premiered in June 1940 before an audience of thirteen thousand at New York's Lewisohn Stadium. The minutes of the 10 July meeting note only that in light of "too many urgent matters pending," it was impossible to arrange a tour for "the composer of 'They Lynched Him to [sic] a Tree.'"[80] Given Still's many other compositions, it is striking that the committee singled out this piece. In fact, it is peripherally connected to cultural diplomacy. Still and Chapin dedicated it to Henry Allen Moe, who had served on the Julius Rosenwald Foundation Fellowship committee, which gave Still funding.[81] Also, the guest list for the premiere included the Librarian of Congress Archibald MacLeish, who had welcomed delegates to the Conference on Inter-American Relations in the Field of Music, and pianist Olga Samaroff, who attended subsequent music advisory committee meetings.[82] Further, Still and Chapin avoided propaganda: although antilynching legislation had floundered in Congress, Chapin believed the work would convince "not [through] propaganda but because it is great music."[83] Copland reportedly admired *And They Lynched Him on a Tree*, on par with his outrage over the Scottsboro Boys.[84] Had he been at the 10 July meeting of the OIAA Music Committee, he might well have advocated for Still's Latin American tour.

If the committee had any illusions about shielding Latin Americans from the savage practice of lynching, they were too late. In *Sur*, Ocampo published a translation of William Faulkner's "Dry September," a short story about lynching.[85] In 1937 Revueltas composed "Canto de una muchacha negra" (Song for a Dark Girl) on a text by Langston Hughes, a terse, dissonant dirge that refers to the "bruised body high in the air" (cadáver balanceante) and that twice repeats, in contrasting ranges, the words "way down South in Dixie" (allá lejos, en el sur).[86] Chávez's "North Carolina Blues," on a text by the Mexican poet Xavier Villaurrutia and dedicated to Langston Hughes, explicitly identifies a region tainted by lynchings, with three repetitions of "en North Carolina" juxtaposed with images of sweat and entrails against an accompaniment that flirts not only with blues but habanera and cinquillo rhythms, all furnishing a "grotesque dance of death," as Stephanie N. Stallings observes.[87] Chávez himself performed *And They Lynched Him on a Tree* in 1944 with the Orquesta Sinfónica de México as "Y lo colgaron de un árbol," having personally overseen the Spanish translation.[88] That the music committee so readily identified Still with this piece—to them, after all, he was "the composer of 'They Lynched Him to [sic] a Tree'"—lays bare the friction between sincere aspirations for equality, the pressures of image making, and the corrosiveness of overly cautious foreign policy.

## "Jumbled proceedings"

Members of the OIAA Music Committee worked hard, and like his colleagues, Copland read a great many proposals. Besides those just described, the committee reviewed (and unanimously rejected) one by the Orpheus Male Chorus of Cleveland to fund a South American tour. Also rejected was a request from the Department of Agriculture to "cover the cost of a half-hour transcription by a symphonic choir" of a *Christ of the Andes Symphony* by one Clough Lighter for distribution in South America. (The matter was finalized when Seeger played excerpts of the score on the piano.)[89] Many applicants wanted to advance their careers. In April 1941 Copland's friend Colin McPhee requested funding to visit Peru, Bolivia, and Brazil, where he would collect "ritualistic music" and then apply its principles to his own compositions. In his proposal, McPhee stressed his experiences in Bali, Java, and Sumatra, emphasizing his good relations with "the natives" and explaining that he had "always managed to get on very well with them, sleeping in their houses, eating their food, and establishing a friendly contact that made work so much easier."[90] He sent a private note to Copland, confessing that his proposal was "the most pompous thing" he had ever written. He also confessed, "Aaron, the reason I want to do this work, apart from its great interest, is that it would establish me, be something I could build on."[91]

In short, committee members were overwhelmed. In an undated memo, Taylor pointed out that it considered "far too many projects," and criticized Smith for running too loose a ship.[92] Certainly minutes betray scarcely a whiff of Robert's Rules; also, Smith, who had a droll sense of humor, occasionally authored shadow minutes in which he poked fun at Seeger, whom he found overbearing. (Smith was no fan of verbosity: once, when a Brazilian university conferred on him an honorary degree in a ceremony, he answered a long-winded address by taking out his flute and playing Debussy's *Syrinx*.)[93] Bartholomew grumbled that the atmosphere was "more like a meeting on the Stock Exchange than that of a committee where important matters are being discussed and decided upon."[94] Convinced that Washington was displeased with the music committee, Bartholomew slammed its "jumbled proceedings."

In fairness to Smith, the bureaucratic structure of the OIAA itself was daunting. The music committee was expected to coordinate with the executive board of the OIAA, the music section of the Pan American Union, and the advisory committee on music to the Department of State, on which Copland nominally served. As a result, multiple authorizations were required for the slightest action. An additional entity also sprang up: the Committee for Inter-American Artistic and Intellectual Relations, consisting of three individuals from the world of private giving. One was Moe (the dedicatee of *And They Lynched Him on a Tree*), with his broad experience in the world of private foundations. The other two "philanthropoids" were David H. Stevens of the Rockefeller Foundation and Frederick Keppel of the Carnegie Corporation. This three-man organization received monies from the OIAA's generous budget and disbursed them as it saw fit, thus lending an "appearance of private giving," as Rockefeller's critics carped.[95] It was this committee that controlled the funds for Copland's 1941 trip.

In short, many matters deemed to "merit further discussion" never resurface in subsequent minutes, instead evaporating into the bureaucratic haze. Yet the OIAA Music Committee did accomplish several things. In addition to tours by the Yale Glee Club tour and the League of Composers Wind Quintet, a generous $140,000 budget was given to the American Ballet Caravan to perform works by U.S. composers in Latin America. Founded by Lincoln Kirstein, the company grew out of the American Ballet, established in 1935 and to which Kirstein had enticed George Balanchine of the Imperial Ballet School in St. Petersburg, mainly to raise the standard of dance in the United States while taking into account U.S. character. Kirstein was convinced that for winning hearts and minds, "dance was the perfect medium . . . since it did not involve speech."[96] The ballets for Latin America included *Filling Station*, about a day in the life of a gas station mechanic with Virgil Thomson's score; *Juke Box*, on U.S. college life with music by Alec Wilder; *Pastorela*, a Mexican-themed work with a score by Paul Bowles; *Time Table*, which used Copland's *Music for the Theatre*; and *Billy the Kid*, which Copland would conduct in Lima.[97]

Private individuals also supported musical Good Neighborliness, including Elizabeth Sprague Coolidge, one of Copland's patrons and who sponsored a Pan American Festival of Chamber Music.[98] There was also Edwin Adler Fleisher of Philadelphia. Having donated a trove of orchestral scores to the Free Library of Philadelphia, in which he paid for paper, ink, and other supplies (the WPA covered copyists' salaries), Fleisher realized that Latin American music was lacking.[99] He decided to spend $10,000 to dispatch Slonimsky, former firebrand of the PACC, to Latin America on a search for scores, a "Pan American fishing trip," as Slonimsky called it.[100] (He and Copland would perform together in Buenos Aires.) The hundreds of orchestral compositions Slonimsky obtained remain at the Free Library for use by scholars, performers, and other interested parties.[101]

## A "Special Envoy": Copland's Projects

Despite bureaucratic confusion, Copland proved one of the OIAA Music Committee's more effective members. He was not its most vocal—an honor Clark seems to have held—but took several initiatives, carrying them forward to the extent possible. Not all came to fruition, such as his plan to commission Latin American works by U.S. orchestras. The same was true of his idea that the committee "promote and, if possible, present a concert" during the May 1941 festival of the International Society for Contemporary Music (ISCM), taking place in New York because of the European war.[102] No program was devoted solely to Latin American music, but the third concert, on 23 May, featured music of the Americas: string quartets nos. 3 and 4 (*Música de feria*) by Revueltas, *Pieza* for string quartet by his compatriot Salvador Contreras, and *Música para trío* (clarinet, trumpet, alto saxophone) by Paz. For Olin Downes, who detected "artificiality and sterility" in the works by U.S. composers, the "best scores" came from Mexico, with Revueltas's third quartet displaying "brilliancy and expert use of telling harmonic colors," and Contreras's music full of "color and idiom."[103] Paz's compositions were already known to connoisseurs. His Sonatina for flute and clarinet was heard at the 1933 ISCM in Amsterdam and at the 1937 festival Charles Munch had conducted his *Passacaglia*, the first twelve-tone work by an Argentine to be performed abroad.[104] Apropos the New York concert, Donald Fuller praised Paz's *Música para trío* for its "pleasing peculiarity of sound."[105] A heftier endorsement came from Thomson, who was "charmed by [the work's] jewelry-like beauty" and by Paz's "precious awareness of musical materials, of intervals and themes and rhythms and counterpoint, of sounds delicate and clear."[106] In chamber music, at least, Latin America fared better than the Colossus of the North.

One of Copland's more successful projects involved libraries. In early 1941 he drafted a project analysis for a series of recordings for Latin American "radio stations, schools, libraries, consulates, etc."[107] (As noted, Copland had drawn up the repertory list.) A grant from the coordinator's office would ensure a contract with Columbia or Victor, "guaranteeing to them in advance the sale of X number of sets of each recording"; Spanish-language commentary would be included. The committee unanimously approved the plan, with Taylor suggesting that Copland's initial plan for twenty sets of recordings be expanded in light of CBS's network of sixty-three Latin American affiliates. Copland's plan wended its way through the bureaucracy and received an allocation of $50,000.[108] Throughout his cultural diplomacy tours in Latin America, he would repeatedly advocate for libraries, convinced that short of live performances, recordings and scores were the best way to disseminate music of the United States.

Since its earliest meetings, the OIAA Music Committee planned to send Copland on a tour as a "composer-lecturer."[109] The committee set forth his obligations: making "South American audiences aware of contemporary American composition, conducting some of [Copland's] own compositions where that might be arranged, lecturing in Spanish on the subject of North American composition, in short proceeding as a special envoy in the interest of contemporary North American composition of a serious nature."[110] Initially, the possibility was floated of Copland traveling with violinist Ruth Posselt, conductor Karl Krueger, and pianists Jesús María Sanromá, Oscar Levant, or John Kirkpatrick, although it ultimately proved too complicated.[111] While his tour took shape, Copland attended to less glamorous committee responsibilities: evaluating more proposals, reading weekly progress reports on OIAA activities in the form of "digests" distributed by Rockefeller's office, and reviewing minutes from previous meetings.

Also before his tour, Copland took the initiative of generating scholarships for young Latin American musicians to study at the Berkshire Music Center. Koussevitzky was sympathetic to musical Pan Americanism, having declared at the opening Tanglewood concert of 8 July 1940, "if ever there was a time to speak of music, it is now in the New World."[112] Copland began the preliminary paperwork, informing Koussevitzky and Margaret Grant, the center's executive secretary, of his plan.[113] The OIAA Music Committee unanimously approved Copland's proposal on the condition that the center provide the scholarships and the OIAA travel and living expenses.[114] The students would be nominated by conservatories in Rio de Janeiro, Buenos Aires, Santiago, and Bogotá.[115] Copland began making contacts in Latin America, writing Antônio Sá Pereira of the Escola Nacional de Musica, in Rio de Janeiro, that "the Music Committee feels that by attendance at this school, Latin American students will be able to come into contact with the musical culture of the United States in one of its finest manifestations."[116] Five young Latin American musicians were eventually selected, representing a range of countries and specializations: Altéia Alimonda, violinist (Brazil); Marcelo Montecino, violinist (Chile); Alejandro Zagarra, violinist (Colombia); Alfredo Ianelli, flutist (Argentina); and Blas Galindo, composer (Mexico).[117]

Still, Copland's project was almost sabotaged thanks to the tortured bureaucratic dance. By mid-June 1941, the plan had been approved at all levels, and the committee was given to understand that funds would be appropriated. Yet as Grant noted, because "the Government cannot make payments before the completion of the plan, the necessary funds must be advanced by some other agency to be repaid later by the Government."[118] In other words, the government had to make a contract similar to those made "between the Government, the Carnegie Corporation, Guggenheim Foundation, and other agencies," in this case, the Boston Symphony Orchestra, which would advance the funds. Grant also cautioned that "if the project were to be abandoned the effect might be the opposite of the good relations which we had hoped to establish." Thankfully (and at the eleventh hour), these obstacles were overcome, and all five young musicians showed up, laying the foundation for future visits to the Berkshires by Latin Americans. The 1941 season began with an exuberant celebration of hemispheric solidarity. A gala benefit concert for the USO and the British War Relief opened with Galindo's *Sexteto* for flute, clarinet, bassoon, horn, trumpet, and trombone, after which the Boston Symphony Orchestra, the Music Center Orchestra, Chorus, Chamber, and Opera divisions, and 250 army bandsmen from nearby Cape Edwards all performed under the direction of the indefatigable Koussevitzky.[119]

## A Citizen Diplomat Prepares

That spring Copland made a quick trip to Cuba, mainly to work on *Our New Music*. He made it a point to listen to popular music, writing Bernstein of the excitement of being in "a crazily mixed-up city with skins of all colors."[120] He also reported,

> I've sat for hours on end in 5¢ a dance joints, listening. Finally the band in one place got the idea, and invited me up to the band platform. "Usted musico [sic]?" *Yes*, says I. What a music factory it is! Thirteen black men and me—quite a piquant scene. The thing I like most is the quality of voice when the Negroes sing down here. It does things to me—it's so sweet and moving. And just think, no serious Cuban composer is using any of this.[121]

Indeed, something was missing in his "field work":

> I have a slightly frustrated feeling in not being able to discuss it with anyone, and a sinking feeling that no one but you and I would think it so much fun. Anyway, I'm bringing back a few records, but they are only analogous to Guy Lombardo versions of the real thing.[122]

In a matter of months, Copland would return to Cuba where he would explore music from a very different perspective. Surely it was with his tour in mind that he also studied Spanish in Cuba, working with a private tutor. By the time he returned to New York, official preparations for his nine-country tour were in full swing. On 6 June 1941, Moe wrote Copland outlining its terms:

> *Purpose*: To study contemporary Latin American music, to lecture on American music and to conduct concerts of American music in several Latin America countries
> *Period:* From August 19 to December 2, 1941
> *Grant:* Three thousand one hundred dollars

In a separate document, Copland learned that he was to "come back with a list of composers and musical scholars who . . . are first-rate and who ought to be given funds to come to the United States for sound musical purposes."[123] Moe, who had known Copland since 1925, when the composer was first awarded a Guggenheim Fellowship, now advised him that although he was "in no sense an official of the U.S. government," he would be "regarded in Latin America as representative of the United States and of your profession; and this is what we desire for we have every confidence in you as a person and as a musician, else this grant would not have been made."[124] Moe also took pains to explain Copland's mission and advised him of possible pitfalls in any goodwill tour. "In Latin America there has been adopted the word 'goodwillings,'" which, Moe explained, "one Chilean scholar called 'an opportunistic attitude'"; Moe added, "We want no 'goodwillings' but "hard and serious professional work."[125] In sum, as a composer of "serious" music in whom the government trusted, Copland would show Latin Americans that U.S. classical music (and by extension U.S. culture) had something to offer. His gracious personality and ability to speak Spanish would enhance the message. Copland was also instructed to purchase health and accident insurance and was advised that "a rather complete report" would be expected of him when he returned.[126]

Administrative cross-talk continued. Although Copland normally attended only OIAA Music Committee meetings, in June 1941 he visited Washington for a meeting of the advisory committee on music to the Department of State. In April he had received a letter of retroactive appointment from no less than Undersecretary of State Welles to serve on the Music Advisory Committee for the period 1 July 1940 to 30 June 1941.[127] At the Washington meeting, Copland asked whether he should "properly be a member of both the Coordinator's Committee and the State Department's Advisory Committee," an idea that met with broad approval.[128] Due to ongoing tensions between the OIAA and the State Department, the OIAA Music Committee was absorbed into the Advisory Committee on Music to the State Department in October 1941, to which Copland was also appointed.[129] By then, he was already in Latin America.

Not surprisingly, Copland wondered exactly which organization he represented.[130] On 10 August 1941 the *New York Times* reported that his trip was sponsored by the Division of Cultural Relations.[131] On 24 August, however, the *Times* noted in an extended article by music critic and Hispanophile Ross Parmenter that Copland was being sent by the "Committee for Inter-American Cultural Relations, an autonomous office working through the office of Nelson A. Rockefeller."[132] Copland asked Moe how he should account for himself, and on 14 August, five days before departure, Moe replied reassuringly that "the truth is of course wholly okay." He then set forth the facts to the composer: "you are a grantee of [the Committee for Inter-American Cultural Relations], which is an autonomous organization whose funds come from the Coordinator of Commercial and Cultural Relations between the American Republics."[133] Moe was adamant on this point. After de Freitas of the administrative staff wrote sixteen letters of introduction to various figures in Latin American music explaining that Copland was "one of the most active members" of the OIAA Music Committee and that his visit was "funded by the Guggenheim Foundation," Moe hastened to correct her.[134] "It is not the fact ... that Mr. Copland's trip to Latin America is 'sponsored by the Guggenheim Foundation' but rather the Committee for Inter-American Cultural Relations," he explained.[135] All sixteen letters were rewritten.

Copland also dealt with musical matters. The first Latin American composer to welcome him was Paz.[136] By this time, Paz had abandoned the ISCM-affiliated Grupo Renovación, which had been promoting modern music in Buenos Aires since 1929. Finding that organization timid, he founded the avant-garde concert series Conciertos de la Nueva Música, also based in Buenos Aires. Well informed about music in the United States, he corresponded with Paul Pisk, Gerald Strang, Henry Cowell, and George Perle.[137] Paz had no use for musical folklore, which he condemned as fit only for "puerile spirits" indifferent to historical progress.[138] Surely Copland was aware of Paz's orientation, so different from his own. In 1940 Lazare Saminsky toured Latin America and interviewed Paz for *Modern Music*, describing him as a "fanatical twelve-tonalist and *Schönbergista*." According to Saminsky, Paz believed that when "the Argentine composer tries to be national ... and invokes the easy folklore of Argentina, his language seems dead, his folkloric style superficial, his creative impotence only too obvious and pathetic."[139] Saminsky and Paz also saw eye to eye on eclecticism (the very quality Saminsky had attacked in Copland). For Paz, eclecticism was the antithesis of modernism, given the aesthetic shilly-shallying it implied.[140]

In a letter of 10 June, Paz greeted Copland warmly, however, assuring him that Conciertos de la Nueva Música was at his disposal.[141] In response, Copland sent Paz his Piano Variations. On 3 August Paz acknowledged receipt, now addressing Copland as "muy estimado amigo" (my esteemed friend) instead of the more formal "distinguido señor" (distinguished sir) of his previous letter. "I knew this stunning work from the Columbia recording in which it appears in your magisterial interpretation," Paz wrote.[142] In a letter of 3 September, which reached Copland in Bogotá, Paz lamented that he had managed to wrangle only a few dates for possible engagements, blaming the "reactionary" views of local musical organizations; a few days later, he wrote yet again, now on the practical details of Copland's visit.[143] Surely Copland appreciated the hospitality shown him by this formidable representative of the Argentine musical community. (Readers familiar with Paz's sharp tongue will be struck by the cordial tone of his letters.) Impressed by the unflinching modernism of the Piano Variations, Paz was eager to assemble for Copland an audience of peers. One wonders, however, how closely the "fanatical Schönbergista" had followed Copland's recent moves. Surely Paz knew—and disliked—*El salón México* and *Billy the Kid*. But in 1941 he kept a discreet silence on Copland the folklorist to support the Copland the modernist.

On 10 July 1941, weeks before Copland was to leave, Kirstein wrote Smith on the challenges of "selling" U.S. culture in Latin America, which Smith passed on to Copland. Allowing that the American Ballet Caravan had been successful so far, Kirstein nonetheless recognized that "the success has been based on Balanchine's classic works which have been wildly received, particularly the old ones. Due to a series of circumstances ... the American scores were either ignored or forgiven. Among these circumstances is the usual prejudice against American art as a whole."[144] Kirstein also noted problems he labeled "political," consisting mainly of tensions between embassy personnel and the coordinator. According to him, the embassy in Rio de Janeiro provided no support, and the ambassador remarked that "he would stop us from playing the scores if he could—but he was not sufficiently interested." Put simply, "the North American music angle is not working out right." Rather dramatically Kirstein added, "If America doesn't take the artistic responsibility for creating new works, then the Germans deserve to take us."[145]

At that point, Copland had little time to ponder geopolitics. On 8 July 1941 Rexach informed him that Durán was researching the possibilities for translating *Our Town* and *Of Mice and Men* and would advise Copland of his findings.[146] Shortly thereafter, Smith asked Copland if he would please drive in his "magnificent car" from the Berkshire Center to Bennington, Vermont, where the League of Composers Woodwind Quintet would launch its Pan American tour. (Robert McBride, the clarinetist, taught at Bennington College.) Besides suggesting that Copland make the two-hour round-trip drive and "supervise some of the practicing and select some of the material," Smith wondered if he could "possibly ... arrange a little concert in Lenox just before the group takes off. It would be a grand thing," Smith continued, "as far as publicity for Latin America is concerned."[147] On 31 July 1941 Durán wrote that the 1939 documentary *The City*, with Copland's score, was available in translation and would be sent to him in Chile. (In response to a query from Copland, he confessed that he did not know its weight.)[148] On 1 August Smith wrote Copland again, now from Durango, Mexico, to report that he was "losing sleep" because both the contract for the quintet and the spending money for the five Latin American students remained unresolved. Again, Smith prevailed upon Copland: could he work out this matter among the lawyers? "You are the one man to straighten out this difficulty," Smith cajoled, also repeating his request that Copland travel to Bennington.[149] By the time Copland boarded the plane on 19 August, weighed down with his own luggage and an extensive collection of records that would accompany him for the next four months, he was probably glad to be getting away.

# PART II

# Copland, Latin America, and World War II

# 4
# Diplomat "in the Field"

In August 1941 the Division of Cultural Relations crafted an internal report, "Radio Activities in Inter-American Cultural Relations." It sounded a warning: activities were curtailed "in view of the fact that no funds have been made available for radio."[1] These bleak words were underlined in thick black ink, likely by some State Department employee. Despite overwhelming optimism over radio's potential in countering Axis propaganda, the division was hamstrung.[2] As Smith had warned, many in Latin America listened regularly to broadcasts from Germany and Italy. Perhaps some listeners even wondered: how could countries that produced Beethoven or Verdi possibly be wrong? Broadcasts from the United States that did reach Latin America showcased European classical music (often performed by the NBC or Chicago Symphonies), popular music, and jazz.[3]

As a cultural diplomat, Copland took full advantage of radio, through which he promoted music of the United States and musical Pan Americanism. His first broadcast in Latin America took place during the 1941 tour in Colombia, where he traveled after spending a week in Mexico. He then visited Ecuador, Peru, Chile, Argentina, Uruguay, Brazil, and Cuba, a total of nine countries. Countries believed to lack cultural clout, such as Bolivia and Paraguay, were not included. Nor was Venezuela: despite (or perhaps because of) Rockefeller's imprint there, Venezuelan oil was a source of conflict.[4] In Cuba, Copland's last port of call, he learned of the invasion of Pearl Harbor on 7 December. Five days later, he left for home.

The State Department generally concentrated on the so-called ABC countries—Argentina, Brazil, Chile—of interest to the Axis for their natural resources and their German and Italian populations (covered in chapters 5, 6, and 7). But other countries also mattered. This chapter examines Copland's visits to Mexico, Colombia, Peru, Ecuador, and Uruguay (on Cuba, see chapter 8). Especially in Colombia and Peru, he tested several strategies that became staples of his cultural diplomacy. Besides giving the first of his twelve lectures of the 1941 tour, he made his radio and conducting debuts, leading Lincoln Kirstein's American Ballet Caravan in *Billy the Kid*. As per his charge from the OIAA, Copland met composers and evaluated them for possible visits to the United States. Undoubtedly, he sensed the fine line between blatant "selling" of U.S. culture and pursuing a propaganda-free "diplomacy of truth."

## "The Foreign Land Right Next Door"

Copland left New York the evening of 19 August, arriving early the next morning in Brownsville, Texas, on the northern bank of the Rio Grande. After a short layover, he boarded a flight to Mexico City on Pan American Airways, then known as the Pan American Airways System.[5] Copland always flew Pan American in his Latin American travels: after Germans infiltrated Latin American aviation by establishing companies such as the Brazilian-operated, German-owned Sindiesto-Condor and Deutsche-Lufthansa Sucursal Perú, Pan American worked closely with the Roosevelt administration to compete with the Germans.[6] Both advertising and Hollywood (as in the movie *Flying Down to Rio*) nudged U.S. consumers to recognize the airline's patriotism, and its Yankee Clipper fleet, showcased in the film, flew regularly to Latin America.[7]

At 12:25 P.M. on 20 August Copland arrived in Mexico City. Surely he was pleased that this "fresh and pure and wholesome" country was his first stop. These qualities were quickly becoming commercialized, however. The OIAA subcommittee on tourist travel was busily studying lodgings, food, and hygiene, calling for more hotels and Pullmans in Mexico, such that by war's end Mexico was being billed as "the foreign land right next door."[8] U.S.-Mexican relationships were generally cordial at this time. The Mexican foreign minister commented that the border with the United States was "a line that unites rather than divides us."[9] Mexicans were hardly unanimous over the European conflict, as some refused to side with the United States under any circumstances. Conservative president Manuel Ávila Camacho, elected in 1940, declared loyalty to the United States, however, and eventually won support even from communists, some of whom opposed Germany's invasion of Russia in June 1941.

Copland's week in Mexico City was fairly relaxed, with no broadcasts, lectures, press interviews, musical performances, or embassy functions. Still, he set to work, meeting composers and establishing the pattern that would serve him in the coming months. Nearly every day, he studied recent compositions, either by perusing scores, listening to recordings, or attending live performances. He would list these compositions in his diary and indicate those he liked best with an asterisk, sometimes conferring two asterisks (on one occasion three) and jotting down strengths and weaknesses. In Mexico he concentrated on the Grupo de los Cuatro (Group of Four). These young men had met while enrolled in Carlos Chávez's class "Musical Creation" at the Conservatorio Nacional, where Chávez taught until 1934.[10] The name "Grupo de los Cuatro" came about in November 1935, when they presented their works together and a critic christened them, perhaps alluding to Les Six in France or the Grupo de los Ocho in Madrid.[11] Like those entities, the Grupo de los Cuatro was united more by common purpose—to promote modern music of Mexico—than by any aesthetic orientation. One, Blas Galindo, had just worked with Copland at the Berkshire Center as a scholarship recipient. Another was Salvador Contreras, whose *Pieza* for string quartet had recently impressed critics at the New York International Society for Contemporary Music (ISCM). The other two were Daniel Ayala and José Pablo Moncayo. All had been performed in the United States. In January 1940 their works were featured on the concert, "Music of the Americas," moderated by Gilbert Chase in New York and sponsored by the Works Progress Administration (WPA).[12]

Writing in his diary about the "loosely knit group," Copland observed that Galindo, Contreras, Ayala, and Moncayo all hewed closely to "the style of the Mexican School, founded by Chávez and Revueltas."[13] (In fact, the young men were considered *chavistas*.)[14] He believed, however, that they had "not exceeded their older confrères," finding them "limited in their use of form, which tends always to be sectionally constructed, and in types of melodic material, which tend always toward the Mexican popular tune."[15] They did excel in orchestration, which Copland attributed to their having played in the Orquesta Sinfónica de México (OSM) under Chávez. (Contreras and Ayala were violinists whereas Galindo and Moncayo, who also played jazz piano, were percussionists.) Of the four, Copland believed that Galindo was the most advanced technically. But because he used "the potpourri style to exaggerated degree," some sections of his pieces were practically interchangeable with sections of others.[16] Copland does not indicate which Galindo scores he studied in Mexico City. But the thirty-one-year-old composer had hardly done badly in the United States. Besides the performance of his sextet at Tanglewood, one of Galindo's chamber works was praised by the Los Angeles–based critic and librettist Verna Arvey in 1938. (She doesn't identify the piece.)[17] Most noteworthy was the performance in May 1940 of *Sones mariachi*, Galindo's orchestration of traditional *sones*. (A *son* is a Mexican folk genre with many regional variants.) It was featured in "Twenty Centuries of Mexican Art," an exhibition and concert series held at that Rockefeller stronghold, New York's Museum of Modern Art (MoMA).[18] *New York Times* critic Howard Taubman enthused over the "gay, flavorsome music of the Central Pacific States of Mexico in a mettlesome arrangement by the talented Blas Galindo."[19]

As for Contreras, Copland studied three works that he found too much alike: *Música para orquesta sinfónica*, *Tres movimientos sinfónicos*, and a suite for string quintet, clarinet, bassoon, trumpet, and piano (probably Contreras's *Suite para orquesta de cámara* of 1938). In a different vein was *Corridos* for soprano, chorus and orchestra, inspired by the traditional Mexican *corrido*, the strophic form and functional harmonies of which generally treat some political or historical event. Contreras's *Corridos* is essentially a medley, complete with shouts from the chorus. Copland found it little more than "a straightforward setting of Mexican popular melodies—none too subtly done."[20] In fact, nothing Copland heard surpassed Contreras's *Pieza*. Copland was equally unenthusiastic about Ayala's music, finding it "picturesque and sectional rather than truly symphonic."[21] He also believed Ayala played up his Mayan background to excess, as in the 1939 ballet suite *El hombre maya*, based on the creation myth *Popol Vuh*. Certainly Ayala's ethnicity was part of his "brand": Chávez told the *New York Times* that Ayala was "of full-blooded Indian descent," adding, "It is a source of pride for the Mexican to know that he is even partly of Indian extraction."[22] Ayala's music was clearly part of the Pan Americanist project, however. His *U-Kayil-Chaac* (Mayan Chant to the Rain), with indigenous instruments and a Mayan text for the soprano soloist, figured at the 1937 Pan American Festival of Chamber Music, and in November 1941 Jacques Singer conducted Ayala's *Panoramas de México* with the Dallas Symphony Orchestra.[23]

In Moncayo, Copland noticed a "distinct flair" (albeit an inconsistent one).[24] He admired *Amatzinac*, for flute solo and strings, which opens with a wandering, sparsely textured statement, leading to an ostinato-based passage. To be sure, Copland registered "a certain French influence of the Milhaud type." But this trait was less conspicuous in Moncayo's *Huapango*, an orchestral rendering of a traditional Mexican dance from Veracruz state in a brisk tempo based on alternating six- and three-beat groupings.[25] Indeed, Copland believed *Huapango* to be Moncayo's best work, an opinion many have shared thanks to the composer's deft balancing of instrumental groupings (spotlighting the harp), gradual introduction of new themes, and overall exuberance. While in Mexico City, Copland also met the principal researcher on the *huapango*, folklorist, author, critic, and occasional composer Gerónimo Baqueiro Fóster.[26] He told Copland that he had collected over fifty huapangos, which Copland described in his diary as a "worthy project." Certainly such undertakings nudged Mexican composers away from "the French influence of the Milhaud type."

Copland also visited with four Spanish expatriates. As the only country besides the Soviet Union that supported the Second Republic during the Spanish Civil War, Mexico was a natural home to these Spaniards.[27] Three were musicologists: Adolfo Salazar, Jesús Bal y Gay, and Otto Mayer Serra (Salazar and Bal y Gay also composed) and, because all had participated in the Republic's cultural program, were decidedly unwelcome in Franco's Spain.[28] The fourth was the composer Rodolfo Halffter, previously sub-secretary of propaganda in the Republican government and among whose works is a set of "elegiac variations" for piano, *Para la tumba de Lenin* (For Lenin's Tomb). Copland studied works Halffter had written in Spain but also perused his violin concerto, commissioned by violinist Samuel Dushkin (Stravinsky's collaborator in the same medium) and scheduled to premiere in Mexico City. It opens with a dramatic cadenza, followed by allusions to the *jota* (a Spanish dance in a quick triple meter), virtuosic double-stops, and string crossings, flavored with the occasional Phrygian tetrachord. Copland deemed Halffter's works "well done in the best European-Spanish tradition" and "clearly written" but concluded that they lacked "real interest . . . because they lack real originality."[29] This did not stop Halffter's music from being played in the United States: his *Danza de Ávila* was published and Joaquín Nin-Culmell played Halffter's *Obertura concertante* for piano and orchestra in a broadcast with the Columbia Symphony, guest-conducted by the Mexican composer and conductor José Yves Limantour.[30]

This first leg of Copland's nine-country trip may not seem to be the most auspicious beginning for a campaign on behalf of musical Pan Americanism. With the exception of Moncayo, he found little that measured up to the standard Chávez had set. Given that Copland would eventually study the music of sixty-six composers, however, many of them young, we would hardly expect him to admire them all. As detailed below, Copland's often critical views were not always shared by other U.S. advocates of musical Pan Americanism. In fact, cultural diplomacy as Copland practiced it was "not a product . . . but a process," to borrow Richard T. Arndt's definition.[31] Meeting one-on-one with musicians, establishing rapport, exploring ideas, and finding stimulation in shared curiosity about music was Copland's "process," not uncovering masterpieces at every turn.

## "Upholding the Ideals of Democracy"

Copland's next destination was Bogotá. Thanks to President Eduardo Santos, elected in 1938, pro-Allied sentiment was gaining ground in Colombia. An avowed Francophile, Santos was convinced that the United States symbolized democratic ideals; an alliance with the United States, moreover, could help Colombia modernize its armed forces. At the same time, Germany eyed the country's platinum reserves and easy access to the Panama Canal. Colombia's approximately four thousand Axis sympathizers would have gladly supported a coup to remove Santos. Like other Latin American nations in mid-1941, Colombia maintained diplomatic ties with Germany.[32]

Copland arrived on 31 August after a night in Guatemala and a layover in Cristóbal (in the Panama Canal Zone). Meeting Copland at the airport were critic Otto de Greiff and conductor Guillermo Espinosa. The latter actively promoted Latin American music. Espinosa studied in Germany with the conductor Felix Weingartner and co-conducted the Berlin Radio Symphony Orchestra in a concert of German and Ibero-American repertory; he then initiated a five-concert series of Latin American music to mark the founding of the German–Latin American Musical Union. When Hitler came to power, Espinosa returned home, however, and in 1936 began directing the Orquesta Sinfónica Nacional de Colombia. Over lunch with Copland, both he and de Greiff lamented musical conditions in Colombia: the orchestra was at a low technical level and the Conservatorio Nacional lacked students. The situation in composition was similarly calamitous, they claimed, with only four individuals "worthy of serious consideration," as Copland noted in his diary. These were Guillermo Uribe Holguín and Adolfo Mejía, both of Bogotá; Antonio Valencia of Cali; and Carlos Posada Amador of Medellín.[33] Copland met Uribe Holguín and Mejía only: on 4 September he traveled to Cali, about 300 miles (470 kilometers) west of Bogotá, to find the conservatory closed and Valencia on vacation. He did not seek out Posada Amador.

In 1941 Uribe Holguín was sixty-one. He had studied in Brussels and then in Paris with Vincent d'Indy at the Schola Cantorum, where Erik Satie and Joaquín Turina were his classmates. In 1903, Uribe Holguín went to New York City and played the violin in various orchestras, taking on odd jobs as well. (When asked to produce a transcription of the overture to *Tannhäuser* for banjo, for example, he learned that instrument on short notice.) All is recounted in his entertaining autobiography *Vida de un músico colombiano* (Life of a Colombian Musician), a copy of which he presented to Copland.[34] Uribe Holguín advocated a cosmopolitan perspective that gave folklore little play, once declaring, "Music knows no country."[35] As such, he was a controversial figure at home and abroad.

Of Uribe Holgúin's approximately 120 pieces, Copland studied about a half dozen, some of which bear out these cosmopolitan aspirations. The loosely structured melodic lines and generous proportions of *Del Terruño* (From the Homeland) are reminiscent of César Franck, for example, despite the title. Copland also studied a Sonata for Violin and Piano from 1939, Uribe Holguín's fourth essay in that genre and also rooted in the Western European tradition. Yet the *Trozos en el sentimiento popular* (Pieces in Popular Sentiment), a series of hundreds of short pieces for piano, often derive from *bambuco* music, a Colombian music-dance genre with three-four/six-eight patterns and an opening upbeat of three eighth notes, accompanied by various members of the guitar family, including the tiple and the *bandola*.[36] Another folkloric work is the *Suite típica*, which Copland assigned an asterisk. He concluded that Uribe Holgúin was "the best Colombian [composer]" and "a force to be reckoned with." Yet Copland found his music "only fairly interesting": besides showing "signs of being written hastily," it did not "seem important—only pleasant."[37] Some in the United States differed. Chase, for example, admired Uribe Holguín's music, as his article on "Colombia's greatest composer" attests.[38] Slonimsky found the *Trozos en el sentimiento popular* "brilliantly written for the instrument."[39] He featured some of them (along with a movement from Uribe Holguín's violin suite) on the set of recordings *South American Chamber Music* (Columbia M-437), another fruit of Slonimsky's "Pan American fishing trip." In May 1940 Uribe Holguín's *Suite típica* was broadcast in a "Salute to the Americas" program that aired on several New York radio stations.[40] After Espinosa conducted it, President Santos greeted the radio audience, telling of his dream for "upholding of the ideals of democracy . . . now endangered."[41]

It was in Colombia that Copland first appeared on Latin American radio. He was featured in two forty-five minutes broadcasts on Radio Nacional (founded in 1940 as Radiodifusora Nacional de Colombia) at the invitation of no less than Gustavo Santos, brother of the president.[42] Like de Greiff and Espinosa, Santos (with whom Copland chatted at a luncheon on 2 September) was pessimistic about classical music in Colombia. Perhaps he hoped that Copland's radio broadcasts would stimulate Colombian musicians while reinforcing democratic principles. For the first program, Copland read a page or so of a greeting in Spanish. He then played the eleven-minute *El salón México* and the thirty-eight minute *Music for the Theatre*, both of which he found in the station's library, a pleasant surprise.[43] On his second broadcast, Copland played a work on which he frequently relied during the 1941 tour, Roy Harris's Third

Symphony. Also part of Copland's traveling record collection was the Harvard Glee Club's recording of Walter Piston's *Carnival Song* for male chorus and brass. Given that the initial cry of "giovinezza!" is also the title of the Italian fascist hymn (the word means "youth") the selection might seem an odd way to show solidarity against the Axis. Yet the piece's riotous humor and snappy articulations were likely appreciated. Copland then featured three piano works by his former student (and heartthrob) Paul Bowles.[44] Like many of his contemporaries, Bowles was fascinated with Mexico, defending its culture and music against "monstrous bastard kitsch," that is, arrangements purveyed by the music industry and played on radio programs of "broadcast horrors," as Bowles dramatically put it.[45] We don't know exactly which of Bowles's pieces Copland played for his Colombian listeners. Likely he selected works inspired by Latin America, such as *Two Huapangos*, or Latin-themed two-piano works, such as "El Bejuco" and "Caminata," both already recorded.[46]

Copland's Latin American radio debut underscores several points. First, he let it be known that U.S. composers, such as Bowles and himself, were eager to supplant European models by taking Latin America as a point of reference. Next, he played music of the "moderate mainstream," omitting the "webs of atonal dissonant counterpoint" against which Arthur Loesser had cautioned. Finally, Copland honed his style of cultural diplomacy. After his second broadcast, for example, he chatted with some of the Colombian musicians connected to the station and played several of his own works for them informally.[47] For Copland, this one-on-one contact proved the most effective and natural form of winning hearts and minds.

On 5 September Copland left Colombia for Ecuador. He spent only two days in Quito, where he visited Juan Gorrell, a "local American" who worked for RCA Victor and managed the music store Reed & Reed, which had branches in Quito and in Guayaquil.[48] Although Copland met few professional musicians, he did visit Sixto Durán, whom he described as an entertaining "old codger" but whose compositions struck him as "childish." Again he was regaled with an account of local musical shortcomings, including the lack of a symphony orchestra and of rigorous training. As in Colombia, Copland was asked for what amounted to musical relief aid: composers "who can teach harmony, counterpoint, and composition in Spanish."[49]

## Copland in Peru

On 7 September Copland flew from Quito to Lima. With its Pacific coastline and oil reserves, Peru was potentially important to the United States. Although

President Manuel Prado, elected in 1939, would prove a solid ally during the war, not all Peruvians wished to take sides in the global conflict. In the 1941 book ¿Hispano-América en guerra? (Spanish America at War?), Peruvian historian and diplomat Felipe Barreda Laos questioned the premise of aiding the United States.[50] Since the late nineteenth century, a substantive Japanese community had lived in Peru, many of whom were deported for internment in the United States after Pearl Harbor.[51]

The welcoming party at the airport comprised Andrés Sas, a Belgian-born composer resident in Peru since 1924; Carlos Raygada, the critic for the Lima paper *El Comercio*; and a Mr. Vargas, who represented the booking agency *Conciertos Daniel*. That evening, Copland attended a party where he heard the Peruvian composer-singer Rosa Mercedes Ayarza, celebrated for her folk-influenced songs. Local newspapers noted his presence with no small fanfare. The day after he arrived, the Lima daily *La Prensa* highlighted his personality and his aesthetic orientation in equal measure, writing, "Aaron Copland is one of those men who proffers great cordiality. He speaks Spanish without difficulty. . . . He belongs to that group of modern artists who, true to their epoch and sensibility, have tried to confer on art the sincere reaction of their spirit in accordance with the resources that contemporary technique has put within their reach."[52] Copland got to work, spending the afternoon with composers Carlos Sánchez Málaga and Roberto Carpio Valdés. Both hailed from Arequipa, a city about 472 miles (760 kilometers) from the capital and known as the "ciudad blanca" (white city) for the pearly white rock from which its colonial-era buildings were built. Copland heard their piano pieces and songs, "all they have written," as he commented dryly in his diary.[53] In fact, Peruvian composers had little incentive to tackle larger forms given the paucity of symphony orchestras and opera companies. Moreover, Carpio Valdés worked full-time teaching and playing the piano for Lima's Radio Nacional whereas Sánchez Málaga was a zarzuela coach, a choral director, and a teacher-administrator at the Conservatorio Bach in Lima, which he founded. With a grander compositional vision was Raoul de Verneuil, back in Lima after a long stay in Paris and whom Copland also met. Copland acknowledged that Verneuil's music was on a larger scale than any he had encountered in Latin America to date. But it struck him as overly complex, "paper music that would give performers a severe headache"; Copland also noted in his diary that, despite some innate ability, Verneuil was "in essence a dilettante."

Copland also met two émigré composers. Rudolf (Rodolfo) Holzmann was born in Breslau, Germany, and studied in Berlin, Strasbourg, and Paris, where he worked with Boulanger. By 1938 he was teaching composition in Lima and playing violin in the Orquesta Sinfónica Nacional del Perú, established the same year and led by another émigré, the Viennese conductor Theo Buchwald. (Holzmann likely played *Billy the Kid* under Copland.) Besides composing, Holzmann published on indigenous music.[54] Copland heard three suites for piano, a Divertimento for piano and orchestra, and some music for woodwind quintet. He recognized superior training and believed Holzmann could do "much good as teacher." Among Holzmann's composition students was Enrique Iturriaga, later one of Peru's main orchestral composers. Also, Holzmann sometimes orchestrated the music of Peruvian composers who felt underprepared to do so themselves. Despite these obvious gifts, Copland tagged Holzmann's music with the dubious epithet "pleasant."

The other emigré composer was Sas, whom Copland saw several times. Born in Paris, Sas lived in Brussels as a child, where he studied music. When the Peruvian government contracted him to teach violin in one of the local academies, he and his wife, the pianist Lily Rosay, established in 1929 the Academia de Música Sas–Rosay in Lima. Like Holzmann, Sas published on indigenous music; he also researched music from the viceregal period.[55] He grumbled to Copland about musical life in Peru, describing an ineffective conservatory and deficient training for composers.[56] Copland saw only a few of Sas's shorter works: songs, piano pieces, and chamber music, which he does not identify. But he may well have studied the four-movement *Cantos del Perú* for violin and piano of 1935, also featured on Slonimsky's recording, *South American Chamber Music*. The second movement, "La Nusta," quotes the melody from the 1913 zarzuela *El condor pasa* (The Condor Flies By) by the Peruvian composer Daniel Alomía Robles, later taken up by the duo Simon and Garfunkel and released (with permission) as "I'd Rather Be a Sparrow Than a Snail."[57] Copland allowed that Sas "writes in a rather expert and musical way." But, he adds, Sas composes "not as a 'real Peruvian,' being a Belgian of nineteen years residence in Lima."[58] Maddeningly, Copland offers no specifics as to what, exactly, betrayed this "profoundly European" temperament or what led him to this essentialist verdict. Sas's music had in fact circulated in the United States, thanks mainly to the firm Southern Music, which published both popular and classical music from Latin America since its founding in 1928. In April 1940 critic Noel Straus heard Sas's *Quenas*, for voice, harp, and flute, calling it "a little masterpiece" with "ravishing color effects."[59]

Again Copland hit the airwaves, appearing in a forty-five-minute broadcast for Radio Nacional de Perú on 11 September. He was introduced by historian Manuel Beltroy, one of the founders of the Instituto Cultural

Peruano-Norteamericano (ICPNA). Established in 1938 with English instruction as its main purpose, ICPNA was then expanding its cultural programs. Copland's talk "Contemporary Music in the United States," which he presented at ICPNA on 9 September, was an excellent fit. It was one of two topics on which he lectured during the 1941 tour, both extracted from *Our New Music*. (The other was "Music in the Films.")[60] He attracted an attentive audience of around two hundred, warmly dressed in winter clothing, who expressed their enthusiasm with "prolonged applause," as he stated in his diary. Copland also noted "much newspaper publicity attendant upon these activities."[61] He wasn't exaggerating: no fewer than four papers either covered or announced the event. *La Crónica*, for example, ran a photo of the composer at the podium, again with Beltroy presiding, who introduced him as "the eminent U.S. composer."[62]

In explaining the music of his native land, Copland offered a narrative of struggle. *La Prensa* quoted long portions of his speech verbatim:

> The first symptoms of a new and healthy movement in the field of creative music presented themselves—in the United States—shortly after the end of World War I. . . . The generation of composers of the pre-war period had sought a typical North American style by basing their music on the melodies of North American Indians or on Anglo-Saxon songs, which one still hears in the mountains of Kentucky or Virginia. Afterwards, Negro spirituals and our own jazz music were considered with some degree of hope as the foundations of an indigenous art. All these attempts have left their traces, but none of them has proven to be a final and definitive solution to the quest for a truly [U.S.] musical style.[63]

Which composer might step up to fill the void? Copland mentioned Piston and Sessions, noting their erudition and training, and who along with Thomson were among "the most original personalities in whom the United States can take pride."[64] He also referred to Blitzstein, who revolutionized the very notion of opera. "His works for the stage," Copland explained, "belong to a type better labeled musical theater than opera . . . created to be presented not by trained singers but by actors capable of singing a little. This lends reality to the drama often lacking in opera."[65]

But Copland also hinted at his colleagues' shortcomings. He dwelt at some length on Harris, highlighting his Piano Sonata, his Concerto for Clarinet, Piano, and String Quartet, his Quintet for Piano and Strings, and his Third Symphony. Harris possessed "a pronounced musical personality," Copland maintained, one of the "strongest" among contemporary U.S. composers (a description Harris would have found gratifying, given his hypermasculine persona).[66] Indeed, his works came very close to approaching a national music. But, Copland maintained, Harris "doesn't always know what to do with his own melodies." Then, with the same "half-diffident charitableness" Theodor Chanler had detected, Copland observed that such limitations were surely due to "the late beginnings" of Harris's musical education, adding that these lapses had "become part of his style, one of its most personal of charms."[67]

Copland then played a portion of the Third Symphony for the Lima public. Accordingly all the newspapers commented on this technological novelty, that is, the "phonographic illustrations" that highlighted Copland's talk. His own *Quiet City*, a parting gesture to his audience, won particular favor. The reporter for *La Prensa* admired its sparse textures and solitary, urgent trumpet solo, calling the work "a true gift, genuinely appreciated by the numerous and select public that filled the performance salon of the Instituto Cultural Peruano-Norteamericano."[68] Perhaps it also answered the question: which U.S. composer was best qualified to offer a "final or definitive solution" to the problem of forging an authentic U.S. style?

## *Billy the Kid* in Lima

The performance of *Billy the Kid* (El Chivato) the following evening surely decided the matter. In fact, Copland may have had some trepidation about leading the orchestra. He had studied conducting only briefly, initially in Fontainebleau with the French conductor Albert Wolff, and then by observing Koussevitzky, who was far from encouraging.[69] In his two rehearsals with the symphony, Copland observed that the ensemble played "only fairly well," with some sections "extremely unequal."[70] Despite these challenges—and the rocky reception of U.S. ballets earlier in the tour, as detailed by Kirstein—the performance proved a rousing success.

On 19 August the American Ballet Caravan arrived from Chile.[71] Not only had the company encountered problems with the embassy in Rio but critics found Thomson's rendering of jazz in *Filling Station* unsatisfactory, and at least one heard "monotony" in Wilder's *Juke Box*; likewise, *Time Table* (Copland's *Music for the Theatre*) was deemed "noisy."[72] In Buenos Aires, the pro-U.S. *Argentinisches Tageblatt* applauded *Time Table*, in which another Argentine critic heard touches of Stravinsky, whereas the pro-Nazi *El Pampero* questioned the "folklore de los negros" in *Juke Box*.[73] Reaction to *Billy the Kid* was also mixed. Although the English-language *Buenos Aires Herald* called it "forceful and gripping fare," a Brazilian critic found it to suffer from "excessive naïveté" (excesiva ingenuidade) and another was frankly bored—at least until the gunshots rang out in the finely calibrated timpani solo in the fifth section.[74] As Kirstein had noted, however, the European classics were immensely successful. In Lima therefore, he took the precaution of bookending *Billy* with *The Bat*, derived from Johann Strauss Jr.'s *Die Fledermaus*, and *Imperial Ballet*, based on Tchaikovsky's Piano Concerto no. 2, each choreographed by Balanchine. Peruvian critics applauded both works, with one reveling in the "spirit and ambience of Imperial Vienna."[75] Another, writing under the pseudonym "Guido d'Arezzo," praised the company's adherence to "classic norms," observed with "great equilibrium and sobriety."[76]

Yet however much they enjoyed the classics, Lima's critics were bowled over by *Billy the Kid*. All its elements seemed to cohere. One critic praised the "rhythm, accent, and musical figures filled with rich folkloric flavor, the rather dramatic intensity that underscores certain moments . . . the confident and animated evocation, of rich color and supple plasticity, of the legendary ambience of the Far West during the middle of the past century."[77] "Guido d'Arezzo" was much taken with the novelty of Eugene Loring's choreography, liberated from stiff tutus and unnatural classical postures; indeed, "Guido d'Arezzo" proposed that the Lima public actually preferred *Billy the Kid* to the classics. "*Billy the Kid*," he wrote, "transports us to an aesthetic plane of much greater interest given the novelty of its choreographic conception, boldly traced on a theme that in itself would seem scarcely appropriate for ballet."[78] The ballet was not without risk: a tale of "persecutions and combats, horse races and killings that sustains a climate of roughness and agitation that barely reaches relief in the occasional lyric scene."[79] Yet all these elements triumphed through the "great innovation" (gran inventiva) of the choreography and Copland's score, which responded with "vigor and dynamism" to movements normally considered incongruous to classical ballet. Further, the music abounded in "multiple feats of realism that translate through audacious combinations of instrumental timbres and interventions, laid bare, by the percussion instruments, the most prominent passages in the adventures that unfold on stage."[80] Thus, with its vigor, dynamism, and daring, *Billy the Kid* drew the Lima public into a completely new realm.

The fact that Copland conducted was also noteworthy: the critic for the Lima newspaper *Universal* appreciated the "capital opportunity to listen to one of the most important compositions of the present day conducted by the composer himself" whereas his counterpart at *El Comercio* (probably Carlos Raygada) reported that Copland "was greeted with affectionate applause."[81]

*Billy* was also a "capital opportunity" for cultural diplomacy. Several dignitaries attended the performance, including the Mexican ambassador to Peru Moisés Saenz; the U.S. ambassador R. Henry Norweb and his wife, Emery May Norweb; and Copland's colleague from the OIAA, Philip Barbour, then on assignment in Peru. Most gratifying of all was the presence of President Prado himself, along with his family, who could hardly help being moved by this celebration of "vigor" and "dynamism." It may not be too much to suggest that Prado, along with the public at large, sensed in the legendary setting of the "Wild West" an environment filled with danger that was comparable to the uncertainties of the present, which demanded the very "audaciousness" showcased in Copland's ballet.

One of the composer's more profound experiences in Lima was listening to a rehearsal of the Conjunto Vacarno, a group of eleven indigenous musicians and a "remarkable girl singer," as Copland described her in his diary. They played violins, rattles, panpipes (a sacred instrument in some Andean communities), and what Copland called "homemade baby harps." It was "the real thing," he wrote, "or almost." We cannot be sure what he found lacking. (It is safe to say that Copland knew next to nothing about Peruvian traditional music.) In the same diary entry, Copland predicted that someday a Peruvian composer would succeed in re-creating this music in "symphonic form" but stipulated that such a day still lay in the future: "No one, to my knowledge, has done it as yet," Copland wrote, adding, "the so-called Inca themes treated by Sas, Sánchez-Málaga, et al., come out thoroughly European in quality, with very few exceptions."[82] Again, "serious" Latin American composers fell short.

Copland left Peru by way of Arequipa, where Carlos Nicholson, a professor of geography and climatology at the Universidad de San Agustín, invited him to enjoy a bit of tourism. A former Guggenheim fellow, Nicholson took Copland to the old Harvard Observatory, thanks to which astronomers had discovered Phoebe, an outer moon of Saturn. By 1941 the original building lay unused, although Professor Nicolson believed it could attract Peruvian and U.S. postgraduate students specializing in archaeology or altitude studies. "The plan seems good to me," Copland acknowledged.[83]

## The "Switzerland of Latin America"

Copland spent only a few days in Uruguay. Sometimes dubbed "the Switzerland of Latin America," Uruguay is known for its economic stability, social welfare programs, public education, and strong central government rooted in democratic premises. (The moniker is hardly congenial to those Uruguayans who find such comparisons irrelevant to Latin America.)[84] Certainly classical music has benefitted from state involvement. The Servicio Oficial de Difusión Radio Eléctrica (SODRE), established in 1931, consisted of a symphony orchestra, chamber orchestra, chorus, ballet company, a theater, radio station, and record library. The full name of the orchestra is the Orquesta Sinfónica del Servicio Oficial de Difusión Radioeléctrica (OSSODRE), which still plays at the Teatro Solís, a charming auditorium in neoclassical style. When Toscanini performed there in July 1940, the Europhile public "went wild" over Debussy's *La mer* and Beethoven's Symphony no. 7, as one chronicler noted; a few days later, crowds of eager Montevideans braved the winter rain and fog to wait for tickets, some standing in line six hours.[85] In 1938 Uruguay had resisted a dictatorship supported by Italy and Germany by electing Alfredo Baldomir as president, generally credited with persuading his compatriots to side with the Allies, although technically from a position of neutrality.[86] Uruguay was much in the U.S. press after a German cruiser, the *Graf Spee*, fought with British warships off Uruguay's coast in a neutral zone, such that the damaged cruiser put in at Montevideo and several wounded German sailors remained interred there until the war ended. To U.S. journalists, the episode suggested anti-Axis solidarity: "Graf Spee Incident Gives Latins Unity," the *New York Times* proclaimed in late 1939.[87]

During Copland's whirlwind visit, the Montevideo press reinforced the Good Neighbor Policy. The day before he arrived, the daily *La Mañana* published an essay by Lange, which highlighted Copland's "dynamic temperament." Unlike any of his U.S. peers, Lange wrote, Copland "has had a manifest inclination toward Latin America and, as a result . . . his friends and supporters, like a great part of the Latin American musical world, receive him as an old acquaintance."[88] For Lange, Copland's presence in Uruguay confirmed "the principles of a positive musical Americanism, represented by the desire to know [one another], to exchange ideas and to fight for the high ideals of culture in our hemisphere."[89] Along with two secretaries of the embassy, Lange greeted Copland upon his arrival. The Uruguayan pianist Hugo Balzo joined Copland and Lange for lunch, after which Copland attended a rehearsal of the OSSODRE and visited the record library.

He spent a fair amount of time with Lange. It is unclear if the two had met previously, but Copland likely knew of some of his Uruguayan colleague's writings, such as the essay "Americanismo musical." Just as Lange had declared to the Montevideo press, he genuinely admired Copland and over the years sent him many a sincere (and lengthy) missive. He also honored him in one of his pet projects, the *Boletín latino-americano de música*, which published articles by scholars from the Americas, with a musical supplement. (Some volumes of the "bulletin" ran to gargantuan proportions of over eight hundred pages.)[90] As if timed to coincide with Copland's visit, the *Boletín*'s musical supplement of October 1941 included Copland's Blues no. 1, Lange's distaste for jazz notwithstanding. The composer also visited "the so-called Instituto Interamericano de Musicología," as he put it in his diary, noting that the institute was "merely a room in [Lange's] house." Although Copland found Lange "definitely a 'case,'" he was impressed with his efforts. Aware that others would likely find him difficult, "due to a complete lack of tact," Copland nonetheless speculated on ways in which the United States might help him, perhaps with funds to pursue his projects as he saw fit. "Despite all his purely personal shortcomings, he has power and drive and knowledge of [Latin American] affairs," Copland wrote. "I should like to see him helped and encouraged in what has been a very uphill job."[91]

Thanks to effective advance planning by the embassy, Copland's four days in Montevideo were packed.[92] Ambassador William Dawson Jr. invited the composer for lunch and held a reception at the embassy in his honor, where Copland met Uruguayan musicians. On the same occasion, he performed the slow movement of Harris's piano trio and Sessions's *Chorale-Preludes*. (It is not known who the other players were.) Two days later, Dawson organized a more formal lunch, again, with the musical community of Montevideo in attendance but also including the Mexican composer Manuel Ponce and the Spanish guitarist Andrés Segovia, then on tour. Copland and Ambassador Dawson later attended a concert of Ponce's works, followed by yet another reception, which featured performances by local musicians of popular Uruguayan selections.[93]

Dawson and his wife were also among the approximately two hundred people who attended Copland's lecture "Trends in Contemporary U.S. Music." It had been a busy day: twice Copland had appeared on the radio, first to discuss the "Influence of Jazz on Modern Music" on a program called *The Good Will Hour* and then later to host a program on U.S. music for the SODRE. In his lecture, sponsored by the Instituto Interamericano de Musicología and la Escuela Nacional de Declamación (ESNADE), Copland explained that he had come to Latin America to learn about its composers and to introduce "serious music" of the United States, an exchange that "should have begun many years ago." Further, "the music of the New World has been ignored . . . for a long time, due to the influence—and the natural anxiety that derives therefrom—exerted by European art. Nonetheless . . . today, we sense many revelatory indications that, in America in the not-too-distant future, the word 'music' will no longer mean an exclusively European product."[94]

Clearly Copland was speaking to that sector of the Uruguayan musical public willing to look beyond established, Europeanized norms of concert life. As if to prove the point, he ended his lecture not with the meditative "gift" of *Quiet City* that had so delighted his audience in Lima but the rambunctious *El salón México*, which, he informed the public, was a mixture of "various Mexican melodies, superimposed by [Copland] that could aptly be titled 'a tourist's impression of Mexico,'" as one journalist reported.[95]

Copland's second lecture in Montevideo was "Music in the Films," presented (appropriately enough) at the Radio City movie house. He concentrated on *Of Mice and Men*, the 1939 film directed by Lewis Milestone with Copland's Oscar-nominated score. John Steinbeck's novella, a scathing portrait of mental illness, despair, and the irrevocable and often tragic bonds between human beings set against the backdrop of the Great Depression, was a far cry from *Argentine Nights* or any of the other frothy Good Neighbor–era musicals that Hollywood relentlessly foisted upon Latin America. One challenge was finding a satisfactory Spanish translation of the title. Steinbeck had taken it from Robert Burns's 1785 poem "To a Mouse," the context of which would be opaque to a native speaker of Spanish. Translators settled on *La fuerza bruta* (Brute Force), alluding to the affable yet deadly Lennie and his protector George, who puts Lennie out of his misery. In 1941 Copland spoke on *Of Mice and Men* in three of his four lectures on film music, discussing the more optimistic *Our Town* (Nuestro pueblo) only once. Unfortunately, the press simply announced these talks or noted the sizeable publics they attracted, rarely commenting in any depth on their content.

In Uruguay, Copland met composers as usual. In his diary, he wondered just how many there were. Carlos Pedrell, a nephew and student of Spanish composer, critic, and musicologist Felipe Pedrell, had died a few months earlier, in Paris. Eduardo Fabini, older than Copland, wrote choral music, piano and chamber music, and orchestral works, such as the symphonic poem, *Campo* (The Country), which Richard Strauss conducted. Luis Cluzeau Mortet, wrote backward-looking yet solid works for orchestra, which the OSSODRE frequently performed and whose piano pieces Artur Rubinstein programmed. Copland met neither Fabini nor Cluzeau Mortet. But one afternoon, at Balzo's house, he heard the music of Carlos Estrada, who had studied in Paris with Henri Büsser. Copland found Estrada "sensitive and well-trained."[96] (He may have heard Estrada's incidental music for Paul Verlaine's play *Les uns et les autres*.) But for Copland, Estrada's music was symptomatic of a trend, namely, "the sweet mood so dear to South American composers," a mixture of sentiment and Frenchified harmonies. Such music was unlikely to figure in "New World music."

Héctor Tosar was another story. With this "quiet, sensitive boy of eighteen," as Copland observed, "music pours out of every pore." Copland studied the *Toccata* for orchestra from 1940, performed by the OSSODRE and published by Ricordi Americana, and the glissando-happy Concertino for piano and orchestra from 1941.[97] Copland also heard a less European-sounding work by Tosar, which he lists in his diary simply as a "dance for piano." Surely this was the *Danza criolla*, by definition about identity: a *criollo* is a person born in Latin America of European parentage while *música criolla* refers to a European genre that is reimagined in Latin America. Its abrupt shifts of register and texture, along with brief melodic fragments juxtaposed with stretches of ostinato that culminate in a breathless coda, impressed Copland. He found Tosar's music "brilliant and facile, full of dash and élan" if "not very original and certainly not profound." But the young man showed such a "vivid musical imagination" that Copland hoped he could study in the United States someday.[98] The next day, again at Balzo's house, Copland heard music by another eighteen-year-old, Sergio de Castro, the son of the Argentine consul and resident eight years in Montevideo. Copland does not discuss in his diary any of Castro's works but believed that he, too, would profit from study in the United States.[99]

In his diary, Copland records an interview with *El Debate*, a Montevideo nationalist and conservative Catholic paper known to be unfriendly to the United States. Although the interview itself does not seem to have been published, *El Debate* put aside whatever reservations it may have harbored about the Colossus of the North and reprinted Lange's glowing essay on Copland, with very minor changes.[100] On 12 October, the day Copland left Montevideo, an editorial in the anti-Nazi daily *El País* proclaimed that the Good Neighbor Policy had "transformed the physiognomy of the Americas," such that "the bitterness, resentment, rancor or resistance that the powerful nation [the United States] awakened among many of the continent have evaporated."[101] Copland, now traveling across the River Plate to Buenos Aires, may well have read these optimistic words and felt that he was part of this effort.

\* \* \*

In considering this portion of Copland's trip, several things emerge. First, the composer made it clear from the outset that he would act as the proverbial Good Neighbor. With events such as the Lima *Billy the Kid* and well-attended lectures on music of the United States, Copland fulfilled his mission just as the OIAA wished. Perhaps most important, he was a quiet force. Neither as outspoken as Kirstein nor as flashy as a Disney cartoon feature, he made the case for U.S. music in no small part through his steady, courteous demeanor. Taking a genuine interest in his surroundings and encouraging the various composers he met—no matter what he actually thought of their music—he persuaded all who encountered him that the United States had good intentions. Thus unfolded Copland's "performance" of cultural diplomacy in the earliest stages of its implementation.

# 5
# Copland in Argentina

No one could accuse Rockefeller of subtlety. As coordinator of the OIAA, he took full advantage not only of his connections in philanthropy but also in business, urging his acquaintances at Ford, General Motors, and General Electric to advertise Good Neighborly feeling. One vehicle was the *Reader's Digest*, available in Latin America. Readers could thumb the pages of *Selecciones del Reader's Digest* or *Seleções do Reader's Digest* and ponder what an eventual Allied victory portended. "Today military, tomorrow washing machines," one ad intoned. Clearly any future hitched to the United States would be filled with television sets, outboard motors, and other objects of consumer desire. Even cosmetics figured in Pan Americanist ad campaigns: one for Michel lipstick touted "eight seductive shades," all "on guard to protect beauty, to protect our hemisphere."[1]

Also safeguarding beauty in the hemisphere was the OIAA Music Committee, whose chief representative was now on his way to the strategically important country of Argentina. This chapter analyzes Copland's approach to this terrain: how he highlighted either his U.S. identity or more cosmopolitan values in an environment where anti-Semitism and anti-U.S. sentiment sometimes surfaced. He also met one of two standout composers from his 1941 tour.

## Argentina as Neighbor

Since the 1920s the United States and Argentina had been at loggerheads over commercial dominance in the hemisphere.[2] Now U.S. officials were convinced that the country was crawling with Nazis. Especially damning was Secretary of State Cordell Hull, who sensed "a seething mass of German intrigue and plotting" there and went so far as to call Argentina "the bad neighbor."[3] More recent scholars have argued that these reactions were exaggerated, with Ronald C. Newton concluding that fear of Nazi influence in Argentina became an "*obsession*" only in U.S. foreign policy circles.[4]

Yet the threat was real enough. Nazi propaganda spread through the country, often via German agents and diplomats. Pro-Nazi youth groups were sometimes violent. Waldo Frank, who gave a strong prodemocracy speech in Buenos Aires, was later beaten up by street thugs who hurled anti-Semitic epithets at him while inflicting a gash on his head. In the U.S. magazine *Collier's*, Frank assured readers that pro-Axis sentiment resided solely in the weak and corrupt government and that the Argentine people craved democracy.[5] German exiles in Argentina sought assiduously to counteract the image of the "bad neighbor," often drawing on the resources of their adopted country. The Argentine press published translations of German writers and one publisher, *Editorial Cosmopólita*, translated the Argentine epic poem *Martín Fierro* into German.[6] Musicians also contributed: in 1934 at the Teatro Colón, the anti-Nazi conductor Fritz Busch led the first performance in Latin America of Bach's *Passion According to St. Matthew*.

Of the many Jews who sought refuge from Hitler in Argentina, approximately a hundred were musicians, some of whom Copland would meet.[7] Conductor Robert (Roberto) Kinsky introduced Stravinsky's *Jeux de cartes* and Schoenberg's *Erwartung* to the Buenos Aires public. Composers included Erwin Leuchter and Wilhelm (Guillermo) Graetzer, the latter a pupil of Hindemith.[8] Some rallied to the anti-Nazi cause. In 1939 the German-born director, actor, and critic Paul Walter Jacob, newly arrived in Buenos Aires, gave a three-day symposium as a retort to the Nazis' event, Degenerate Music of May 1938 (Düsseldorf), which fingered composers most threatening to the Third Reich's cultural values: Hindemith, Krenek, Schoenberg, Webern, and Weill. Jacob included all in his symposium, adding Halévy, Mahler, Mendelssohn, and Offenbach.[9] On 16 June 1941, at Buenos Aires's Teatro Astral, several Jewish émigré musicians gave a benefit concert for prisoners in internment camps.[10]

Any role for U.S. culture here was doubtful. It was reported, for example, that the antidemocracy Argentine Foreign Minister Enrique Ruiz Guiñazú was convinced that the Colossus of the North was rife with cultural decadence.[11] Even some pro-Allied intellectuals were also unpersuaded. The conductor and composer Juan José Castro, with whom Copland would enjoy a long association, was as ardent a defender of the United States as any. Yet after spending a year in New York on a Guggenheim Fellowship, he observed that despite financial support and genuine interest, U.S. music itself lacked "great values."[12] In 1941 the British Embassy took a poll on cultural attitudes in Argentina. It revealed no particular antipathy toward the United States but confirmed that despite insulting films such as *Argentine Nights*, the mass public craved U.S. consumer products and popular culture.[13] As images of Blondie, Betty Boop, and Mickey Mouse (el ratón Mickey) graced the press, cultural elites feared a U.S. "invasion." In November 1941 the Argentine film critic César Fernández Moreno registered the "remaking of our sensibility—namely, Latin—in favor of the coarsely pragmatic, which is coming to us from the north in films, the *Reader's Digest*, jazz, and milk bars."[14]

## Copland and the Buenos Aires Press

Copland arrived in the Argentine capital on 26 September. The Third Secretary of the American Embassy met him at the airport and promptly whisked him away to a tea party at the home of Ambassador Norman Armour, recently transferred from Chile. Shortly thereafter, Copland spoke with *El Mundo*, a Buenos Aires daily that ran Spanish translations of anti-Hitler editorials by U.S. journalist Walter Lippman. Under the headline "Aaron Copland Endorses a Strong Pan American Musical Bond," *El Mundo* outlined the composer's objective: "creating effective, sincere, and cordial bonds between the musicians of the American nations." In the extravagant language of the era, *El Mundo* added that "among the merits that adorn this ambassador of art from the sister nation are his fruitful work as teacher and composer and excellent command of our language."[15] Then the reporter described Copland's vision of a Pan American musical bond, to which the "democratization" of music was central, adding, "in the opinion of our guest, the radio and the phonograph will help in inestimable ways the work of Pan American unity in which he and his U.S. colleagues are involved. . . . In music, radio and electronic sound represent a revolution that is as important as the advent of the printing press for letters, Copland says. The radio and the phonograph are democratizing music to an incredible degree—he continues—vastly expanding the listening public, and creating a 'new musical taste.'"[16]

In other words, the effects of these democratizing media went beyond mere numbers. The "new musical taste," moreover, jointly developed by composers and the public, would take the Western Hemisphere as its laboratory. As Copland explained, "it's not difficult to predict . . . that within ten years, the radio and the phonograph will have created their own musical literature and that very few composers will be unaffected by this fundamental transformation in the social function of music. The inevitable law of the influence of the medium on the artist's works will have fulfilled itself once more, and in that evolution—which will be historical—we musicians from the Americas will surely be in the vanguard."[17] Of course, Copland was simply repeating ideas he had been developing for years, most recently in *Our New Music* ("The Composer and Radio") but also in a radio address he had given a few months earlier, in which he applauded the medium's potential for expanding the "democratic bases of music."[18] Now these bases embraced the entire hemisphere.

In conversation with a reporter from one of Buenos Aires's Jewish papers, however, Copland showed another facet of his personality: the cosmopolitan modernist. The reporter for *Mundo Israelita* described Copland as "tall, slender, with a pleasant smile . . . limiting himself to offer, in his Mexican-accented Spanish, succinct information about himself."[19] Not surprisingly, Copland mentioned his piano trio *Vitebsk* to the readership of *Mundo Israelita*. He then explained, "I cultivate . . . modern music in its serious form and on rare occasions I make use of folklore as a theme for inspiration, as in the case of [*Billy the Kid*], in which I use motives from cowboy songs."[20] (He does not mention the Hassidic song in *Vitebsk* or the tunes in *El salón México*.) In surveying Jewish composers in the United States, he further downplayed musical identity-consciousness. Neither Frederick Jacobi, Bernard Rogers, David Diamond, Marc Blitzstein, Louis Gruenberg, nor Israel Citkowitz use Jewish material, Copland pointed out (chiding Lazare Saminsky for doing precisely that); rather, they "contribute to the general cultural scheme." Copland also related the triumphant story of Jewish musicians from Europe—Ernest Bloch, Milhaud, Pisk, Schoenberg, Weill—who had fled Nazism and now enjoyed the liberties the U.S. afforded. He concluded with an optimistic remark on his "mission," through which he hoped to take advantage of "the means of diffusion" and benefit "the composers of Latin America, a selection of whose works I can deliver to the Rockefeller committee."[21]

With the antifascist newspaper *Argentina Libre*, Copland took a more nuts-and-bolts approach, giving readers a glimpse into the life of a U.S. composer. His interviewer was Argentine musicologist Leopoldo Hurtado, affiliated with the prestigious Colegio Libre de Estudios Superiores and precisely the sort of "Latin American elite" the State Department wanted to target. Hurtado was deeply committed to modern music, as his essay "In Defense of Atonality" makes clear.[22] He was also witty and well-read. In a review of Virgil Thomson's irreverent *The State of Music,* Hurtado declared, "It's no secret to anybody that the United States is rapidly marching toward musical hegemony."[23] The reader discovers soon enough that, far from a militant provocation, Hurtado's attention-grabbing gambit complements Thomson's humor. Yet Hurtado tacitly acknowledged the threat of U.S. cultural hegemony, whether through Hollywood's missteps or watered-down articles in the *Reader's Digest.* In interviewing Copland, he also wondered about classical music in the United States, of which many Argentines were ignorant. Did that ignorance point to something larger? As Hurtado remarked to the composer, "you [U.S. Americans] have imposed fashions and customs of the contemporary world: of dressing, of eating, of dancing, in turns of phrase, modern journalism, radio, 'jazz,' the movies, cars. Everything that has transformed the face of the world in recent years is of Yankee origin. Why has this not occurred with serious music?"[24]

Copland's reply was matter of fact. "It's much more difficult to write serious music than popular music," he explained. "The diffusion and imposition of North American dance music is exactly what make progress in the field of serious music seem slower and less noticeable."[25] Nonetheless, Copland glimpsed some essential qualities in the music of his native land, including "a certain rhythmic structure . . . perceptible in all [U.S. composers]," which, he acknowledged, may come from jazz. Thanks also to works by Depression-era researchers, "new elements and previously unknown materials" in folklore were already bearing fruit. When Hurtado asked how U.S. composers further their music, Copland mentioned two possibilities. The first was to disseminate new works by radio. The second possibility, raised nowhere else during the 1941 tour, was to write for young people. That market, moreover, would remind composers of their duty to the broad public:

> It is calculated that there are more than 5,000 school orchestras [in the United States] endowed with complete instrumentation. . . . Those orchestras don't have good music to play. . . . We [U.S.] composers need to write music for such ensembles: simple and clear, with easy appeal, but also with a modern technique and our own style of composition. This is a very important experience because there—as here—we musicians tend to find ourselves stuck in our own little corner waiting to write great works and are very infrequently offered the opportunity to actually do so.[26]

Here, Copland was doing a bit of advance publicity for his *An Outdoor Overture*, soon to be performed at the Teatro Colón under Juan José Castro, one of the theater's regular conductors.

In each of these interviews, Copland's focus shifts. In one, he's a democratic populist eager for symbiosis between the composer and a broad public through new media. In another, he's a representative of the vanguard dedicated to "serious" music who is rarely inspired by folk music. Or, he's a professional composer attuned to the practicalities of musical life in his own country. As it turned out, Copland's Argentine public would take this chameleonic finesse more seriously than any other Latin American country.

Copland also gave three lectures in Buenos Aires. On 7 October, when he spoke on "Modern North American Composers" before an audience of around two hundred, he addressed Roger Sessions and Walter Piston, expressing admiration for both. Each was a university professor and each was "supremely erudite." Their music showed the influence of "current neoclassical tendencies," with Sessions a "friend of the well worked-out, of the meticulous and the perfect," who wrote music that was "grave and pessimistic, of a profoundly human quality and consummate technical perfection." For that reason, Copland explained, "it is heard very little."[27] Evidently erudition promised few rewards in the United States.

## Folklore: A "magnificent trough"

Surely aware of Paz's revulsion to folklore, Copland now met other Argentine composers who felt essentially the same way. Honorio Siccardi, who had studied in Italy with Gian Francesco Malipiero in the 1920s, was an original member of the Grupo Renovación. He penned the organization's founding documents, railing against "slaves to Folklore . . . situated in sweet and soporific sinecures where the singsong of tedium murmurs" and who "lacking ideas . . . have found in autochthonous elements [i.e., folklore] a magnificent trough in which to refresh themselves."[28] In fact, the Grupo Renovación allowed that composers with technical savvy could at least in principle use folklore to good effect.[29] (That many who did so trained in Europe, often at the Schola Cantorum, lent credence to Jorge Luis Borges's quip that in Argentina even nationalism was imported.)[30] Nonetheless, Juan José Castro, also a founding member of the Grupo Renovación, criticized his peers for "abusing the all-too-familiar habit of folklore."[31]

Siccardi's music, which Copland perused one evening after a reception at the U.S. Embassy, avoided this "magnificent trough." Impressed with Siccardi's "excellent technique," Copland detected two principal styles in his string quartet, songs, and piano pieces: either "a rather severe form of modern academicism, where the workings of the theme are of greater interest than the theme itself" or "a kind of emotional music vaguely reminiscent of the neo-Italian school." (Here, Copland probably meant Malipiero, Vittorio Rieti, Idelbrando Pizzetti, and Alfredo Casella.) Despite the lack of a "marked personality" in Siccardi's music, Copland concluded, "All his stuff is highly playable."[32] His works were never widely known in the United States, although his *Deux chansons de Amado Villar* was performed at the 1939 ISCM Festival in Warsaw and Nicolas Slonimsky added seven of his works to the Fleisher Collection.[33] Saminsky found "something very personal and highly attractive" in Siccardi's music and programmed his "Ave Maria" at a three-choir festival at Temple Emanu-el that featured music of the Spanish baroque and "the two Americas."[34] For Copland, other Argentine composers seemed even more restricted by European models. On 3 October he met Roberto García Morillo, also a critic and author, who had studied in Paris. In García Morillo's music, Copland observed "continual repetition of formulas" despite "a certain gift for neo-Stravinskian rhythms."[35] Copland also visited Carlos Suffern, later a formidable critic. Copland admired Suffern's verbal agility and likened him to an armchair athlete: just as "some people talk a good game of tennis, Suffern talks a good composition," he quipped. Among the works Suffern played for Copland—"with much explanation"—were *Tres poemas de Gide* for voice and piano, a piano sonata, and a chamber suite, *Los juegos rústicos* (Rustic Games). Whatever Suffern's "excellent sense of a musical line," Copland ultimately found his music derivative, as in the Gide settings, which seemed "hardly more than a well-executed pastiche."[36]

One of Copland's least favorite Latin American composers was the prolific Jacobo Ficher. Born in Odesa (today Ukraine), Ficher studied violin with Leopold Auer and composition with Alexander Tcherepnin at the Leningrad Conservatory before emigrating to Buenos Aires in 1923. He wrote choral music, ballets, piano works, ten symphonies, and film scores.[37] In 1928 his orchestral *Poema heróico* received an award from the Leningrad Philharmonic, and his second string quartet took first prize out of sixty-five entries in the 1937 Pan American Festival of Chamber Music, on whose jury Chávez sat.[38] In February 1941 Ficher's oboe sonata, which Saminsky called Ficher's "best work" and "in an even more 'neo-classical' vein than his symphonies," was performed at a chamber music concert at the New York Public Library. Downes called it "plausibly put forward," extravagant praise for one so skeptical of neoclassicism as he.[39] Generally uninterested in the folklore of his adopted country (he wrote a set of Argentine dances for piano in 1943), Ficher occasionally drew on his

Jewish heritage, as in his *Tres danzas hebraicas* for two pianos, which conclude with a lively "Hora." In 1933, the year Hitler came to power, Ficher composed his Second Symphony in response to growing anti-Semitism. Saminsky admired its "imagination and power," and Slonimsky found it "emotional and rhapsodic . . . with Hebraic thematic undertones."[40] Copland, however, was unmoved. After studying the work, he observed that despite the "occasional bow to modern harmonies or rhythm" in the Second Symphony, Ficher's music was fundamentally *vieux jeu* (old hat). In other words, Ficher simply revisited "the usual academic models with occasional dissonant chords" with "nothing in particular to say." As if this were not damning enough—and at odds with other opinions—Copland believed that Ficher was "not very clever and probably now composing the best music he is capable of producing."[41]

On 2 October, the same day as his visit with Ficher, Copland attended Paz's lecture on modern music at the Teatro del Pueblo. Only a handful of listeners attended. "Paz speaks poorly," Copland reported in his diary, without elaborating. Afterwards, he and Paz dined with colleagues, and on 6 October Paz played Copland several of his works, including *Diez piezas sobre una serie dodecafónica* (Ten Pieces on a Dodecaphonic Series). Copland was intrigued, if wary:

> Paz strikes me as a typical figure of the modern music movement—serious, learned, solitary, and somewhat heroic. His music is not without personality. . . . One respects his work, without loving it very much. It is clearly done, without great variety of manner or mood, but it is at the same time the only example I know of the Latin temperament attaching itself to the German musical line.

"The music [Paz] now writes can mean very little to the general musical public," Copland commented, likely with some empathy.[42] He was also curious to see Paz's pre–twelve-tone music and on 22 October got his wish. Copland studied *Movemiento sinfónico* of 1930, with its polytonal sonorities, long pedals, and contrapuntal lines with different tonal centers.[43] In all, Copland heard a total of eight works by Paz, three of which he assigned asterisks: the *Obertura para 12 instrumentos* of 1931–32, *Concierto no. 1* (piano, flute, oboe, clarinet, bassoon, trumpet) from 1932, and the Sonata for clarinet and piano (later withdrawn). He acknowledged Paz's "excellent technical equipment" and "terrific tenacity." He also concluded that Paz was "in many ways a remarkable musician." Nonetheless,

> One would like to add that he is also a remarkable composer, but that would hardly be true. . . . He has some striking lacunae in his artistic make-up—practically no real lyricism, and a very dry kind of fun. This gives all his music a kind

of pallor which is *tiring* in the end. He is, above all things, enamored of music that looks well on paper. His scores are always a pleasure to look at, but not always a pleasure to hear. A quiet, reserved, and lonely man—one feels sorry for him, for he is somewhat of a "genius manqué."[44]

Paz's music was nonetheless worth following. "It would be interesting to see what would happen to his style," Copland wrote, "if his works were performed as often as they deserve to be," suggesting a degree of feedback between creator and public of which Paz himself was likely skeptical.

Copland also visited the Castro family, Argentina's musical dynasty. Juan José Castro Sr., a cellist and instrument maker, had emigrated from Spain in the late nineteenth century and raised his five sons in greater Buenos Aires, four of whom became musicians. Prior to receiving the Guggenheim Fellowship that took him to New York, Juan José Jr. studied at the Schola Cantorum with d'Indy.[45] He made his mark principally as a conductor: Stravinsky, who rarely had anything good to say about conductors, called him "an impeccable master of the baton."[46] His career as a composer was not insignificant: in 1931 Ernest Ansermet conducted Castro's *Allegro, lento e vivace* in London, and his large-scale *Sinfonía Bíblica*, which Saminsky called a "spacious and luminous work," was performed at Carnegie Hall.[47] In nearly all his compositions, Castro embraced neoclassicism to such a degree that Argentine critic Jorge D'Urbano called him "the great Argentine exponent . . . of 'neoclassicism,'" due not to the allure of "any school but to temperament."[48]

Copland may have met the younger Juan José in New York but seems to have been unacquainted with his music before visiting him and his wife Raquel at their home on 16 October. There, he heard Castro's recently completed piano concerto. The first movement, a jolly *moto perpetuo*, which unfolds in a sonata form, borrows themes from Castro's own *Toccata* of 1940. The second movement, "Trágico," is punctuated with a two-note pattern, thickly harmonized, and the third, the most dissonant, reawakens the relentless energy of the first with more than a touch of humor. Copland felt, however, that his Argentine colleague's "musical intelligence [was] far ahead of his creative urge" and that he generally produced "a resoundingly good version of a well-worn model."[49] Was Castro aware of his limitations? In his diary, Copland recalled that Raquel "said laughingly—'Juan José is ashamed of his compositions.'" Here, Copland reflected, "one understands why—despite the exaggeration such 'shame' implies. Perhaps I am judging him on too small evidence, but I rather doubt it." In any case, many of Juan José's compositions, including the concerto, are well worth hearing today.

## "At last: A composer with a fresh style"

Copland also met Washington Castro, the youngest of the musical brothers. A thirty-two year-old cellist then studying composition with Siccardi, he was "still immature," according to Copland. The eldest was José María. Unlike Juan José, the renowned conductor, José María lived quietly in Buenos Aires, where he had completed his studies. He worked as a cellist, conducted a radio orchestra and a municipal band, and at one point was employed in a bookstore. Copland heard some of his compositions at a concert of the Grupo Renovación and was "struck favorably" by "the young Castro."[50] (In fact, in 1941 José María was forty-nine, eight years older than Copland.) On 21 October Copland visited José María and, in a marathon session, heard more of his music. Later, he enthused to his diary, "So far, [José María Castro] is the best composer I have found in South America. At last, a composer with a fresh style and personality, added to an excellent technique. None of the usual Gallicisms or nostalgia or 'effect' music—so current down here . . . He seems a simple and direct soul . . . perhaps less cultured than Juan José, but more real creative instinct."[51] None of the music Copland heard was folkloric, however. Rather, José María's works fell into "two categories . . . either frankly neo-classic (but of the bright and happy kind), or . . . neo-romantic with a bitter-sweet flavor entirely personal to the composer. He understands the secret of a good melodic line, and of allowing a musical phrase to flower naturally. . . . He does not seem to know too well just what direction he is taking artistically speaking; but seems rather to trust his musical instinct."[52]

In the first category, of bright and happy neoclassicism, was the bustling Concerto Grosso of 1932, José María's first orchestral work and a hyperenergetic accounting of the baroque form. Copland assigned it an asterisk (Slonimsky called it Castro's "most effective work").[53] In the "bittersweet" category was José María's Third Piano Sonata, from 1939, and subtitled "Spring." "The best piece of South American music I have yet heard," Copland exulted, assigning the *Sonata de primavera* three asterisks, the only piece so designated in all of his 1941 tour. Its meandering harmonies, fluidity of form, and occasionally enigmatic melodic lines recall Copland's own words about Gabriel Fauré, whom he called a "neglected master" in an essay of 1924. Like Fauré, José María exercises restraint: rather than exploiting the full resources of the piano, he resists "lusciously full or dazzlingly brilliant" sonorities, instead maintaining "ascetic reserve."[54] The result is a discursive, highly personal utterance, having little to do with typical Pan Americanist "vigor" or "dynamism." Copland also studied José María's piano concerto, a Sonata for Two Cellos, portions of a ballet-pantomime *Georgia* (the title refers to the female protagonist), and a *Concerto for Orchestra*, performed at the Colón just days after Copland left Buenos Aires and revised in 1944, the same year the Boston Symphony Orchestra premiered Béla Bartók's celebrated essay of the same name.

Should we be surprised that Copland found "freshness" in José María's music, despite its indebtedness to Europe? For Copland, individual personality evidently transcended the often long-winded debates over identity, folklore, universalism, and modernism. Once during the 1941 tour, Copland visited José María at home, finding him comfortable in his own skin: a "serious, simple, sympathetic artist—happy in his work and happy in his home life."[55] In principle, José María was interested in visiting the United States, although he knew no English. Nothing came of this idea, however, and he remains largely unknown outside of Argentina, a far more "neglected master" than Fauré.

## "A natural flair for Argentinian musical phraseology"

Closer to the Pan Americanist musical ideal was Alberto Ginastera, then twenty-five years old. Unlike Siccardi, García Morillo, Ficher, Paz, and the Castro brothers, he reveled in local color. He was still a student at the Conservatorio Nacional Superior de Música when his ballet suite *Panambí* was premiered at the Teatro Colón, a colorful evocation of an indigenous community on the banks of the Paraná River in which Ginastera combines French impressionism and ostinati à la Stravinsky. Besides examining *Panambí*, Copland looked over the *Cantos del Tucumán*, four songs for flute, violin, harp, soprano, and "native drum" on folk poetry by Rafael Jijena Sánchez that pay homage to Tucumán, a northern province of Argentina.[56] Another work was Ginastera's graduation piece, a setting of Psalm 150, which Copland judged "well written, somewhat in the style of Honegger's *Roi David*." (Given the success of *Panambí*, it's surprising that he calls Psalm 150 Ginastera's "only work . . . with any pretensions to serious musical content.")[57] Copland also studied two works that Ginastera later withdrew: a piano concerto from 1935, the *Concierto argentino* (Hugo Balzo had just premiered it in Montevideo) and another that Copland lists as "Sinfonía—two movements," probably Ginastera's *Sinfonía porteña* (Buenos Aires Symphony), Ginastera's initial foray into the genre.[58] With the exception of Psalm 150, all the Ginastera works Copland studied had a decidedly regionalist bent. So did Ginastera's most recorded, performed, and arranged work, the in-progress ballet *Estancia*, Ginastera's homage to life on the pampas for the American Ballet Caravan.[59] During the 1941 tour, Kirstein evidently discovered that "Buenos Aires was not the [entire] country" and commissioned a score that would reflect some of Argentina's regional variety.[60] Today, *Estancia* (the name means "ranch") is heard most frequently as an orchestral suite, with its most celebrated movement the *Malambo*, Ginastera's rendering of the traditional gaucho dance and demonstration of manhood, enlivened with frequent metric alterations, sharp accents, and a long, breathless coda.[61] Much the way the Brooklyn-born, Jewish, left-leaning, homosexual Copland became rather implausibly identified with the U.S. West, Ginastera, born in Buenos Aires and based there for most of his career, declared, "I am a man of the pampas."[62]

Surely aware that Ginastera's "brand" would satisfy the OIAA's informal criteria, Copland dubbed him "the white hope of Argentine music . . . far ahead of any of the young men his age here." Further—and despite the fact that Copland would likely have been at a loss to identify a *vidalita* or a *chacarera*, two Argentine genres—he insisted on Ginastera's innate gift for "Argentinian musical phraseology." Still, he maintained, Ginastera was not yet "a heavyweight." A skilled orchestrator with "a knack for writing effective, sure-fire music," Ginastera boasted a talent that was merely "pleasant," the same category Copland had assigned to Uribe Holguín, Mejía, and Holzmann. Copland also admired Luis Gianneo, whom he met at a "musical party" at the home of the pianist Orestes Castronuovo. Gianneo composed over a hundred works and was active in radio and youth orchestras, writing several sets of piano pieces for young musicians. He played one such set at Castronuovo's, likely *Música para niños*, from 1941, which combines folk genres with a prelude and fugue and also an invention. Copland found it "charming" and noted that "everyone" believed Gianneo was one of the best composers in Argentina, even though he lived in Tucumán, far from the musical activity of the capital.

## Copland's Music in Buenos Aires: Two Publics

On two occasions Argentine musicians played Copland's music. On 15 October Juan José Castro conducted *An Outdoor Overture* at the Teatro Colón, the final rehearsal of which Copland attended. He commented in his diary that the players did "very well" and that Castro's conducting was "excellent."[63] Also on the program were Cimarosa's Overture from *El matrimonio secreto*, Mendelssohn's *Italian Symphony*, *Three Chorales for Organ by Bach* (in Castro's orchestration), and Ravel's *Rhapsodie espagnole*.

Unfortunately it was a meager public: "gallery full—seats downstairs empty," Copland acknowledged. Critics addressed *An Outdoor Overture* at some length, however. One imagined a "[U.S.] fair . . . bathed in dazzling sunlight" and another heard "the energetic soul of [Copland's] people," filled with "dynamic optimism"; the pro-U.S. *Argentinisches Tageblatt* noted the work's "fresh, life-affirming" quality.[64] Another critic (probably García Morillo) noted that Copland had rejected aggressive modernism in favor of "an art that is fresher and cleaner" (un arte más fresco y depurado) such that *An Outdoor Overture* crystalized Copland's aim to "make [his music] easy to understand by the public through the simplicity and clarity of its writing: which seems to be, as it appears, the ideal now being pursued by the majority of U.S. composers."[65] In other words, Copland had not only democratized music but persuaded his compatriots to do the same. Indeed, the critic for *La Vanguardia* wrote that "the 'open doors' of this overture refer not only to the fact that it is conceived for performance far from the habitual confines of the concert hall but that it is dedicated to the masses and is therefore accessible both to initiates and ordinary listeners."[66]

To be sure, not all critics found sunshine and freshness in Copland's score. Héctor Chiesa wrote for *El Pueblo*, an anti-U.S. daily read mainly by authoritarian Catholics. He hinted at what Saminsky called Copland's "absorbing rather than creative nature," opining that Copland achieved "absolutely no originality in [*An Outdoor Overture*], in which the influence of Mussorgsky and Stravinsky are noticeable."[67] Upping the ante was the right-wing, anti-Semitic tabloid *La Fronda*, financed by local agencies of the Third Reich. Its critic had nothing but praise for Castro's arrangement of the Bach chorales and deemed the Cimarosa overture "one of the jewels of the great classical era."[68] Two works by Jewish composers on the program merited little more than sarcasm, however:

> [Bach and Cimarosa] shared the concert program with the greatest of Jewish musicians, Mendelssohn, whose well-known *Italian Symphony* we heard in an agile and sympathetic interpretation by Castro. . . . Mendelsohn was and continues to be a minor figure, one quarter, as Nietzsche said, of Schubert. The other Jew was Ravel, whose enchantingly vacuous *Rhapsodie espagnole* follows, in the scale of values, well behind Chabrier, who, without wanting to make anything other than music, without trying to create a mysterious "atmosphere," was far closer to essential Spanishness than this sonorous spiral, mathematically, precisely, and preciously realized, by Ravel.[69]

That left "the third Jew" on the program:

This was Aaron Copland, a musician who is visiting us, and whose *An Outdoor Overture* was heard for the first time here. The piece reveals a romantic inclination and a modernity of design that don't succeed in coalescing. It's a motley work, with an excess of sound that amounts to grandiloquence, since behind it one finds no idea that merits expression with this sort of language. To our judgment, he's a romantic disguised as a modernist. The influence of Stravinsky, more than obvious, is oppressive.[70]

Thus the familiar stereotype, according to which Jews merely cobbled together the inspirations of others—in "motley" fashion—followed Copland to Latin America. Another Argentine paper funded by the Reich was *El Pampero*. It did not review the concert but did announce it, mentioning all the composers but Copland. Although that may be merely an oversight, at no point does the paper acknowledge the composer's presence in Buenos Aires. There was, however, space to report on other artistic events, such as "The Reich's Week of Culture," along with the upcoming radio broadcast of *Tannhäuser* on the program *Music of All Germany*, and Hitler's campaign against "degenerate art" influenced by "the Jew, Freud."[71] Further, although *El Pampero* overlooked Copland, it took aim at U.S. cultural diplomacy. The editorial "Another Yankee-Jewish Chicanery" characterized the Good Neighbor Policy as "a powerful hand that moves in the darkness" dedicated to "sowing confusion in the fraternity of Latin American nations, in setting them one against the other . . . in making them fight. . . . And to achieve that end [the United States] doesn't hesitate in its choice of means, certainly not when it can count on the powerful arm of the media, organisms that are nothing more than instruments of penetration and domination."[72]

The main tool in this quest for cultural domination? None other than the OIAA, headed by Rockefeller, "the magnate of Standard Oil." As the editorial proclaimed, "The committee charged with 'culturally' coordinating the American nations, that committee driven by the magnate of Standard Oil, which is so prodigal in distributing money among the newspapers of the American nations and information agencies, are the fingers of that claw that moves in the shadows. . . . And this is how Uncle Sam puts into practice his 'Good Neighbor' policy."[73] Thus *El Pampero* warned Argentine readers still vacillating between the Allies and the Axis: they could opt for the time-tested culture of the Reich or one engineered by a corrupt oil magnate from the Colossus of the North.

Copland's second concert in Buenos Aires was of a very different order. It took place at the Teatro del Pueblo under the aegis of Paz's Nueva Música. Now wishing to prove himself as one who cultivates "modern music in its serious form," Copland gave the public premiere of his Piano Sonata, the economy of materials and clamoring dissonances of which are a far cry from the winsome *An Outdoor Overture*.[74] Also participating was Slonimsky, then on the Argentine leg of his "South American fishing trip." He and Copland led off the program with Sessions's *Chorale-Preludes*, an organ work transcribed for piano four hands. The rest of the program came about thanks to the Jewish musical community of Buenos Aires. Slonimsky played Harris's piano trio with the violinist Anita Sujovolsky, born in Buenos Aires but resident in Berlin until 1933, and the cellist Germán Weil, born in Kherson (Ukraine).[75] Two Austrian-born musicians, the pianist Sofía Knoll and the flutist Esteban Eitler, performed Gerald Strang's *Three Pieces for Flute and Piano*.[76] The final work on the program was Henry Cowell's "United" String Quartet, played by Sujovolsky and Weil; violinist Ferencz (Francisco) Heltay, who had arrived in 1938; and Berlin-born violist Hilde Heinitz.[77] Perhaps on that occasion more than any other, the "United Quartet" lived up to Cowell's aspiration to reconcile European genres such as the string quartet with what were then considered "primitive" musics.[78] Here, however, the "cultivated" genre was performed by four Europeans who had fled a madman now leading a country long considered the height of civilization.

With the exception of Strang's *Three Pieces*, these works were unfamiliar to the Buenos Aires public.[79] Critics noted "highly dissonant combinations [of sound]" in the *Chorale-Preludes*; "noble sentiment" in the Harris trio, and "felicitous combinations of timbres" in the first movement of Cowell's quartet.[80] As for Copland's sonata, gone were identity-conscious tropes of "the energetic soul of [Copland's] people" or the "dynamic optimism" of the United States. One critic emphasized the work's intellectual dimension, including the "inevitable logic in [its] working-out" and "extreme sobriety . . . manifested with noble and apt means."[81] Another described it in language Stravinsky would have welcomed: "essentially objective music, stripped down, which makes not the slightest concession to sentimentality, or to expressivity, and which zealously adheres to a strictly musical logic."[82] Paz also applauded the Piano Sonata. In an extended survey of Copland's accomplishments, published in *Argentina Libre*, he echoed the truism Hurtado had raised in the same publication: "We've heard ad nauseum that the United States is not a musically creative country for the simple fact that it hasn't produced a Monteverdi, a Beethoven, or a Mussorgsky."[83] Copland, a member of a "radical group" of U.S. composers then working to reshape the language of U.S. music, was "a primary figure in this movement of renewal."[84] As an example of Copland's "radicalism," Paz addressed the Piano Variations, which he found "strong, aggressive, magnificently dissonant . . . simple and sharp, and moreover laconic," music that could "never be accepted as a model in academic institutions plagued by professorial mummies."[85] When it came to the Sonata, heard at the Nueva Música concert, Paz called it "a masterpiece" and complimented the "rough dissonances the composer implacably fires at the ears and nerves of the public . . . full of tragic force." In sum, Copland was a "consummate master."[86]

As for how one might account for the gulf between, say, the Sonata and *An Outdoor Overture* or *Billy the Kid*, Paz allowed tersely that sometimes "the music of Copland deliberately seeks touches of the popular." Another critic elaborated on this phenomenon as well. Copland, blessed with an "extraordinary ability to adapt his music to the most diverse styles," had simply given free rein to his multifaceted personality.[87] Capable of balancing modernism and populism, he defended the "democratic bases of music" with infinite flexibility.

\* \* \*

Argentina was one of Copland's more challenging diplomacy assignments. Having impressed interviewers with his command of Spanish and easygoing charm, he offered the full variety of his compositional styles. He also put aside his preference for folklore to be genuinely thrilled by both the "happy neoclassicism" and "bittersweet romanticism" of José María Castro, a true "find" for Copland. In addition, he emerged unscathed by diatribes against Rockefeller and the OIAA, speaking out boldly on behalf of democracy and even assigning a role to the mass public in developing "a new musical taste." He also took pains to situate composers of the Americas at the forefront of this project. In Brazil, Copland would pursue similar activities. But he would also encounter a new task, one that proved trickier than some of his other obligations in cultural diplomacy.

# 6

# Copland in Brazil

At the 1939 World's Fair, the first of two "Brazilian nights" took place on 5 May in the Hall of Music. After the Brazilian and U.S. national anthems, the New York Philharmonic-Symphony followed with the Overture (*Protofonia*) to the 1870 opera *Il Guarany* by Antônio Carlos Gomes, widely regarded as Brazil's first composer of international stature despite the obvious Italianisms in his style. Other works on the program included *Fantasia Brasileira* for piano and orchestra by Francisco Mignone; *Batuque* by Oscar Lorenzo Fernândez; and *Fantastic Episode* by Burle Marx, who along with his three talented siblings would be known in the United States as one of "Brazil's Marx Brothers."[1] Dominating the proceedings was Heitor Villa-Lobos with his *Choros* no. 8. A fanciful expansion of the *choro*, a Brazilian urban serenade traditionally involving members of the guitar family, tambourine, and flute, Villa-Lobos's rendering drew on such a massive orchestra that one critic exclaimed, "A *Sacre du printemps* of the Amazon!"[2] Rosenfeld, however, heard "opacity and turbidness," and Edward O'Gorman deemed *Choros* no. 8 "eight times louder, eight times longer, and eight times more complex" than necessary.[3] Oscar Thompson had little to say about *Choros* no. 8 but observed that "the name of Bach figured rather curiously" in two additional compositions by Villa-Lobos. These were *Bachianas brasileiras* no. 2 for orchestra, with its humorous final movement, and the gentle Aria from *Bachianas brasileiras* no. 5 for soprano and eight cellos, performed by Bidu Sayao.[4]

U.S. critics may have been divided on Villa-Lobos's music, but few would deny his large-than-life presence.[5] This chapter explores Copland's experience in Brazil with Villa-Lobos. In 1941 Brazil was vacillating between the Axis and the Allies, and U.S. cultural diplomats eagerly courted Villa-Lobos in the hopes of bringing him to the United States. Along with other duties, it fell to Copland to accomplish this great coup for cultural diplomacy.

## "A possible source for fresh musical experience"

Copland had met Villa-Lobos many years earlier, in Paris. At that time, Copland had no idea Latin American classical music even existed. But he surmised that it might prove "fresh":

> One afternoon in 1923 I was introduced to a short and dynamic individual at the Paris apartment of my composition teacher, Nadia Boulanger. Someone told me that this gentleman with the dark complexion and the fiery eyes was a composer from Brazil by the name of Heitor Villa-Lobos. This was the first inkling I had that there might be such a thing as Latin American [serious] music. Up to that time we all naturally assumed that the exciting new music would come from Europe. A few daring spirits had the temerity to hope that the United States might someday contribute to the stream of world composition. But practically nobody had given a thought to South America as a possible source for fresh musical experience.[6]

In 1923 Copland could hardly have dreamed that one day he would be recruiting Villa-Lobos for the U.S. State Department. At the time of his tour, the Brazilian government was headed by the dictator-president Getúlio Vargas, who came to power in 1930 in a military intervention over a disputed election. Calling himself the "father of the poor" (o pai dos pobres), Vargas initially served as the civilian head of a provisional government (1930–34). In 1937 he began to preside over the authoritarian Estado Novo (New State), a centrist, corporatist, nationalist, and anticommunist regime that scholars have compared to those of Benito Mussolini of Italy and Antônio de Oliveira Salazar of Portugal.[7]

Vargas flirted with Nazism. The German-Brazilian magazine Intercâmbio ran photographs of him alongside the Hitler Youth (it was rumored that he once sent Hitler birthday greetings) and Axis sympathizers in Brazil joined Ação Integralista Brasileira (Brazilian Integralist Action), a group that marched about in jackboots at rallies.[8] Brazil was also home to the largest bloc of Germans and people of German descent in the Western Hemisphere, many of whom lived in prosperous communities in Santa Catarina state, where the city of Blumenau celebrates Oktoberfest amid half-timbered, Schwarzwald-style buildings.[9] As Smith had warned the OIAA music committee, Axis cultural diplomats had already made headway. The U.S. consul in Santa Catarina, Reginald S. Kazanjian, confirmed these fears. In a report to the Division of Cultural Relations, he observed that among Nazi sympathizers were pastors, teachers, members of women's organizations, and "technicians" (individuals who organized clubs and activities to cement group solidarity). Kazanjian also acknowledged the power of ideas, the "philosophy of 'Pan-Germanism,'" which he described as a "fanatical and mystical belief in the superiority of their race."[10] A visit such as Copland's might encourage Brazilians to embrace other values.

Vargas was not especially interested in the arts himself. But his government's strong cultural program helped him present the Estado Novo as a modern, unified state rather than as one more impoverished Latin American nation. Cultural administrators inculcated *brasilidade* (Brazilianness), which focused on national unity: under the Estado Novo, Brazil would see itself as one nation rather than as a congeries of individual states with competing interests. In the arts, this modern state would adopt those international trends most compatible with Brazilian character but which also bespoke universalism.[11] For example, the two principal architects of the era, Lucio Costa and Oscar Niemeyer, took as a model the International Style, with its sleek lines and unadorned surfaces. But they enhanced these "unmarked" buildings with presumably Brazilian features, such as landscaping, ensuring that their internationally acclaimed creations were seen as "unmistakably Brazilian and, at the same time, universal," as one historian notes.[12] At the 1939 World's Fair, the Brazilian Pavilion won praise for this approach.[13]

In music, concert life in Rio de Janeiro had long been dominated by France. French-language music magazines circulated, and artists programmed works by Massenet, Chabrier, and Saint-Saëns, all to satisfy Francophile appetites.[14] In 1915 Villa-Lobos presented his debut concert there, establishing himself as an enfant terrible.[15] In 1922 he represented music at the Week of Modern Art, a symposium of lectures, concerts, and exhibits in the coffee boomtown of São Paulo, at which participants preached no single aesthetic but advocated upheaval and change.[16] Shortly thereafter, Villa-Lobos departed for Paris, where he assaulted listeners with "savagery," *"bruitisme"* (noise), and "lawless rhythm" in mammoth primitivist works, such as *Choros* no. 8.[17] In 1930, the year Vargas came to power, Villa-Lobos returned home and, like other Brazilian artists and intellectuals, surveyed the new political reality and his likely place in it. Some, such as the author Jorge Amado, were silenced or harassed in the Estado Novo. But moderates and leftists of various stripes could receive contracts and positions, olive branches the Ministry of Culture held out to a potentially rebellious constituency.[18] Villa-Lobos, who admired certain aspects of Mussolini's regime, had few compunctions about throwing in his lot with Vargas.[19] He began directing the Superintendência de Educação Musical e Artística (known by its Portuguese acronym SEMA), which mainly targeted youth. In essays on musical Brazilianness, he advocated folk music as a conduit to "an authentic Brazilian musical conscience."[20] (After Vargas was overthrown in 1945, Villa-Lobos's writing on music's political or patriotic music abruptly ceased.)[21] In his customary supersized style, he led choruses of thirty-thousand to forty-thousand young people in folk and patriotic songs accompanied by orchestras of a thousand players, which he called "orpheonic singing." Thus, as an administrator and educator, Villa-Lobos emphasized the Brazilian aspects of brasilidade.

As a composer, however, he addressed its universalist dimension. Just as architects sought the "unmistakably Brazilian and, at the same time, universal" in their buildings, Villa-Lobos attempted something similar in his *Bachianas brasileiras*, surely the most blatantly universalist opus by any Latin American composer. He composed the nine-work series between 1930 and 1945, the exact time frame of the first Vargas regime. (Vargas served again as president from 1951 to 1954 but committed suicide in office.) With bruitisme now behind him, Villa-Lobos paid homage to Johann Sebastian Bach, in whose music he claimed to detect striking similarities with Brazilian traditional music. As he saw it, Bach was "a kind of universal folkloric source, rich and profound . . . linking all peoples."[22] Few took this rhetorical sleight of hand seriously, even if Baroque features do occasionally surface in the *Bachianas*. (No. 5, for example, contains sequences.) Along with other works by Villa-Lobos, the *Bachianas* were played regularly in the United States in the early 1940s, with nos. 5 and 2 remaining popular today.

## Courting Villa-Lobos

Copland arrived in Brazil on 6 November, planning to divide his time between Rio de Janeiro and São Paulo. He was not the first U.S. cultural diplomat to approach Villa-Lobos. John W. Beattie and Louis Woodson Curtis, leaders of the music education team dispatched by the Pan American Union, had observed the Brazilian composer's chorus rehearsals. In the *Music*

*Educators Journal*, they described him as "dynamic, egocentric, energetic, self-sufficient, opinionated." They also referred to "heated arguments" over pedagogical techniques. To be sure, they managed to emphasize the amiability of these exchanges.[23] But privately, Beattie told Charles Seeger that Villa-Lobos was "not at all interested in a trip to the States," adding, "in fact, his chief interest is in Villa-Lobos." More significant, in Villa-Lobos's gargantuan choruses "the tone quality he wants and gets is terrible," hardly a selling point. Beattie and Curtis agreed, however, that Villa-Lobos could be brought to the United States as "one of the world's greatest composers [but] certainly *not* as a music educator."[24]

Aware of these challenges, Copland visited Villa-Lobos a total of eight times, lavishing more attention on him than on any other individual during the 1941 tour. Their first visit is illustrative. On 8 November at 4:00 P.M., Antônio Sá Pereira, who had welcomed the Yale Glee Club to Rio de Janeiro earlier that year, accompanied Copland to Villa-Lobos's office to make the necessary introductions. Villa-Lobos then regaled Copland with recordings of miscellaneous "pieces for children; songs, piano pieces, choruses" and a work Copland lists in his diary as "Fantasie for Violin and Orchestra" (probably the *Fantasie de movimentos mistos* of 1921).[25] After dining at Villa-Lobos's club, they went to his home, where Copland heard a piano reduction of Villa-Lobos's early orchestral work *Amazonas*, played by José Vieira Brandão, Villa-Lobos's assistant. (It cannot have been easy to evoke on the piano the timbres of Villa-Lobos's unusual instrumentation, which calls for viola d'amore and violinophone, the latter an instrument that amplifies the sound of the violin through a metal horn.) Next, Brandão essayed part of *Choros 11*, which Copland described in his diary as "a forty-minute Piano Concerto for Artur Rubinstein." (The final version of this single-movement work, which takes over an hour, is scored for two harps, E-flat clarinet, soprano and alto saxophone, two contrabassoons, vibraphone, celesta, xylophone, and Brazilian percussion in addition to the standard orchestra.)[26] All told, Copland's first session with Villa-Lobos lasted from 4:00 P.M. until midnight.

Similar marathons followed. On 13 November Copland attended an all-Villa-Lobos concert of piano pieces, again performed by the tireless Brandão. Copland does not identify these works but commented that "artistically [these pieces] have very little that is new . . . but as a healthy influence on Brazil's composers one can see their importance."[27] On another occasion, Copland heard a reading of Villa-Lobos's sixth string quartet, a work loosely based on classical models, with hemiolas, mild dissonances, and fleeting moments of counterpoint. Copland called it "simple and unpretentious . . . excellent for radio performance" and whose "plain melodies and cute Brazilian rhythms" lent it accessibility. "It is characteristic," he remarked, "that no movement is entirely bad, just as none is entirely good."[28]

Negotiating with Villa-Lobos was another matter. Despite Copland's repeated blandishments—he told his Brazilian colleague that he was "à la mode just now" in the United States and that a visit there would be a "golden opportunity"—Villa-Lobos imposed conditions that seemed to shift daily. Sometimes he presented himself as an idealist, agreeing to come in principle but only if he could remain independent of government. On other occasions, he claimed to desire commercial sponsorship so that he could be accepted or rejected on his own merits as artist. To that end, he stipulated that there be no "receptions or banquets of any kind in his honor," explaining, "if they wish to honor me, let them play my music." Other times he sought deliberately to provoke. Copland roughly transcribed one such conversation: "if ever [Villa-Lobos] came to the States he would publicly denounce educators Beattie and Curtis as 'criminals' as 'misleaders of youth—who *d'ailleurs* [moreover] says he, are both charming gentlemen' (!)."[29]

Copland was annoyed both by Villa-Lobos's coquetry and his ego, the "considerable size" of which he compared to Koussevitzky's. To be sure, after their initial meeting he admitted, "I liked him more than I thought I was going to." After much back and forth and increasingly mystified by Villa-Lobos's mercurial behavior, Copland took the delicate step of broaching the topic with various Brazilian musicians. They intimated that Villa-Lobos's hesitation stemmed from lack of confidence in his own conducting ("according to all reports with reason," Copland added). Eventually, he lost patience with Villa-Lobos and decided that "it would be dangerous to bring [him] in any official capacity, as he . . . prides himself on his honesty and outspokenness and exercises both on the slightest provocation." Neither composer, however, closed off the possibility that some arrangement could be agreed upon. They remained on cordial terms.

## A "tough life"

Villa-Lobos's assistant Brandão was not only a fine pianist but composed three hundred works. When he died in 2002, one obituary read: "It's a tough life being a composer in a country where a single towering figure epitomizes its music both at home and abroad. Even now, Finnish composers still feel Sibelius looming over them. . . . For Brazilian musicians it is Heitor Villa-Lobos who hogs the limelight."[30] Many of the composers Copland met in Rio and São Paulo likely felt the same way.

Copland dismissed some of them out of hand. He found none of Brandão's works "interesting," due to lack of "real composer temperament."[31] (Slonimsky, on the other hand, merely noted that Brandão wrote "in a simple unassuming style without attempts at modernism.")[32] Copland also met Jayme Ovalle, a former street musician who was largely self-taught and later became a customs inspector. Copland felt Ovalle had "no future to speak of" as a musician. In 1945, however, Ovalle's song "Azulão" (Bluebird), was published and later recorded by Victoria de los Ángeles, Kathleen Battle, Montserrat Caballé, Angela Gheorghiu, and Gérard Souzay, all of whom negotiated with aplomb the challenges of Portuguese diction.[33] Newton Padua, a cellist who studied church music in Rome and taught harmony in Rio de Janeiro, struck Copland as a "composer of no consequence"; Padua did, however, compose several chamber works, the opera *A Lenda do Irupê* (based on a Guaraní legend), and various orchestral works, including the symphonic poem *São Paulo e Anchieta*. More interesting to Copland was Radamés Gnattali, originally from the state of Rio Grande do Sul and then directing the orchestra for Radio Nacional in Rio de Janeiro. He composed for radio serials but also in more "serious" genres, turning out a concertino for piano and orchestra, a piano trio, a cello sonata, and a string quartet. Gnattali struck Copland as "a very musical chap," albeit "with a kind of slick musical talent such as we are accustomed to in composers like [Robert Russell] Bennett or Morton Gould."[34]

Copland had mixed feelings about Mignone, a native of São Paulo who studied in Milan and then taught at the Escola Nacional de Música in Rio de Janeiro. By 1941 Mignone had many compositions to his credit, including about a dozen symphonic works. He invited Copland and Sá Pereira to dine at his home, where they heard "numerous songs and piano pieces." Then, at a concert of Brazilian music in Copland's honor sponsored by the Ministry of Foreign Affairs, Mignone's new piano sonata was performed. Digesting the work's many episodes and virtuosic flourishes, Copland ultimately found the piece unsatisfying: he questioned its "improvisatory manner" and predicted that the work was "certain to go stale, despite the pretty *trouvailles* [discoveries] at every corner."[35] Yet, Copland admired Mignone's *Maracatú de Chico-Rei* (The Maracatú of the Little King), a ballet score for chorus, orchestra, and enhanced percussion that pays homage to the *maracatú*, an African processional dance in which a royal couple is crowned.[36] Copland also liked Mignone's *Fantasia brasileira* no. 4, scored for piano and orchestra and commissioned by Kirstein when the American Ballet Caravan was in Rio. As Jennifer L. Campbell explains, it remains one of the unsolved riddles of the dance world: Balanchine choreographed *Fantasia brasileira* no. 4, and although the company premiered it in Chile later in the tour, the choreography was lost, and the score remains unpublished.[37] Copland assigned it an asterisk. Mainly, he found Mignone's music "full of color and life, not profound, always on the theatrical and brilliant side." If "carefully chosen," Copland believed, Mignone's works would "make a good impression" [in the United States].[38] Mignone's music had already "made a good impression": four of the five movements of *Maracatú de Chico-Rei* were performed at the 1939 World's Fair, whereupon New York critic Jerome D. Bohm praised them as "highly effective" for the "Stravinskian influence . . . frequently encountered in Brazilian music," and his colleague Irving Kolodin observed "remarkable felicity."[39] In April 1940, when *Maracatú de Chico-Rei* was performed at Carnegie Hall, Colin McPhee admired its "naive and pleasant noisiness."[40]

Copland also met Cláudio Santoro, then twenty-five years old. Born in Manaus, the site of the famous belle époque opera house built in the heart of the rainforest during the rubber boom, Santoro moved to Rio de Janeiro to study violin at the Conservatório de Música do Distrito Federal. As a composer, he was then exploring twelve-tone composition with his mentor, the German-born émigré Hans Joachim Koellreutter, who had studied at the Berlin Academy of Music and concertized throughout Europe as a flutist before arriving in Brazil in 1937. Over the ensuing years, Koellreutter introduced the twelve-tone method to his students in Rio de Janeiro and São Paulo. Copland found Santoro's most recent music "difficult to evaluate because of the system" but nonetheless believed it had "sincerity behind it, and a certain personality."[41] (Copland does not say which works he studied but a likely candidate is the terse Sonata for Violin Solo, published earlier that year and written according to strict twelve-tone procedures.) Copland met Koellreutter at a musical gathering in São Paulo, where he heard several of his works, including a pre-twelve tone sonata for flute and piano.[42] Copland praised Koellreutter's "firm technique" and "nice sense of melody," all of which added up to a "definite leaning toward the Berg side." He decided—mistakenly, it turns out—that Koellreutter's was a "pretty talent rather than an important one."[43]

## Camargo Guarnieri: "Everything it takes"

It was also in São Paulo that Copland met the second of the two composers who captivated him during the 1941 trip. Having enthused about José María Castro, Copland now visited Mozart Camargo Guarnieri. (Surnames of famous individuals—Edison, Milton, Wagner—are not uncommon as first names in Brazil. Guarnieri eventually dropped "Mozart," signing his name "M. Camargo Guarnieri" so as "not to offend a master," he explained.)[44] Guarnieri enrolled at the conservatory in São Paulo but in 1938 began studying composition and aesthetics with Charles Koechlin in Paris. When he returned to Brazil a year later, he discovered that his reputation now extended beyond his native city. By 1941 he was teaching at the São Paulo conservatory.

"Guarnieri is a real composer," Copland declared in his diary. "He has everything it takes—a personality, technique, and a fecund imagination with plenty of work to show." Copland knew what he was talking about: that day, he had listened to no fewer than twelve of Guarnieri's compositions. On five, he conferred asterisks: the *Dança selvagem* (Savage Dance) for orchestra, the Concerto for Violin and Orchestra, *Encantamento* (Enchantment) for Violin and Piano, the Second Sonata for Violin and Piano, and the *Ten Ponteios* (Preludes). Two had already won Good Neighborly acclaim. In 1940 the violin concerto took first prize in a contest funded by Samuel Simeon Fels (like Edwin Adler Fleisher, a Philadelphia-based philanthropist) and on whose jury Howard Hanson and Koussevitzky sat. The violin piece *Encantamento* was written on a commission from the Pan American Union.[45] (Guarnieri later transcribed for orchestra this brief, thoughtful statement, with its hesitant opening theme.) Guarnieri also played Copland three sonatinas for piano, which Brazilian critic Eurico Nogueira França had called a "happy compromise . . . between the great universal forms and native content."[46] For Copland, Guarnieri was "without any doubt one of the few real talents in S.A. [South America]—and along with José María Castro, one of the few composers who deserves to be far better known than he is." His music balanced technique, personality, and national identity:

> [Guarnieri's] gift is a more orderly one than that of Villa-Lobos without being the less Brazilian. It has the typical traits of abundance—(Brazilian composers seem to have no musical inhibition)—, the typical romantic bias, and the typical rhythms of the country. Guarnieri's use of folk material is less conscious . . . but it makes a clearly indigenous impression nonetheless. All his music is highly playable—it would go over with any audience. One likes most its healthy emotional expression—it is the honest expression of how one man feels. . . . In short, his work is that of a highly musical person who knows how to express what he has to say.[47]

Whereas Villa-Lobos gave free rein to "typical abundance"—a Brazilian trait, according to Copland—to produce many a sprawling and incoherent work,

Guarnieri was "healthy" because his musical gifts complemented his own character. The fact that Copland likely had only a fuzzy notion of "typical rhythms" did not prevent him from sensing a "clearly indigenous impression" in Guarnieri's music. "Of all the composers I have met," he concluded in his diary, "I should say that Guarnieri is first choice for a visit to the States."

## "The heart is a dead muscle"

On 24 November Copland gave his lecture on film music at the Associacão Brasileira de Impresa (Brazilian Press Association) before a "numerous public," as he reported in his diary. He focused on *Of Mice and Men*, known in Portuguese as *Caricia Fatal* (Fatal Embrace).[48] Another event was a concert of U.S. music in his honor, at Rio de Janeiro's Escola Nacional de Musica, which attracted a good-sized audience. Soprano Cristina Maristany performed two songs by Ives ("Evening" and "Walking"); Thomson's *Stabat Mater* for soprano and string quartet; and Copland's *As It Fell upon a Day*. Also on the program were Piston's Violin Sonata, Harris's Piano Quintet, and Copland's own Piano Sonata, which the composer performed.

Copland later wrote in his diary that "the program was somewhat heavy considering the tastes of the audience and the heat." This was an understatement. To be sure, *As It Fell upon a Day* went over well, with one critic praising Copland for investing the pastorale with "the resources of modern technique."[49] But another found Thomson's *Stabat Mater* "too clever by half and destitute of sensibility" (cerebrino e destituido de sensibilidade); for another, the entire program was full of "hard and unexpected harmonizations, polytonal audacity, brusque and deliberately confusing effects," all suggesting "the agitated, nervous, and clamorous life of North America."[50] That reviewer also noted lack of emotion, complaining, "The heart is a dead muscle, one never heeded. It's only the brain that works and produces, out of an eagerness to grow something new and different within this formidable imaginary that is characteristically and essentially [U.S.] American."[51]

Unfortunately Copland's Piano Sonata was part of this trend. The same critic argued that "the sonata is a work of solid structure, but absolutely lacking in any emotive sense. Above all, it's the result of technical feats and disordered desires, deftly transplanted to staff paper and perfectly acceptable, in the final analysis, as modern music."[52] A critic for the *Correio de Manha* was even more outspoken. Looking back on Rio's Francophile past, he invoked the French nineteenth-century pianist and composer of salon music Francis Thomé:

"Évidement, ce n'est pas du Francis Thomé!" (Clearly, it's not Francis Thomé!) apropos the Sonata. Again, despite "solid musical construction," the Sonata was "a product of sound combinations exclusively for obtaining certain timbral effects . . . resulting in disconcerting encounters and unexpected shocks to our . . . ears."[53] Far from proclaiming Pan Americanist solidarity, the Sonata contained "moments in which we seem to see between the staves of Copland's sonata an entire army of goose-stepping warriors!" the critic observed, adding sarcastically, "it's marvelous."[54] Only one critic touched on hemispheric solidarity, calling the concert "a beautiful night of spiritual alliance between our musicians and the great republic of the north."[55] Clearly nothing could be taken for granted in musical Pan Americanism.

## Good Neighbor in Brazil

Throughout, Copland advocated for hemispheric solidarity. On one occasion, he greeted a reporter from the *Diario de Noticias* in his hotel in Rio de Janeiro, who interviewed him about musical developments in the United States and his association with Rockefeller's organization. Omitting any mention of modern music or the "unexpected shocks" of which critics had complained at the Escola Nacional concert, Copland remarked that because "cinema, radio, and recordings, for their part, have all effected great transformations with respect to the public, music has been democratized, so to speak."[56] In describing his "mission," Copland insisted that "there was no better way to get to know the music of a country than through direct contact." He especially praised Brazilian music's "extremely rich folklore with something of Black, Portuguese, Spanish, and indigenous musics," all of benefit to composers of the Americas seeking inspiration.[57]

He took a similar tack on the radio program *A Hora do Brasil* (Brazilian Hour), a nightly feature of the Vargas regime. Broadcast by the government radio station, the program proffered entertainment and its own account of the news. The average Brazilian had little hope of escaping *A Hora do Brasil*, which often blared from loudspeakers in public places.[58] As Smith reported, some Brazilians mocked the propaganda-filled program, calling *A Hora do Brasil* the "Hour of Silence" due to its strict censorship.[59] Copland's broadcast was arranged by Ayres de Andrade, a critic for the Rio newspapers *Diario Carioca* and *O Jornal*, who also worked in the music wing of "the Governmental propaganda agency," as Copland described it.[60] For the broadcast, Copland read a prepared text in Portuguese, probably with coaching on pronunciation from a native speaker. Copland urged his audience to reflect on the "clear indications that in the near future the word 'music' will no longer mean a purely European product." His Brooklyn-accented Portuguese likely echoed throughout the markets and town squares of many a distant part of Brazil.

Occasionally Copland enjoyed a tourist outing. In his diary entry of 23 November, he registered a "visit to Petropolis" in Rio de Janeiro state, without specifying who, if anyone, accompanied him to the so-called Imperial City, where the former emperors of Brazil once lived. In Rio de Janeiro, he lunched with the U.S. anthropologist Charles Wagley, whose knowledge of rubber production would prove valuable once the United States entered World War II. Villa-Lobos continued to extend hospitality toward Copland, despite the oddities of their relationship, and on 22 November he invited Copland to accompany him to one of Rio de Janeiro's samba schools. These entities, more like neighborhood clubs than actual schools, had been springing up in the favelas since the 1920s. Mainly, their members prepare for Carnaval (Mardi Gras), celebrated on a grander scale in Brazil than anywhere else in the world.

Carnaval also lays bare the glaring contrast between fleeting opulence and the poverty of everyday life. As Orson Welles's frustrated film project made clear, samba was a catalyst for racial conflict. The Brazilian singer and dancer Carmen Miranda, for example, appropriated the dress, music, and idioms of the northeastern state of Bahia, sometimes known as the "Africa of the Americas" for its large Black and mixed-race population. After conquering Hollywood, in her native land she was alternately applauded for her star power or condemned for her "vulgar negroid sambas."[61] The government sent a mixed message: although Vargas admired Miranda and believed samba could unify the country, his plainclothesmen came close to arresting the French anthropologist Claude Lévi-Strauss for having himself photographed with Brazilian Blacks and giving the impression that Brazil was inhabited by "dark-skinned people."[62] At other times the administration trumpeted *mestiçagem* (miscegenation) as a national strength.[63]

Taking Copland to a favela would therefore have to be finessed. Just as Hollywood movies were expected to avoid images of abject poverty in Latin America, it would hardly do to expose the eminent U.S. composer to a slum. He and Villa-Lobos went to Estação Primeira de Mangueira, founded in 1928 and located near the middle-class neighborhood of Maracaná, the site of a stadium in which Villa-Lobos often presented his thirty-thousand-voice extravaganzas. (Villa-Lobos had taken Smith to the same locale, who found the "Negro music schools" to be "highly respectable.")[64] The journalist Francisco de Assis

Barbosa, known as "Chico," wrote up his visit in a piece that appeared under the headline "Mister Copland Falls for the Samba." According to Chico, Copland immersed himself completely in the experience. "Copland's blue eyes didn't miss a single movement of the dances," Barbosa observed.[65] The composer asked numerous questions. How, exactly, were the schools organized? What were its members' obligations? An informant explained: "We're a society. Every member pays 2000 *réis* a month," adding that rehearsals for Carnaval would begin in November, at which point "we start in on a disciplined regime."[66] At one point, Copland mused, "North American Negros sing differently," a phenomenon he found "very curious." When Chico invited him to elaborate, Copland thought at some length. Finally he told Chico that the singing and dancing of Brazilian Blacks were more "gentle" (mansos) than that of their Northern counterparts.[67] The community remained largely indifferent to the two classical composers in their midst. When Villa-Lobos inquired about a *cuica* (friction drum) of a small boy, the lad simply shrugged.

Copland greatly enjoyed the experience. He wrote in his diary that he was "struck by the similarity [in] rhythm to what I had heard in Cuba," adding that he heard "no harmony of any kind—only rhythm and melody. Pretty overpowering in a small room."[68] This experience in Estação Primeira de Mangueira was only the beginning of Copland's fascination with Brazilian popular music.

## "The Negro Problem"

In São Paulo, Copland visited the ethnomusicologist and critic Mário de Andrade, of mixed race. (Andrade was also an experimental poet: Slonimsky relates that once when he attempted to use Portuguese in a lecture in São Paulo, a woman remarked to him afterwards that he sounded just like Mário de Andrade. Since Andrade was known as "the James Joyce of Brazilian literature" for his liberties with syntax, Slonimsky understood that this was not necessarily a compliment.)[69] Earlier in his career, Andrade served as chair of history of music and aesthetics at the São Paulo Conservatory, with Guarnieri among his pupils.[70] In launching ethnomusicology as a discipline in Brazil, Andrade addressed music's social role. The best-known of his numerous books and monographs is *Ensaio sôbre a música brasileira* (Essay on Brazilian Music), an analysis of the relationship between folk, popular, and classical music published in 1928.[71] In the mid-1930s he began heading the Department of Culture in Rio but in 1941 returned to São Paulo, having clashed with the Vargas administration. Smith knew Andrade and admired the "brilliance" of his mind. He also proposed that U.S. students research the music of Brazil's northeast under Andrade's direction, with its "wild religious gyrations ... considered 'uncivilized' and unworthy of urban life."[72] When Copland returned to Brazil in 1947, still in search of "freshness," it was that region—the Africa of the Americas—that most fascinated him.

Another of Andrade's projects was the public record library (discoteca) in São Paulo, one of the more comprehensive in the hemisphere and anticipating similar efforts worldwide. Copland was bowled over. "It is, of course, an admirable institution," he commented. "It would be fine if every city had such Discotecas."[73] Small wonder that Copland admired Andrade. As he wrote in his diary,

> Mário de Andrade is a highly cultured musicologist of mixed Negro and white blood. I spent an evening with him at his house and found him to be very sympathetic. I have no way of judging the quality of his work as yet but opinion seems unanimous that he has contributed valuable research material on the Negro contribution in Brazil. He has never been outside Brazil and would benefit enormously by a visit *chez nous*. (There is the Negro problem to be considered, of course.) Also, he speaks French, not English.[74]

In committing to his diary those three words—"the Negro problem"—Copland was relying on a ready-made phrase. Just as speakers of American English insert into ordinary speech phrases from the Bible ("go the extra mile," Matthew 5:41) and Shakespeare ("good riddance," *Troilus and Cressida*) without being aware of their sources, Copland was likely ignorant of the twisted lineage of "the Negro problem." In 1891 the lawyer, future Democratic U.S. senator of Maryland, and Pulitzer Prize–winning author William Cabell Bruce published *The Negro Problem*, a racist screed in which he argues that "the Negro problem" was attributable to the inherent inferiority of Blacks.[75] In a 1903 lecture "The Negro Problem: Is the Nation Going Backward?" author and philosophy instructor William Mackintire Salter insisted that Blacks, despite their "animal habits and instincts," called for humanity's better instincts, largely because they were incapable of reasoned judgment.[76] W. E. B. Du Bois turned the matter around, asking pointedly in an *Atlantic Monthly* essay, "How does it feel to be a problem?" and observing that while it was a question no one dared ask, many "flutter round it."[77] As we have seen, such "fluttering" attended the OIAA's discussion of *And They Lynched Him on a Tree*.

\* \* \*

In hesitating over Andrade, Copland was surely thinking of the difficulties the distinguished scholar would encounter in the United States. To be sure, Andrade would have avoided the Deep South, since State Department–sponsored visitors from Latin America generally visited Washington, DC; New York; New England; the Midwest; and sometimes California. Of course life in those regions was also segregated, either by law or custom. This brief phrase—"the Negro problem"—spontaneously jotted down by Copland, encapsulates "the social reality of racism" in the Americas.[78] In Chile, one of the so-called White republics of Latin America, critics would connect this social reality with Copland's music.

Meanwhile, Copland could take satisfaction in his Brazilian sojourn. Even if he was unsuccessful in pinning down Villa-Lobos for a U.S. tour (which Copland clearly did not see as a great loss for cultural diplomacy) and even if his Piano Sonata had failed to inspire positive views of the United States, Copland steadfastly upheld musical Pan Americanism in the press and over the airwaves, reaching into remote parts of the country. In Guarnieri he found another standout Latin American composer. He also listened to Brazilian popular music, perhaps for the first time in any sustained way.

# 7
# Copland in Chile

In the early 1940s the U.S. author Erna Fergusson visited South America. In *Chile*, one of her books on the Spanish-speaking world, she took stock of the strong presence there of U.S. business. Fergusson was frankly disappointed in her compatriots, especially corporate wives. "Yanqui women do not read Chilean history or literature," she observed tartly; further, "their knowledge of Chilean politics is extremely sketchy." They talk of "chitchat of their own group or of affairs at home . . . [as if] on an island of the U.S.A. mysteriously transported into a foreign land." Fergusson compared their Chilean counterparts, whom she saw as a possible target for U.S. goodwill efforts. "I thought of the fascinating, alert Chilean women, busy with politics, education, all the arts," she commented. "What a foreign legion of good feeling our women could be if they would learn Spanish, know Chilean women!"[1]

Any number of Chileans, women and men, would have agreed with Fergusson. Many believed the United States was little more than a bully, with recent conflicts including the 1930 Smoot-Hawley Tariff Act, which barred Chilean products from U.S. markets.[2] Other Chileans, however, admired the United States, especially its popular culture. Others were curious about classical music of the United States, even those partial to the "occidental" aesthetic rooted in European values that Domingo Santa Cruz so zealously promoted. This chapter tracks Copland's negotiations among these groups.

## "All of South America Must Repel the Nazis"

With its long, undefended coastline and substantial German immigrant community, Chile was a high priority for the U.S. State Department. In July 1940, the *New York Times* speculated that the Nazis would conquer the country and, after seizing its abundant metals, timber, and animal products, spread to southern Brazil, Uruguay, Argentina, and Paraguay.[3] When Copland arrived in Santiago in mid-September 1941, headlines in the pro-U.S. Santiago daily *Las Últimas Noticias* reflected such anxieties. "All of South America Must Repel the Nazis," read one.[4] Another looked optimistically to an Allied victory, proclaiming, "After the War the German People Must Be Detoxified."[5] Anti-Nazi cultural elites wished to further ties with the United States. Eugenio Pereira Salas, cofounder of the U.S.-Chilean Institute, published his chronicle of landmark events in U.S.-Chilean musical relations, such as the Chicago debut of the Chilean soprano Isidora Martínez King in 1887, along with New York recitals by Chilean pianists Carlos Hucke and Enrique Soro.[6] During Copland's visit, Santiago's Museum of Fine Arts featured an exhibit of paintings by U.S. artists, including Philip Evergood, Ernest Fiene, and Edward Hopper. Reactions by Chilean critics were mixed. According to one, these works exuded a "vital accent, young and energetic" although "the aura of a great painting" was absent, due to lack of "profundity."[7]

U.S. popular culture made tremendous inroads, however. Had Copland opened a newspaper or two during his first few hours in Santiago, he might have imagined he was back in New York. Playing at the local cinema, in all its technicolor glory, was the "spectacular musical super-production" *That Night in Rio* (Aquella Noche en Rio), a Good-Neighbor movie in which Don Ameche and Carmen Miranda riotously extend "felicitations to our South American relations."[8] Also playing was *Blondie Goes Latin* featuring the Mexican singer Tito Guizar.[9] In addition, santiagueños could look forward to two upcoming dance competitions, one for rhumba and conga and another for swing.[10]

## Copland Meets Chilean Composers

Shepherding Copland around Santiago was Santa Cruz. They likely met in New York during Santa Cruz's visit earlier that year. A foremost figure in Chilean musical life, Santa Cruz had initially pursued a career in law. In 1917, however, he founded the Bach Society, which performed Renaissance polyphony and introduced works such as J. S. Bach's *Christmas Oratorio* to the Santiago public.

He then worked as a diplomat, serving in the early 1920s as the secretary for the Chilean Embassy in Madrid, studying composition with Conrado del Campo of Madrid's Real Conservatorio in his spare time. Upon returning to Santiago, Santa Cruz devoted all his energies to music, joining the faculty of the Conservatorio Nacional in 1928. Shortly thereafter, the government asked him to reorganize music instruction in Chile, whereupon he converted the conservatory into a Facultad de Bellas Artes (Fine Arts Department), that is, part of the university system. Copland admired Santa Cruz's administrative acumen and the organization of his program. Given the strict separation between university and conservatory in Latin America, he correctly believed it was "unique."[11] Santa Cruz also helped found the *Revista musical chilena*, still an important journal. During Copland's visit, he was extremely attentive to his U.S. colleague. He also kept him plenty occupied. Once, Santa Cruz invited Copland and several other composers to his house, where they spent an afternoon playing recordings and discussing music. As Copland was leaving, Santa Cruz bestowed on him a "pile" of scores by Chilean composers for him to take back to his hotel and study.[12]

As noted, Santa Cruz repeatedly asserted Chile's fealty to Europe, which he called the "seal of civilization, discreet and all its own, that stands out among the positive flowerings . . . of occidental civilization."[13] What did it mean to write "occidental" music in one of Latin America's so-called White republics? Despite some late-romantic proclivities, Santa Cruz's style is often described as neoclassical: not for nothing did Slonimsky dub him "the Chilean Hindemith." In his choral music, songs, piano works, symphonies, and string quartets, Santa Cruz drew on European models. Only one work even hints at folklore: the second movement of the *Cantata de los Ríos de Chile* (Cantata on Chilean Rivers) contains a rustic tune in the oboe, which Santa Cruz claimed to recall from childhood.[14] A more emblematic work is *Five Pieces* for string orchestra, completed in 1937. It intrigued Kirstein, who envisioned choreographing it as a plotless ballet for the American Ballet Caravan under the title *Noble Dances of the Viceroy*. A nod to occidental culture? According to Kirstein, the dance would portray "the irresistible, cold earnestness of the white conqueror" and the "steady sun . . . beat[ing] on his hot armor." Ultimately, the land would be returned "to the heirs of conqueror and conquered" so that all could live in harmony.[15] The project, rooted in historical fantasizing, never came to fruition.

Copland initially believed the *Five Pieces* should be published. But after hearing a locally produced recording, he changed his mind, pronouncing the work "merely a neoclassical pastiche."[16] He also examined Santa Cruz's *Three Pieces* for Violin and Piano, a string quartet, and the Four Poems by Gabriela Mistral, the latter on texts by that Chilean poet-diplomat and future Nobel laureate. In general, Santa Cruz's style struck Copland as "distinctly dated—which gives all the music a rather derivative air"; further, Copland found that unnecessary complexity substituted for "a real freshness of feeling and . . . ends up by becoming annoying."[17] Not everyone agreed: Chase found the Chilean composer's music to contain "much originality and great technical finish" whereas Smith considered it "capable of making a profound impression."[18]

Copland did, however, admire Santa Cruz's protégé, Juan Orrego-Salas. Only twenty-two, Orrego-Salas had trained in architecture, which he was still practicing when he and Copland met in Santiago. They lunched together on 25 September, after which Orrego-Salas played his "collected works," a fact Copland likely noted with a smile, given that the young man's modest oeuvre at that point consisted of only a handful of small-scale pieces. Copland found Orrego-Salas musically sensitive and a good candidate for study in the United States.[19] In fact, he had an immensely successful inter-American career. During the 1940s Orrego-Salas traveled to the States on various grants, returning periodically to Chile. After the Latin American Music Center at Indiana University was founded in 1961, with Rockefeller Foundation funding, he returned to serve as its director. For decades he and Copland nourished a mutually respectful friendship.

Several Chilean composers Copland met had day jobs. Alfonso Leng may be the only individual in history to receive awards in both periodontics and music. His symphonic poem La muerte de Alsino (based on the novel Alsino, by the Chilean author Pedro Prado) is rooted in the tradition of Richard Strauss, with violin solos that hint at Ein Heldenleben. By the time of Copland's visit the engineer and musical autodidact Próspero Bisquertt had written two operas, several songs, and piano pieces. Copland found him "a typical South American figure—naturally musical but hardly a trained or experienced composer" and whose many works "all tend to be French in character."[20] Still, Bisquertt's opera Sayeda of 1929 was performed more than once in Santiago, and Paris heard his symphonic poem Procesión del Cristo de Mayo. Alfonso Letelier, who took a degree in agricultural engineering, composed around sixty works and eventually taught at the Conservatorio Nacional. Upon studying one of his string quartets and several piano pieces, Copland observed that Letelier seemed "eager for criticism and eager to learn."[21]

Full-time musicians Copland met included Samuel Negrete, the director of the Conservatorio Nacional, who showed him a string quartet and a symphonic work. Copland found both competently written but lacking "any great personality."[22] He detected no shortage of personality in Acario Cotapos, however, an original member of the Pan American Association of Composers (PAAC), who lived in New York City between 1916 and 1925.[23] His works were never performed on a PAAC concert, but in 1918 Eva Gauthier performed his *Le détachement vivant* (The Surviving Regiment) for voice and chamber ensemble at New York's Aeolian Hall, and in 1922 the International Composers Guild presented his *Philippe l'arabe* (Philip the Arab) for baritone and chamber ensemble.[24] His most successful work for the New York public may have been his *Three Preludes*, in which Downes heard moments of a "perceptible degree of imagination and . . . suggestion" when the guild featured it in February 1925.[25] Copland assigned the *Preludes* an asterisk but spent more time digesting "symphonic fragments" of Cotapos's opera *Voces de Gesta* (Epic Voices), based on the eponymous "pastoral tragedy" by Spanish author Ramón del Valle-Inclán. It had already premiered in a concert version in Madrid, where Cotapos lived during the 1930s and where Raymond Hall of the *New York Times* highlighted its cosmopolitanism, remarking that the work "reflects no Chilean or any other specifically American character."[26] Despite some deft orchestration, Copland believed *Voces de Gesta* had not worn well over time, however, and that ultimately it seemed "sputtery like [Cotapos] himself, though containing fine things."[27] Making a less favorable impression was René Amengual, then thirty, and whose string quartet and piano concerto Copland examined, along with piano pieces and songs. Although Slonimsky found Amengual's Sonatina for Piano of 1938 "Ravelesque" but still "finely done," Amengual's music prompted Copland to reach a general conclusion about Chilean music: it was "romantic and chromatic . . . always tinged with Ravelian chords and always rather more complex than necessary."[28]

What, exactly, might "occidentalism" mean to Chilean composers? Perhaps surprisingly, part of its mystique lay in the indigenous presence. Here, Carlos Isamitt is worth examining. One of the country's more successful composers, he staked a good part of his career on an idealized view of the Araucanians, the name generically applied by the Spanish to the indigenous peoples of southern Chile and used into the mid-twentieth century.[29] (The current term is "Mapuche," albeit with some debate over the geographical region encompassed and claims of other indigenous groups.)[30] To the colonial imagination, the Araucanians exemplified the "noble savage," most notably in the epic poem "La Araucana" by the sixteenth-century Spanish poet-soldier Alonso de Ercilla. Heirs to this notion upheld Chile's status as a "White republic," which in turn depended on the trope of the mestizo, the descendant of the brave and virtuous Araucanians who intermarried with Europeans and was largely accepted as racially unmarked (i.e., White).[31] This selective mestizaje effectively erased the Afro-Chilean heritage, however.

Isamitt drew on this mystique in his music, extolling the "extraordinary rhythmic and melodic richness" of Araucanian music.[32] Among his several Araucanian-inspired works are *Mito araucano* (Araucanian Myth) for orchestra, *Símbolos araucanos* (Araucanian Symbols) for solo piano, and *Friso araucano* (Araucanian Frieze), seven songs for soprano and baritone soloists and orchestra, which the Spanish expatriate musicologist Vicente Salas Viu called "a synthesis of salient aspects of the being and the life of Araucanian Indians."[33] Copland assigned it an asterisk. He was far less impressed with Isamitt's non-Araucanian works: a sonata and sonatina for piano, a violin concerto and violin sonata, and a suite for orchestra. In one of his harsher diary entries, he questioned Isamitt's creative process, noticing "a rather naïve air, which results not in a music as simple as he is personally, but . . . in a highly fussy harmonic background, like a child pleased at the complicated shapes it is able to draw." In short, Isamitt was "a complicated case of the pure-naïve who is rather spoiled by knowing either too much or not enough."[34]

Copland also met Isamitt's teacher, Pedro Humberto Allende. Then fifty-seven, Allende taught at the Conservatorio Nacional, having composed piano pieces, chamber music, vocal works, and orchestral music. His symphonic poem *La voz de las calles* (The Voice of the Streets), in which cries of street vendors are woven into the orchestral texture, was evidently "in demand" on concerts at the Pan American Union.[35] One Allende work Copland examined was the series of piano miniatures, *Doce tonadas de carácter chileno popular* (Twelve Tonadas in Popular Chilean Character). A *tonada* is a song with guitar accompaniment (often strophic and sung in parallel thirds). Both it and the *cueca*, a dance of variable rhythmic structure accompanied by guitar, accordion, or harp, are symbols of Chilean identity, specifically, rural identity.[36] Allende composed them after a visit to Europe, where he met Felipe Pedrell, whose views on musical nationalism meshed with his own.[37] Ricardo Viñes, the Catalan pianist and advocate for new music, premiered the *Tonadas* in Paris.[38]

The *Tonadas* are a vehicle for some of Allende's ideas on folk music and national identity. In 1931 he addressed folklore in the *Bulletin of the Pan American Union*, arguing that "The author of a stylized composition does not copy pure folk art, but taking his inspiration from its essence, dignifies it with beautiful harmonization and enshrines it in approved forms."[39] Allende was also convinced that Chilean folk music was rooted in Spanish tradition, which despite some Arabic and incidental African traits, had remained "absolutely untouched by native [American] music."[40] Reinforcing this aesthetic of untrammeled purity was the Argentine critic Gastón Talamón, who rhapsodized, "Allende, inspired [by the tonada], extracts the essential folklore of his race to elevate it to a superior rank: universal for its category and Chilean for its materials."[41] To be sure, such notions have far more to do with racialized mythologies and less with the nature of musical transmission and intercultural exchange. In defending this "superior rank," representative of the "Chilean race" and uncontaminated by dubious influences, Allende added another criterion, insisting that "pure folk music springs from the folk or country dweller."

From here it was but a small step to identifying the enemies of "pure" Chilean folkore: the "brutal stridency of the jazz band, an imported Negro music" was inimical to the values of "European, occidental countries."[42] In a 1935 essay in the Catholic daily *El Mercurio*, Allende railed against "the out-of-tune music of the North American Blacks [that] displace our noble Chilean tonadas and cuecas."[43] In pursuing this ardent defense, Allende could count on backing from "scientists," that is, folklorists such as Rodolf Lenz, who sought to determine which elements of Chilean music hailed from the Spanish "fatherland" and which reflected the racially unmarked "noble savage."[44] All complemented the notion of a Chilean "race," one that exalted the virtues of occidentalism and Whiteness.

Reinforcing rural Chilean identity was the *huaso* (cowboy), also racially unmarked due to "assumptions of Whiteness," as Juan Eduardo Wolf puts it.[45] Singing huasos performed tonadas in close harmony, accompanying themselves with guitars. The most celebrated among them were Los Cuatro Huasos, established in 1927. None of its four singers was a cowboy or even from a rural background (three were lawyers, and one was an architect).[46] Yet, their "pure" folk music both emblematized rural values and offered an alternative to jazz. Mistral, for example, hailed Los Cuatro Huasos for "winning the battle" against jazz, now infiltrating "all of Spanish America" (some critics even described their harmonizations as "Germanic").[47] These clean-cut young men were also cultural diplomats. In August 1939 Los Cuatro Huasos performed at New York's Waldorf Astoria Hotel and at the Chilean Pavilion at the World's Fair, traveling on diplomatic passports to represent the Chilean government.[48] When they disembarked at the dock in New York, in full huaso regalia, they announced their mission of introducing authentic Chilean music in the United

States. The following year, they enhanced a radio address by Chilean president Pedro Aguirre Cerda. After the president exhorted the Americas to form "an indestructible unit" on behalf of democracy, Los Cuatro Huasos performed "typical Chilean music."[49]

Rhetorical battle lines were thus drawn. For some Chileans, musical identity was rooted in rural values that, in combination with certain local traits derived from Europe, enshrined Whiteness. For them, the principal threat to Chilean identity was U.S. jazz, widely identified with Blackness.[50] In examining Allende's *Tonadas*, Copland could hardly have suspected that he was in the presence of music so freighted with national and racial ideologies. He merely commented in his diary that despite Allende's innate musicality, a "Parisian veneer—heritage of the 1920s post-impressionist school" clung to his works, which "tend[ed] to be poetic and nostalgic" and which showed "a definite lack of variety—even possibly of vitality."[51] Some of the issues just discussed, however, would surface in critical reaction to Copland's own music.

## Pablo Garrido and the Chilean Jazz Scene

Copland also met Pablo Garrido, a composer, violinist, journalist, author, activist, and all-around iconoclast. Garrido, whose effusive prose can be compared with that of Paul Rosenfeld, was a leader in the Chilean jazz scene. Despite the weight of U.S. hegemony, jazz had been wildly popular in Chile for decades, coexisting at least in some circles peacefully alongside the tonada and the cueca. In other words, it was possible to enjoy national genres but also dance the Charleston, the shimmy, or the foxtrot, all of which belonged to a category of jazz known as *melódico*.[52] Garrido, on the other hand, took a more intellectual approach. From his native city of Valparaíso, he launched the Royal Orchestra (its English name conferring a cosmopolitan air), which he led with his violin, sometimes adding dissonances so startling that listeners dubbed him "Pablo Gar-ruido" ("*ruido*" meaning "noise"). The Chilean poet Neftalí Agrella even described Garrido's "cubist violin," affirming these modernist inclinations.[53] Tellingly, the ensemble focused on hot jazz, considered "less sweet and more Negroid" than "jazz melódico."[54] Hot jazz also rested on several stereotypes. Because it was seen as intensely expressive, it reinforced the notion that Blacks, unencumbered by intellect, were capable of a range of emotions inaccessible to Whites; similarly, its forward-thrusting rhythmic impulse, which invariably culminated in improvisation, fed into the myth that Blacks, musically illiterate, compensated with formidable spontaneity.[55] Hot jazz spread beyond Valparaíso. In March 1939, the Hot Club de Chile convened for the first time in Santiago (it was later known as the Club de Jazz de Chile), and Garrido himself moved to the capital. He also translated *Le jazz hot*, the 1934 book by French critic Hugh Panassié, into Spanish.

Most Chileans were not only unfamiliar with Afro-descended musical traditions of their own country but lacked direct experience of Black musicians. In the 1940s, for example, Pereira Salas dug up accounts of a nineteenth-century minstrel troupe from the United States performing in Valparaíso and Santiago. In referring to the spirituals he believed they performed (he gave several titles), Pereira Salas applauded the emotive quality of "Negro melody."[56] In fact, the performers were in blackface and none of the titles cited are of spirituals.[57] Similarly uninformed critics addressed jazz. According to one, swing originated in Harlem to remind its Black inhabitants of "warm lands, lost in the memory of their ancestors now gone," even though this style of music had quickly degenerated.[58] In other words, Black music was well and good in its place (the "warm lands" of Africa), but once transplanted, it betokened all manner of social ills. The same critic fretted that "in Chile, [swing] is danced all over and its grotesque attitudes, sometimes filled with all manner of suggestiveness, have dominated today's youth, who are incapable of thinking of any other diversion without invading the atmosphere with its torrid notes."[59] Similar anxieties greeted the handful of Black musicians who visited Chile in the twentieth century. In 1928 Josephine Baker included Chile in her Latin American tour, whereupon Mistral brazenly attacked her "simian gesticulations."[60] Artistic miscegenation also offended: when the White musician Kerry Keller ("Lady Crooner") performed at the Club de Jazz de Chile, she was criticized for trying to "sound Black."[61]

As a journalist covering some Black artists, Garrido took the opposite tack. He interviewed the vaudeville performer Helen Justa, whom he described as "an authentic star from Harlem."[62] Further, he asserted that Justa was in Chile for no lesser purpose than to represent Blackness itself: "to tell us the marvelous message of her race, to sing to us the tender melodies of South Carolina, and to strew hither and yon the perfervid currents of modern swing that cultivate those eminences called Duke Ellington, Cab Calloway, Count Basie or Jimmie Lunceford."[63] Among the numerous questions Garrido hurled at Justa was, "Which artists do you most admire?" "Billie Holiday" was her prompt reply. In his report, Garrido did not refer to "Strange Fruit," the antilynching song *par excellence* with its horrifying account of "blood on the leaves, blood at the root," and which he surely knew.[64] However sincere, Garrido's overheated rhetoric recalls the words of James Baldwin: "I have tried . . . to convey something of what it felt like to be a Negro, and no one had been able to listen: they wanted their romance."[65] The "romance" generated from Garrido's energetic pen not only obfuscated the actual status of Black people in the United States for Chilean readers but also careened into his ideas on social justice, a crusade in which he gave Copland pride of place.

## "Believe It or Not"

One morning, Garrido stopped by Copland's hotel to interview him for the Santiago paper *Las Últimas Noticias*. Copland found Garrido a "good guy" even if his "proletarian sympathies sometimes [got] in the way of his better artistic judgements." Garrido, who confided to Copland his desire to obtain a Guggenheim Fellowship "to study Negro music comparatively in the U.S.A.," opened his report with a flourish.[66] Referring to the widely syndicated newspaper column that reported on all manner of bizarre events and coincidences, he announced, "As in a 'Believe It or Not' . . . by Ripley we marvel at the presence of Copland in this distant Latin American capital."[67] Covering the usual biographical data in short order, Garrido proceeded to his main point, namely, Copland's own "proletarian sympathies." As he reported, "We follow Aaron Copland attentively, ever since 800 workers sang his robust proletarian hymn 'Into the Streets May First,' on the simple and magnificent poem by Alfred Hayes, at the Second Workers Music Olympiad of 1934. A shining landmark of music for the people."[68]

Garrido explains that Copland writes in an "authentic American idiom." Yet he links the composer not to "freshness" nor "vigor and dynamism" but to the despair and squalor of the community to which jazz owes its existence:

> Right alongside Copland, without him being aware of it, runs the warm blood of hot jazz. Louis Armstrong and Coleman Hawkins and a hundred anonymous figures with dark faces scrape out the soul of the lowest rungs of society with melodies and miraculous rhythms, coming from the high heavens: inspirations and improvisations of the lived moment. Then, and without Copland necessarily being aware of it, Duke Ellington's band is born, and the African jungle has blended with the rivers, the trees, and the birds of the field and towns . . . which will typify a [Black] nation desirous of its own expression.[69]

Hot jazz is thus a natural outgrowth of a "nation" of "anonymous figures with dark faces," of which Copland had been an honorary citizen ever since he penned "Into the Streets May First." "Aaron Copland is the magnificent result of such delirium and such desire," Garrido declared. Further, "like all genuinely gifted individuals, Copland is extraordinarily plain. There is no ostentation in his person, his dress, his speech. He extends his hand and welcomes everyone as an equal."[70] Forging bonds with Blacks and downtrodden workers alike, Copland was also far removed from the rarefied world of the concert hall. This image of Copland, according to which he privileged jazz and proletarian music, was a far cry from the OIAA's charge that Copland advance "serious" music in the hemisphere.

Not surprising, Garrido wanted to know Copland's opinion of jazz. "What do you think of swing?" he asked. Here, Copland employed a narrative of degeneration. "Swing is the result of a decadent hot jazz," he replied. "Or to put it better, it's a timely appropriation of all the splendor jazz possessed in its golden age."[71] But, he hastened to add, swing was only one "mode" of jazz, and the other, hot jazz (*el agitado*) "has triumphed." This was due in part to "vigorous color" and "dynamism," qualities inculcated by Ellington, who "taught all of us that with brass instruments it's possible to achieve exquisite, velvety tones, comparable to those of woodwinds or strings."[72] Garrido then asked which jazz orchestras Copland most admired. Ellington, certainly, Copland replied. But Copland also mentioned double bassist John Kirby and his ensemble, to which he once introduced to Koussevitzky (also a bass player). "Imagine," the composer remarked to Garrido, "that one night I took Koussevitzky, the renowned symphony conductor to listen to these jazzmen. I didn't succeed in convincing him, although I made him see the marvelous sense of improvisation of those men." Copland's final words on the subject? "I believe in jazz and I salute its contribution to our contemporary music."[73]

This was a rather different position from the one Copland took in *Our New Music*, where he described jazz's "limited emotional scope." In another interview in Santiago, Copland discussed jazz with a reporter from *La Opinión*, who asked, "From what sources have you taken the substance of your musical works?" Far from "saluting" jazz's contributions, Copland gave his now-familiar reply. "The first influence I received was of Black music, primordial origins of jazz, which has so impassioned the masses in the United States and of which, it can be said, establishes the characteristic of the present century, all movement and dynamism," he recalled. As for its role in his development, he added, "But since jazz is such a limited field . . . it inevitably had to follow this route."[74] Effectively, it exhausted itself, overtaken by other creative forces.

## The "blackest of Black music"

Critical reaction to Copland's performance of his jazz-inflected piano concerto with the Orquesta Sinfónica de Chile hardly clarified these conflicting views. It is not clear whose idea it was to program the work, Copland's or conductor

Armando Carvajal. Perhaps, after his interview with Garrido, Copland calculated that the Chilean public would enjoy it. He planned to split the program with Carvajal (whom Smith considered one of the best in South America).[75] Copland would conduct *An Outdoor Overture*, *Quiet City*, and *El salón México*, and Carvajal would lead the ensemble in two works by Wagner: the Prelude to Act III of *Lohengrin* and the "Good Friday" music from *Parsifal*. Carvajal would also conduct Allende's *Escenas campesinas* (Country Scenes), which, like his *Tonadas*, evoked the imagined Chilean folk in all its "purity." One critic applauded "traces of rustic songs" therein, calling the *Escenas campesinas* "the first [work] . . . in our musical literature that succeeds in establishing an undeniable whiff of racial character."[76] Copland enjoyed the rehearsals, finding the orchestra responsive and Carvajal "an intelligent musician."[77]

Among the reviewers of Copland's music was the demanding and often blunt Albert (Alberto) Goldschmidt, a German-Jewish immigrant, who wrote for various publications and invariably signed his reviews "Dr. Goldschmidt." Many in the Chilean musical community resented him, complaining of his "tank-driver's prose" (prosa de tanquista). The allusion to military equipment was not idle: Goldschmidt had served in the German army in World War I and was later summoned to Bolivia to advise the country on the Chaco War (1932–35). His detractors believed that his main failure as a critic was judging Santiago by the standards of Vienna or Berlin.[78] According to *Time* magazine, Goldschmidt was so despised that he carried a revolver at all times.[79]

Yet he reacted most cordially to Copland, devoting his entire review to him with nary a mention of Wagner or Allende. Goldschmidt starts off with high praise for musical Pan Americanism, calling Copland's presence in Santiago "a cultural event of true transcendence."[80] He also commends Copland for rejecting "experimentalism" and approaching a "U.S. symphonic style," one that "must constantly reveal its own nature if it is to avoid losing itself in the mere imitation of European ideas."[81] Goldschmidt then showers praise on Copland's music. He found *An Outdoor Overture* "sublime" (a term not often associated with that work) and the more profound *Quiet City* "contemplative." In *El salón México*, he acknowledged some lack of formal clarity but nothing that sabotaged the work's inherent humor, in part because of Copland's skill as an orchestrator.

That left the concerto. Again, Copland showed his "extraordinarily rich" orchestral palette, "his way of distributing the sonority within the [orchestral] groupings, his great wisdom, his mental discipline, his vast flexibility and his taste within his intentions"; further, "his independent manner of handling the rhythm as a relative functional element constitutes one of the most interesting phenomena of our modern musical creation and exploration." In the final movement, Goldschmidt opined, this concept was "realized on a level that is practically fantastic, without altering the perspective of sound quality or construction."[82] Yet, Goldschmidt admitted, "apart from that movement . . . the work seems the weakest of those presented: the way of fusing the expressive (cantabile) phrases between the orchestra and the piano part has not been felicitous; the instrumentation is, in part, thin, and especially in the Molto Moderato, long stretches are ultimately tiring."[83] Moreover, the piano part never really "takes off." Still, "the idea of improvisation and the super-rhythms of jazz are very good and treated with consequence at the beginning and the end of the work."[84] In short, this exacting European, receptive both to jazz and to Pan Americanism, judged Copland's concerto according to the criteria of occidental music: form, structure, orchestration, and balance.

By contrast, the anonymous reporter for *La Nación* overlooked such technicalities to focus on race. He heard Blackness not just in Copland's concerto but in all the Copland works performed. The critic also attempted to buttress his argument by recalling the recent visit of the League of Composers Woodwind Quintet, whose repertory, he claimed, also reflected the legacy of Black music that U.S. composers inevitably shared: "Like Adolph Weiss, Alvin Etler, David van Vactor and [Robert McBride]," he wrote, "the composer of *An Outdoor Overture, Quiet City, El salón México*, and the concerto for piano and orchestra writes music following the tendencies staked out by the race of color of his native land."[85] Given the quintet's repertory—European classics, some Latin American music, and a few original works—this was a bizarre conclusion to draw. Might we surmise that this critic concurred with R. Nathaniel Dett, who argued, "[Black] music . . . has been the basis of [U.S.] music," and that "if American culture is to be carried to the other Americas . . . Negro music should be acknowledged"? In fact, the critic takes Copland's music as little more than a platform for the familiar narrative of degeneration—although with a new twist. To be sure, *authentic* Black music (such as spirituals and other "folk music") was all well and good. Jazz, however, had enervated the very community it represented, leaving it bereft of dignity. "Jazz is the blackest of Black music," the anonymous critic proclaimed. "It's the stridency that importunes the conversation of neighbors in a canteen or café. It's the voluptuous syncopation of tipsiness, the total chaos, music with neither backbone nor vital marrow." Consequently, jazz had done "the most damage in the domain of art and to the immaculate field of music of the people."[86] Just as jazz threatened "occidental" identity in Chile, so too did it inexorably seep into the "serious" music of the land from which it arose. Marshaling such rhetorical strategies, racist critics North and South made short work of the enterprise of "American music."

* * *

Copland's one radio broadcast in Santiago was an hour-long program on Radio La Americana. He also lectured at the Universidad de Chile, on two consecutive days.[87] In addition, he gave a press conference, in which he explained his work for the U.S. government. "Music is one of the most important means to inter-American understanding," he affirmed. Copland also opined on musical Pan Americanism:

> Actually, the concept of Pan Americanism is somewhat poorly understood. Pan Americanism exists as a reality and not as a mere word, mindlessly bandied about. I can't explain, either for myself or for other U.S. musicians, the reason for the almost total lack of awareness between the two parts of the American continent. Before the present war, no one ever mentioned a word in favor of cultural exchange. But now the idea is quickly spreading [in U.S. musical circles] that South America and Central America do indeed exist, and that Europe is only a secondary matter. In the field of music, all possible efforts are being made to arrive at a balanced understanding of common problems and, moreover, a better comprehension of Chilean, Argentine, Bolivian, Peruvian, Brazilian, etc., composers.[88]

The idea that Europe was now "only secondary" likely ruffled a few feathers. And naturally Copland kept a discreet silence on what he believed were the limitations of Chilean composers. Evidently their penchant for complexity, reliance on European forms, and "romantic and chromatic music" could all be traced to occidentalism. If occidentalism attaches itself to "assumptions of whiteness," does that make all its defenders racists? When Santa Cruz, one of its staunchest champions, visited Boston in 1941, he was shocked to discover that he had to argue with hotel staff to allow a Black Chilean acquaintance, now in the United States, to enter through the main door with him.[89] If some in the United States saw Latin America as a continent of "half-breeds" and "dark-skinned" peoples, some Latin Americans saw—or heard—Blackness at every turn in U.S. music even as they were well aware of the pervasive racism in the Colossus of the North. As this brief survey of Chilean music suggests, jazz stood in for what many in the United States called "the Negro problem," one that also plagued the "other American republics" in myriad ways.

# 8

# The Americas at War

In early December 1941 Copland was in Havana, the last stop of his cultural diplomacy tour. At that time, Juan José Castro was in New York conducting the NBC Symphony.[1] A legend persists with respect to Castro, the orchestra, and the attack on Pearl Harbor. As Castro tells it, on Sunday, 7 December, he arrived at the NBC studio for one of his scheduled broadcasts. Immediately he was informed that President Roosevelt would address the nation by radio to announce that the United States was at war. Castro was asked to conduct "The Star-Spangled Banner." "I was glad to do so, naturally," Castro later recalled, "pleased by the honor that in a moment of such transcendence my baton would lead the first hearing of the national anthem after the country entered the Second World War." He also claimed to have joked with the players that "without a doubt, listeners to our concert that night included Hitler, Mussolini, and Stalin."[2]

In fact, Castro never conducted the NBC Symphony on 7 December. His broadcasts took place on 2, 9, and 16 December; moreover, Roosevelt did not request a declaration of war until the next day, before a joint session of Congress.[3] Castro did perform in New York on 7 December, however. That evening, he played his *Sarabanda* with the violinist Remo Bolognini and accompanied Elsie Houston in several of his songs in a concert at the MoMA, sponsored by the League of Composers. Writing in the *New York Times*, Howard Taubman found in Castro's music "a modest, craftsmanlike, sometimes daring talent." He also noted the brevity of the program, dwarfed by the events of the day.[4]

Castro's anecdote, repeated by various biographers, is thus pure fiction.[5] But by inserting himself into "the date which will live in infamy" on behalf of a nation long at odds with his own, Castro effectively declared his Good Neighborly feeling. This chapter traces some of the events in musical Pan Americanism after the United States entered the war, emphasizing those in which Copland participated.

## Copland in Cuba: "América indivisible"

Copland learned of the attack in Havana but makes no mention of it in his diary. Nor does he refer to local reaction. But Cuba was so pro-U.S. that on 11 December it declared war on Germany and Italy.[6] Mexico immediately broke diplomatic relations with the Axis and in Argentina, the editorial staff of *Sur* defied its government by dedicating the entire December 1941 issue to the attack.[7] A strongly worded lead essay by Victoria Ocampo, "América indivisible," sought to rally the Americas.[8]

In Cuba, Copland pursued his usual activities. Among the composers he met was Gustavo Morales, whose music he dismissed as "undistinguished."[9] He also visited Gilberto Valdés, who conducted a radio orchestra and who often based his compositions on Cuban materials. For Copland, Valdés could be "the George Gershwin of Cuba" but lacked the technique.[10] To be sure, Copland realized that Cuban classical music had been dealt a serious blow with the premature deaths of Amadeo Roldán and Alejandro García Caturla, who died in 1939 and 1940 at age thirty-nine and thirty-six, respectively. They were among the most frequently performed composers on PAAC concerts.[11] Roldán, writing in Henry Cowell's 1933 essay collection, *American Composers on American Music*, urged his colleagues to compose music that would be "a contribution of the New World to the universal art."[12]

José Ardévol, another Cuban composer, marked out a different path to universality. Born in Barcelona, Ardévol emigrated in 1930 and when Roldán died, took over his class at the Havana Conservatory. At the time of Copland's visit, Ardévol was promoting neoclassicism, which he called a vehicle of "universal contemporaneity" (lo contemporáneo universal) and saw as a guarantee of technical competence: composers who could negotiate the demands of sonata form or fugue would be taken seriously beyond their native country.[13] Copland studied Ardévol's concerto for three pianos and orchestra, two concerti grossi, an instrumental suite, and a *Sonata à 3* for two flutes and viola, assigning asterisks to two of these five pieces. He detected a certain sameness in Ardévol's works but felt they deserved wider recognition. Ardévol, he believed, "would profit by a visit *chez nous*."[14]

Copland was also interviewed by the journalist Nena Benítez, who scolded him for having visited Cuba the previous April without telling anyone. "¡Esto se llama 'jugar una mala pasada!'" (That's called "pulling a fast one!"), she exclaimed, laughing as the composer methodically repeated this idiom, new for him. When he shrugged that "he really didn't really speak Spanish," she found his confession overly modest.[15] Benítez asked Copland about the role of folklore in U.S. music. Having downplayed it elsewhere in his tour, he told her, "Right now, we are making great use of folkloric materials. In the United States we have Black music, music of Native Americans, 'spirituals,' jazz. . . . It's all a question of time. From these sources, composers take their themes." Still, he added, "the day will come when we get tired of folklore and something new will arise, possibly something unexpected."[16]

Copland gave his two lectures in Havana: on contemporary music in the United States (3 December) and on film music (11 December); also on 11 December, he participated in a concert of U.S.-Cuban works with members of the Orquesta de Cámara de la Habana (Chamber Orchestra of Havana). Before an ample public, Copland performed his Piano Sonata; other works representing the United States were *Quiet City* and Roy Harris's Piano Trio. The Cuban portion consisted of music by Ardévol, Roldán, and two of Ardévol's students, María Isabel Rubirosa and Harold Gramatges.[17] Copland's final activity as a cultural diplomat in 1941 was a broadcast in Havana, billed rather hyperbolically as "a musical event of the first magnitude." He play his tried-and-true repertory—piano works by Bowles, Piston's *Carnival Song*, Harris's Third Symphony, *El salón México*, and *Music for the Theatre*—and then packed up his record collection and left for the airport.[18]

## "Remarkable that we have never thought of South America before"

Perhaps on the long flight to New York (or during his layover in Miami) Copland jotted down several impressions in his diary, under the heading "Finale." Mainly, he wanted to fix certain items in his memory. His list of "Sights remembered" includes "the faces of the players in the Conjunto Vacarno in Lima" and the tango orchestra at the Café El Nacional in Buenos Aires with its "hard, dry sonority—sudden contrast of *secco* staccatos and legatos." Especially compelling was a scene from Ecuador, where he had scarcely any cultural diplomacy duties. At the top of his list of "Sights remembered" is "the crowd of Indians outside Reed & Reed," the Quito branch of that music store. What was it that spoke so directly to Copland? The fact that in a city such as Quito, with its strong indigenous population, White U.S. visitors will experience their Otherness far more keenly than in Buenos Aires or Santiago? Although this "sight remembered" remains confined to these few words, Copland felt the moment keenly. His final diary entry ends with the thought, "It is remarkable that we have never thought of South America before . . . " His ellipsis dots quietly hint that the matter is far from closed.[19]

Copland's initial foray as a cultural diplomat was successful from many standpoints. His lectures, media appearances, and friendly one-on-one conversations struck the right tone. He had made a strong case for U.S. music, including his own. The president of Peru had applauded him, and the broad public heard "vitality," "optimism," and "freshness" in his works, all presumably reflecting U.S. character. But Copland also succeeded with musical elites, especially in Buenos Aires, with his Piano Sonata. In sum, Copland more than achieved the objectives of the OIAA Music Committee as set forth in its initial charge: to "increase solidarity and understanding of the peoples of the various Latin American countries by us here in the United States through the medium of music."[20]

If these were the high points of Copland's trip, were there any lows? To judge from his diaries, the greatest challenge for Copland was the very music he was sent to Latin America to evaluate. To be sure, given the quantity of music he heard, the likelihood that he would have admired all of it is slim; moreover, he was aware of the pitfalls of "goodwilling" and mindful that at least part of his mission was quality control. Yet he identified two exceptional cases—José María Castro and Guarnieri, both established composers—and some promising younger talent, such as Santoro, Orrego-Salas, Ginastera, and Tosar. He was also convinced of the potential of others (Siccardi, Mignone, Moncayo, Isamitt, and even Paz) while acknowledging those out of the mainstream, such as Gianneo. If Copland was unmoved by the great majority of the works he studied, he remained polite and encouraging in public while keeping his criticisms to himself. In other words, he behaved like a diplomat.

Less straightforward is Copland's tailoring of his message for different constituencies. On the one hand, he advocated for achieving a "whole new musical taste" by collaborating with the listening public through radio and the phonograph. On the other, he tells the cognoscenti of his aim to "cultivate so-called modern music in its serious form," clearly not tailored to the mass audience. To one interviewer, he recognizes the virtues of jazz, and to another he questions its viability. As always, folklore is a wild card: either he employs it "only on rare occasions" or applauds its potential. None of these positions is strictly untrue nor incompatible with Copland's actual beliefs, which were many-sided and conflicted. But one can only wonder how many points of view on the same issue a public figure can present, sometimes within the space of weeks. All point to the question: who was Copland?

## State Department Duties

Now back home, Copland fulfilled his assignment to write the "rather complete report" the State Department expected. Running forty-five pages, it replicates many passages from his diaries. Copland also offers several suggestions for future cultural diplomacy with Latin America. Chief among these was that the State Department distribute scores, recordings, and books on music, either in libraries or "centers of distribution," such as the cultural institutes he visited in Chile and Peru. Copland also stressed the importance of radio libraries, maintaining that his Latin American contacts were eager to broadcast works by U.S. composers.[21] He also recommended eight composers to visit the United States. Topping the list is Guarnieri, followed by José María Castro, with Ginastera in third place. (Copland also recommended Radamés Gnatalli, despite his reservations about his "slick musical talent," along with, Isamitt and Uribe Holguín.) Among eight student-composers are Tosar (in first place), Orrego-Salas, and Villa-Lobos's assistant José Vieira Brandão. (The others were Santoro, René Amengual, José Pablo Moncayo, Sergio de Castro, and Salvador Moreno of Mexico, who is not mentioned in Copland's diary.) Pablo Garrido is absent from the category "musicologists, conductors, critics," which is topped by Mário de Andrade.[22] In other words, Copland remained steadfast in his willingness to challenge the "Negro problem." Villa-Lobos is conspicuously absent.

Copland had three additional suggestions. One was to launch a magazine on classical music in English, Spanish, and Portuguese. Another was to establish a fund for publishing Latin American music in the United States. Last, Copland sought greater exposure for music of the United States. Trips such as the one he had just taken should not be isolated phenomena, he argued, but should be complemented by other U.S. musical visitors to Latin America. On that hopeful note, Copland's debut as a cultural diplomat for the U.S. State Department concluded.

## To preach or to learn?

Something odd happened next, however. In early 1942 Copland's article "Composers of South America" appeared in *Modern Music*. As noted, throughout his trip, Copland had largely followed the model established by his colleague Waldo Frank, who visited Latin America "not to preach." Now, however, Copland assumed the role of critic. Acknowledging the difficulties of infrastructure, education, and support under which most Latin American composers labored, he informed the readers of *Modern Music* that after examining "the work of about sixty-five [Latin American] composers," he failed to "find a Bach or a Beethoven among them" and advises those who "thrive exclusively on masterpieces" to "stay away" from Latin American music.[23] Open-minded listeners had a good chance of someday being rewarded, however: "present accomplishment is completely overshadowed by the tremendous possibilities of the future."[24] Cautioning his readers to "stop thinking in terms of The South American Composer"—at least not a Bach or a Beethoven, one surmises—Copland permits himself certain generalizations. Chief among these is his conviction that "the countries that have developed most quickly are those with the richest folklore."[25] As we have seen, many Latin American composers rejected folklore precisely *because* they saw it as an obstacle to "development."[26]

Copland approaches the matter with uncharacteristic heavy-handedness. Surveying the musical scene in Chile, for example, he describes Santa Cruz as "a very energetic and competent musician." But like Sessions, he is "more the philosopher-composer than the composer pure and simple." As a result, Santa Cruz's music had "a scholarly look that makes one respect rather than love it." Chilean music as a whole was not in much better shape. As Copland contended, "Chilean music lacks outside air. . . . Chilean composers influence each other too much. Their music is not as fresh as it might be. . . . [It is] thickened by complex chromatic chords that seem more complex than is absolutely necessary. I miss the bold and affirmative note that one expects in the music of a newly developing country."[27] Given centuries of indigenous music making, along with the rich traditions of the colonial period, one wonders how many Chilean musicians saw their country as "newly developing," especially compared with the United States.[28]

In Brazil, on the other hand, Copland found "unusually rich" folklore, one to which "almost without exception Brazilian composers have frankly addressed themselves."[29] Might not a high level of "development" be expected? Here, Copland resorts to essentialism. Whereas Mexican composers are "more fortunate" than their Brazilian colleagues in that their "temperament is far more disciplined and therefore closer by nature to the generally sober line of new music," Brazilians exhibit an "uninhibited, abundant, non-critical, romantic" temperament and thus "confine themselves to the languorously sentimental or the wildly orgiastic mood, with very little in between" such that their works lack authentic "musical *ambiente*."[30] Epitomizing these shortcomings was Villa-Lobos, to whose defects Copland devotes almost an entire paragraph. Acknowledging the sheer number of Villa-Lobos's compositions, Copland observes that these works may be "enormously picturesque, free of musical prejudices, full of rhythmic vitality, sometimes cheap and vulgar with an overdose of figuration formulas—and sometimes astonishingly original" with a "way of being most effective on first hearing." Copland's damning conclusion? "The Villa-Lobos music has one outstanding quality—its abundance. This is its primary virtue."[31]

Yet all is not lost for Brazil. At least one composer, Guarnieri, managed to capture the proper *"ambiente"* in "fresh" works, more "orderly" than those of Villa-Lobos yet "touched by a sensibility that is profoundly Brazilian."[32] Again, Copland does not elaborate on this sensibility or how he came to detect it. He makes short work of Uruguay, Cuba, Ecuador, Peru, and Colombia, speaking warmly of Tosar and sympathetically registering Cuba's loss of Roldán and Caturla. From Peru and Colombia, only Sas and Uribe Holguín were "worth serious consideration" although both betrayed their French training to too great a degree; further, in dealing with indigenous music, Sas fell short of the standard Chávez had set.[33]

That left Argentina. Copland found its composers "more cultivated and more professionally prepared" than their counterparts elsewhere in Latin America, even if in the absence of a "strikingly indigenous profile" one could not identify an Argentine school.[34] Epitomizing this professional preparation was Paz, whose "formidable" intellect and work ethic Copland praised. Yet repeating verbatim words previously confided to his diary, Copland reported that Paz's "attachment" to the "Schönberg twelve-tone line" was "mental rather than emotional" and that his music was "as cool and detached and precise as any diagram, the kind of music that is always a pleasure to look at, if not always a pleasure to hear," exuding a "greyish pallor" that "in the end [was] tiring... distinguished rather than exciting."[35] An antidote to "pallor" was Ginastera, thanks to "natural flair" and an "unusual knack for bright-sounding orchestrations."[36] Having stated in his diary that Ginastera was the "white hope" of Argentine music, Copland now affirms that "all groups are agreed" on this point. (In 1943 Leopoldo Hurtado would describe Ginastera as "a youthful composer about whom any definitive judgment would be premature.")[37] Copland also praises the "refreshingly simple and direct" music of José María Castro, albeit without reference to "indigenous profiles" or "local phraseology."

It is difficult to know how Copland imagined his article would be received in Latin America. Having conversed with composers and critics knowledgeable about the United States—Hurtado, Santa Cruz, Paz—he surely realized that his comments would circulate in Latin America. In Buenos Aires, at any rate, there were repercussions. A few months after Copland's essay appeared, Paz reviewed the premiere of Ginastera's *Sinfonía porteña*, performed by Fritz Busch and which Copland had examined in 1941. Surely Paz's reaction influenced Ginastera's eventual decision to withdraw the work: he condemned the *Sinfonía porteña* as a hodgepodge of derivative features ranging from the "elemental rhythm of the Stravinsky of *Petrushka* . . . the fairy-like atmosphere of the Ravel of *Daphnis et Chloe* and *Rhapsodie espagnole* . . . the insinuating climate of *Iberia* . . . the vibrant trumpet noises of *Turandot*"—and plenty more.[38] This tirade against eclecticism was the opening volley in a polemic Argentine musicologist Esteban Buch has dubbed "el caso Ginastera." Shortly thereafter, Juan José Castro stepped in on Ginastera's behalf, and soon the mild-mannered Ginastera entered the fray himself, tagging Paz a Beckmesser, a "Dr. Goebbels," and a self-appointed "führer" of Argentine music. In addition to these anti-German epithets, Ginastera called forth as his principal defense Copland's *Modern Music* article. "Paz's manner of composing," Ginastera declared, "is like solving a crossword puzzle or an anagram: mix the twelve tones among themselves . . . coldly, like a calculator," concluding, "how right Copland is!"[39] This was an unexpected turn for Copland's cultural diplomacy.

## Musical Pan Americanism at Home

Copland's bluntness aside, musical Pan Americanism flourished in the coming months, now against the backdrop of Pearl Harbor. In January 1942 Latin American foreign ministers met in Rio de Janeiro to debate the pros and cons of breaking with the Axis, decisions that depended on trade relations; the presence of German, Italian, or Japanese communities in a given country; internal politics; and intra-American relations.[40] All but Chile and Argentina severed diplomatic ties. In May, after two acts of German aggression on the seas, Mexico declared war.[41] Next came Brazil in 1942.[42] Cultural diplomacy marked the occasion: on 23 August, the Disney-OIAA cartoon feature *Saludos Amigos!* premiered in Rio de Janeiro in its Portuguese incarnation (*Alô, Amigos*).[43] That the film was first shown in Rio rather than Hollywood, as was the norm, sent a strong message of hemispheric solidarity. *Saludos Amigos!* then played in Argentina and Chile before opening in Hollywood that December.[44]

The U.S. music industry also took advantage of the newly consummated alliance, whether through cover art or advertisements hailing "contemporary music in the country of our neighbor and ally, Brazil."[45] The music publisher G. Schirmer released *Latin-American Art Music for the Piano by Twelve Contemporary Composers*, edited by Lange and whose contributors included Sas, Guarnieri, Amengual, Manuel Ponce, Roberto García Morillo, Carlos Suffern, Ginastera, José María Castro, Villa-Lobos, Juan Bautista Plaza, and Paz (who offered a pre-twelve-tone work). The collection combines European-influenced works, such as Castro's *Piezas breves*, with its erratic repetitions à la *Pulcinella*, and folk-based pieces, such as Sas's *Himno y danza*, based on the Andean music-dance genre, the *wayno*. All offered the intermediate-level U.S. piano student the potent suggestion that music could unite the Americas. Classical music of the Americas was also available at the turn of a radio dial: NBC's *Music of the New World* offered Good Neighborly music appreciation lessons, with scripts by Gilbert Chase.[46] The inaugural program in this three-year series, "The First American Music" and broadcast on 10 October 1942, presented not the music of European-descended Puritans but indigenous peoples of South America. Other episodes featured works by some of the composers Copland had met: *Tribu* (Tribe) by Daniel Ayala and *Danza de las fuerzas nuevas* (Dance of New Energies) by Blas Galindo, both for orchestra.[47] All were carefully chosen by Chase.

Copland was directly involved in several Pan Americanist projects.[48] He served on the jury for the 1942 International Society for Contemporary Music (ISCM) festival, held in Berkeley, California. Fellow jurors were the Belgian-born conductor Désiré Defauw; the composer and University of California faculty member Albert Elkus; the Polish-born conductor and composer Grzegorz Fitelberg; and Milhaud, then teaching at nearby Mills College. They selected six Latin American composers for the program, "probably the highest in the history of the ISCM," as the critic Alfred Frankenstein observed.[49] Besides Fructuosa Vianna of Brazil and Pedro Sanjuan of Cuba were Chávez, Ficher, Gianneo, and José María Castro. As a jury member, Copland either put aside his distaste for Ficher's music or was outvoted. Indeed, critics praised Ficher's sonata for oboe and piano, finding it "perky, brief, almost Bach-like"; Frankenstein also admired Gianneo's *Music for Children*, which he described as "a bright, bell-like set of piano miniatures." Yet Frankenstein relegated José

María Castro's *Sonata de primavera*, the work that had so captivated Copland, to a secondary category: of "works one may describe as interesting and worth hearing but . . . not as important as those mentioned above."[50]

Having advocated for radio in his State Department report, Copland reiterated this point at a meeting of the OIAA Music Committee of 16 January 1942. He and Davidson Taylor drafted a proposal to send record libraries to thirty Latin American radio stations, complete with program notes (in Spanish and Portuguese translation, one assumes). They estimated that $9,000 would cover packaging and shipping. "We believe this is extremely urgent and should be done at once," both insisted.[51] The radio division of the OIAA, previously sluggish, now snapped into action.[52] It sent surveys in Spanish, Portuguese, and English to Latin American listeners, asking them to compare major U.S. radio stations such CBS, General Electric Company, NBC, Crosley Corp., and Westinghouse Radio Stations (along with the BBC and Soviet stations) with those from Germany, Italy, and Japan. Several survey participants agreed with listener Alizo Antonio of Mérida, Venezuela, that there was too much "Afro-Cuban music, for examples, rumbas, sones, etc., etc." From Bogotá, a listener resistant to the antidemocratic broadcasts from Berlin and Rome, observed, "We want more music . . . more N.B.C. Symphony, Cincinnati, New York, etc." Another Colombian listener, Mateo Espinel Blanco of Pamplona, opined that "in the news, we find a good dose of optimism and faith in the future of the democracies over the Axis. And in classical music, in your beautiful programs, I find solace and repose [for] our spirit, exhausted by the cares of the day."[53] It is not too much to suggest that Copland's success with and advocacy for radio during the 1941 tour helped prod the OIAA to redouble its efforts in this medium.

## "Round, Round, Hitler's Grave"

Copland also welcomed several Latin American musicians to the United States. Pianist Hugo Balzo, whom Copland met in Montevideo, was now a guest of the Pan American Union, mainly to give recitals. After one performance in Washington, DC, he was hailed as an "official representative of his country in furtherance of neighborly relations."[54] Balzo generally combined "standard" repertory with works by Chávez, Sas, or Ginastera. Some programming was rather unusual, however. At New York's Town Hall, Balzo shared the stage with the Almanac Singers, the folk group noted for topical songs on union struggles, militarism, and racism. Surely their lusty rendering of "Round, Round Hitler's

Grave" made a strange contrast with Balzo's sensitive interpretations of Ginastera, Villa-Lobos, and Federico Mompou.[55] Another guest was Plaza, the distinguished Venezuelan composer, educator, and musicologist, and whose three-month visit was also funded by the Pan American Union.[56] He and Copland likely met in New York, where Plaza arrived in March 1942. He presented a paper to the Greater New York Chapter of the American Musicological Society, in which he urged further research on Venezuelan colonial music.[57] He also enhanced his talk with live music. In that era, when businesses organized amateur theater groups or musical ensembles, the New York Public Library boasted its own madrigal chorus, which Smith put at Plaza's disposal, hastily assembling an orchestra as well. Plaza led them in a performance of colonial-era music: the Gloria from the Mass in D and *Popule Meus* by Ángel Lama; *In monte Olivetti* by Cayetano Carreño; *Pésame a la Vírgen* by Pedro Nolasco Colón; *Salve* by Juan José Landaeta; and a *Cristus factus es* by José Antonio Caro de Boesi, likely the first time this repertory was heard in New York. The radio division of the OIAA recorded the performance and distributed the disks to various stations.

Mignone visited the United States as well. In February and March 1942, he spent six weeks on a State Department grant, conducting the CBS Symphony Orchestra (broadcast to Brazil) and performing in a League of Composers concert, which Copland surely helped organize.[58] It featured works by Gianneo, Tosar, Guarnieri, Juan José Castro, Ardévol, and Mignone (including the piano sonata Copland heard in Rio). Unfortunately it was less than successful. Downes sensed "drawing-room fashion" in Mignone's sonata and expressed surprise that Villa-Lobos, whose music was "head and shoulders" above the others, was omitted. He also commented that the composers chosen by the league were "ignoring their own birthright and imitating European music, modern twenty years ago, as sedulously as a large number of our North Americans have done, and with as unfertile ... consequences," the same conclusion Copland had often reached.[59]

Also in early 1942, Santa Cruz returned to the United States. En route from Chile, his ship passed through the Canal Zone, blacked out as a military precaution. In New York he visited Copland, Smith, Kirstein, and Barbour before heading off to Washington, where he met up with Seeger, Gustavo Durán, and Chase.[60] He then traveled to Ohio to participate in the opening ceremonies for an exhibit of Chilean art at the Toledo Museum, a project he had organized with the OIAA Committee on Art. From the stage of the museum's peristyle, Santa Cruz again promoted Chile as an "occidental country: unlike Mexican,

Brazilian, or Peruvian art, so easy to be charmed by," Chilean art was "a result of the growth of an occidental country in an American land."[61] Then he was off to Milwaukee to attend the Biennial Convention of the Music Educators National Conference (MENC), the motto of which was "American Unity through Music."[62] A grant-in-aid from the Rockefeller Foundation enabled an entire Latin American delegation to attend: besides Santa Cruz were Mignone, Plaza, Sá Pereira, conductor Jorge Castañeda (Guatemala), composer Luis Sandi (Mexico), and educator and women's rights advocate Esther de Calvo (Panama). All were curious to know about music education in the United States. Was it really a vehicle for democracy, as some believed? Did it ensure that music was available to all children rather than only the talented few, in contrast to the European conservatory system adopted throughout Latin America?[63] The visitors also sensed the presence of the free market, registering the sheer array of music education products, such as textbooks, teacher guides, and games. Some details were amiss, however. When Santa Cruz examined a children's songbook that presumably contained four Chilean folksongs, he discovered that one song was not Chilean at all and that two others suffered from an incongruous four-part harmonization resembling "the very serious form of a Protestant chorale."[64] He was quick to point out this lapse.

## Guarnieri in the United States

One of the more fortunate beneficiaries of Good Neighbor cultural diplomacy was Guarnieri. Starting in late 1942, he spent several months in the United States, also with funding from the Pan American Union. Because the union did not completely cover his expenses, Esther Mesquita, a wealthy *paulista* (resident of São Paulo), stepped up and commissioned a new work, and in June of 1942 Guarnieri led the São Paulo Orquestra Sociedade de Cultura in his *Abertura concertante* (Concert Overture), which he dedicated to Copland.[65] In late October he left Brazil, remaining in the States until May 1943. Highlights of his trip included two CBS broadcasts and a concert at the MoMA on 7 March, where Leonard Bernstein, mezzo soprano Jennie Tourel, and violinist Samuel Dushkin performed his works. The critic for the *New York World Telegram* observed that Guarnieri "writes with directness, his aim apparently being to tell his story in as unaffected manner as possible," echoing Copland's view that Guarnieri's music was "the honest expression of how one man feels."[66] In a review titled "Excellence from Brazil," Thomson praised Guarnieri's music for its "authority and amplitude," adding with his usual flair for provocation that such qualities were "rare in any hemisphere, particularly in this one."[67] Also in March, the National Symphony performed the *Abertura concertante* in Washington, DC, which Chávez conducted along with Moncayo's *Huapango* and his own *H.P.* (Horse Power) in the Hall of the Americas at the Pan American Union. The event was a special "All American" program, attended by United Nations representatives, members of the diplomatic corps, congresspeople, and Supreme Court justices. Representing the United States in this all-American embrace was *Billy the Kid*.[68]

Guarnieri also visited the Eastman School of Music, where Howard Hanson invited him to conduct the orchestral version of *Encantamento* and his *Dança brasileira* with the Eastman Philharmonia. (Apparently the latter caused such a stir that Guarnieri repeated it, starting the tradition of playing the *Dança brasileira* twice each time it is heard.) He then traveled to Boston for a chamber music concert of works by Guarnieri and Villa-Lobos, organized by Slonimsky. Surely the peak moment of the entire tour was Guarnieri conducting his *Abertura concertante* with the Boston Symphony Orchestra.[69] The piece's metric juxtapositions, exuberant coda, and vigorous motives made a fine impression: the critic for the *Christian Science Monitor* called it an "amiable, ingratiating piece, well designed to cultivate good will between good neighbors."[70] Appropriately, Guarnieri's *Abertura concertante* shared the program with a still-new work by its dedicatee. Copland's *Lincoln Portrait*, for orchestra and speaker, was one of several pieces he completed in the aftermath of his cultural diplomacy tour. It would prove significant in Latin America.

## From *Lincoln Portrait* to *Retrato de Lincoln*

During 1942 Copland composed some of his most celebrated works. Two came about at the request of a conductor. *Fanfare for the Common Man*, for brass and percussion, was one of a series of curtain raisers that Eugene Goossens of the Cincinnati Symphony Orchestra commissioned from various composers to buck up the nation's morale. (One of these, Henry Cowell's *Fanfare to the Forces of Our Latin American Allies*, celebrates hemispheric solidarity.) *Lincoln Portrait* was part of a similar multicomposer project. André Kostelanetz asked Copland, Thomson, and Jerome Kern to each commemorate musically a national hero. Copland's choice of Abraham Lincoln was apt: in his Fireside Chats, President Roosevelt frequently quoted Lincoln, and during the war he read Carl Sandburg's extensive biography of the sixteenth president.[71] Clearly the American Civil War, which Lincoln once described as "the fiery trial through which we pass," held lessons for the present.

Copland brought to *Lincoln Portrait* some well-tested strategies. These include his signature wide-interval melodic lines, "open" harmonies, and musical quotation, here, of the songs "Springfield Mountain" and "Camptown Races." The central element of *Lincoln Portrait*, however, is the speaker, who declaims against the orchestral backdrop some of the sixteenth president's most memorable words, including portions of the Gettysburg Address and the annual message to Congress of December 1862.[72] Copland pieced them together with his own transitional texts, repeatedly asserting Lincoln's narrative agency: "This is what he said"; "This is what Abraham Lincoln said"; or simply, "he said." For even greater emphasis, Copland sometimes places two such declarative sentences back to back, as in "This is what he said: He said."[73]

*Lincoln Portrait* was not without risk. Copland opted for narration out of concern that it would be impossible to capture Lincoln's wisdom in music. As he confessed in the program note for the Boston performance, he "secretly" hoped to circumvent this challenge by "doing a portrait in which the sitter himself might speak."[74] To at least some listeners, however, the narration might have conjured up the Soviet oratorio, which often incorporated a speaker.[75] The spoken text was even likelier to evoke melodrama, a moribund art involving speaking over music that had largely died out in the nineteenth century.[76] (Some notable exceptions are twentieth-century "speaker pieces" such as Schoenberg's *Gurrelieder*, Stravinsky's *Oedipus Rex* and *Perséphone*, and Milhaud's *Cristophe Colombe*.) For this reason, some critics would disparage *Lincoln Portrait* as "movie music."[77] Much depended on the delivery. Because he disliked "hamminess," Copland added instructions in the published score, urging speakers to depend not on acting but "sincerity of manner."[78] Copland observed: "how Lincoln spoke these words we can never really know, but certainly we can all sense how *not* to read them."

Copland took pains to ensure that the spoken text would have the desired impact. The narrator's entrance, in the final third of *Lincoln Portrait*, is aptly timed. The orchestra repeats the "Springfield Mountain" motive in C major whereupon the tonal center drops to A-flat, heard against a G natural and darkened with the tam-tam. By now, listeners have digested quotations of U.S. traditional music—including the minstrel song "Camptown Races," precipitously swept aside—along with shifts of mood, color, and tempo. All have led to this critical moment, in which "the sitter speaks" to address a national calamity and to majestically celebrate the principles of democracy to which Copland was committed.

Throughout the Americas, Lincoln was a potent symbol for many different constituencies. In the United States, advocates of the New Deal emphasized his humble circumstances, with members of the American Communist Party looking to Lincoln for social justice, whereas volunteer combatants in the Spanish Civil War joined the Abraham Lincoln Brigade. Conservative U.S. Americans, especially Whites in the rural South, needed a "safe" Lincoln, however. To win over that group, Roosevelt and his followers minimized the racial dimension of Lincoln's legacy, generically insisting that Lincoln was an "emancipator—not of slaves alone but of those with heavy hearts everywhere."[79] In Latin America, Lincoln had enjoyed renown since 1845, when as a young Whig congressman, he dared oppose the imperialist U.S.-Mexican War. Unlike his debate opponent Stephen Douglas, who saw "the tropics" as ripe for the expansion of slavery, Lincoln argued that the United States should resist the temptations of manifest destiny and set an example as "the last, best hope of earth."[80] One Latin American admirer of Lincoln was Argentine statesman Domingo Faustino Sarmiento. Exiled to Chile for defying the dictatorship of Juan Manuel Rosas, Sarmiento was sent to the United States in the 1840s to study the U.S. educational system. Having described the United States as a land with "no kings, nobles, privileged classes," he published a biography of Lincoln, the chief representative of such egalitarianism.[81] Lincoln even came to be seen as "the precursor of the Good Neighbor." At least this is the title of a book by Cuban author and politician Emeterio Santovenia, who tells of two Cuban brothers who fought in the Union army.[82]

To further the Good Neighbor policy, Hollywood took advantage of Lincoln's stature in Latin America. Unlike Axis newsreels that reveled in images of military preparedness and Lebensraum, U.S. films would inspire rather than intimidate, offering Latin Americans movies such as *Young Mr. Lincoln* (1939) and *Abe Lincoln in Illinois* (1940).[83] Most celebrated was the big-budget *Juárez* (1939), the story of the reformist Mexican president Benito Juárez, who served during the American Civil War. Juárez, who sought to lift agrarian workers out of poverty much the way Lincoln eventually emancipated Black people from slavery, has been called "the Lincoln of Mexico."[84] In 1864, when Napoleon III sent the Austrian archduke to govern Mexico as Emperor Maximilian I, Juárez was directing what amounted to a guerrilla war. Although preoccupied at home, Lincoln sent arms to Juárez, managing to keep the war-torn United States neutral in the Mexican conflict.[85]

The film portrays Juárez as a thoughtful and decisive leader, thus challenging Hollywood's usual array of stereotypical Latin Americans—greasers, bandidos, horse thieves, or somnolent Indians snoozing under their sombreros.[86] Throughout, references to Lincoln abound. These include the Mexican president's stovepipe hat and the portrait of Lincoln in Juárez's study (which

Juárez calls the *gringo*), all enhanced with frequent quotations of the "Battle Hymn of the Republic" in Erich Korngold's score. Napoleon III, played by a slimy Claude Rains, spits out snide allusions to Lincoln: "Democracy! The rule of the cattle by the cattle for the cattle!"[87] As for persuasiveness, one U.S. critic observed that those Latin Americans wondering about how to comport themselves vis-à-vis the European powder keg would find *Juárez* easy to "read between the lines"; another found in the film an "amazing parallel to current events . . . the contrast of plumed dictatorship with democratic idealism."[88] Most important, Latin Americans applauded *Juárez*, including Mexican president Lázaro Cárdenas. That the film was temporarily banned in Peru until after the elections of October 1939 attests to its import.[89] (It was these elections that brought to power President Manuel Prado, the U.S. ally.)

Clearly Latin Americans would listen to *Lincoln Portrait* with interest. It was only natural that it be translated into Spanish—as *Retrato de Lincoln*—to spread democratic ideals throughout the hemisphere. An undated manuscript, probably from around 1943, shows several hands at work, with the translator unidentified.[90] As discussed in subsequent chapters, *Retrato de Lincoln* would enjoy an unusual trajectory in several Latin American countries.

## The Real Copland?

Several of the works Copland wrote during this unusually fruitful period were performed on future trips to Latin America.[91] These include *Rodeo*, from 1942, another "cowboy ballet," with Agnes de Mille the choreographer.[92] Another is *Danzón cubano*, also from 1942 and originally conceived for two pianos. Its musical materials came not from anthologies but from Copland's own jottings during his Cuban sojourns.[93] (The orchestral version, which calls for claves, maracas, gourd, and cowbell, dates from 1946.) To be sure, some scholars propose that Copland's understanding of the danzón is less than accurate.[94] Yet his creative process—combining rhythmic and melodic cells in various configurations—corresponds to the genre's basic format, as manifested in Ernesto Lecuona's *Danzón* or Arturo Márquez's multisectional "Danzón no. 2," for example.[95] Also present is syncopation, a frequent feature of danzón that makes it a close cousin of ragtime and thus a Pan American genre. At the premiere on 9 December 1942, Copland played *Danzón cubano* with Bernstein. Copland, who moderated the concert, acknowledged that like *El salón México*, *Danzón cubano* was a tourist's impression. "No objection," Taubman observed in his review, "if the tourist has a lively mind and a sense of humor."[96]

The Sonata for Violin and Piano was a different matter. Copland worked on it in Hollywood, where he wrote the score for *The North Star*, like *Of Mice and Men*, directed by Lewis Milestone. The sonata capers from placid melodies to rhythmically active passages to angular motives à la Prokofiev, striking some listeners as inscrutable. Colin McPhee, for example, described the work as "both recherché and baffling in its simplicity."[97] During this time, Copland also began what is arguably his most beloved work, *Appalachian Spring*, the felicitous collaboration with choreographer Martha Graham that remains at the forefront of his so-called Americana style. Copland first composed the version for chamber ensemble, performed at the Library of Congress in 1944, and then the more familiar format, the suite for full orchestra.[98] Copland's transparent, accessible music was ideally suited to this tale of community spirit and idealism, giving voice to the homespun values—"simple gifts"—that inspired so many U.S. Americans during the war. It earned him a Pulitzer Prize and a New York Music Critics' Circle Award.[99]

In 1944 Copland began the Third Symphony, a large-scale, forty-minute work in the traditional four-movement format. He set forth his intentions in the program booklet for the Boston premiere (October 1946). Remarking, somewhat dryly, that in the 1920s he had been typed as a "composer of symphonic jazz" and later "as a folk-lorist and purveyor of Americana," he now aimed "to let the music 'speak for itself.'"[100] Several critics considered the work on these terms, noting "complex design" or "lucidity and logic."[101] By heralding the fourth movement with his own *Fanfare for the Common Man*, a wartime exhortation to triumph, however, Copland suggests something other than "the music itself." Some critics pounced on this decision. One called the *Fanfare* quotation "kitschy"; another complained of Copland's fondness for "brassy choirs."[102] Others believed that the Third Symphony as a whole revived the specter of eclecticism, finding not only that *Billy the Kid* and *Appalachian Spring* were too present in the work but also Mahler, Rimsky-Korsakov, and "hackneyed" allusions to Tchaikovsky. Looming largest was Shostakovich: Warren Storey Smith's moniker for the Third Symphony, "Shostakovich in the Appalachians," is for better or worse part of Copland lore. (Smith also heard a hint of Strauss's "Of Science" fugue from *Also sprach Zarathustra* and the Mussorgsky-Ravel "Great Gate of Kiev.")[103] None of these observations exactly places the symphony in the vanguard of musical composition.

Another work Copland would introduce in Latin America was *The Cummington Story*, a film with his score released in 1945 by the Office of War Information (OWI). It recounts the true story of forty European refugees displaced by the war and given shelter in Cummington, Massachusetts, a project spearheaded by the Congregationalist minister and conscientious objector Carl Sangree. Among the refugees were many Jews but also Catholics, Protestants, and freethinkers. Most were professionals (lawyers, insurance managers, physicians, and a newspaper editor). Upon arriving in the idyllic New England town, the refugees are struck by the fact that references to Ralph Waldo Emerson and scores by Mozart are encountered in the simplest of homes. They also learn that freedom of worship and speech are taken for granted, perhaps an allusion to the Four Freedoms Roosevelt articulated in his state of the union address of 6 January 1941.[104] The film belies its propagandistic intent by touching on less noble aspects of life in the United States: the townspeople, wary of the Other, forfeit several opportunities to be hospitable. Yet they ultimately embrace the refugees, a point driven home one Sunday morning in the plain New England church where Sangree preaches from the book of Leviticus: "The stranger that dwelleth with you shall be unto you as one born among you and thou should love him as thyself." Throughout, Copland's score juxtaposes counterpoint, musical quotation, and what Neil Lerner calls the composer's "pastoral" style. If the Third Symphony hinted that Copland's star might be fading, the musical language of *The Cummington Story* conveyed the clear, optimistic message that so gratified his public during the war.

Not all was bright. In a U.S. House of Representatives' report, *Investigation of Un-American Propaganda Activities in the United States*, from 1944, Copland's name appears five times, once apropos his prize-winning mass song "Into the Streets May First!" which as noted, had been performed in April 1934 at the Second Workers Music Olympiad, a competition of workers' choruses.[105] A happier moment was the full premiere of *Statements*, which finally took place in January 1942. Despite meanings some have attached to the movement titles ("Militant," "Jingo," and the like), no critic of the premiere seems to have detected any political content. Thomson called the work "a manly bouquet, fresh and sweet and sincere and frank and straightforward" and for Taubman, *Statements* showed that Copland was a "man who knows his own mind," adding, "and an original mind it is."[106] Manliness and self-assurance were the watchwords of the hour.

## Pan Americanism and Approaching Victory

Latin American composers continued to visit the United States. In 1943 René Amengual, whom Copland met in Chile, arrived as a guest of the Institute of

International Education. Also, Copland's "mission impossible" in Brazil came to fruition. In November 1944 Villa-Lobos arrived in Los Angeles to spend three months in the United States. The sponsorship was as complex as the Brazilian composer could have desired: the Southern California Council of Inter-American Affairs, the music section of the Motion Picture Academy, and Occidental College all funded his trip.[107] Besides conducting, Villa-Lobos received various honors, including an honorary LLD in a ceremony on the Occidental campus. Serving as translator was the Brazilian author Érico Veríssimo, then a visiting professor at the University of California, Berkeley. He could not refrain from embellishing the composer's acceptance speech, mostly at the expense of Vargas's Estado Novo and Villa-Lobos's exalted status within it. When Villa-Lobos claimed that he had "learned the song of liberty" in the Brazilian rain forest, Veríssimo added, "and I believe it, because today liberty in Brazil exists only in the rain forest," provoking giggles from the public.[108] In New York, Villa-Lobos's great champion Olin Downes published a lengthy interview with the Brazilian composer. Gone was Villa-Lobos's rhapsodizing over "the power of nationalities." Rather, he perorated on universalism to all who would listen.[109]

Cultural diplomacy continued to be debated. In a memo to Charles Thompson, who replaced Ben Cherrington as chief of the Division of Cultural Relations, Reginald S. Kazanjian, the U.S. consul based in Santa Catarina, Brazil, ventured beyond gray administrative prose and spoke from the heart:

> Should anyone say that these are war days and there is no time or money to spend on cultural "trifles," I wish to put myself on record as affirming that the cultural policy as being pursued by your Division is not only the most natural basis for avoiding wars and misunderstandings but is also the key foundation for a world peace and civilization. . . . Let those that put forward such arguments compare the expenses and destruction of the present war with the blessings and enlightenment of the self-paying cultural program. If they are still not convinced, I suggest that they come to [Santa Catarina] and let me show them first hand.[110]

Gauging the trickle-down effect of cultural diplomacy on the broader public remained an inexact science, however. A contest for high school students from greater Boston, jointly organized by the New England Institute of Inter-American Affairs and the *Boston Globe*, posed questions such as (1) "Latin America is three times, five times, or ten times as large as the United States?" or (2) "Name two of the cities where conferences for cooperation among the

Americas have been held since 1930."[111] (One of these quiz kids, Leonard B. Horwitz, would later receive a collegiate fellowship for Latin American studies and interview Copland during his next visit to Buenos Aires.) The fact that every youngster missed the question "Name two Latin American artists" suggests that cultural diplomacy had a ways to go.[112] As an Allied victory came to look increasingly likely, U.S. cultural diplomacy widened its purview. Copland now served on the State Department's Sub-Committee on Musical Interchange with the U.S.S.R., which met for the first time on 11 February 1944. Chaired by Downes, the subcommittee convened in the editorial board room of the *New York Times* even though no funds had yet been placed at its disposal.[113] Downes reminded the subcommittee that theirs was not a wartime assignment, nor were they "under the pressure" the OIAA and the Division of Cultural Relations had confronted.[114]

Latin Americans, sensing that the war was winding down, digested the transformations it had wrought in the hemisphere. Not all were as fortunate as Venezuela, whose oil production had increased 358 percent, making it one of the few countries in Latin America that could now pay for modernization programs. Mexico emerged from the conflict more unified, which helped facilitate President Manuel Ávila Camacho's plans for industrialization. In March 1945 the Inter-American Conference on Problems of War and Peace took place in Mexico City, resulting in the Inter-American Treaty of Reciprocal Assistance and Solidarity. Emphasizing "principles of sovereignty and non-intervention," the treaty anticipated the United Nations charter.[115]

In Brazil, Vargas resigned in a bloodless coup. Elections were held in December 1945 (the first since 1934), in which Eurico Dutra, perceived as Vargas's hand-picked candidate, prevailed. Chile, long neutral, finally declared war on the Axis in early 1945 on notice from the U.S. State Department that failure to do so would mean exclusion from the United Nations.[116] As for Argentina, U.S. officials were still disinclined to recognize that neutrality did not necessarily mean "pro-German." But when firefights with British warships in coastal waters made Argentines nervous, the country switched from neutrality to nonbelligerency. In June 1943, when a military coup removed the faltering Argentine government, Juan Domingo Perón took a central role, first as Secretary of Labor and then in other positions. Perón's quirky blend of left-wing populism, right-wing international alliances, and corporatism increased tensions between Argentina and the United States. Yet it was that government that broke relations with the Axis in 1944, declaring war on Germany in 1945.

Thanks to Secretary of State Hull and his backers, however, Argentina has never quite lived down its reputation as a hotbed of Nazi intrigue.

* * *

In 1947 Copland would return to Latin America. By then President Roosevelt, chief architect of the Good Neighbor policy and beloved in much of Latin America, was dead. No longer did movie stars, musicians, and ballet dancers relentlessly spread good will in Latin America, nor did the phantasmagoric array of Disney cartoons or movie musicals replete with banana-laden headdresses and percussion-heavy soundtracks offer up a cheery view of inter-American harmony. Neither did concerts, art exhibits, or essay contests vie for the attention of cultural elites. Rather, new priorities fell into place and U.S. cultural diplomacy in Latin America would never be the same. The next chapter explores Copland's approach to these new realities.

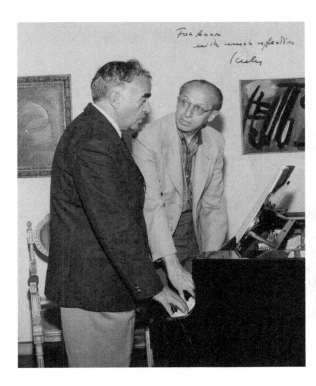

Figure 1. Carlos Chávez (left) and Aaron Copland. Note on photo says, "To Aaron, With much affection, Carlos." Library of Congress, Music Division, Box Number 479/6. The image of Aaron Copland is reproduced by permission of the Aaron Copland Fund for Music, Inc.

Buenos Aires 3_agosto 941.

Sr. Aaron Copland
New York. U.S.A.

RECEIVED
AUG 1 1941
P. L. BARBOUR

Muy estimado amigo,

gracias por su amable carta del 22 de julio y por el ejemplar de sus "Variaciones" para piano, que mucho le agradezco. Yo conocía esta hermosa obra por los discos "Columbia" en que aparece ejecutada magistralmente por Vd. Así que, sin Vd. saberlo, estaba Vd. en mi estudio, listo a deleitarme con la audición de su obra en cuanto yo tuviera deseos y tiempo para oirla. Igual amabilidad y en iguales circunstancias actúan cerca de mí Ernst Krenek, Hindemith, Milhaud y otros más, siempre listos a satisfacer mis caprichos auditivos.

Me parece entender que no recibió Vd. mi carta y programas de "Conciertos de la Nueva Música", que yo le enviara al Hotel Empire N.Y., dirección que me facilitara en Bs. Aires mi excelente amigo William Berrien. En ella le hacía saber que si Vd. tuviera la intención de venir a esta ciudad, seríamos encantados de recibirle y nos veríamos muy honrados si Vd. deseara actuar como ejecutante, dando a conocer alguna de sus obras, o pronunciando una conferencia sobre música norteamericana, que gustosamente sería ilustrada por los excelentes artistas que actúan en nuestras audiciones. Como por su carta me entero que Vd. ofrecerá cuatro conferencias en ésta, retiro en parte mi ofrecimiento, quedando de todas maneras en pié el ofrecimiento de nuestra colaboración como ejecutantes, a la vez que la invitación a ejecutar alguna obra de Vd. en nuestras audiciones. Vd. lo decidirá de la manera que a su juicio sea más conveniente. Nos alegramos anticipadamente de su próxima estadía entre nosotros. Aquí hallará Vd. amigos sinceros que contribuirán en lo posible a hacerle agradable el mes que pasará Vd. en Buenos Aires.

Le saluda cordialmente, con mucho aprecio,

Juan Carlos Paz

P.S. — Gracias por haberme hecho enviar la crónica de Virgyl Thomson, sobre el Festival de la I.S. for C.M, en New York. —

DOS DE ESTAS HOJAS Y UN SOBRE DE VIA AEREA PESAN 5 GRAMOS

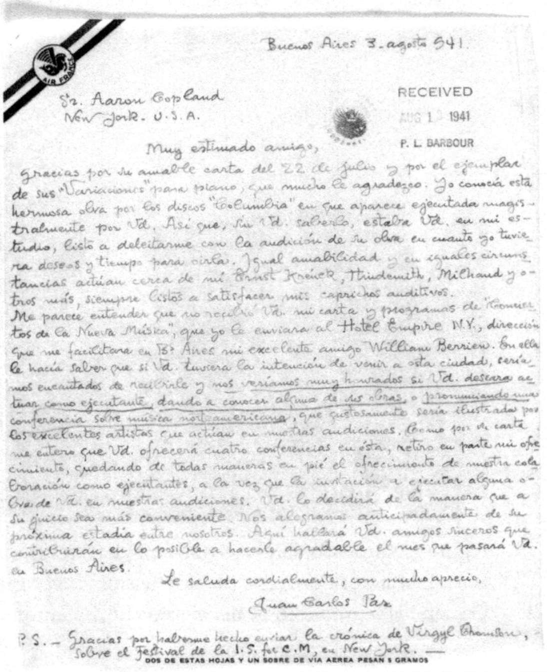

Figure 2. Juan Carlos Paz to Aaron Copland, 3 August 1941. Library of Congress, Music Division, Box Number 260/16. Reproduced by permission of the Aaron Copland Fund for Music, Inc., successor to Aaron Copland.

Figure 3. Aaron Copland arrives in Lima, September 1941. Library of Congress, Music Division, Box Number 483/18. The image of Aaron Copland is reproduced by permission of the Aaron Copland Fund for Music, Inc.

Figure 4. Aaron Copland (second from left) on the lecture circuit, Lima, Peru, September 1941. Library of Congress, Music Division, Box Number 483/18. The image of Aaron Copland is reproduced by permission of the Aaron Copland Fund for Music, Inc.

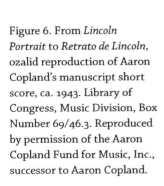

Figure 5. Aaron Copland's script in Portuguese for *A Hora do Brasil*, Rio de Janeiro, November 1941. Library of Congress, Music Division, Box Number 216/8. Reproduced by permission of the Aaron Copland Fund for Music, Inc., successor to Aaron Copland.

Figure 6. From *Lincoln Portrait* to *Retrato de Lincoln*, ozalid reproduction of Aaron Copland's manuscript short score, ca. 1943. Library of Congress, Music Division, Box Number 69/46.3. Reproduced by permission of the Aaron Copland Fund for Music, Inc., successor to Aaron Copland.

Figure 7. (Left to right) Aaron Copland, Heitor Villa-Lobos, and Brazilian ambassador at Waldorf Astoria, New York. Library of Congress, Music Division, Box Number 479/5. The image of Aaron Copland is reproduced by permission of the Aaron Copland Fund for Music, Inc.

Figure 8. Music of the Americas, Montevideo, Uruguay, 1947. Library of Congress, Music Division, Box Number 359/12.

En la cultura de sus compositores
tiene la musica argentina la posi-
bilidad de desarrollar una obra
de significacion universal

Aaron Copland

Para Buenos Aires Musical

Nov 14 1947

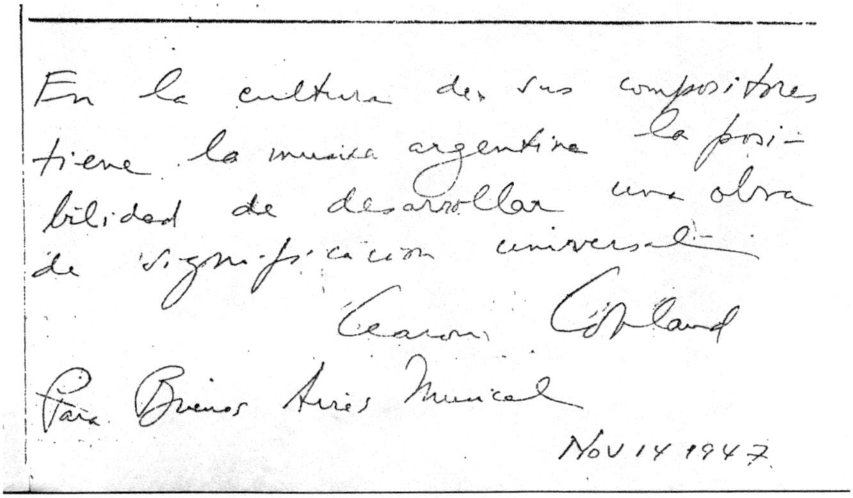

Figure 9. Handwritten note in the Argentine music magazine *Buenos Aires Musical*, 17 November 1947.

Buenos Aires 11 de noviembre de 1947

Maestro Copland, sería muy
grato para mí poder recibir su
fotografía autografiada como recuerdo
de su estada en mi país, donde
tanto se admira su música y
su obra de difusión americana.
Agradeciendo desde ya
su amabilidad, lo saluda
cordialmente

Olga Susana Pardo

Concordia 2794 _ Villa del Parque _
Capital

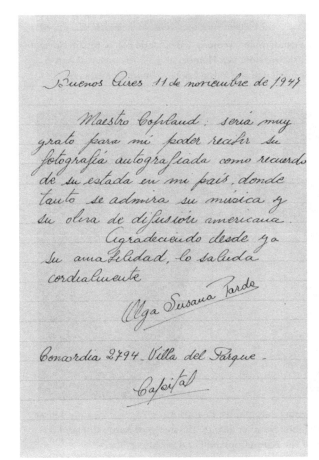

Figure 10. Fan mail from Olga Susana Pardo of Argentina. Library of Congress, Music Division, Box Number 359/10.

Figure 11. Aaron Copland at a candomblé ceremony, Salvador de Bahia, Brazil, November 1947. Library of Congress, Music Division, Box Number 483/15. The image of Aaron Copland is reproduced by permission of the Aaron Copland Fund for Music, Inc.

Figure 12. Aaron Copland signing autographs, Buenos Aires, Argentina, 1963. Library of Congress, Music Division, Box Number 483/15. The image of Aaron Copland is reproduced by permission of the Aaron Copland Fund for Music, Inc.

Figure 13. Aaron Copland and Domingo Santa Cruz, Santiago, Chile, 1963. Library of Congress, Music Division. The image of Aaron Copland is reproduced by permission of the Aaron Copland Fund for Music, Inc.

Figure 14. Aaron Copland at the podium in Bogotá, Colombia. Library of Congress, Music Division, Box Number 477/4. The image of Aaron Copland is reproduced by permission of the Aaron Copland Fund for Music, Inc.

Figure 15. Aaron Copland and Latin American composers (left to right, standing): Domingo Santa Cruz, Alberto Ginastera, Juan B. Plaza; seated: Copland and Carlos Chávez (confirmed on the back of the photo). Library of Congress, Music Division, Box Number 479/6. The image of Aaron Copland is reproduced by permission of the Aaron Copland Fund for Music Inc.

# PART III

# Copland, Latin America, and the Postwar

# 9
# The Early Cold War

In late summer 1947 the Inter-American Conference for the Maintenance of Continental Peace and Security got underway in Rio de Janeiro. With the war over and a new U.S. president in power, leaders throughout the hemisphere took stock of prior alliances. Many Latin Americans assumed that President Harry S. Truman would uphold Roosevelt's vision of Pan American solidarity. They also expected recognition for their solidarity during the conflict, such as the raw materials, bases, and personnel provided on behalf of the Allies. One evening during the conference, a party was held at a nearby luxury hotel, the Palácio Quitandinha. In a newspaper column titled "Samba para Mr. Copland!" radio personality and journalist Fernando Lôbo reported that various Brazilian bandleaders played "boogies," thinking they were pleasing their U.S. visitors. The guests clamored for sambas, however, a request the Brazilian musicians were happy to oblige. Confident in the future, cosmopolitan citizens of the Americas were unafraid of losing their local identities. Internationalism, modernization, and universalism were the new watchwords: as Lôbo declared, "we are no longer a lame version of our grandparents."[1]

Copland was then on his second government-sponsored cultural diplomacy tour. Traveling under the auspices of the Visiting Professor Program, a new State Department initiative, he arrived in Rio on 19 August. At the exuberant gathering, he chatted with Lôbo. Because Copland was among those who requested sambas, Lôbo assured him of a "command performance" later in his stay, a promise Lôbo kept. This chapter details the ways in which Brazil was the highlight of Copland's 1947 trip, thanks in part to serendipitous moments such as these. Besides Rio de Janeiro, São Paulo, and Porto Alegre, he ventured off the beaten path to Brazil's northeast, hearing music completely new to him and which he found entrancing. He also paid a brief visit to Uruguay and spent a month in Argentina, all the while pondering the challenges of universalism in the postwar world.

## Aftermath of the Good Neighbor Policy

Now that the Axis was vanquished, communism was the new enemy of the hemisphere. At least, this was the view of the United States. In Brazil, communism was enough of a presence that Ambassador William D. Pawley warned Truman, "There is hardly a town in Brazil of over 1,000 inhabitants that does not have a Communist office."[2] In March 1947 Truman expounded before a joint session of Congress on the need to contain Soviet influence, an address subsequently known as the Truman Doctrine. The same month he signed Executive Order 9835, which purported to rout out federal employees with ties to organizations considered subversive, and in July 1947 he signed the National Security Act, creating, among other entities, the Central Intelligence Agency (CIA).

In Latin America Truman made little effort to fill his predecessor's shoes.[3] At the Rio conference, he left delegates nonplussed by giving them to understand that not even a fraction of the funds allocated to the Marshall Plan would find their way to Latin America. The Inter-American Treaty of Reciprocal Assistance, crafted during the conference, essentially urged its erstwhile neighbors to support the United States in its new role as a superpower, whereupon the Mexican journalist Narciso Bressols griped that Latin American nations had been invited to become "compulsory" allies rather than equal partners.[4] In addition, Truman's Point Four Program ensured that the special relationship among the American Republics would be subsumed into a global scheme, according to which Latin America, Asia, and Africa were relegated to the category "underdeveloped" and therefore "breeding grounds" for communism. The worst fears of many Latin Americans were confirmed: the entire Good Neighbor policy was not only insincere but had depended entirely on Roosevelt.[5]

The OIAA was shut down by executive order and its activities absorbed by the State Department.[6] Some Roosevelt-era government programs for U.S.–Latin American cultural exchange remained in place, however. Among them was the Buenos Aires Convention for the Promotion of Inter-American Cultural Relations, established just as the Good Neighbor Policy was gaining ground. One postwar grantee was musicologist, pianist, and composer Robert M. Stevenson, one of the first U.S. scholars to specialize in Latin American music and who received a fellowship for research in Mexico.[7] The result was his authoritative *Music of Mexico: A Historical Survey*, published in 1952 and still consulted. As in the Good Neighbor era, the private sector also stepped forward: Reichold Chemical was a Detroit-based company whose music-loving German immigrant CEO Henry Helmut Reichold funded a prize for symphonic composers of the Americas. In general, however, U.S. cultural diplomacy set its sights globally, guided by a vision of "One World."[8] But whose world and whose culture? This utopian proposition set the stage for either the Western democracies or the Soviet bloc to prevail, with very little in between. Copland too branched out. By now he had served not only the State Department's Sub-Committee on Musical Interchange with the U.S.S.R. but also private organizations such as the National Council on American-Soviet Friendship, sometimes in leadership positions.[9] Over the coming years, he would visit Italy, the Soviet Union, the People's Republic of China, Eastern Europe, Japan, the Philippines, Australia, New Zealand, Portugal, Yugoslavia, West Germany, Austria, Turkey, and Norway as a cultural diplomat, all reinforcing the concept of One World.[10]

First, however, Copland returned to Latin America. In 1947 his ties there were still strong. The Spanish translation of *Our New Music* (*Música y músicos contemporáneos*) had just appeared, and in a warm introduction, Leopoldo Hurtado noted Copland's centrality in the current contemporary music scene. He also praised his U.S. colleague's willingness to confront head-on the central question of modern music: how can composers marshal contemporary techniques without alienating the mass audience?[11]

## Latin American Composers in the Berkshires

Also reinforcing U.S.–Latin American friendship was the Tanglewood Festival. Having closed in 1942 due to the war, it was now set to reopen for the summer 1946 season. (The festival would not close down again until the 2020 pandemic.) At the first concert, an overflow public leapt to its feet to applaud Koussevitzky as he approached the podium to lead the Boston Symphony Orchestra in Beethoven's *Eroica* Symphony. Later in that triumphant season, the ensemble performed the orchestral version of *Appalachian Spring*.[12]

No fewer than nine Latin Americans composers were in attendance, as was Eleazar de Carvalho, a twenty-five-year-old Brazilian conductor who studied with Koussevitzky. Ralph Hawkes, the senior director of Copland's publisher Boosey and Hawkes, found the Latin American presence "evidence of flourishing musical culture."[13]

Amid the sweet-smelling greenery and cheerful hum of insects, the "class of '46" busied itself with seminars, lectures, concerts, and leisure.[14] Thanks to consecutive grants from the Rockefeller and Guggenheim Foundations, Juan Orrego-Salas was already in the United States, where some of his works were performed.[15] Also on a Guggenheim fellowship was Héctor Tosar, who on 1 December 1946 gave at the Pan American Union what was likely the first all-Ginastera recital in the United States.[16] Among the works he played were the *Doce preludios americanos*, a series of twelve miniatures from 1944. In the four "portrait preludes" from this set, Ginastera musically depicts three Latin Americans (Roberto García Morillo, Juan José Castro, and Villa-Lobos) but also Copland, clearly a citizen of the Americas. Ginastera told him that the work was but a "little homage," reflecting "only a minimum of all the respect and admiration I feel toward you."[17] Listeners can easily imagine the ebullient opening gesture in Copland's orchestration. Ginastera, whose own Guggenheim had been delayed because of the war, arrived in the United States in December 1945.[18] Early in his stay, he wrote Copland, addressing him respectfully as "Mr. Copland" and in his courtly English, expressed the hope of spending "lovely moments" together.[19] Because Copland was immersed in his Third Symphony, he had little time for "lovely moments" with Ginastera or other visitors for that matter, although they did see one another in New York.

Another Guggenheim fellow was Julián Orbón, born in northwest Spain but resident in Havana since 1940.[20] Also traveling from Cuba was Harold Gramatges, a member of Ardévol's class and winner of the Reichold Symphony of the Americas contest. Claudio Spies, born in Chile of German-Jewish parents, was also present (it is not clear that he studied with Copland) as was Blas Galindo, now well acquainted with the Berkshire Music Center.[21] Antonio Estévez of Venezuela also attended, as did Roque Cordero of Panama, the latter on a grant from the Institute of International Education and enrolled at the University of Minnesota, where he studied conducting with Dimitri Mitropoulos and composition with Ernst Krenek, then teaching at Hamline University in St. Paul.[22] All recognized that young composers of the Americas no longer had to cross the ocean to Paris or Vienna to perfect their technique.[23]

Those halcyon days proved rich in memories. Once Copland was driving around some of the Latin American students in his Buick, of which he was rather proud. As Orbón recalled, "One day, I was riding in Copland's car together with Héctor Tosar and Ginastera. Copland said, 'My God, I have to drive very carefully, because I have with me the hope of Latin American music!' And Ginastera said, 'Well—and the reality of North American music!'"[24] Ginastera too looked back on that remarkable summer. "Like many young composers," he wrote, "I discovered the secret path to my future musical life" at the Berkshire Music Center.[25] Ginastera also found respite from Argentine politics. In mid-1945 Perón was removed from government by the Argentine military and imprisoned for assuming too much power as vice president. His followers, however, demanded his release in a massive demonstration.[26] When Ginastera signed a petition opposing Perón, he lost his teaching job at the Liceo Militar General.[27] In an essay for *Modern Music*, "Political Shadow on Argentine Music," Ginastera detailed the dire effects of *peronismo*, including the cessation of concerts by the Grupo Renovación.[28] For solace, Ginastera turned to composition, writing the gripping, three-movement choral work, *Hieremiae prophetae lamentationes* (Lamentations of the Prophet Jeremiah), a glimpse into his state of mind and which he finished in 1946, perhaps in the Berkshires.

Ginastera also defended Juan José Castro, whose anti-Peronism exceeded his own. Like Ginastera, Castro signed a petition and lost employment, namely, his conducting position at the Teatro Colón.[29] With another orchestra, Castro programmed *Retrato de Lincoln* (Lincoln Portrait) in 1945, probably the first Latin American to do so. The speaker was radio personality Alberto Aguirre. According to Ginastera, who reviewed the concert, Aguirre "performed the role . . . with great austerity and nobility," evidently meeting Copland's exacting criteria. Ginastera also praised the work's "simple but strong character," reflecting "the qualities of a typical, strong U.S. personality."[30] Emboldened, Castro planned another performance of *Lincoln Portrait* as part of a patriotic celebration organized by an anti-Peronist women's group, which never took place, however, possibly because of political tensions.[31] Castro and Ginastera celebrated their pro-U.S. sentiment in Ginastera's Second Symphony, subtitled "Elegíaca" and dedicated "To Those Who Died for Liberty," which Castro conducted on 31 May 1946.[32] By then, Perón had been president for several months.

By fall 1946 Copland was preparing to return to Latin America. As on the eve of his earlier trip, he advocated for young composers. He was now serving as chair of the New York–based U.S. Group for Latin American Music, a private organization whose executive director, Erminie Kahn, managed to persuade the Empire Tractor Company to fund Latin American composition students to study at the Berkshire Music Center.[33] Applicants for the "Berkshire bolsa" (scholarship) had to be younger than thirty and residents of Argentina, Brazil, or Uruguay, the three countries Copland planned to visit. (Additional countries could be added in the future).[34] Established Latin American composers would screen the initial submissions and submit their evaluations to Copland during his tour. Final decisions, however, would rest with Copland and a subcommittee of Chase, Cowell, Smith, and an Ethel Cohen, a procedure that did not sit well with the Latin Americans.[35] All came about because of a generous farm-equipment manufacturer and a resourceful administrator.

## An "enlightened and cordial opinion"

The new Visiting Professor Program sent qualified individuals from various disciplines to live abroad for up to six months. Grantees were expected to take advantage of State Department–sponsored cultural centers. In Latin America these totaled around thirty and featured activities ranging from lectures by distinguished experts to informal Song Nights, in which Latin American adolescents gathered to learn songs from the United States. Many centers had libraries and record players. The overarching goal was to encourage "an enlightened and cordial public opinion [of the United States] based on familiarity with the intellectual aspects of American life," thus counterbalancing U.S. "material development," of which the world was well aware, according to a State Department booklet.[36] In 1947 Copland was one of six grantees for Latin America.[37] He does not seem to have applied in any formal sense; rather, his name was "suggested to the Department as a person qualified to accept such a mission," as Francis J. Colligan, assistant chief for the Division of International Exchange of Persons, informed him.[38] Colligan initially suggested that Copland visit Cuba, Colombia, Chile, Peru, and Brazil, all countries with at least one cultural center. Copland decided to spend not the six months available to him but just over three, however. He was also reluctant to present very many Spanish-language talks. "Although my conversational Spanish is adequate," he told Arthur E. Gropp, of the Biblioteca Artigas–Washington in Montevideo, "I could give only one or two formal talks in Spanish, reading from my own texts. Any other talks would have to be in English."[39] He agreed to speak Spanish on the radio. For Brazil, Colligan mapped out a series of lectures for the Instituto Brasil–Estados Unidos (IBEU) in Rio de Janeiro, assuring Copland that despite some advantages to presenting in Portuguese, the "clientele" would be perfectly happy to listen to him speak English.[40] As it turned out, Copland ended up using a good deal more Portuguese than he anticipated.

Compared with 1941, his schedule was far more demanding: nineteen radio addresses, twenty-eight lectures, and performances in all three countries, as both conductor and pianist. Copland also met informally with composers, although this time he was under no obligation to identify potential visitors to the United States. On both ends of the trip, he would spend approximately a week in Washington, DC, to consult with State Department officers.[41] He was paid $500 a month and received first-class, round-trip airfare; travel throughout Latin America; $6 per diem during his pre- and post-trip stays in Washington; $7 per diem in Latin America; costs incurred by excess baggage, passport fees or incidentals; and a budget for "stenographic services" and supplies. In a flyer, "Information for a Visiting Professor," Copland learned that just as in 1941 he would not be considered an official representative of the U.S. government but that "statements and activities may frequently carry different and even unexpected connotations when made abroad."[42] Copland highlighted this passage.

## "His music is universal"

Copland spent only a week in Uruguay, then in the midst of what some historians consider a "golden era" under President Luis Batlle Berres.[43] The economy was strong and the arts were thriving, including the orchestra, which Copland conducted on 1 November in a program of music from Uruguay and the United States. Guido Santórsola, formerly a violist with the orchestra, conducted the Uruguayan portion: Tosar's Concertino for piano and orchestra, which Tosar performed, and Santórsola's own *Two Symphonic Movements*, a "philosophical-musical" work that paid homage to ancient Greek philosophers, as Santórsola explained in his program notes. Copland chose *An Outdoor Overture*, *Appalachian Spring*, and *Lincoln Portrait*, with actor Hugo Dualde as speaker.[44] At the Biblioteca Artigas–Washington, the composer listened to the recording of Koussevitzky and the Boston Symphony Orchestra (with the actor Melvyn Douglas as speaker).[45] He believed the Montevideo orchestra lacked "discipline" and that the players were unused to "modern rhythms," a liability for *Appalachian Spring*.[46]

On the eve of the concert, Copland wrote his older sister Laurine, who had long encouraged him to conduct. "I'm carrying out your plans for me by conducting the orchestra here," he told her.[47] Despite having led ensembles in Lima and Santiago, Copland had recently undergone a moment of truth: in 1946 Eugene Goossens became too ill to lead the Cincinnati Symphony in *Appalachian Spring* and Copland realized that he was unqualified to step in on short notice. He vowed that he would learn to conduct at least his own works.

Before long, he gained confidence to the point that when observing others on the podium, he sometimes had "the distinct impression" he could do better himself, as he wrote in his diary in Rio de Janeiro.[48] In Montevideo, he jotted down brief progress reports. "I think I'm improving rapidly as a conductor," he reflected on 28 October. Or, "Tosar says my conducting is influenced by L. B. [Leonard Bernstein]; also I was reported to have a left hand like Bruno Walter!" Alternatively, he might confess, "I made some mis-beats—damn!"[49] It cannot have been easy to run rehearsals in Spanish. (In Brazil he probably used some mixture of Spanish and French). On-the-job training in Latin America paid off, however, and by the 1950s Copland was regularly performing three kinds of programs throughout the world: all-Copland, all-U.S., and U.S. with other repertory, establishing what Emily Abrams Ansari calls his "global reputation as a conductor."[50]

The Montevideo concert exceeded Copland's expectations. He exulted in his diary that the audience greeted him "warmly and from there on, it was a cinch." There was "lots of excitement backstage, including a visit from the American Ambassador and . . . Mrs. Briggs." "Seems I communicate something," he acknowledged with satisfaction.[51] Nevertheless, the house was small, a fact some Uruguayan critics attributed to the beginning of summer vacation when no longer "does music form a part of what is ordinarily indispensable for the spirit and for culture," as one chided.[52] Not all the works on the program fared equally well: Santórsola's "philosophical-musical" *Two Symphonic Movements* came off "pompously," as one critic carped, whereas another found its "Satie-like Hellenism" incongruous.[53] Tosar's Concertino, already familiar to the Montevideo public, was cordially received, however. With regard to Copland's music, one critic noted the "true symphonic value" of *Appalachian Spring* and another enjoyed its "highly varied rhythms and frequent changes of tempo."[54] According to Copland, *Lincoln Portrait* brought "bravos" from the audience. Yet critical reaction was mixed. The reviewer for *La Razón* found it "the most interesting and exciting" work on the program.[55] *El País* found the narrated text "antimusical," however.[56] Similarly, *El Diario* doubted *Lincoln Portrait*'s intrinsic musical values, noting that despite the "sincerity" of this "hymn to Democracy," the work "doesn't escape from being, at bottom, art with a message" (un arte dirigido).[57] To be sure, no critic bandied about the term "movie music." Still, it seemed clear that Copland had rejected the realm of absolute music, thus ensuring that *Lincoln Portrait* was excluded from the pantheon of High Art.

In fact, *An Outdoor Overture* garnered the most praise. The critic for *El País* preferred it to all the other pieces on the program, and *El Diario* called it the "freshest." Also weighing in was the Uruguayan folklorist and musicologist Lauro Ayestarán, who attached unusual significance to this unassuming work:

> *An Outdoor Overture* . . . is the key to all the composer's future works. It's music of precise shapes and limpid objectivity, representing in the highest degree his authentic and deeply felt modernity. Its orchestral writing defines itself through a perfect equilibrium. . . . Not a single false step . . . nor excesses of density among the sonorous amalgams. The sun passes in strong rays of light across an orchestral texture that is muscular yet transparent. On the other hand, a healthy and athletic dynamism in clearly youthful rhythm is on full display.[58]

Coexisting with "authentic modernity" are the typical values of U.S. music: "healthy and athletic dynamism," "clearly youthful rhythm," and "muscular yet transparent" orchestration. This "perfect equilibrium" of the national and the modern, the absence of "excess," suggested that it was *An Outdoor Overture*, not Santórsola's puffed-up homage to Hellenism, that laid greater claim to classical values. One critic explicitly identified these traits as "universal":

> Those who went to the Auditorium yesterday with the idea that they were going to hear typical American music, with jazz and folkloric themes, certainly came away disappointed, for those characteristics are always absent in the music of the celebrated U.S. composer. [Copland's] music is universal, with symphonic vigor and agile rhythms, and with ideas that unfold with great finesse and inspiration.[59]

Copland also appeared live on the radio and taped a broadcast "for later use." With Tosar, he stopped by the Instituto Interamericano de Musicología, which Copland had visited in 1941 and where Lange showed them ("naively," Copland thought) ten bound volumes of his own correspondence, ready to take their place in the annals of history. Copland also met Enrique Casal Chapí, a Spanish expatriate who had organized concerts for Republican troops during the Spanish Civil War and whom Copland found "an intelligent man." Upon visiting Hugo Balzo and his "pals," Copland sensed the passage of time, as they all struck him as considerably older.[60] Ambassador Briggs lavished plenty of attention on the composer. Besides attending the Copland-Santórsola concert, he arranged a special dinner for the composer at the Jockey Club, along with the tedious reception at the embassy mentioned in chapter 1, after which Copland "fell into bed, pooped."

## "Everyone seems genuinely glad to see me again"

For Buenos Aires, Copland had envisioned a "festival of American music" with shared conducting responsibilities along the lines of the Montevideo program. He hoped it could take place at the Colón.[61] As detailed below, however, any such plan had to take politics into account. In 1947 Perón was at the height of his power, having won the presidency, partly because he stood up to the United States. Still resentful of Argentina's conduct during the war, Assistant Secretary of State for Latin America Spruille Braden (the "good Yale man" Marshall Bartholomew described) attempted to derail the election by compiling a "blue book" of Perón's presumed Nazi connections. Peronists not only ridiculed these machinations but crafted a pithy campaign slogan—¿Braden o Perón?—all the more embarrassing to the United States when Perón handily won. As president, Perón gave impassioned speeches from the balcony of the Casa Rosada, the official residence. He also promulgated legislation on behalf of the poor and the working class while his equally charismatic wife, Eva Duarte (Evita), headed a charitable foundation bearing her name. Like Castro and Ginastera, intellectual elites opposed Perón, in part for his restriction of civil liberties but also for his administration's profoundly anti-intellectual tone.[62] Yet no viable alternative to Perón arose.[63]

Copland and the State Department thus had to tread with care, as did Ginastera, who now replaced Paz as Copland's main musical contact in Buenos Aires. Copland arrived in Buenos Aires on 22 October. After dining with Ginastera and his wife, Mercedes de Toro, he swung by José María Castro's bookstore, where Ficher, Gianneo, and several others were waiting. "In all, a very pleasant reunion," Copland wrote, adding, "everyone seems genuinely glad to see me again."[64]

Besides two concerts, Copland presented six radio broadcasts and seven lectures. He also gave a book signing and was made first honorary member of the newly founded League of Composers (Liga de Compositores).[65] Among the composers he visited was Sergio de Castro, whom he had met briefly in Montevideo in 1941 and who was now based in Buenos Aires. With his "child-like innocence and purity of spirit," Castro reminded Copland of Israel Citkowitz. Copland also wrote in his diary, "We [the State Department] should take a chance on [Castro]," evidently forgetting that he was no longer obliged to identify candidates to visit the United States.[66] Among Ginastera's students, Copland met Pía Sebastiani, a fine pianist who had premiered her own piano concerto at age eighteen under Albert Wolff. (Copland's former conducting teacher spent some of the war years in Buenos Aires.)[67] Copland hit it off especially well with twenty-six-year-old Astor Piazzolla. He was struck by the fact that this "simpático, warm-natured Italian boy" had spent ten years in Brooklyn: in the early 1930s, Piazzolla, then twelve and fluent in English, served informally as a personal assistant to Argentine movie idol Carlos Gardel (then shooting at the Paramount studios in Queens) by helping Gardel shop at Macy's and Gimbel's and running other errands throughout the city.[68] In 1947 Piazzolla had yet to revolutionize tango, although he was already performing at the Tango Bar on Corrientes, a famously lively street in Buenos Aires. Copland examined one of Piazzolla's piano sonatas but "didn't get much of an impression," as he noted in his diary.

Music by the Spanish expatriate Julián Bautista was disappointing. "Stuff expertly done but shows no originality whatsoever," Copland concluded, after studying Bautista's clarinet concerto and the song cycle *Catro poemas galegos* (Four Gallegan Poems) for soprano and chamber ensemble. "I always feel like commiserating with the composers like Bautista," he despaired. "They come so close to having everything it takes—and then their music adds nothing."[69] On 14 November, Copland's birthday, he "fell out of bed" to attend a choral concert featuring two choruses by Ficher. His opinion remained unchanged: "The man just isn't smart enough," Copland insisted.[70] At an embassy reception, Copland met members of "the Jewish contingent," as he put it.[71] They included the Dresden-born Michael Gielen, then studying with another émigré composer Erwin Leuchter, a champion of Schoenberg's music. Gielen, later a respected conductor, struck Copland as "very German . . . with a thorough German competence."[72] On another occasion, Copland heard a string quartet by Guillermo Graetzer, which he judged "good but not remarkable." He was much taken with the Argentine writer and activist María Rosa Oliver, who assisted Spanish expatriates and founded a support organization for women. A wheelchair user, she attended Copland's impromptu talk for the American Women's Club on 12 November, "which made it worthwhile," as he wrote. By his own account, he gave a "terrible lecture" at the Colegio Libre de Estudios Superiores: having nothing prepared in Spanish, he was reduced to reading from his book. "Should never have agreed to do it," he sighed.[73]

Copland's presentation at the Sociedad Hebraica (Hebrew Society), where he showed the Spanish-language version of *The Cummington Story*, was far more successful.[74] It was an apt choice for that public, which surely saw itself in the film. Like the refugees in Cummington, they too were professionals with a healthy appreciation for high culture. They too had felt the pain of separation from their home countries and knew the sting of prejudice, of being perceived as Other. Cummington, however, enjoyed the benefits of wise leadership: Copland's audience could observe Reverend Sangree's quiet persuasion—enhanced by the subtleties of Copland's score—in an environment where freedom of expression thrived. These values seemed worlds away from Peronist Argentina.

In a press conference at the Continental Hotel, Copland opined on the state of contemporary music, which the English-language Buenos Aires daily the *Standard* covered under the headline "Anti-Revolutionary Trend in Music." Copland pointed out that "composers following in the footsteps of Schönberg, 'father' of atonality, have little following today," a point more than one Argentine composer would have challenged. "Music has become much less dissonant," Copland explained, to which the reporter added, "It has been noticed that Copland's music has mellowed in style and become less dependent on the striking and shocking."[75] This comment effectively set the stage for hearing Copland's latest works.

## "Naiveté, sentimentality, sweetness, and realism"

In planning his concert at the Colón, Copland relied on Albert B. Franklin, the embassy's cultural officer, who tipped him off on the musical ramifications of the political situation. Juan José Castro, he explained, could not collaborate in a U.S.-Argentine program, since any members of the Colón Orchestra playing under him would lose their jobs. Franklin also discouraged Copland from sharing conducting duties with the less-controversial Ginastera or even programming one of his works.[76] Copland decided to focus on his own music: besides *An Outdoor Overture*, favorably received in 1941, he would offer the Third Symphony, *Appalachian Spring*, and *Lincoln Portrait*. Rehearsals went well enough. "Everybody on their best behavior," Copland reported, although he found the orchestra "not very smart about rhythms"; he also observed that "the percussion section leers." Still, at the final rehearsal everyone "sat up and played."[77]

Had Copland's music really "mellowed in style," as the reporter from the *Standard* proposed? *Lincoln Portrait*, with the actor Jorge Dantón as speaker, held a few surprises. Author and critic Jorge D'Urbano, already familiar with the work, commented, "This mug-shot of Lincoln has never struck me as especially gratifying," adding, "at least in Spanish, the effect is quite dreadful."[78] Journalists for Peronist papers had no such compunctions, however. One, employed by the rabidly anti-U.S. tabloid *Democracia*, set aside its usual antagonism to the United States to applaud *Lincoln Portrait*, finding it a "magnificent, clear, and expressive evocation."[79] Why did an unabashedly *peronista* paper praise a work that so blatantly symbolized the United States? In fact, Perón's working-class base venerated its leader much the way the U.S. public did Lincoln. Like Lincoln, Perón was born far from the metropolis and rose to power from outsider status ("He was born in Kentucky; raised in Indiana, and lived in Illinois"). Like Lincoln, Perón was hailed as an emancipator ("As I would not be a slave, I would not be a master"). Like Lincoln, Perón took ownership of the spoken word: "This is what he said" (Eso fué lo que dijo); "This is what Abraham Lincoln said" (Eso fué lo que dijo Abraham Lincoln); or simply, "He said" (Dijo). The exhortations in *Lincoln Portrait* on toil, work, and bread, moreover, would have been entirely at home in any of the rousing speeches Perón routinely delivered from the balcony of the Casa Rosada. Thus Abraham Lincoln found one more signification in Peronist Argentina. It was not one the State Department would have encouraged.

As for the Third Symphony, some critics perceived it as an "intellectual work," with one calling it "pure music" (the opposite of "un arte dirigido").[80] Ginastera, however, heard "freshness," that favorite Good Neighbor trope.[81] Writing in *Sur*, he took pains to clarify that this quality resulted not from eclecticism but was "molded through long years of diverse influences and transformed by [Copland's] exceptional critical faculty" and "forceful personality."[82] As in 1941 *An Outdoor Overture* conveyed "freshness" as did *Appalachian Spring*, which another critic called one of Copland's "freshest" orchestral works.[83]

D'Urbano elaborated on all these themes. But he also considered *Appalachian Spring* according to the composer's own criteria, including Copland's desire to reach a broad public. This D'Urbano deemed an act of valor:

> Copland's action on behalf of an ideal of popular music (that is, a means of direct expression for the great public) and that resonates with the U.S. public, is open to dispute but it marks him as a creator of forms and methods that are rather original. He has had the courage, if you like, to express himself freely on a topic that, of all others, is by far the most ungrateful for any artist.... I have the impression that the resistance occasioned by such a declaration is stronger than any that might arise to any other aesthetic statement.[84]

Key here was folklore, a cornerstone of Copland's aesthetic. As D'Urbano saw it, Copland may have initially been drawn to folklore but ultimately surpassed its basic requirements. After all, D'Urbano observed, "one is inclined to say ... that Copland is a folkloric composer, an affirmation that Copland defends himself from with plenty of energy." Yet, D'Urbano continued, "a good part of [Copland's] *oeuvre* extracts elements beyond . . . American folklore, [drawing instead on] solid and realistic American life, which is rather different. Few musical works can express with greater clarity that complex of naiveté, sentimentality, sweetness, and realism that characterizes the U.S. social environment more than *Appalachian Spring*."[85]

However much naiveté, sentimentality, and sweetness conveyed the "realism" of U.S. sensibility, they were hardly markers of the avant-garde. Although D'Urbano was skeptical of Copland's aesthetic orientation, he respected the skill with which the composer realized it. No mere *pompier*—an epithet Stravinsky called on more than once to decry blind adherence to hackneyed tradition—Copland instead tapped the essence of U.S. character. None of these distinctions bothered the public, however. As Copland reported in his diary, after the concert the green room was "packed."

## "Being a pompier is no crime"

Copland's second concert was a retrospective organized by the Liga de Compositores. The program consisted of the *Two Pieces* for string quartet, the Piano Variations, the Sonata for Violin and Piano, and the two-piano version of *Danzón cubano*, which Copland played with the Argentine pianist Raúl Spivak. Some participants were from the Jewish refugee community, such as violinist Ljerko Spiller, "a fine artist" in Copland's estimation and with whom he performed the Violin Sonata. "The house was packed," Copland wrote in his diary, adding, "I apparently have a public here."

Critics paid the *Two Pieces* little heed but wrote at length of the Piano Variations, with their "audacious, astringent, and laconic language" (su lenguaje audaz, áspero y lacónico).[86] Another explained that "the controversial Variations" dated from a period when Copland had grappled with modernism, a problem he "seized with an iron grip," thus rewarding an elite public able to grasp the work's nuances.[87] Among these elites was Carlos Suffern, whom Copland had met in 1941. Suffern marveled over the Variations: "supremely intelligent, aggressive at times, always logical" and with a "peremptory language [that] imposes itself rather than attracts," all features of Copland's modernist "manner," the "most interesting" stage of Copland's evolution.[88] That stage, however, proved ephemeral.

In describing the works that followed, Suffern was by no means pleased. Whereas several critics admired the "great simplicity" of the Violin Sonata, for Suffern, the work amounted to little more than a "pretty bakery cake" (bonita torta de confitería) with "sugary effusions" and misguided attempts at humor: "we would have taken it for a joke . . . but we saw that this was not the author's intention and were perplexed."[89] The humor of *Danzón cubano*—its syncopations, unexpected silences, and stretches of static harmonies—left Suffern cold: the work was but a cliché, one on which models such as Milhaud's *Saudades do Brasil* could be blamed. Suffern also dug into the pieces performed at the Colón. In *Appalachian Spring*, he heard movie music, "a silent documentary, in very nice Technicolor" with "lovely landscapes, regional songs, from the mountains, complete with pulpit and morning stars"; similarly, *Lincoln Portrait* was "a movie dubbed in Spanish" thanks to which, Suffern quips, "we now know that the great Lincoln was one meter 90 centimeters tall."[90]

What prompted Copland to compose this way? Suffern finds the answer in the Third Symphony. Like Ginastera, Suffern considers the work a "portrait of the composer." Yet the composer's personality is anything but "forceful." Rather, the symphony reveals that Copland, a "cultivated man" with "eclectic tastes," likes "beautiful songs . . . if they happen to be melodious and sentimental, all the better, with a touch of ingenuousness, even of the commonplace, and to digest them without commotion, as befits a good and inoffensive man."[91] Suffern also pinpoints Copland's "eclectic tastes," observing, "It is said that Mr. Copland is very fond of the cinema . . . of listening to the best music, none more than Russian: some Prokofiev; a great deal of Stravinsky—he adores *Petruchka*—a fair amount of Mussorgsky, whose prelude to *Khovantchina* he can't get out of his head: how that rosy sky and clarinet melody pursue him! Furtively, he likes to wink at the bearded old deadpan Rimsky Korsakov."[92]

Much the way Paz rattled off the welter of influences in Ginastera's *Sinfonía porteña*, Suffern catalogues in the Third Symphony "dancelike turns in Bartók" (los giros danzables de Bartok), the "burnished trumpet-calls" (trompetas espejeantes) of Mahler, "melodic passages of Puccini" (pasajes melodiosos de Puccini), and even isolated "*fleurs de mal* of Schönberg (flores del mal de Schömberg [sic]). Copland's "absorbing rather than creative" nature betrays a profound inner conflict, however. "Pity that Tchaikovsky is so romantic!" exclaims Suffern. "Because [Copland] likes him quite a lot and can't come out and say so."[93] Another liability is Copland's sensitivity to the market. He admires Shostakovich "not so much for his music but for his conformity and ad-worthiness"; just like his Russian counterpart, Copland recognizes that "music, although it comes from intelligence, is also a product and must adjust itself to the best prices in the marketplace."[94] In short, Copland rejected the forward path opened up by the aggressively modernist Piano Variations to "adjust" to a confused, eclectic style conscious of its marketability.

Yet Suffern concludes on a bizarrely empathetic note. Acknowledging Copland's inner conflict and inability to reconcile himself with the trends of his own day, the composer, nonetheless, manages to sustain himself. His particular case of modernism manqué need not diminish our regard, however, for as Suffern acknowledges, "at the end of the day, being a pompier is no crime."

> After the concert, Mr. Copland, a man of simple habits, goes back home, reads a few lines from various music magazines, an article from the *Reader's Digest* to stay up to date, writes down his impressions, drinks his glass of milk, and then goes to bed and sleeps like an angel. . . . If only he could at least compose what he feels, if he could repeat without blushing the songs, the beautiful melodies, the persistent harmonies, the thick timbres that he hears and loves! But he can't, he's a radical musician. What a dilemma! "To be."[95]

Concluding his plaint with the words "To be" (in English), Suffern leaves little doubt over the weight of modernity on Copland's shoulders. A clean-cut Hamlet poring over the *Reader's Digest* while sipping a wholesome glass of milk to assuage his existential doubts, Copland feels all too keenly the chasm between elite and popular tastes. At the same time, he instinctively mirrors "that complex of naiveté, sentimentality, sweetness, and realism" of U.S. life, as D'Urbano had put it. Suffern thus hints at the question that would bedevil Copland in the coming years: how to respond to the slings and arrows of a burgeoning aesthetic crisis.

Shortly before leaving Argentina, Copland was interviewed by Enrique Valenti Ferro, a powerful figure in musical life. Having encouraged regional identity during the Good Neighbor period, Copland now alluded to universalism, declaring that "the work of Argentine composers is quite similar to that of composers from my own country. We have the same problems with regard to folkloric melodies and rhythms as in Argentina. This doesn't happen, by contrast, in Brazil, so rich in these elements. In Argentina and the United States, however, we possess greater possibilities to develop music of universal significance."[96]

Bypassing the fact that many Argentine composers were hardly preoccupied with the "problem" of folklore, Copland added a handwritten note, which reads: "In the culture of her composers Argentine music has the possibility of developing an *oeuvre* of universal significance." For Copland, whether a market-driven eclectic, pompier, purveyor of Technicolor music, or representative of fresh-faced U.S. dynamism, folklore still lay at the heart of that future. Now, however, it no longer symbolized Pan American solidarity but suggested the concept of One World, however tentatively Copland upheld it.

## "I would not be surprised"

Copland spent about a month in Rio de Janeiro. He prepared a concert with the Orquestra Sinfônica Brasileira (OSB), appeared on the radio, gave fifteen lectures, and met various composers. He also worked on a concerto for the clarinetist Benny Goodman, one of several classical works the King of Swing commissioned.[97] These activities and others are discussed below.

Copland's Brazilian diary leaves his biographers a mystery that has yet to be unraveled: he refers repeatedly to an individual identified only as "H," with whom he enjoyed several outings in Rio. (Variants such as "HR," "Heitor," and "Heitor R" arise in similar contexts.) In private writings, Copland generally used initials only for intimates, referring to his lover Victor Kraft, for example, with whom he had recently begun living in a house on the Hudson River, as "V."[98] For acquaintances and professional associates, Copland uses surnames (Villa-Lobos) or in the case of long names, an abbreviation, as with "E. d. C" for Eleazar de Carvalho, the conductor of the OSB. When Copland arrived in Brazil in 1947, "HR" met him at the airport, obviously someone he previously knew even though no "HR" appears in the 1941 diaries. Copland also mentions an "Heitor" who accompanied him to the movies on 23 September. On another occasion, he saw "H. (Bolero)," with "Bolero" either a nickname or a way of distinguishing more than one "H." Nor is it clear that "HR," "Heitor," and "H. (Bolero)" are the same "H" who enjoyed at least six outings with Copland, including a taxi dance (a dance with paid partners). Which "H" "dropped in and stayed on" on 4 September? If "H" is a romantic interest, Copland keeps that detail confidential.[99]

To work on the concerto, Copland needed short-term lodgings with a piano. The search for housing required a good many phone calls, for which he probably needed the help of a Portuguese-speaking acquaintance. After two weeks of looking, Copland moved to the neighborhood of Santa Teresa, where Carvalho had tracked down an apartment with a piano. A week later, by which time Copland had given three lectures, he was wondering "if the trip makes any sense." "No composing so far—difficult to settle down to it. Rio distracting—piano lousy," he added.[100] Yet shortly thereafter, Copland wrote Bernstein from his hard-won digs in Santa Teresa. "I've just begun work on the B[enny] Goodman piece," he reported. "Had a hard time getting settled—but now I'm installed in my own ap't on top of one of those fantastic hills right plunk in the center of Rio, with a picture postcard view . . . from the bedroom window. It's fun to lean out the window with a friend and admire the view."[101]

It was in that charmed environment that Copland scored the concerto for solo clarinet, harp, piano, and strings. The work consists of two movements, slow-fast, played attacca. Despite having renounced jazz, he enlivened the work with a Charleston rhythm, a swung version of one principal theme, and boogie-woogie. In Brazil, Copland was asked if his new piece would be influenced by his surroundings. Would he write a piece titled, say, *Impressões brasileiras* (Brazilian Impressions)? the host of Radio Roquete Pinto asked Copland during one broadcast. More than once, Copland would reply, "Since I am writing [the concerto] here, I would not be surprised if some Brazilian rhythms got into it."[102] Years later, he mentioned that a "phrase from a currently popular Brazilian tune, heard . . . in Rio, became imbedded in the secondary material in F major" (i.e., mm. 297 ff.).[103] Yet the wide, chromatically altered intervals of that section are barely singable, and no scholar has satisfactorily identified any Brazilian tune in the concerto.[104]

If an actual tune remains a mystery, other elements of the piece hint at Brazilian influence. One is the cadenza. It may well be a souvenir of the "command performance" arranged by Lôbo, the journalist who covered the diplomats' party at the Palácio Quitandinha. On 12 September in a private home, Copland heard the singer, guitarist, and composer Dorival Caymmi and the flute player Benedito Lacerda; also present was Alfredo da Rocha Viana Filho, the saxophonist, flutist, and arranger known as Pixinguinha.[105] Caymmi was known for his ballads and sambas celebrating the Brazilian state of Bahia, and Lacerda specialized in the *choro*, the genre that Villa-Lobos so exuberantly distorted.[106] Copland was especially delighted with Caymmi, the composer of one of his favorite sambas, "Você já foi à Bahia?" (You've Been to Bahia?) and who sang "beautifully with his guitar."[107] Copland also found Lacerda "wonderfully inventive."[108] "Highly pleased" with this musical extravaganza, Copland stayed out until 3:00 A.M. and later, in one of his more substantive diary entries, reflected on the music. Its "real interest," he wrote, was the "melodic invention, the large curve of the line, the unequal and unexpected phrase lengths (especially fine), and the rapidity of the execution in sixteenth-notes, staccato tunes." In fact, the cadenza of the clarinet concerto crystallizes these impressions. Copland alternately truncates and lengthens motives, manipulating "unequal and unexpected phrase lengths," a "sixteenth-note" theme (after the fermata) that maintains intact the "large curve of the line" and the "melodic invention," and a "staccato tune," spanning a generous register and marked "incisive," which leads to a glissando-like passage that invites the orchestra to rejoin.[109]

One other Brazilian element surfaces in the concerto. *Saudade* is the Portuguese term for a condition more acute than "nostalgia" and more profound than "memory." It has no easy translation in English. The aching first movement, in which harp and plucked lower strings introduce a lonely melody sung by the solo clarinet, so moved U.S. composer and author Phillip Ramey that he asked Copland point-blank if its "bittersweet lyricism" reflected the isolation of being a homosexual in the first half of the twentieth century, when homosexuals were not only branded as "deviants" but subject to arrest in the United States. "You might have something there," the famously circumspect Copland replied.[110] It is not too much to imagine Copland drawing inspiration for the concerto from a variety of sources: Brazilian music, the "picture-postcard" vistas of Rio de Janeiro seen from his window in Santa Teresa in the company of his unidentified friend, and his own experience as a gay man in a hostile environment.

## Defending U.S. Culture

Besides his scheduled lectures, Copland volunteered to give two additional talks. One, "The Role of Culture in the United States," took place at the IBEU's International Relations Club. He discussed photographer Alfred Stieglitz, the Group Theatre, and Paul Rosenfeld and in handwritten notes listed additional talking points. These included "the usual idea" that "America pays for its commercial development by its lack of cultural development" and "our fear" that "ideas of America will be derived solely from Hollywood movies, Time magazine, jazz recordings or even: Hemingway."[111] Copland, who admired Hemingway's "The Old Man and the Sea" (he later scored the television series *The World of Nick Adams*, based on the same author's short stories) nonetheless seems to have recognized Hemingway's dubious status at mid-century. Critics inveighed with growing intensity against middlebrow culture, increasingly associated with the newly prosperous—but shockingly uncultivated—middle class of postwar consumerism, with Hemingway often a whipping boy.[112] Russell Lymes, for example, attacked those "writers and painters who set out to be serious men, as Hemingway did, but then become popular in being taken up by the middlebrows" whereas Dwight Macdonald declared Hemingway "intellectually . . . a Philistine," given the "baby talk" of his characters.[113]

Copland's lecture was thus another point of conflict between his own practices and his State Department mission. The "good and inoffensive man" with less than daring tastes was expected to showcase a high level of intellectual achievement in the United States even as he increasingly risked association with the "middlebrows" himself, justly or not. Copland's other "extra" lecture better reflected his priorities. A benefit for a local hospital, his talk would have to "make itself accessible and agreeable to a public interested in music yet without deep knowledge of it," as the organizers requested.[114] He gladly accommodated: after showing clips of *Our Town* and *The Cummington Story*, Copland explained the challenges of film scoring, enhanced with demonstrations at the piano. A large and enthusiastic public attended.[115]

Some of Copland's scheduled lectures did not always attract the desired numbers, however. His first, at the Ministry of Education, drew what he deemed "a smallish crowd" of about 150, leading him to wonder if "maybe people aren't that interested in the subject matter." The audience for his second lecture was even smaller.[116] "One of two reasons," Copland reasoned: "bad publicity or no interest in the subject matter."[117] Thanks to a flurry of press announcements in the main Rio papers, bigger audiences attended his multilecture series, "A Panorama of American Music." It lived up to its name: Copland took 1776 as a starting point and concluded with the younger generation of the present. Some composers he identified as "primitives." William Billings, for example, was "a short, ugly man, with a shriveled arm and a bad leg—a man with no sense of touch, but with an invincible desire to write music," a description we would avoid today but which Copland likely intended as a metaphor for the challenges of birthright and culture U.S. composers have confronted.[118] Copland devoted almost an entire lecture to Ives, portraying him as a strong individual misunderstood by his contemporaries.

No longer, however, did Copland take pains to draw links between the music of North and South America or offer an alternative to Europe. Rather, he looked to a musical future in which Europe and the Americas would be equal players. "Of one thing I am convinced," he declared. "The history of music in the future [will] be written from both sides of the Atlantic."[119] Copland's lectures also established a bond between himself and critic Eurico Nogueira França, once a composition student of Villa-Lobos's and who covered these lectures in a series of long, detailed essays for the *Correio da Manhã*.[120] Nogueira França would become one of Copland's most enthusiastic supporters in Brazil.

Copland also became acquainted with the IBEU library. Having described record libraries as "urgent" during the war, he remained convinced of their importance in the postwar. He considered, for example, the ordinary Brazilian curious about U.S. music and eager to enjoy it at home through a lending library, a system not generally in place in Latin America at that time and which he recognized would be complicated to implement. On 10 October Copland attended a meeting to formulate ways to increase circulation in the IBEU library. Although he realized that "no precedent in Rio for borrowing books or music in our sense" existed (nor open stacks), he persisted in his belief that libraries and cultural centers were models for international relations.[121]

## A "mess!"

On 13 September the OSB performed Copland's Third Symphony on an all-U.S. program that also included William Schuman's *Symphony for Strings* and Peter Menin's *Folk Overture*. The still-new orchestra had given its inaugural concert on 11 July 1940 under its first music director, the Jewish émigré Eugen Szenkar (Jenö Szenkár), who was about to step down.[122] Now the ensemble was trying out guest conductors: earlier in his stay, Copland heard the orchestra under the direction of Jaroslav Krombholc (of the former Czechoslovakia), which to Copland sounded "about like the Rochester Symphony playing on tour."[123] Carvalho, recently returned from the Berkshire Music Center, would conduct the all-U.S. program. A photograph in the Rio de Janeiro daily *A Manhã* showed him joining hands with Koussevitzky and Bernstein under the headline "A Resounding Victory for the Artistic Vocation"; other press reports gave similarly glowing accounts.[124] After sitting in on several rehearsals, Copland found Carvalho "very heavy-handed" and at the concert itself, only the slow movement of the Shuman and the first movement of the Third Symphony "came out O.K."[125] The rest, he believed, was "a mess!"[126]

Some critics agreed. Among them was Marc Berkowitz, who wrote in the English-language *Brazil Herald* that Carvalho's gestures were so "flashy, almost 'sporty'" that one "felt tempted to shout 'Goal!'"[127] Despite the rough performance, the Third Symphony confirmed Copland's recent turn toward a "mellow" style. Registering not eclecticism, as critics in the United States had done, Berkowitz simply noted that "those who expected a daringly modern composition, filled with dissonances and strange instrumental combinations" must have found the symphony "rather tame" given its "frankly melodious" music, "serene undertone," and "almost romantic" lyricism.[128] Another critic, Ademar Nóbrega, compared the symphony to the Piano Sonata, so unenthusiastically received in 1941, and observed that of the two compositions, the Third Symphony was "without a doubt, the more human work, deeply felt, more a work of art."[129] Some overlooked these essentially romantic qualities and heard national identity in Copland's score, citing the usual Good Neighbor–era tropes of "evident vitality," "vibrant atmosphere," "vigor," and a "reserve of energy" typical of "Yankees."[130] Nogueira França also linked the symphony to the composer's native land: Copland's music, with its "overwhelming emotional color," displayed "a healthy vitality, a decided optimism, an affirmation of faith in life itself . . . the traits of U.S. character."[131]

One outlier had another take, however. Writing for the newspaper *Brasil Portugal* under the evocative pseudonym "Oberon," this critic dissected the entire program from "the land of Uncle Sam." Schuman, for example, was a "Yankee composer" with "an agitated soul" whereas Menin's "street songs" suggested the "turbulent" life of New York City through "barbaric motives." The Third Symphony, filled with "the racket of machines" (barulho das máquinas), only aggrandized these tendencies. "Oberon" even suspected Copland's motives. As he wrote: "And to end this 'mechanical concert,' we heard Symphony No. 3 by Aaron Coplan [sic] . . . forty-five minutes of an attempt to be understood by a public with a Latin soul. We do not know why a man as talented and inspired as Coplan [sic], who succeeds in writing beautiful and expressive themes within that symphonic confusion, as in the Andantino quasi molto, insists on pulling one over on the public."[132] In proposing that Copland suppressed his natural inclination to give free rein to heartfelt emotions "Oberon" may have disagreed with some of his Brazilian colleagues. But he saw eye to eye with Suffern, who also targeted Copland's conflict between modernity and feeling ("Pity that Tchaikovsky is so romantic! Because [Copland] likes him quite a lot and can't come out and say so"). "Oberon," however, was less convinced of Copland's inner turmoil.

At a Brazilian-U.S. concert organized by the Brazilian Chamber Music Society on 26 September, the public heard Copland's Sonata for Violin and Piano, *Two Pieces* for string quartet, *Vitebsk*, and Piston's tonally restless Piano Trio no. 1. Launching the program were two atonal works by young Brazilians: a Sonata for Oboe by Cláudio Santoro, whom Copland had briefly met in 1941, and a Duo for Flute and Violin by César Guerra-Peixe, both studying twelve-tone music with Koellreutter. Neither work seems to have made much of an impression on critics. Nogueira França, for example, focused on the "versatile Copland," whether in the "neoclassicism" of the Violin Sonata or the "pathos-filled accents" of *Vitebsk*. He saw these ostensibly conflicting approaches not as eclectic but as an expression of "personal modernism" (modernismo pessoal), which enabled Copland deftly to negotiate different styles.[133] Berkowitz, delighted that the Chamber Music Society programmed only contemporary music ("still quite a risky thing" in Brazil), again alerted diehard modernists to Copland's "personal" modernism. Apropos the Violin Sonata, for example, he observed that "those who expected to hear a very arid modern sonata must have been quite astonished to discover that modern music could also be melodious, at moments even lyrical."[134]

## "If men will but keep the Peace"

In Rio de Janeiro alone, Copland appeared on the radio eight times. He tested a variety of presentation formats. On one occasion, he read aloud five pages of commentary in Portuguese. "Not a pleasant sensation!" he later acknowledged in his diary. More frequently, he prepared brief remarks in English and had them translated so that he could simply read a few lines. Folksy expressions were difficult to capture: when Copland described Marc Blitzstein's *Airborne Symphony* as "fresh off the griddle," the translator rendered it as "a real novelty" (realmente uma novidade). Perhaps Copland was amused when, scripted to sound like a radio host, he would close a program by saying, "I'll be back again next Monday evening at 10:30 P.M. to present another program of modern music by contemporary North American composers. Until then, this is Aaron Copland wishing you a very pleasant good evening."[135] Sometimes he would respond in Spanish to questions the host posed in Portuguese. This was the procedure for one broadcast, in which Copland gave a rather long history lesson that covered Billings, Francis Hopkinson, *Dwight's Journal*, and George Bristow, along with more recent composers. One host, Shelia Ivert of Radio Roquete Pinto, interviewed him in English.[136]

Copland also planned the nuts and bolts of each broadcast, calculating the timing of whatever works he planned to play. In his notes for Radio Gazeta, he listed timings for Billings ("When Jesus Wept"), Charles Griffes (*Poem for Flute and Orchestra*), Harris (Third Symphony), Piston (Prelude and Allegro, Finale of Sinfonietta), Samuel Barber (*Capricorn Concerto*), Bernstein (*Jeremiah Symphony*), and Copland (Piano Sonata).[137] Since many programs went on the air at 10 P.M. or later (his 12 September broadcast on Radio Nacional ran from 11:15 to midnight), he had to be resilient. Copland was also a good sport: one station experimented with a "technological enhancement" that caused *Appalachian Spring* to fade unexpectedly into *The Cat and the Mouse*, a bizarre juxtaposition that he likely took in stride.

Broadcasts were a platform for Copland to stake out his positions. On Radio Nacional, he told listeners that you can like both Wagner and Brahms "for the simple reason that they are different but equally valid musical expressions."[138]

In other words, doctrinaire, black-and-white thinking leads nowhere, an apt position for one frequently bruised by charges of eclecticism. On the same program, Copland devoted thirty minutes to the *Airborne Symphony*. Scored for tenor and baritone soloists, male chorus, orchestra, and speaker, the work had recently premiered under Bernstein with Orson Welles as the speaker (identified in Blitzstein's score as the Monitor).[139] Copland, who likely concentrated on the instrumental portions of this text-heavy composition, explained to his listeners that Blitzstein treated the subject of flight from two equally intriguing perspectives: flight was a thing of beauty and a triumph of science but also a tool for annihilation. In other words, human thought and action were shaped by a spectrum of possibilities rather than simplistic dichotomies. Copland also asked his listeners to weigh the costs and benefits of "man's conquest of the air—the terrible role that conquest played in the second World War—and the magnificent role it can play in the world of the future—if men will but keep the Peace."

Sometimes Copland echoed Good Neighborly rhetoric in his broadcasts. He told Ivert that Brazil was "the first [South American] country to develop a music of its own" due to "the rich folklore which is at [the] disposal of [its] composers," adding "other countries are not so fortunate."[140] Yet more often than not he backed away from regionalism. No longer seeking solidarity among "we musicians of the Americas," Copland consistently took Europe into account, reiterating the point made in his lectures, namely, that in the future, "the history of music will be written from both sides of the Atlantic."

## "Dullards" Making Music

Union with Europe was all well and good—except when it came to Brazilians writing twelve-tone music. Copland soon recognized that Koellreutter and his class were an increasingly formidable presence both in Rio and São Paulo.[141] In November 1946 they founded Música Viva, a new music society based in Rio that advocated "all that favors the birth and the growth of the new," as declared in its manifesto.[142] Its members held that music should reflect social reality but eschew national identity, given the danger posed by "sentiments of nationalist superiority . . . egocentric and individualist currents."[143] Música Viva spread its message through a journal, radio broadcasts, and in the presumably identity-neutral twelve-tone compositions of its members.

In Rio, Copland saw Koellreutter at a recital by Ernesto Xancó, principal cellist in the OSB, who was playing a work by Santoro.[144] Although Copland didn't immediately recognize him (an "embarrassing moment"), Koellreutter greeted him and told him of his growing class of pupils. Besides Santoro and Guerra-Peixe, other students included Eunice Katunda, Edino Krieger, and Heitor Alimonda (brother of the violinist Altéia, who had studied at the Berkshire Music Center in summer 1941 through the scholarship Copland established).[145] All were adherents of Música Viva. "[Koellreutter] seems to have all the young pupils," Copland wrote in his diary, adding, "one doesn't know whether to trust his judgments or not."[146] Later he commented, "My impression is that Koellreutter has managed to corner the market in young composers. Only around him do they seem to get stimulation. . . . A curious situation in which Brazilians are being brought up by a typical German."[147] More than once, he wrote of "twelve-toners," suggesting a herd mentality. He found further evidence of this tendency on 5 October, when he attended a concert by Koellreutter's students. "The master and the pupils make a singularly humorless impression," Copland complained. "The main reaction was one of dullness. No apparent care for the type of melody worked with. All emphasis on counterpoint."[148] After another concert of Koellreutter's class, in São Paulo, he exclaimed, "Dreary!"[149]

There were exceptions. Copland admired the music of Eunice Katunda, a fine pianist who would later study conducting with Hermann Scherchen.[150] (Her *Homenagem a Schoenberg* was performed at the 1950 ISCM in Brussels, the only work from Latin America performed at that festival.)[151] Copland also thought well of Guerra-Peixe, then thirty-three, and Edino Krieger, then nineteen, both of whom visited him in his hotel on 1 September, bringing scores.[152] The twenty-eight-year-old Santoro continued to impress Copland. Since 1941 Santoro had composed the non-twelve tone *Impressões de uma fundição de aço* (Impressions of a Steel Factory), an homage to 1920s machine music, and which took second prize in an OSB composition contest.[153] In 1947 Copland felt that Santoro was "certainly the most gifted young composer around" and "on his way to something."[154] On that point, Copland was correct.

Copland reflected in his diary that "Koellreutter can't harm gifted young people but he certainly can encourage a lot of dullards to imagine they are composers!" He was similarly irritated by Música Viva, with its "many pious pronouncements about . . . the social role of music. All very German and rather jejune. I can't warm up to Koellreutter's personality."[155] The fact that Copland devoted so much space in his diary to the "curious situation" of a "typical German" in Brazil confirms that whatever collaboration between Europe and the Americas he envisioned and whatever the promise of One World may have portended, he was nonetheless captive to essentialism.

## Other Brazilian Composers

Copland visited several of the composers he had met in 1941, including Villa-Lobos. Copland found him as much the grand old man of Brazilian music as ever: after lunching with Villa-Lobos on 22 September and listening to a lot of inflated talk, he wrote, "[I] should think that he would get awfully bored with himself!"[156] Copland also visited Oscar Lorenzo Fernândez, who invited him to his home for *feijoada*, a weighty meal of black beans served over rice with pork ingredients, such as feet and tail, once the food of enslaved Africans.[157] After the leisurely meal, Fernândez showed Copland two symphonies and several piano pieces, which Copland described as "honest music of no particular originality." Later in his stay, Copland attended an all-Fernândez concert of orchestral music that included "Batuque," from Fernândez's suite *Reisado do pastoreio* (Epiphany of the Shepherds) of 1930. This appealing work, filled with off-beat accents, strident brass, and jostling melodic fragments, had launched the 1940 goodwill tour by Toscanini and the NBC Symphony, who recorded it in Constitution Hall on the eve of departure; Bernstein later programmed it on his Young People's Concerts. Copland allowed that Fernândez's works based on Brazilian folk rhythms were "highly effective" but found the rest of his music "basically dull and non-exportable."[158]

Copland's visit with Francisco Mignone was perplexing. Since 1941 the Brazilian composer had produced relatively little, due in part to health problems and excessive work at the radio station. Copland believed self-sabotage was also to blame, finding Mignone "strangely dissatisfied." He showed Copland his *Quatro Amazônicos* (Four Amazon Sketches) for small orchestra, which Copland thought "looked pretty good."[159] Copland also met Luiz Cosme, who had studied at the Cincinnati Conservatory in the late twenties. At an OSB concert Copland heard his *Oração a Teiniaguá* (Prayer to Teiniaguá) and *Falação de Anhanga-Pita* (Death of Anhanga-Pita). Finding his "ideas and orchestration pleasant," Copland believed Cosme "should write more."[160] He was already studying twelve-tone technique, which came to fruition in his *O lambe-lambe* (The Strolling Photographer), a ballet that combines serialism with Afro-Brazilian music and elements of the choro, and which Scherchen performed in Zurich the following year.[161]

Among Copland's social activities were a luncheon to hear the U.S. journalist Eric Sevareid speak on foreign policy, a dinner with Burle Marx, and a visit with the Brazilian neorealist painter Cândido Portinari, several of whose murals grace the Hispanic Reading Room at the Library of Congress. In his limited leisure time, Copland took in local sights, such as the Quinta Boa Vista park and the

Church of Our Lady of Penha, where visitors ascend more than three hundred steps to the main sanctuary. He also heard an all-Beethoven recital by the German pianist Wilhelm Backhaus. "Honest piano playing of the old school" with "no glamourizing," he commented in his diary. "Very pleasurable."[162]

## The Search for "Freshness"

Copland spent four days in São Paulo. Besides appearing on the radio and lecturing on *Our Town* and *The Cummington Story*, he spoke to the press. When one interviewer asked his opinion of Brazilian popular music, Copland recalled the late-night "command performance" in Rio, remarking that Caymmi, Lacerda, and Pixinguinha were "all splendid."[163] Of course, he visited Guarnieri, whom he had not seen since 1943. Both composers were honored in a chamber concert of their works at the Teatro Municipal on 19 October, featuring the Sonata for Violin and Piano, which Copland and Altéia Alimonda performed, along with *Two Pieces* and Copland's Piano Variations. One critic tagged Copland's gift for expressivity, remarking that the Violin Sonata was "noble in its conception, sober in its melodic eloquence, and impregnated with undeniable poetry and profound lyricism."[164] The second half consisted of Guarnieri's Second String Quartet, which had earned him a prize awarded by RCA Victor and the Chamber Music Society of Washington, DC. For Copland, this "good, playable" work was rich in "definite Gershwin touches," which Guarnieri told him were "pure Brazilian," a coincidence Copland attributed to "the Negro influence on both our musics."[165] Such sounds were far from the abstractions of Koellreutter and his "twelve-toners."

On 20 October Copland left São Paulo for Porto Alegre, where Consul William Belton met him at the airport. His lecture the next day attracted around two hundred people, who were swallowed up in the thousand-seat Teatro São Pedro.[166] At a reception, he met Villa-Lobos's mischievous translator Érico Veríssimo, whose 1945 book on Brazilian literature Copland had read. (This was probably *Brazilian Literature: An Outline*.) It contains valuable lessons about essentialism: Veríssimo cautions that just as "we Brazilians must not sum up the United States as a country of Babbitts, gangsters, greedy businessmen, and wailing crooners" neither should U.S. Americans "go on thinking that Brazil is just a land of lazy Indians, poisonous snakes, and lush palm trees."[167] Copland also spent a morning at the local conservatory, where he found a "very nice atmosphere." There he met a young composer, Ênio Freitas e Castro, who showed Copland some of his works, which Copland believed evinced "a certain freshness."[168]

Then he went on to Salvador de Bahia, capital of Bahia state, in whose historic center tourists can see both the cathedral and the *pelourinho* (pillory), where enslaved Africans were flogged.[169] The U.S. consul escorted Copland to a reception, where according to Copland, "everyone seemed awed—and silent. No local composer of any account."[170] He made a positive impression, however.[171] Musician and sometime reporter Paulo Jatobá, who wrote up Copland's visit in the local press, reiterated his own belief that the United States was more than a country of "Babbitts and gangsters," recalling previous visitors such as Orson Welles or the Disney team, whose 1944 cartoon feature *The Three Caballeros* (a follow-up to *Saludos Amigos!*) contains a Bahian sequence. Jatobá even wondered if Copland, a "representative of U.S. civilization," had first learned of Bahia through Walt Disney. He took pains to clarify for his readers the basis for this surprising question: "Instead of isolating himself at home and writing his symphonies, concertos, sonatas, and [other music] within classical forms," Jatobá explained, "Aaron Copland went out in search of other fields of musical performance, and found . . . vast possibilities for sonic undertakings."[172]

In talking to the Bahian press, Copland waxed enthusiastic about Brazilian popular music and another "command performance" was arranged on his behalf. The next evening, after hosting a short program on Radio Sociedade de Bahia, he was treated to an on-air homage.[173] First were some Bahian songs and then a demonstration of *capoeira*, the physically demanding yet playful dance-fight traditionally performed by enslaved Africans with music of the *bateria*: a tall, wooden hand drum (*atabaque*), a scraper (*reco-reco*), and the *berimbau*, a hollowed-out gourd attached to a musical bow made of wood and enhanced with a small shaker (*caxixi*).[174] Copland could observe at close range several capoeiristas, taking in the sweep of their devastating kicks and jubilant cartwheels while listening to the "fascinating sounds" of the berimbau, an instrument completely unfamiliar to him.[175] He found it all "really fresh."[176]

After the homage, Copland went to a nightclub with Marshall Levins, a Brooklynite living in Bahia, and heard a "remarkably good" jazz band. The next morning, Levins took him to the seventeenth-century Benedictine monastery São Salvador da Bahia de Todos os Santos, prompting Copland to reflect that monastic life "seemed appealing, particularly if one removed the religious claptrap."[177] Copland then endured a lunch at the local Rotary Club—"dull!" he complained to his diary—followed by his lecture on the music of the United States and yet another musical tribute to his visit, this one more modest. "Incredible performance by a lady singer doing 'Because' in English," Copland wrote. (It was probably the 1902 song by Guy d'Hardelot.) After the "lady singer" concluded, the director's son performed Blues no. 2.

The climax, however, was a late-night *candomblé* ceremony, again, arranged especially for Copland. Like its Cuban counterpart *santería*, candomblé syncretizes African religious expression (forbidden during slavery) with images of Catholic saints, which assumed new identities in Latin America.[178] Amid steady drumming, call-and-response singing, and dance, worshippers may undergo possession, manifested in paroxysms of shaking or more tranquil states of trance. In observing this sacred ritual, Copland found the "noise of the drums . . . intolerable in that room," although he recognized that he was the only one discomfited. The drumming itself, "quite complex," interested him, as did the worshippers' response to it. He was struck, for example, by the "long trance-like dance, definitely related to the drumming" performed by a young woman who, after dancing in a circle with other women, underwent possession. For Copland, she was *"l'élue"* (the protagonist of Stravinsky's *Rite of Spring*). She "takes a fit, self-induced but real," he observed, as did a boy of about seven. If Copland was skeptical about the authenticity of the proceedings—how could he verify if a trance was "self-induced" or not?—he was impressed by the participants' sincerity. He wrote, "I was taken by the faces of the onlookers—complete identification, it was. In retrospect it was quite impossible to separate the spectacle aspect from the 'magical' one . . . During the trance-like dancing a woman and a man looked on, really worried about what harm the *élue* is liable to do to herself. When the spirit is exorcised they are led away or so it seemed."[179] Suspicious of "religious claptrap" and nonobservant himself but respectful of the human dimension of spiritual rituals, Copland was far more open-minded about candomblé than he was about Brazilian twelve-toners.

The next stop was Recife, capital of Pernambuco state, and whose numerous rivers, small islands, and some fifty bridges have earned it the moniker "the Venice of Brazil." Copland had his usual obligations: upon arriving at the airport, he was escorted directly to the radio station, where he talked for fifteen minutes and played two excerpts from *Rodeo*. The same day, he gave a lecture at the IBEU, "at their request" in English, which he imagined was useful to Brazilians seeking to improve their foreign-language skills. After the lecture, yet another homage commenced. This time, it was a "four-ring circus," as Copland described it—at considerable length—in his diary.[180]

"Act 1," he began. "Some guitar players played delicate choros and modinhas" (the latter a quietly introspective song in Portuguese). "Act 2"was devoted to *frevo*, a dance-march accompanied by band instruments and relatively new in 1947: the term, based on the verb "ferver" (to boil), had first appeared in a musical context only thirty years earlier, in a Recife newspaper.[181] The ensemble consists of E-flat and B-flat clarinets, trumpets, saxophones, valve trombones, bass tubas, various types of drums, and tambourine. As Copland wrote, "the army band—twenty-eight men—sat in a room and played . . . in a very fine way." Further, although "based on march rhythms, the frevo has a style of its own," whether in the dialogues between winds and brass or "upward-thrusting phrases and sudden single accented notes," like any good jazz band. "All this energy," Copland noted, "was being produced by a group of men with deadpan faces, on army pay and army rations." "Act 3"took the celebration outdoors, such that "the whole neighborhood turned out to watch":

> Down the street came a Clube Carnevalesco—one of the four rival clubs in the town. Everyone dressed to kill, their club band playing frevos, followed by the dancers of frevo. . . . To dance the frevo is no cinch. You do it alone, and it seems to consist of a continual falling backwards, the idea being to come as near to falling on your ear as possible. . . . So many dancers deliberately crowded into one small space while dancing down the street! So that added to the hazards of falling are the hazards of bumping your fellow dancers. . . . No one ever had a fight about it. Recife in carnival time is said to outrival Rio and I can well believe it.

"Act 4" was a maracatú. Already familiar with Mignone's evocation of the African processional dance, Copland had some inkling of the genre's significance. It was especially associated with Recife: an account from 1666 explains that several hundred Africans went to mass in Recife, "elected a king and queen [and] marched through the streets singing and reciting verses they themselves improvised."[182] In Recife, Copland heard eight drummers. Amazed, he wrote, "I've never seen such energy pounded onto drumheads—simply phenomenal. The gestures of playing are quite different—each stroke starts from above the head. (Much dissatisfaction among the players because one instrument was missing, though how we could have heard it is a mystery.) Gradually was able to distinguish a basic 4/4 rhythm, but boy, what they packed into that 4/4." He also commented on the general atmosphere. "Everyone," he remarked, wore "outlandish finery, like a Harlem drag." We can't be sure if Copland likened the maracatú to a Harlem drag ball because of its African roots or because of the unfettered abandon of such balls, often held in gay bars, where White men sometimes blackened their faces and competed for the most flamboyant costumes. "I'd like to go back to Recife," he concluded. "For a twelve-hour stay I think I did pretty well."

From that peak moment, however, the rest of Copland's activities were routine, even tedious. In Fortaleza, the capital of Ceará state, he had to sit through a "god-awful concert" given by a Mr. Wiggington that he "couldn't get out of."[183] At the IBEU in Fortaleza, he lectured to a good-sized crowd but noted their "provincial reactions," rather a surprising reaction for Copland. Seeing "not much point" to having stopped in Fortaleza, he was up at 4:30 A.M. on 24 November to board a 6:00 A.M. plane for Belém, the capital of the state of Pará and known as the gateway to the Amazon. He found it "pleasant to be in a town without official tie-up for a change."[184] After a delay of several hours, he finally took off for San Juan, Puerto Rico. From his seat in first class, he observed that the Amazon River looked "amazingly long."[185] After arriving in San Juan, he connected to Miami and then to Washington, DC, for his post-trip debriefing. He broke up the flight by chatting with the pilot in the cockpit, who was "reading a magazine!" as Copland anxiously noted. A State Department employee met him at the airport, and once in his hotel, Copland telephoned Kraft. On 27 November, in the final diary entry of his 1947 cultural diplomacy tour, he wrote in exuberant capital letters "THANKSGIVING DAY!"

## "A truer picture"

Although the State Department had instructed Copland to submit separate statements on all the institutions he visited, he wrote only a single report.[186] It ran fifteen pages, one-third of the document he had turned in six years earlier.[187] Again, he offers recommendations. First, the State Department should send more classical composers to Latin America. As in 1941 a trip such as his was still "an isolated phenomenon." Copland proposed Barber and Piston, both of whom "talk French and Italian." He also listed a few candidates for visits to the United States: José María Castro, Gianneo, Fernândez, Guerra-Peixe, and Hurtado. Also as in 1941 Copland urged the State Department to exploit radio more fully, noting that he had found a reasonable selection of U.S. classical music only in Rio de Janeiro and hardly any in the State Department centers.

Copland had high praise for the State Department, however. "The Department of State's visiting professor program cannot be measured as to value," he declared, but "the mere presence of an American scholar or artist in the midst of the cultural life of a Latin-American city is in itself important. It gives stimulus . . . as well as adding to the prestige of America in a sphere where it is most needed."[188] Copland added, "The State Department is to be congratulated on the level of cooperation extended by the staffs in the Embassies, Consulates and cultural missions with whom I came in contact."[189] Copland also went public with his gratitude. His remarks appeared in the State Department newsletter *The Record*.[190] In addition, he acknowledged the State Department in "Composer's Report on Music in South America," an article on his travels that appeared in the *New York Times*. In it, he declared,

> The Department of State sponsored my tour through these provincial capitals under its program of exchanging professors in various fields with Latin American countries.... Our government cooperates with local persons to maintain cultural centers for the teaching of English and the spreading of comprehensive ideas about our civilization. The cultural centers lend books, phonograph recordings, printed music [and] organize lectures and concerts and in general help give the local citizen a truer picture of the United States than can be obtained from a Hollywood movie.[191]

To be sure, Copland no longer invoked Western Hemisphere identity; rather, "our civilization" (that of the United States) was now the selling point of cultural diplomacy.

Yet in his *New York Times* piece Copland emphasized not his experiences in major cities but the "vast possibilities for sonic undertakings" he had encountered elsewhere. After a full paragraph on Caymmi, whom he described as "Brazil's finest composer in the popular style," Copland devoted a paragraph to the berimbau and two paragraphs to the frevo. About a third of his piece treats "serious music." "The situation as regards [U.S.] music seemed somewhat better than it was six years ago, when I first visited Latin America," he explained, adding "people in the know are familiar at least with the names, if not with the music, of our composers." Yet the overall picture was uneven. Live performances of U.S. music rarely take place, except occasionally on concerts by the Argentine League of Composers or the Brazilian Chamber Music Society. Because orchestras lacked parts, "the 'big public' gets its contact with American music solely through recordings." Gershwin remained a favorite but Barber, Harris, Piston, and Schuman were only gradually becoming known; further, Copland exclaimed, "no one seemed ever to have heard of Leonard Bernstein!" As for up-and-coming Latin American composers, Copland found plenty of natural talent but few good teachers, especially in Rio de Janeiro. (He was likely thinking of Koellreutter and his "dullards.") To be sure, Copland told his readers that "music of the French school no longer exerts so exclusive and pervasive an influence on the younger generation as was true of their elders," an encouraging sign, in his view. Copland addressed those "elders" in a single sentence, observing simply, "Composers like Camargo Guarnieri, Luis Gianneo, José María Castro, and Alberto Ginastera are worth anybody's time."

Members of that younger generation soon showed up at the Berkshire Center. The three winners of the Empire Tractor Contest were Pía Sebastiani of Argentina, Edino Krieger of Brazil, and Tosar, now a Berkshire Center habitué. (Piazzolla, who entered his *Rapsodia porteña* for orchestra, was evidently crushed not to have been chosen.)[192] During summer 1948 they worked with Copland and Milhaud. All three went on to successful careers. Sebastiani, for example, enrolled at the Paris Conservatory; then, even while employed as a cultural attaché in Belgium and France, she managed to concertize in prestigious venues such as London's Wigmore Hall. (While in the Berkshires, she had the honor of being mentioned in the *Boston Globe* for her uncertainty as to the ingredients of a peanut butter sandwich.)[193] Krieger worked with Peter Menin at the Juilliard School and in 1949 conducted the New York Philharmonic before moving to London, where he studied with Lennox Berkeley and worked for the BBC.[194] Tosar spent two years in Paris studying at the Conservatoire and the École Normale, later receiving commissions from the Koussevitzky and Fromm Foundations. Another young composer Copland had found promising was Santoro, as noted. He had the good fortune to receive a Guggenheim Fellowship to study with Schoenberg in Los Angeles. Unfortunately, he was unable to use it: upon applying for a visa, he refused to renounce his links with communism, which he then embraced, and his application was denied.[195] As discussed in chapter 10, there could hardly have been a worse time for a young communist to visit the United States.

\* \* \*

Before Copland's next visit to Latin America, the governing board of the Pan American Union drafted a charter for the "improvement and strengthening of the Pan-American system," which in 1948 resulted in the Organization of American States (OAS).[196] The charter emphasized the "unilateral character" of the Monroe Doctrine, giving the United States more latitude than many Latin Americans would have liked.[197] Two years later the U.S. statesman and anticommunist strategist George Kennan visited Latin America. In a confidential, thirty-five page report to Secretary of State Dean Acheson that effectively shreds Good Neighborly ideals, Kennan relies on racism and imperialism in equal measure:

It seems to me unlikely there could be any other region of the earth in which nature and human behavior could have combined to produce a more unhappy and hopeless background for the conduct of human life than in Latin America. ... The large scale importation of Negro slave elements into considerable parts of the Spanish and other colonial empires, and the extensive intermarriage of all these elements, produced other unfortunate results. . . . The shadow of a tremendous helplessness and impotence falls today over most of the Latin American world.

In fact, according to Kennan, it was Latin America that now threatened the hemisphere. "Most of the people who go by the name of 'communist' in Latin America are a somewhat different species than in Europe," he wrote. Moreover, "because their Latin American character inclines them to individualism, to indiscipline and to a personalized, rather than doctrinaire, approach to their responsibilities as communists, they sometimes have little resemblance to the highly disciplined communists of Europe."[198] In other words, Latin Americans were so inept that even communism was beyond them. The following chapter explores the shifting political winds Copland encountered at home, their effects on his career, and aesthetic polemics in the Americas.

# 10
# Shifting Ground and the Crisis of Modernism

In 1948 Cláudio Santoro found himself in Europe. Having impressed Copland as "the most gifted young composer around," the young Brazilian decided to study with Boulanger after the United States denied him a visa.[1] In May he traveled to Prague, where he served as a delegate to the Second International Congress of Composers and Music Critics along with others from Eastern Bloc and Western countries with a significant communist presence. Like them, he faced a dilemma. The Soviet cultural commissar Andrei Zhdanov had declared the avant-garde an enemy of the state, and folk-tinged "music of the people" was in the ascendancy. Nonetheless, established composers East and West—including Santoro himself—were writing atonal and twelve-tone works.[2] Perhaps not surprisingly, his address to the Prague conference, "The Problem of the Contemporary Composer and his Social Position," was less than decisive. In the aftermath of the congress, however, Santoro decided there could be no middle ground: one was either a "Zhdanoviano or a charlatan," he roundly declared.[3] Further, as he opined in the Brazilian journal *Fundamentos*, "today, in the socialist countries, the people are in power and the revolutionary class is in the front line"; moreover, "the artist who marches alongside the proletariat must . . . never be on the side of the latest bourgeois trend."[4]

These ideas were essentially the same as those Copland espoused in the 1930s, when he called music "a powerful weapon in the class struggle." That was also the decade in which Copland had discovered the power of folk music in "serious" composition. This chapter contextualizes some of the ways in which these statements and others came back to haunt him at the same time that he struggled with the crisis of modernism then unfolding throughout the Americas.

## Folklore and the "musically unwashed"

Much has been written on the so-called Cold War style of composition, whose adherents pursued objectivity and abstraction, often through twelve-tone technique.[5] As it turned out, certain buzzwords associated with this aesthetic shift also figured in the vocabulary of U.S.–Latin American relations.[6] Two such terms were "progress" and "modernization." "Progress" emerged in the economic plan crafted for Latin America by the administration of President John F. Kennedy, the Alliance for Progress (AFP). It went hand-in-hand with the widely accepted "modernization theory," which held that if Latin America could only modernize, problems of resource distribution would disappear, and dictatorships would be less likely to take hold.[7] Neither progress nor modernization unfolded as foreseen. The AFP's strong anticommunist component was recognized in Latin America early on (as were the gains for U.S. business that resulted from its implementation), and it was the more "modernized" countries that ultimately suffered the most brutal military dictatorships, such as Brazil (1964), Chile (1973), and Argentina (1976).[8]

Another buzzword doing double duty in politics and music was "nationalism." In Cold War geopolitical discourse, nationalism could be equated with either anti-U.S. sentiment or communism. In 1952 journalist Herbert L. Matthews wrote that the sort of nationalism taking hold in Latin America was "a destructive and above all . . . 'anti-Yanqui' force."[9] In a 1953 speech, President Dwight D. Eisenhower proposed that those American nations that had overcome "the temptations of heedless nationalism" were the least vulnerable to "forces threatening this continent" (i.e., the Soviets).[10] Another was "freedom," the prerogative of Western countries. It manifested itself in the Congress for Cultural Freedom, a CIA-backed concatenation of offices, publications, and events that promoted an anticommunist agenda in the name of freedom.[11] The concept of "the individual," who embodied the benefits of liberal society, spilled over into aesthetic discourse. In Henry Cowell and Sidney Cowell's 1955 biography of Ives, for example, the composer is no longer a mere eccentric but a Cold War individualist, representing "a bastion of autonomy . . . free of ideology" (i.e., the United States).[12] Scientific objectivity, on which liberal society rested, also became an aesthetic ideal, as composers engaged in the presumably neutral investigation of tones, rhythms, and mathematical relationships, like research scientists unencumbered by political dogma. Rather than "learn from the masses," composers largely avoided the broad public, given what they saw as its limited capacity for intellectual engagement. The title of Milton Babbitt's infamously titled essay "Who Cares If You Listen?" sums up this position.[13]

"Folklore," which would brand a composer as a nationalist, had little place in this scheme. Some U.S. music critics assaulted the "innumerable 'Hoe-Downs,' 'Hayrides,' 'Square Dances' and the like" of the 1930s and 1940s, all "within the listening grasp ... of the musically unwashed."[14] Others conflated folklore with communism, which they blamed for the "disastrous vulgarization of cultural life."[15] Yet despite much talk of artistic freedom in the West, artists were often unconcerned with actual *human* freedom—of religion, assembly, political affiliation—caring mainly that their communist brethren were free to be "cubists, surrealists, dodecaphonists and existentialists."[16] Paradoxically, composers willingly sacrificed "freedom" to submit to the rigid strictures of twelve-tone music. Neither were creative minds "free" to paint landscapes or quote folk-tunes in tonal symphonies.[17] In a striking reversal of Arthur Loesser's exhortation to the OIAA Music Committee, compositions showcasing Latin American folklore were "definitely *out*."

## U.S. Cultural Diplomacy and the HUAC

When Copland returned from Latin America, he took on new assignments, including another "speaker piece." *Preamble for a Solemn Occasion* marked the first anniversary of the United Nations' Universal Declaration of Human Rights, drafted by a committee that Eleanor Roosevelt chaired. Copland's text consisted of portions of the preamble to the United Nations charter. He enhanced its affirmations ("faith in fundamental human rights ... of all nations large and small") with percussion, hymn-like utterances in the woodwinds, and his "brassy choirs." The premiere took place on 10 December 1949, with Bernstein conducting and the British actor Laurence Olivier as speaker. Likely, Copland believed that the State Department would continue promoting these ideals unhindered.[18] His optimism was short lived.

Emboldened by Executive Order 9835 (sometimes called the "Loyalty Order"), public figures stridently compared U.S. "decency" with Soviet "depravity."[19] Shallow binaries—"civilized and primitive, modern and backwards, white and nonwhite, masculine and effeminate, mature and juvenile, normal and perverse"—made it uncommonly easy to tell who was a virtuous U.S. American and who was not.[20] They also fed into a host of resentments the political right had long harbored: Roosevelt's so-called sellout at Yalta, Mao Zedong's victory, and the Soviet testing of the atom bomb in August 1949. All enabled the ascent of U.S. Senator Joseph McCarthy of Wisconsin, who made the State Department a principal target. Besides distrusting "foreign ideologies" on principle, McCarthy and his followers considered diplomats bookish, Eastern-establishment types. Not only that, but because these effete individuals engaged in negotiation in lieu of more "macho" behaviors, many were believed to be gay. These "cookie pushers in striped pants," as some called them, were therefore unduly susceptible to blackmail, especially by the Soviets, "strong believers in homosexuality," as Representative Arthur L. Miller, Republican of Nebraska claimed.[21]

Various State Department employees, gay and straight, had already aroused suspicion.[22] Some were directly involved with Latin America, such as Sumner Welles, Undersecretary of State under Roosevelt and a principal adviser on Latin America. In 1943 he had to resign for propositioning a Black Pullman porter.[23] Welles, in turn, had protected Laurence Duggan, chief of the Latin American Division and instrumental in establishing the Division of Cultural Relations. (As noted, during the 1930s Duggan became interested in Soviet culture, like many of his generation.) After Welles departed, Duggan went to work for the Institute of International Education in New York City but remained a target of investigation. In December 1948 the forty-three-year-old Duggan was found dead outside the institute, presumably having fallen from his office on the sixteenth floor. To be sure, many suspected foul play.[24] Another defender of U.S.–Latin American cultural diplomacy caught up in the tentacles of the House Un-American Activities Committee (HUAC) was Gustavo Durán. Having helped coordinate Copland's 1941 trip and various other Pan Americanist musical projects, Durán was now accused of jeopardizing relations with Latin America through alleged communist ties, largely because of his role in the Spanish Civil War. Charges against him were ultimately dropped, but as late as 1995, conservative William F. Buckley called that decision "a shabby expedient," a conclusion he reached on the flimsiest of evidence.[25]

## "The only way to have a friend"

No scholar has ever found that the HUAC explicitly targeted Copland's homosexuality. Mainly, it was his activities in the 1930s that raised suspicions. Yet his travels on behalf of the State Department to Latin America also caught McCarthy's eye, as the senator himself would reveal.[26] Neither did it help

## 10. Shifting Ground and the Crisis of Modernism

that after his 1947 trip Copland went public with his praise for the State Department. None of those statements, however, resounded as forcefully as his speech in March 1949 before the Cultural and Scientific Conference for World Peace at New York's Waldorf Astoria Hotel. One conference guest who attracted a good bit of media attention was Shostakovich; U.S. musical figures included Bernstein, Blitzstein, and Downes; also attending were Charlie Chaplin, Albert Einstein, Lillian Hellman, Arthur Miller, several professors, and members of the clergy.[27] On 4 April 1949, in a story titled "Red Visitors Cause Rumpus," *Life* magazine told of proceedings "dominated by intellectuals who fellow-travel the Communist line." Accompanying the article were two pages of photographs of these individuals, including Copland, all in mug-shot style to enhance the danger they posed.

It was before the fine arts panel of the conference, moderated by Downes, that Copland delivered his speech "Effect of the Cold War on the Artist in the U.S."[28] It proved one of the strongest "performances" of his career. In it, he gave cultural diplomacy pride of place. Identifying himself as "a democratic American artist, with no political affiliations of any kind, and not at all interested in doctrinaire communism," Copland decried the "attitude that has turned the very word 'Peace' into a dirty word," one abetted by fanaticism that, if left unchecked, would result in another world war. He also assailed the repression and incrimination then prevailing in the United States, with its stultifying impact on artists. Central to this mindset was the tendency to think in terms of binaries:

> There is a concerted effort on the part of press and radio to convince the American people that nothing remains for us to do but make a choice between two diametrically opposed systems of thought. We are being taught to think in neat little categories—in terms of blacks and whites, East and West, Communism and the Profit System.

Copland reflected further:

> In historical perspective, one can find plenty of precedent for that kind of schematized thinking, however wrong it may be. During the religious wars of the 16th century it must have seemed inconceivable that Catholicism and Protestantism could ever peacefully coexist in the same world. . . . In the field of music there was a time when you were supposed to make up your mind between Richard Wagner and Johannes Brahms. To find some virtue in both was considered impossible. Nowadays a similar cleavage is supposed to exist between the mass-appeal music of Shostakovich and the musical radicalism of Schoenberg.[29]

As we've seen, Copland had criticized mindless partisanship in Latin America, telling his Brazilian radio audience that Wagner and Brahms were "different but equally valid musical expressions" and that listening to both would ensure an open mind. Also on Brazilian radio, he had expounded on the need for peace—far from a dirty word. Copland thus gave the opposite message of that promoted at Prague, according to which one was either a Zhdanoviano or a charlatan, period.

Copland also discussed specifics of cultural diplomacy. He mentioned the committee, organized in 1944 by "our own State Department," through which he and Downes helped enhance cultural relations between the United States and the Soviet Union, then allied in the global struggle against fascism, along with an American-Soviet friendship committee. He also chided the Soviet mindset apropos cultural diplomacy: "I have no wish to embarrass our distinguished composer-guest from the Soviet Union, but I see no reason why we should not point out in a friendly way that all cultural interchange becomes difficult, if not impossible, when all foreign music from the West is condemned in advance." As he explained,

> It makes no more sense to reject the artistic findings of a foreign composer than it would to reject the scientific investigations of a foreigner.... If a brilliant new composing talent emerges from Tadjikistan we all want to hear what his music is like. If a bright new composing star rises out of the Kentucky Mountain area we think the Russian people should know what his music is like.

Copland also noted recent progress in U.S. music, remarking that not long ago, "we had very little music that was worth exportation" but that in recent years "we have earned the right to have American music heard throughout the world." It was thanks to cultural diplomacy, of course, that the world had experienced these achievements. With humankind in the grip of the Cold War, an "invention of men who have lost faith—men who are intent upon stirring up fears and hatreds that can only breed destruction," the future was bleak, however. In a dramatic conclusion, Copland invoked President Roosevelt, visionary-in-chief of Good Neighbor–era cultural diplomacy.[30] Roosevelt, Copland insisted, "understood these principles well" and recognized that "[peaceful] relations via the arts only symbolize what should be taking place on the plane of international politics." As a parting shot, Copland quoted Roosevelt's final inaugural speech, delivered on 20 January 1945, days after the Soviet army wrested Warsaw from German control. Copland reminded his audience how on that occasion, the thirty-second president argued, "'We cannot live alone

## 10. Shifting Ground and the Crisis of Modernism

at peace." Rather, Roosevelt affirmed, we have "learned to be citizens of the world, members of the human community,'" adding, "We learned the simple truth, as Emerson said, that the 'only way to have a friend is to be one.'" Thus Copland closed his speech by upholding one of the cornerstones of international relations and which his own practice of cultural diplomacy confirmed.

Throughout the speech, Copland's personal idealism was much in evidence.[31] Certainly he had been a "friend" to many a Latin American composer, including those whose aesthetic views differed from his. He also spoke from his firsthand experience of the demands cultural diplomacy exacted. In this remarkable utterance, free of "diffident half-charitableness" and "softness of critical fibre," Copland made several strategic errors, however, which the HUAC could easily flag. Not the least of these was praising Roosevelt, whom the red-baiters were eager to malign. Also, by reiterating his enthusiasm for the work of the State Department, Copland allied himself with its phalanx of snooty, hyperintellectual diplomats. In addition, he dared to censure binaristic thinking, the mindset that found such favor with McCarthy and his followers. Finally, he exalted the thing McCarthy most feared: receptivity to practices other than one's own. Having tortuously defended an often murky middle ground in aesthetic debate, Copland now expressed himself with perfect clarity on civil liberties and world peace. All the while, accusations flew and lives around him were shattered.

A "rumpus-causing red," Copland suffered additional mishaps. Months after the peace conference, Thomson printed in his weekly column for the *New York Herald Tribune* some remarks by Schoenberg, resident in the United States since 1933. "You cannot force real artists to descend to the lowest possible standards to give up morals, character and sincerity, to avoid presentation of new ideas," Schoenberg argued. "Even Stalin cannot succeed and Aaron Copland even less."[32] Irritated, Copland hastened to draw a distinction between himself and the Soviet dictator, which Thomson also printed. "Unlike Stalin," Copland declared, "I have no desire to suppress [Schoenberg's] music! True, I can't be listed as an apostle and propagandizer for twelve-tone music; but since when is that a crime?"[33] Eventually the two composers reconciled by letter.[34] But new troubles followed. In 1950 a right-wing organization accused Copland of plagiarism in his Oscar-winning film score *The Heiress* (1949), and shortly thereafter he earned a substantial entry in that Who's Who of suspected communists, *Red Channels: The Report of Communist Influence in Radio and Television*.[35] Soon the Federal Bureau of Investigation (FBI) opened a file on the composer.[36]

## A "state of flux and semiconfusion"

During the 1951–52 academic year, Copland presented his Charles Eliot Norton lectures at Harvard, later published as *Music and Imagination*. Far less decisively than in his speech for the peace conference, he considered the musical fallout from ongoing aesthetic and political polemics. Surely with his exchange with Schoenberg in mind, Copland observed that "sharply drawn" lines between twelve-tone composers and populists had entered the world of musical composition. In lecture 4, for example, "Tradition and Innovation in Recent European Music," he told his Harvard audience that the twelve-tone composer is constantly aware that "whether he likes it or not he is writing *against* a vocal and militant [communist] opposition." However much Copland longed to occupy a middle ground, he had come to realize that inhabitants of that elusive space lived in "a state of flux and semiconfusion, trying to avoid the brickbats from both parties."[37] Clearly he was talking about himself.

Copland also drew on his experience in Latin America. In lecture 5, "Musical Imagination in the Americas," he focused on folklore, a less than felicitous subject for one unwilling to be typecast as a "purveyor of Americana." Wrestling with the meaning of musical identity, he echoed some precepts he had tested in the Latin American press. Expressing identity musically (he refers to a "profile") required three conditions. As Copland explained, "First, the composer must be part of a nation that has a profile of its own—that is the most important; second, the composer must have in his background some sense of musical culture and, if possible, a basis in folk or popular art; and third, a superstructure of organized musical activities must exist—that is, to some extent, at least—at the service of the native composer."[38] Indeed, Copland equivocated. The composer "must" have a grounding in folk or popular art but only "if possible"; likewise, Copland asserted that a musical superstructure "must exist" but adds the empty caveat "that is, to some extent, at least." In discussing folklore in "serious musical composition," he vaguely mentions both cowboy songs and the "certain order of feeling" a hymn tune conveys.[39] Might all these elements contribute to the "Western hemisphere music" Copland once so avidly promoted? He now confessed uncertainty, acknowledging that many "disapprove heartily" of searching for American qualities in contemporary music. As a point of reference, he took the music of Sessions, Piston, and Barber:

> There is a universalist ideal, exemplified by their symphonies and chamber music, that belittles the nationalistic note. I myself lose patience with the . . .

music lover who wants [U.S.] music to be all new, brand-new, absolutely different. They forget that we are, as Waldo Frank put it, the "grave of Europe," by which I suppose he meant to suggest that we have inherited everything they are and know; and we shall have to absorb it and make it completely our own before we can hope for unadulterated American creation. Nevertheless, there is a deep psychological need to look for present signs of that creation. I know this to be true from my own reactions to the music of other nations. . . . [W]e inevitably look for the note that makes it characteristically itself. This attitude may be narrow and wrong, but it is an unpremeditated reaction which rightfully should be balanced by the realization that not all the composers of any country are to be limited to an obviously indigenous expression.[40]

Whatever the pitfalls of universalism, the values Copland once held dear were now potentially "narrow and wrong." Yet he makes an exception for Latin America. He asserts, for example, that Chávez and Revueltas are of a piece with Mexico's ancient past: even those lacking prior knowledge of "the Amerindian man," Copland insists, can infer "his essential nature" from the music of these two composers.[41] In heeding the "deep psychological need" a musical identity could satisfy, were the two Mexican composers "limited to an obviously indigenous expression"? Even in what seems to be Copland's valedictory to "Western hemisphere music," he vacillates. Lacking a "triumphant resolution," Copland raised questions while ultimately hedging his bets.[42]

## A "perverted stance"?

Latin American musicians also grappled with identity. Having introduced twelve-tone music in Brazil, Koellreutter now had to defend himself. In November 1950 Guarnieri, whose music Copland found "profoundly Brazilian," penned a fiery "Open Letter to the Musicians and Critics of Brazil" (Carta aberta aos músicos e críticos do Brasil). It appeared in the respected newspaper *O Estado de São Paulo* and was reprinted in four other national papers. Nothing less than the well-being of the nation was at stake:

> To import and attempt to adapt in Brazil this caricature of music, this method of anti-artistic and cerebral contortionism, one that has nothing in common with the specific characteristics of our national musical temperament, destined to nourish the perverted stance taken by a small elite of paranoid initiates, constitutes a crime against the nation! . . . Like monkeys, like vulgar imitators, like creatures without principles [some composers] prefer to import and copy harmful, foreign novelties, thus pretending to be "original," "modern," and "advanced."[43]

Guarnieri's letter made waves throughout Latin America. Chávez, for example, tersely observed that "in a certain South American country there is no shortage of those who claim that composers who [write twelve-tone music] are traitors to their country."[44] Koellreutter, clearly the object of Guarnieri's rant, responded with a courteous invitation to a debate. When Guarnieri refused, Koellreutter proposed a roundtable discussion. Again, Guarnieri turned him down. Perhaps something told him that Koellreutter, with his formidable intellect, would be the victor in any battle of wits.[45] At that point, Koellreutter had little choice. Weeks later, the perpetrator of this "crime against the nation" and leader of "monkeys" wrote his own open letter, warning against "exalted nationalism" and the blindness it incurs, essentially echoing Música Viva's precepts. For good measure, Koellreutter called Guarnieri's arguments "incompetent and tendentious," which, in light of Guarnieri's rhetorical excesses, was an easy case to make.[46]

Increasingly, Guarnieri found himself in the minority in Latin America's classical music circles.[47] Roque Cordero, a member of the Berkshire "class of '46," confronted the crisis in contemporary music in his vigorous essay "¿Nacionalismo versus dodecafonismo?" Bent on "progress," Cordero was unmoved by the needs of the uneducated listener. He assaulted his readers with a barrage of rhetorical questions. "Should the fact that men of today compose in the language of their time be considered illogical?" Cordero demanded. "Why censure the composer of today who expresses his musical thought through the technical advances of recent decades?"[48] In short, ignoring twelve-tone technique and specialized training can only denigrate "the progress achieved by the artistic disciplines over the years."[49] In Mexico City, Rodolfo Halffter began writing twelve-tone music, and Chávez introduced the works of Luigi Dallapiccola to his public, just as he had done for Copland twenty-five years earlier. In Santiago, the composer and violist Eduardo Maturana completed several twelve-tone works, prior to the arrival of Fré Focke, a Dutch émigré serialist who studied with Anton Webern.[50] Stefan (Esteban) Eitler of Austria, who also emigrated to the Chilean capital, promoted twelve-tone composition as well. With their new Chilean colleagues, these emigrés founded the new-music organization Tonus in 1952. In Lima, Andrés Sas began writing twelve-tone works, as did Rodolfo Holzmann, who in 1941 had shown Copland only "light and pleasant music." In 1958 the first electroacoustic studio in Latin America attached to an academic institution, the Estudio de Fonología, was established at the Universidad de Buenos Aires. Its director was Francisco Kröpfl, a former student of Paz; another Argentine studio would follow in

Córdoba along with others elsewhere in Latin America in the ensuing years.[51] The most wide-ranging venture in avant-garde music was the Centro Latinoamericano de Altos Estudios Musicales (CLAEM) in Buenos Aires, a center for advanced composition studies that Copland would visit during his final cultural diplomacy tour in Latin America.[52]

With the support of critics such as Eurico Nogueira França and Jorge D'Urbano, Copland retained a loyal following in Latin America. But some musical elites subjected him to new scrutiny. Central here was his perceived attunement to market forces, which Suffern had pointed out at such length. The Spanish expatriate Adolfo Salazar addressed the matter as well, albeit less hyperbolically. He argued that although Copland might not be a major composer, he was no mere crowd pleaser. Rather, Copland was a "musical artificer, a worker who, with certain rhythmic, harmonic, melodic, and especially sonorous materials, fashions musical goods," just as composers prior to Beethoven wrote "music made to order."[53] Thanks to Copland's expert hand, *An Outdoor Overture* is "a school exercise composed by a master" whereas *Appalachian Spring* and *Rodeo* "serve the client who has come to solicit [music] in Copland's factory." To be sure, Salazar left open the question of whether the laws of supply and demand inevitably corrupt artistic creation.

Paz left no such doubt. Surely one of Guarnieri's "small elite of paranoid initiates," the Argentine serialist spewed forth another one of his pronouncements against musical folklore, now with Copland as his target. In *La Música en los Estados Unidos* of 1952, one of few books by a Latin American on the music of the United States, Paz railed against *El salón México* and *Danzón cubano*. He damned both works as little more than "travel-agency brochures" and insisted that they were the "nadir of Copland's total oeuvre, for their sentimentalist conformity and perpetual and keen condition of folkloric banality."[54] Paz did not stop at folklore, however. He also charged Copland with "aesthetic nomadism"—eclecticism—a practice that confirmed Copland's vulnerability to the "laws of supply and demand."[55] Indeed, Copland went beyond amicably accommodating his "clients," as Salazar proposed. Rather, he abandoned the principles of serious, contemporary music: in lieu of the "strong, aggressive, magnificently dissonant" Piano Variations or the "rigorous distillation" of the Piano Sonata, Copland had fallen prey to an "aesthetic of opportunism," ensuring that works such as *Appalachian Spring* and *Rodeo* betrayed "more concession than conviction and more vulgarity than intrinsic merit."[56] Compare Ives, whose forward-looking music not only defied the market but avoided "the sentimentality of a Foster, the mediocrity of a Gershwin . . . the vulgarity of a Shostakovich." (Paz also found it remarkable that Ives had composed such music at all given the "exceptionally limited environment of sensibility and culture" in the United States.)[57] Once, Copland had met similar aesthetic challenges with aplomb. The fact he now chose to ignore them made his descent all the more despicable.[58]

## Copland as Twelve-Toner

Confronting "flux and semiconfusion," Copland now tried various compositional strategies. He dismissed the *Preamble for a Solemn Occasion* as a "potboiler" (a curious position for one who could be expected to give his best efforts to a paean on world peace) and in 1949 began the song cycle *Twelve Poems of Emily Dickinson*, that series of introspective mood-pictures on death, an uncertain afterlife, and the transience of worldly honors.[59] Each of the twelve songs is dedicated to a composer-friend, three of whom are Latin Americans: Santa Cruz ("Dear March, come in!"), Guarnieri ("I felt a funeral in my brain"), and Ginastera ("I've heard an organ talk sometimes"). Nowhere in these three songs do we find the slightest allusion to Latin American identity—"folkloric banality," as Paz would have it—and throughout, the universe is benign. Despite paradox and sorrow, Copland and Dickinson portray "Nature the gentlest mother" soothing even her "waywardest" children to sleep.[60] These were surely comforting thoughts to a man turning fifty and reevaluating his place in the creative world.

In 1950 Copland completed the Piano Quartet (piano, violin, viola, and cello), his first essay as a "twelve-toner."[61] He began working on it shortly after the confrontation with Schoenberg and finished it just in time for its premiere in Washington, DC, in October 1950.[62] As Jennifer DeLapp-Birkett demonstrates, the score suggests rapprochement between the very binaries— the "neat little categories"—Copland had disparaged.[63] For one thing, his row consists of eleven rather than twelve notes. More important, the row's strong tonal implications yield whole-tone patterns, thus inviting "a reconciliation of serialism and tonality."[64] (The third movement even has a key signature.) Perhaps what strikes the ear most readily are Copland's signature "open" sonorities. If these wide intervals once evoked the vast spaces of the western United States, they now imprint his musical personality on an idiom he once resisted but now saw fit to test. Given Copland's distaste for the music of Schoenberg, Paz, and Koellreutter—not to mention all those Brazilian "dullards"—writing the quartet was a big step. He would maintain that his reasons for taking it were strictly musical.[65]

Another work from the same period took a different turn. Surely Paz would have found "sentimentalist conformity" in Copland's backward-looking opera *The Tender Land*, begun in 1952. With his librettist Erik Johns, Copland based it on *Let Us Now Praise Famous Men*, the WPA-funded photojournalistic book by James Agee and Walker Evans about the lives of tenant farmers in the southern United States. A tale of youth, family, and coming of age in uncertain times, *The Tender Land* evokes some of the themes Copland's public so enthusiastically applauded during the war. With its focus on rural life (the opera is set not in the south but in the Midwest), *The Tender Land* also lends itself to Americana-style melodies and quotation of folk music; indeed, the hymn "Zion's Walls" concludes the first of its two acts. As a souvenir of those ideals for which Copland was so warmly applauded only a decade earlier, *The Tender Land* was largely unsuccessful as an opera, although Copland arranged an orchestral suite from its materials. Tellingly, part of the plot involves a false accusation.[66] Thus, like other stage works from this period (most notably Arthur Miller's *The Crucible*), *The Tender Land* does more than merely hint at McCarthy's tactics.

## Citizen Diplomat Turns Enemy of the State

Doubts over Copland continued to grow, and at least some of his movements were monitored. In June 1951, when he returned to New York after six months abroad, FBI director J. Edgar Hoover tipped off his counterpart at the CIA on Copland's return flight information.[67] On 11 December 1952, Copland's name came up in a hearing called by a Select Committee of the House of Representatives to investigate tax-exempt foundations. Harold Keele, counsel to the committee; Representative Donald Lawrence O'Toole (Democrat, New York); and Representative Sid Simpson (Republican, Illinois) questioned Henry Allen Moe, who had shepherded Copland's first State Department trip to Latin America and served as Guggenheim Foundation secretary for almost three decades, overseeing the disbursement of Copland's fellowship in 1925. Their colloquy contains some chilling moments.

Mainly, the committee was interested in the foundation's selection process. When Keele asked for the names of "outstanding" grantees, Moe named three Nobel laureates, all in the sciences. He acknowledged that a small number of grantees did not live up to their potential and that other cases were complicated for different reasons. On the latter point, Moe singled out Alvah C. Bessie, the novelist, screenwriter, and volunteer in the Abraham Lincoln Brigades, who in 1950 served ten months in prison for contempt of Congress for refusing to confirm or deny his involvement in communism.[68] Although Bessie had received his fellowship fifteen years prior to these incidents, Moe told the Select Committee that in his case, the foundation had made its "most grievous mistake of all," adding, "we have no pride in that record."[69] Moreover, Moe noted, "There are others." When pressed on this point, the dedicatee of *And They Lynched Him on a Tree* named Langston Hughes, who, like Bessie, supported Republican Spain; Hughes had also visited the Soviet Union. "As a matter of hindsight," Moe confessed, "we would have to say that we wish we hadn't made that one."[70]

Keele then referred to a widely shared belief that "if a person was committed to the Communist ideology, they [would be] unable to be objective either in the arts or the sciences." Did Moe agree with this premise? Moe replied, apparently without hesitation, "We have no doubt about that."[71] Simpson sought confirmation on what Moe described as "borderline" cases, asking whether "a man [who] is an avowed Communist or known to be to your satisfaction to be a Communist sympathizer would be considered for a fellowship." "We wouldn't have any truck with him at all," Moe insisted.[72] To be sure, as to the question of whether artists were especially prone to "foreign ideology," Moe did allow that "the great artists and writers and composers of all time have never been exactly cozy members of society."[73]

Again, Keele prodded him on the foundation's "mistakes." "None leaps to mind," Moe answered. "Well," Keele continued, "I was thinking of . . . perhaps . . . Aaron Copland."[74] Moe leapt to the composer's defense. He told the committee that

> Mr. Copland was, of course, a participant . . . in that so-called Scientific and Cultural [sic] Conference for World Peace held at the Waldorf Astoria in New York in 1949. He has since served as Charles Eliot Norton professor in Harvard University, which is, so far as the arts are concerned, probably the highest distinction that can be attained by an artist or writer in America. He is recognized to be one of the foremost of American composers.

Moe, whose OIAA missives to Copland read "Dear Aaron" (rather than "Dear Mr. Copland"), spoke of the composer with affection:

> I well remember when we granted our first fellowship [for composition] to Mr. Copland in 1925. . . . He had been born and brought up in Brooklyn and by his undoubted musical abilities had pulled himself up and was engaged in musical composition. We gave him $2,500 a year for two years and he has gone on from success to success in his profession. As a man, sir, I don't know that there is anything wrong with him and I have known him for over a quarter of a century.[75]

At that point, Keele intervened. "Well, neither do I have any knowledge whether there is anything wrong with him," he said. He added, however, "I do note that he has been identified pretty closely with *New Masses*, the *Daily Worker*, and that he has allied himself apparently in a number of instances with Communist-front organizations."[76] Again, Moe defended Copland. "Mr. Keele," he said, "I . . . think you have to relate this kind of thing to the climate of opinion that existed at the time when Mr. Copland, as you say, wrote for *New Masses*. I don't know whether he did or not." Recalling the political and economic turmoil of the 1930s, Moe continued. "I remember those days very well, sir," he said, adding, "we are not God and cannot foresee the future. But with respect to Mr. Copland, sir, I would not think there could possibly be anything wrong with him from the point of view of this committee."[77] Keele was satisfied, and the session ended on a light note. "After all, it's a free country," Moe observed. "And from my point of view everybody has a right to make a damn fool of himself in his own way if he wants to."[78] Both he and Keele agreed that such behavior was not uncommon.

However gentlemanly in tone, the hearing gives one pause. Moe readily admitted that funding Bessie and Hughes had been a mistake, either because he was actually convinced that communist sympathizers in the arts or the sciences were incapable of objectivity (a premise he unhesitatingly affirmed to the subcommittee) or because rewarding such individuals reflected poorly on the foundation. For Copland, on the other hand, who had maintained a lower profile in the 1930s and had more than proved himself as an artist since then, allowances could be made, given "the climate of opinion that existed" when the young man from working-class Brooklyn first rubbed elbows with communists. Indeed, the transformation from impressionable leftist to settled, renowned composer reflected Copland's fulfillment of the American dream yet again. That gratifying narrative was enough to assuage the committee's doubts, at least for the moment.

Weeks later, however, came the *Lincoln Portrait* debacle. Scheduled for performance in January 1953 to mark President Eisenhower's inauguration, the work was eliminated from the program thanks in large part to Republican Congressman Fred E. Busbey of Illinois, who habitually attacked intellectuals associated with the State Department.[79] On the floor of the House of Representatives, Busbey acknowledged his ignorance of music. That, however, did not stop him from advocating for "fine, patriotic and thoroughly American composers"—obviously disqualifying Copland.[80] Reaction in musical circles was swift and unequivocal. Members of the League of Composers, various public figures, and music critics the stature of Paul Hume and Howard Taubman united in a passionate defense of Copland. Under the headline "*Portrait* of President Deeply Patriotic—Composer's Stature Not in Doubt," Taubman expressed "outrage" over "censorship and blacklisting through the whims of one individual or a handful."[81] Although the inaugural concert went off without *Lincoln Portrait*, on 12 February (Lincoln's birthday) the work was aired on WABF, a progressive New York radio station.[82]

Shortly thereafter, Copland suffered another a gross injustice. In April he learned that his works would be barred from all 196 U.S. libraries worldwide. Having labored for years to furnish Latin American libraries with recordings and scores by U.S. composers (especially during the war) and having aided the libraries in the State Department cultural centers, Copland surely recognized that this action, besides diminishing him personally, was a frontal assault both on U.S. music and cultural diplomacy. It was also clumsily executed. Roy M. Cohn, a twenty-six-year-old graduate of Columbia Law School (himself a closeted homosexual), toured U.S. information centers around the world with his colleague David Schine (the two were known as Rosencohn and Guildenschine) to rout out allegedly objectionable materials. They operated without specific criteria, however.[83] One reporter, for example, learned that *Witness*, Whitaker Chambers's account of the Alger Hiss trial, had been removed from the Abraham Lincoln Library in Buenos Aires, a colossal blunder on the part of the inquisitors.[84] Reporting on another investigation, one headline stated laconically, "Mark Twain Is Cleared."[85]

The worst indignity for Copland was being called for a closed-door session of a Senate Permanent Subcommittee on Investigations.[86] On 26 May 1953 he confronted three senators (McCarthy, Karl Mundt of South Dakota, and John McClellan of Arkansas), a representative from the State Department, and three government lawyers, including Cohn. Copland, who later set down his impressions of the encounter, found all participants very mannerly, although such behavior seemed stressful for Cohn, whom Copland judged to be spoiling for a fight. Copland also noted "little personal animus" on McCarthy's part but recalled that when the senator entered the room, "it was similar to the entrance of Toscanini—half the battle won . . . through the power of personality."[87] Throughout the hearing, Copland managed to be both evasive and courteous, with "softness of critical fibre" now a strategic advantage. For example, when Cohn asked, "do you feel Communists should be allowed to teach in our schools?" the composer replied, "I haven't given the matter such thought as to come up with an answer."[88] When asked if he had ever been a "communist sympathizer," Copland feigned failure to understand the question. "I am not sure that I would be able to say what you mean by the word 'sympathizer,'"

Copland said. "From my impression of it I have never thought of myself as a Communist sympathizer," adding, "I have never sympathized with communists as such." Distancing words ("as such," "from my impression") cloaked his comments in a defensible vagueness, as did answers such as "I don't know," "I don't remember," and "I may have."[89] Apropos the hearing, the *New York Times* quoted Copland's statement that he had never been a communist and that "as a composer and free man," he had always opposed Soviet restraints on personal freedom.[90] One of McCarthy's reasons for having interrogating Copland in the first place also came to light. "Senator Joseph R. McCarthy, Republican of Wisconsin, the committee chairman, announced that Mr. Copland had made a lecture tour of South America in 1947 as a cultural representative of the State Department," the *Times* noted. This, McCarthy said, "brought the Pulitzer Prize–winning composer within the scope of his inquiry."[91]

Fully expecting to be called back before the subcommittee, Copland made a list of nine of his contributions to the United States under the header "My Record." He emphasized his activities on behalf of cultural diplomacy: "advisor to the State Department's Cultural Program," "participant in that program," "musical ambassador," and "worker in that field in Latin America and Europe."[92] He never had to reappear, however, and his case was eventually dismissed for insufficient evidence. In what seems to be McCarthy's final reference to Copland in the media, cultural diplomacy figures. In July 1953 the senator was taking aim at one of its crown jewels, the Fulbright Program, established in 1946 under legislation proposed by Senator J. William Fulbright (Democrat, Arkansas) to encourage mutual understanding among nations.[93] In a budget meeting, McCarthy sniped that the "half-bright program," as he called it, might well be aiding communist sympathizers. When Fulbright observed in his soft Arkansas drawl that McCarthy had failed to finger very many communists, McCarthy insisted that he had ensnared "a sizeable number." Among these, he blustered, was the "composer Aaron Copland," who had a "great record of Communist activity."[94] Within a year, McCarthy's smear tactics would meet their ignominious end.

McCarthy did no permanent damage to Copland. To be sure, like many victims of the red scare, Copland initially had a difficult time renewing his passport; also, the universities of Alabama and Colorado rescinded invitations for lectures, along with a few other cowardly withdrawals of support from other institutions. In 1954, however, Copland was made a member of the American Academy of Arts and Letters, among other honors.[95] Still, paperwork and emotional stress cost the composer valuable time for his creative projects, not to mention legal fees. Perhaps most galling was the realization that the government he had once optimistically served had stooped so low.

When it came to eliminating cultural diplomacy and reducing exposure to "foreign ideology," however, McCarthy failed spectacularly. On the contrary, President Eisenhower undertook the most robust foray into "soft power" in U.S. history. Borrowing the approach Roosevelt had taken with the OIAA, Eisenhower accessed his own emergency fund to establish the President's Special International Program for Cultural Presentations, among whom were various "musical ambassadors" sent abroad.[96] Other Eisenhower-era cultural diplomacy projects were the People to People Program and the American Specialist Program, both of which could involve music. As Eisenhower himself acknowledged, music was one means to redress the reputation of U.S. Americans as "bombastic, jingoistic, and totally devoted to the theories of force and power."[97] Like their counterparts during the Good Neighbor period, Cold War cultural diplomats debated whether classical or jazz musicians should be sent abroad and whether "goodwilling" slighted poorer countries. A major challenge was the "Negro problem," now enshrined in a Carnegie Corporation–funded book, *An American Dilemma: The Negro Problem and Modern Democracy*.[98] While trumpeter Louis Armstrong and singer Marian Anderson toured the world as cultural diplomats, searing images of Blacks being hosed or attacked by police dogs circulated internationally as the U.S. government reacted in fits and starts.[99] Despite these blatant lapses in credibility—and despite McCarthy's best efforts—U.S. cultural diplomacy reached its peak.

## Private Citizen in Caracas

Copland's brush with the HUAC passed largely unnoticed in Latin America, although Santa Cruz affirmed, "Copland means more than ten senators."[100] In 1954 he went to Venezuela to serve as a juror in the First Caracas Festival of Latin American Music. The festival was the brainchild of the Cuban-born critic, novelist, and musicologist Alejo Carpentier, then living in Caracas.[101] Carpentier wanted nothing less than to replicate the international festivals at Bayreuth and Salzburg, and to that end, enlisted the Orquesta Sinfónica de Venezuela, founded in 1930.[102] He admired both Copland and Boulanger, once joking that "in every North American city there's at least one drugstore with a soda fountain and one Boulanger student," adding, "Aaron Copland was one of these."[103]

Copland went to Caracas without U.S. government funding. Instead, the generous Venezuelan music lover Inocente Palacios paid the jurors' expenses, salaries for orchestra personnel and staff, and generous prize money for the winning compositions ($10,000 dollars for first prize and $5,000 dollars each for second and third). Copland and his fellow jurors stayed at the Hotel Tamanaco at the rate of $100 per night, then the highest in Latin America. In his Venezuelan travel diary, the habitually thrifty Copland took note of his "swanky" surroundings and marveled at the cost of a bottle of champagne—"$30.00 each!"[104] All was possible because of Venezuela's oil-rich economy. Presiding over it, however, was the military dictator General Marcos Pérez Jiménez.[105]

While in the Venezuelan capital, Copland may well have picked up a copy of the 4 December 1954 edition of the English-language daily *Caracas Journal*. He would have rejoiced—and perhaps rolled his eyes—at the front-page headline: "McCarthy Censured: Split Creates Party Concern." The bottom left-hand corner of the *Caracas Journal*'s front page shows a photo of Copland, appearing not with his usual boyish grin but in a serious mood, and the accompanying column describes him as "the number 1 composer of the United States."[106]

Musically, the festival disappointed Copland. He unleashed his frustrations in his diary: two Villa-Lobos works, *Choros* no. 9 and *Erosão. Origem do Rio Amazonas* (Erosion. Origin of the Amazon River) were "inexcusable"; he even accused Villa-Lobos of "getting away with murder." As for Antonio Estévez, who had studied at the Berkshire Center and with Otto Luening, he had not yet lived up to his potential, Copland felt (at least not in his *Cantata criolla* for soloists, chorus, and orchestra, his best-known work today). Copland also found the all-Cuban program irritating: allowing that Ardévol's *Tríptico de Santiago* was "not so bad as [he] was led to believe," he nonetheless noted "some striking moments alongside inexplicably ineffective ones." To be sure, there were bright spots. Copland was pleasantly surprised by *Homenaje a la tonadilla* by Julián Orbón, another member of the "class of '46"; also, Tosar's Concertino "held up well." Most impressive was Chávez's Symphony no. 3, written on a commission from Clare Boothe Luce, the first woman in the United States appointed to major ambassadorial positions (Italy and Brazil) and whose nineteen year-old daughter had been killed in an accident. In the symphony's first movement, grief staggers under its own weight, with an elongated final cadence suggesting only the most ephemeral of conclusions; movements 2 and 3 recall the cool woodwind timbres of Stravinsky's Octet, and movement 4, which starts with a recitative-like solo for English horn and harp, ends in anguish.[107] Chávez's symphony thus distinguished itself from much of the rest of the program in that it lacked any hint of folklore. It proved but a brief oasis. As Copland confided to his diary, the vast majority of the Latin American works he heard at the 1954 festival suffered from sounding "too Latin American!"[108]

As with previous trips to Latin America, Copland wrote up his experience. In a short essay in the *New York Times*, he told his readers of Venezuela's vast wealth and of Caracas having "put itself on the contemporary musical map."[109] He also praised the festival organizers and thanked Palacios for his generosity. Still, "a few gripes" were in order. The forty-odd works performed were not only too much alike but they tended to "over-emphasize the folklore-inspired side of Latin American music." Copland also lamented the lack of "an experimental note," noting, "of dodecaphonic music there was not a trace." Gone is any exhortation to Good Neighborly "freshness," "truly indigenous music with universal significance," or "rich folklore." Most obvious is that instead of disdaining "twelve-toners" infiltrating Latin American "temperament," Copland made a complete about-face. Any Latin American composer reading these words alongside Copland's *Modern Music* article would have been surprised.

* * *

Copland continued to distance himself from folklore. His Piano Fantasy, begun in 1952 and completed five years later, is a rigorous, thirty-minute, one-movement work deriving from a ten-note row. Like the Piano Quartet, it hints at reconciliation: Copland explained that its "overall tonal orientation" of E major coexists alongside twelve-tone procedures.[110] He also took pains to explain both the work's general scheme and his apparent stylistic inconsistencies. As with the Third Symphony, the Fantasy "belongs in the category of absolute music." It too is situated in a narrative of misunderstanding:

> [The Piano Fantasy] makes no use whatever of folk or popular music materials. I stress this point because of a tendency in recent years to typecast me as primarily a purveyor of Americana in music. Commentators have remarked on my "simplicity of style" and my "audience appeal" in such a way as to suggest that that is the whole story, and the best of the story. As a matter of fact a composer in our time is comparatively helpless as to the picture of himself that will be presented to the public.[111]

Yet shortly after writing these words, Copland began his *Three Latin-American Sketches*, finishing two of the three, "Paisaje mexicano" and "Danza de Jalisco." Their premiere took place in 1959 at the Spoleto festival (Italy). Each could easily be said to "over-emphasize the folklore-inspired side of Latin American music." Chapter 11 considers the ways in which Copland came to see Latin America in the early 1960s and how Latin America came to see him. By then, much ground, both aesthetic and political, had shifted.

# 11
# The Sixties

On 25 April 1961 Copland conducted his Nonet for strings at the Cramton Auditorium of Howard University in Washington, DC. Dedicated to Boulanger, the Nonet was commissioned by the Dumbarton Oaks Research Library and Collection in honor of the golden wedding anniversary of Robert Woods Bliss and Mildred Barnes Bliss, who in 1939 had opened their home to attendees of the first Conference on Inter-American Relations in the Field of Music. Copland's performance took place under the auspices of the Inter-American Music Festivals, a private-public venture launched in 1958 that ran intermittently for over two decades. Overseeing the project was the Colombian conductor Guillermo Espinosa, whom Copland met in Bogotá in 1941 and who was now heading the music division of the OAS.

Unlike the Caracas Festival, the Inter-American Music Festivals featured few works that sounded "too Latin American." Rather, composers of the Americas took pains to display their more abstract creations. Among them were Estévez (*Concerto for Orchestra*), Cowell (Symphony no. 14), Santa Cruz (Woodwind Quintet, op. 33), and the Argentine avant-garde composer Mauricio Kagel (*Metapiece*).[1] In fact, any composer venturing into folklore earned censure: one critic condemned Guarnieri's *Choros* for Clarinet and Orchestra as an example of the "rum and Coca-Cola" school of composition. Ginastera, on the other hand, caused a "sensation" with his serialist String Quartet no. 2, cementing his status in the United States as a musical cold warrior.[2]

We might expect that as musical Pan Americanism's principal advocate, Copland would figure prominently in the festivals. *El salón México*, *Danzón cubano*, or the two completed *Latin-American Sketches* would be out of place in this cerebral company, however. The only Copland work performed over the entire history of the festivals was the Nonet. Scored for three violins, three violas, and three cellos, it offers a terse succession of dark hues, dense textures, and themes that seem to struggle for life.[3] Nevertheless, it was with the Nonet, unlike any of Copland's other works, that he presented himself as a composer of the Americas in the 1960s. This chapter unpacks the details of Copland's changing profile in Latin America.

## "A living refutation to communist-inspired lies"

U.S.–Latin American relations continued to deteriorate. In 1951 the left-leaning, legally elected president of Guatemala Jacobo Arbenz expropriated land claimed by U.S. business (United Fruit). Three years later, a CIA-organized invasion force overthrew the Arbenz government, annihilating "a stammer of freedom," as the Guatemalan poet Luis Cardoza y Aragón put it.[4] In Cuba, after revolutionaries overthrew the right-wing U.S. ally Fulgencio Batista on New Year's Day 1959, the island became a litmus test: each Latin American country was expected to declare loyalty either to Fidel Castro or the United States, with no middle ground possible. In March 1961 President Kennedy unveiled the Alliance for Progress and, at a White House reception for Latin American delegates and members of the U.S. Congress, pledged to "build a hemisphere where all men can . . . live out their lives in dignity and in freedom."[5]

Surely older delegates were reminded of Good Neighborly sentiment. Yet only a month later, Kennedy called on CIA-trained Cuban exiles for an amphibious assault on the island to rally Cuban citizens against communism. The failed Bay of Pigs invasion only buttressed the communist cause, however. In August 1961 the AFP was formalized at Punta del Este, a seaside Uruguayan resort. At a late-night social gathering Kennedy aide Richard N. Goodwin and Ernesto (Che) Guevara, now Cuba's finance minister, met face to face. Wearing his customary fatigues, Che thanked Goodwin profusely for the Bay of Pigs, which he claimed had inspired the revolutionaries like nothing else. He even presented Goodwin with some Cuban cigars as a token of appreciation for President Kennedy.[6]

U.S. cultural diplomacy's global mission continued to include Latin America.[7] In 1955 the Everyman Opera Company's production of *Porgy and Bess* toured several Latin American cities, as did the U.S. violinist Joseph Fuchs.[8]

Dance was still "exportable": the San Francisco Ballet mounted a thirty-two-city tour in 1958, visiting less-traveled locales, such as Tegucigalpa, Honduras, and Valencia, Venezuela. Tensions over what amounted to "goodwilling" persisted. After the New York Philharmonic visited the Soviet Union and Europe in 1955, the U.S. Embassy in Lima fielded complaints that "top U.S. performers are sent to Europe . . . and the lesser-known ones to Latin America."[9] Black artists also toured Latin America. Among the university ensembles to travel there was the Howard University Choir in 1960. Especially memorable was the visit of jazz trumpeter Dizzy Gillespie, intensely interested in Latin American music. He later recalled audiences and media who had "heard about blacks being lynched and burned" expressing surprise that they had just listened to a band of "half whites and blacks and a girl playing . . . and everybody [seeming] to be getting along fine."[10]

Copland's final State Department–sponsored trips to Latin America took place in 1962 and 1963. Both were under the auspices of the American Specialists Program, which sent abroad educators, journalists, academics, political figures, and artists to lecture, participate in meetings, or, in the case of musicians, perform. American Specialists were also expected to challenge communist propaganda. Rather than preach the virtues of democracy, however, they would inspire through example and "provide, through their personality living refutation to communist-inspired lies about [the United States]," as one internal document explained.[11] Clearly the U.S. government believed Copland was qualified for this task despite his inglorious communist past.

The two trips were originally planned as one. The American Embassy in Mexico City requested Copland's presence during the 1962 musical season. The State Department passed on the invitation to the composer, then in Yugoslavia. When other Latin American embassies were informed, personnel in Lima, Buenos Aires, Bogotá, Rio de Janeiro, Santiago, and Montevideo bombarded Copland with so many inquiries regarding his availability that at one point, Manuel Sánchez, the program officer of Cultural Exchange, confessed, "I am afraid I am becoming a nuisance with my almost daily letters to you but that is the way the communications are coming from the field."[12] It was then decided to spread Copland's American Specialist grant over two years, since a trip to Japan in February 1962 made for too much travel.[13] Thus, in 1962 Copland visited Mexico, Brazil, and Uruguay. In 1963 he returned to Brazil and also traveled to Argentina, Chile, and Colombia.

Besides his usual lecturing, Copland planned to conduct, offering his second and third types of programs: all-U.S. or U.S. plus "standard repertory." Embassy personnel tipped him off on the various orchestras. Edward T. Purcell, the cultural affairs officer of the American Embassy in Montevideo, told Copland that the OSSODRE was "probably the best [orchestra] in South America," adding that the players were used to guest conductors, having recently played under Howard Mitchell of the Washington, DC–based National Symphony and Kyril Kondrashin of the Soviet Union.[14] Edgar Borup, the acting cultural affairs officer at the American Embassy in Rio de Janeiro, went into more detail, warning of the technical limitations of the Orquestra Sinfônica Brasileira (OSB) even under Eleazar de Carvalho's "expert guidance."[15] He recommended programming only one difficult work, such as Copland's Third Symphony, which, Borup noted, the orchestra had once played. This was the 1947 performance that Copland called "a mess."

The Latin American trips of the 1960s reveal fissures in Copland's musical legacy. In coming to grips with the multiple and, to him, often incoherent directions that classical music was taking, he had already expressed his frustration at being known solely as a "purveyor of Americana." Many Latin American cognoscenti also saw him this way, even as *El salón México* and *Appalachian Spring* continued to delight the broader public. Yet several critics identified a middle ground, which they variously called "sensible modernism" or even "an avant-garde for the masses." As noted, Copland himself came to acknowledge "two different publics" even if he did not say as much in public. He also confronted the fact that, now over sixty years old, he was somewhat more sensitive to the strain of travel: overnight flights, layovers, and the abrupt change from the summer heat of the United States to the bitter winter rain of the Southern Hemisphere sometimes took their toll. There was also the customary 9:30 P.M. curtain, "always a tough assignment," as he acknowledged. Was Copland serious when he told an Uruguayan journalist in 1962 that he was at heart a "stay-at-home"? It's hard to take him at his word. Still, the composer had just moved to his final residence, on Rock Hill Road in Peekskill, New York, about an hour from Manhattan. Away from congestion and bustle, he found in this oasis the fortitude to dedicate himself anew to the power of music, despite "flux and semiconfusion" and rapidly decaying relations between erstwhile "neighbors."

## Copland and Ives: U.S. Universalists

As in 1941 Copland started out in Mexico. Victor Kraft, no longer Copland's lover but a good friend, saw him off at Idlewild Airport, just as he had thirty years earlier.[16] Arriving on 15 July Copland was greeted at the airport by

Chávez, accompanied by James H. Webb, cultural attaché of the American Embassy, and Orbón, who had left Cuba after the 1959 revolution. A host of newspapers and magazines covered Copland's activities: *Novedades*, *Atisbos*, *La Prensa*, *Excelsior*, *Diario de México*, *Diario de la Tarde*, *El Nacional*, *Política*, and *El Universal* (including its English-language section "Colony Events and People"), and the English-language the *News*, along with the magazines *Audiomúsica* and *Tiempo*. These publications hailed "the great composer A. Copland" (*Excelsior*, 16 July 1962) and "Friend of Our Country and Advocate for Our Music" (*El Universal*, 17 July 1962). Among the amenities Copland enjoyed was an interpreter, Dorothy Lailla, who appears at his side in press photographs.

The next day, Copland plunged into rehearsing. Besides *Statements* and Suite from *The Tender Land*, he would conduct the Orquesta Sinfónica Nacional in Bernstein's Overture from *Candide*, Ives's *Unanswered Question*, Haydn's Symphony no. 95 in C Minor (H. I: 95), and Ravel's *Le tombeau de Couperin*. Unfortunately, the first rehearsal was a bit of disaster: no one was in the hall to meet Copland and the parts had not been distributed.[17] Subsequent sessions were equally frustrating. On 18 July, two days before the concert, Copland arrived at the 8:00 A.M. rehearsal to find "no proper lights, chairs disarranged, etc." As a result, things started late and the "orchestra couldn't concentrate," rendering the four-and-a-half-hour session essentially useless, as he wrote in his diary.[18]

Early in his stay, Copland addressed communism. He described to journalist Angela Muller his positive experience visiting the Soviet Union, adding that in Poland, "a country under the communist yoke," there was nonetheless "considerable musical movement."[19] Here, Copland was politely disagreeing with Chávez, who had recently commented that certain Soviet composers were "incredibly bad" (malísimos), especially Aram Khachaturian, who was "vulgar on a grand scale" (en grado apoteótico).[20] Copland felt this verdict was "too severe," adding that "although surely some [Soviet] composers write exclusively under the orders of the government, others freely cultivate their own styles."[21]

The mutual esteem between Copland and Chávez, strong as ever, now took a new turn. Chávez praised the universality of Copland's music and in this light, paired him with Ives (quite a contrast from Paz's scathing comparison). A year earlier, Chávez had hosted a piano recital by William Masselos showcasing the two composers. It took place at the Colegio Nacional, established in 1943 with the goal of furthering knowledge throughout Mexican society. As the only musician among its founders, Chávez constantly sought a balance between Mexican music and "universal classical [music]" to encourage a "well-rounded and well-educated public in our country," as he stated.[22] Masselos played Ives's First Piano Sonata and Copland's Fantasy. Shortly thereafter, Chávez published the essay "Ives and Copland," echoing the trope of the Cold War individualist or "autonomous man" necessary to uphold universalism, at least according to the then-current lexicon of musical-political buzzwords.[23] Chávez quotes Gilbert Chase, who held that Ives's music "proceeds from the local to the regional, thence to the national, and finally to the universal."[24] Like Ives, Copland had synthesized national and universal influences such that both composers had "conferred upon the music of United States a new dimension: the dimension of universality."[25]

Chávez reiterated these points when Copland lectured at the Instituto Mexicano-Norteamericano. In introducing him, Chávez explained that Copland was "already universal," and that like Ives, had made "essential and new contributions to music."[26] Four hundred people braved inclement weather to hear Copland speak, and to judge from photographs, many were young. More established representatives of the musical community included Julián Carrillo, Luis Sandi, Rodolfo Halffter, Blas Galindo, Francisco Agea, and Lan Adomian, the Mexican-Armenian composer who, like Copland, had been involved with the Composers Collective in New York thirty years earlier.[27]

Throughout his lecture, "Contemporary Trends in Music Today," Copland nudged composers toward a global perspective.[28] He reflected, for example, on music in relation to the universal human condition, observing that "music is not a refuge or escape from the realities of existence, but a haven wherein one makes contact with the essence of human experience."[29] He also referred to "African tribes for which rhythm is music; there is little besides rhythm in their music."[30] "But what rhythm!" Copland marveled. "The minds that conceive such rhythms have their own, special concepts: it seems incorrect and even unfair to call them primitive."[31] As for "contemporary trends," Copland briskly surveyed three principal approaches: twelve-tone writing ("the most difficult to understand"), aleatory, and computer music. "Fortunately," he added, "not all new music is forced into the category of 'hard-to-understand.'"[32] He also hinted at the possibility of a modern music that a broad public could appreciate, preferably without regard to "political barriers."

Copland's concerts, however, revealed that universalism still eluded the United States. One critic remarked that the program was "divided into two parts: music of U.S. composers and works from the universal repertory"; the same critic claimed—under the headline "Haydn Was Monotonous"—that no one had shown up to hear Copland conduct Haydn and Ravel.[33] Another observed that the programming "had the effect of two respectable persons invited to a social gathering in which they don't know anyone at all."[34] On the other hand, Copland's own music went over well. The critic who panned the Haydn called *Statements* (Declaraciones) "six little musical jewels . . . [that] have few rivals in contemporary music" and found the Suite from *The Tender Land* (La tierra tierna) an example of "a sensible modernism, that in no way quarrels with logic, giving pleasure from beginning to end."[35] Another, writing in the communist magazine *Política*, came close to suggesting that Ives's *The Unanswered Question* was superior to any Copland work on the program, however.[36] To be sure, *Statements* was from "the group of prestigious compositions, that while offering musical respectability don't accrue the popularity of his scores with a picturesque bent."[37] Still, the "heart of the concert . . . was *The Unanswered Question* by Ives," the most significant composer of the United States, in that critic's view.[38] However much critics found U.S. music to fall short of universalism, the public was delighted. Two days later, when Copland repeated the program, he took seven bows.

## "Known only as the composer of *El salón México*"?

Among Copland's many social activities in Mexico was lunch with Chávez and Anita Brenner. Brenner was fortunate to have returned to the country of her birth some years before. Had she remained in New York, she likely would have faced the HUAC for her on-site reporting on the Spanish Civil War and friendships with "fellow travelers." The three had much to chat about: shared memories of New York in the 1920s, Copland's impressions of Mexico past and present, and the future of music. Salón México, the dancehall mentioned in the 1932 edition of Brenner's guidebook, came up more than once during Copland's 1962 trip. According to one reporter, the first question Copland asked upon arriving was, "Is it true that the Salón México dancehall no longer exists?" He was evidently disappointed when his doubts were confirmed.[39] Its mystique was nonetheless part of Copland's public persona. A "human interest" photo in the *Diario de la Tarde* shows him kneeling alongside a little girl named Olga in typical Michoacán dress, presenting "the composer of *El salón México*" with a bouquet of yellow, red, and white dahlias.[40] A reporter for *Excelsior* trumpeted the work's importance, noting that "Mexican soil" had inspired several compositions by Copland.[41]

Repeatedly Copland told the press that *El salón México* was nothing more than a tourist's impressions (una obra de tipo turístico) and insisted, "I don't want to be known only as the composer of El salón México."[42] Rafael Fraga reinforced this point in El Universal: "It seems that Maestro Copland is not entirely pleased to be known in the world of music for El salón México . . . [and] with this we are in complete agreement, since Copland has written a great many works of far greater merit, in their development as much as in their orchestration."[43] Reporters ignored Copland's efforts. According to Daniel Dueñas, on 24 July, when Copland left for Brazil on an Aeronaves de México DC-8, he remarked that the first of his works that brought him "international prestige was El salón México," adding, "it continues to be my favorite!"[44] This doubtful account surely appealed to many readers, especially those who favored Copland's "scores of a picturesque bent."

## Copland and Aesthetic "Totalitarianism"

Copland arrived in Rio de Janeiro at 9:00 A.M. on 25 July 1962, with layovers in Guatemala City (2:30 A.M.) and Panama City (6:30 A.M.). After a night of "sitting-up sleep," as he called it, he began rehearsing the OSB at 10:30 A.M. In summer 1962 the United States was alert to the communist presence in Brazil. President João Goulart, elected in 1961, advocated greater state intervention in the economy and reform of tax profits garnered by multinational companies. He was also open to bringing Cuba back into the Pan American fold, a point on which he urged "hopeful vigilance."[45] Goulart and Kennedy, both young and handsome presidents of the hemisphere, initially enjoyed a honeymoon. But increasingly the CIA began to feel that Goulart was "giving the country away to the communists," and in July 1962 Kennedy sized up possibilities for a Guatemala-style coup.[46] In an Oval Office meeting Lincoln Gordon, now the U.S. Ambassador to Brazil, advocated "mak[ing] clear, discreetly, that we are not necessarily hostile to any kind of military action." Tensions were sufficient that Frank H. Oram, a foreign service officer, was asked to leave his post in Madrid and "help counteract anti-U.S. feeling," as Copland wrote in his diary, having become friends with Oram and his wife, Mary. He also noted the fall of the cruzeiro, making everyone nervous about the economy, "with reason."[47]

As in Mexico City, Copland's program for Rio combined "universal" repertory with works from the United States. In the first category was the Adagietto from Mahler's Fifth Symphony, which he programmed because his first choice, Fauré's Pelléas et Mélisande Suite, was not in the orchestra's library; he also performed Brahms's Variations on a Theme by Haydn. The U.S. part of the program contained the same selections as in Mexico City but with Lincoln Portrait, in

Portuguese translation, instead of *Statements*. The speaker was Paulo Santos, a radio, television, film, and theater actor who had honed his musico-dramatic skills in such works as Prokofiev's *Peter and the Wolf* and Benjamin Britten's *Young Person's Guide to the Orchestra*. Copland found rehearsals encouraging, and the 28 July concert was greeted with a standing ovation. Indeed, such a crush of well-wishers besieged Copland afterward that his safety seemed threatened: he wrote in his diary that the "autograph hunters were so numerous and insistent in the green room that the Embassy staff people got frightened and hurried me away."[48] Reviewers were equally enthusiastic. Nogueira França alone wrote two articles on Copland in the *Correio da Manhã*. In one, a short review of the concert, he called *Lincoln Portrait* "music of political-social action, the equivalent of an enthusiastic hymn to democracy." He also noted (possibly with the current political instability in mind) that "at the climactic profession of faith in the government of the people by the people [sic], the applause of the audience rang out."[49]

Nogueira França's second article is a front-page, four-column essay, "Aaron Copland: Musician of the Quotidian." In it, he argues that far from indulging in "sentimentalized conformity," as Paz would have it, Copland was actually a rebel. Disinclined to dwell in the ivory tower, the composer pleases his public by drawing on "the daily experience of life to produce music for posterity." Such experiences consisted of attending high school (*An Outdoor Overture*), listening to jazz (*Music for the Theatre*), or traveling (*El salón México*), each work reflecting the expert training Boulanger had imparted. How did this make Copland a rebel? Because he defied the musical "totalitarianism" that had politicized the creative world. "In an era close to our own," Nogueira França declared, "totalitarianism promulgated an aesthetic slogan equivalent to lowering creativity to the level of the masses. Copland, on the contrary, has total creative independence and does what he wants, through conscious deliberation, attending to music's interest in participating in daily life, far removed from the solemn circles of concert life."[50]

In other words, in defying both the avant-garde and Zhdanovismo, Copland marked out his own path, one that spoke to many listeners but also instilled hope for the future of music. Copland likely addressed some of these matters in his first appearance on Latin American television.[51] Alongside him were Santos, the speaker in *Lincoln Portrait*, and Edino Krieger, one of the winners of the "Berkshire bolsa" and who studied with Copland during summer 1948. The broadcast took place on a typical day for a busy cultural diplomat: after a three-hour rehearsal with the OSB, Copland took part in a roundtable discussion covered by the media followed by a cocktail party at the American Embassy. Finally, at 10:30 P.M. Copland arrived at the television studio. The fifteen-minute clip was scheduled for broadcast two days later (i.e., on 28 July) although neither transcript nor tape seems to have been preserved.[52]

## "Too Much Brass"

The morning of 29 July 1962 Copland left Brazil for Uruguay. His erstwhile OIAA colleague Carleton Sprague Smith, then in Brazil for a conference, "Tensions in Development in the Western Hemisphere," saw him off at the airport.[53] After the short flight to Montevideo, Copland conferred with Purcell, the cultural affairs officer, to plan his activities. Chief among these was rehearsing the orchestra, often in three- or four-hour sessions that were filmed on television for the SODRE archives.[54] Copland found the orchestra "considerably less good" than in 1947, in part because it lacked a permanent conductor. In his diary, he grumbled that it was "irritating to see players, especially young ones, playing with absolute boredom in their faces."[55] Another challenge was the difficulty of the program, which consisted of Barber's *School for Scandal* Overture, Harris's Third Symphony, Schuman's *New England Triptych*, Ives's *Unanswered Question*, Copland's own Suite from *The Tender Land* and *Orchestral Variations*, his orchestration of the Piano Variations. "Big mistake!" he acknowledged, realizing that asking the audience to "swallow" six new works was simply too much.

Reviewers agreed, with one calling the concert a "trial by fire." The repertory itself also left something to be desired: as one Uruguayan critic argued, U.S. composers were overly fond of the brass section. In his review, titled "Too Much Brass," this critic informed the Montevideo musical public that "Copland . . . has an infectious enthusiasm for the American material he selected and displayed with energy and conviction. Too *much* energy, no doubt, in the service of music overloaded with brass and explosions of percussion, all of which made the little work by Ives [*The Unanswered Question*] an oasis in an afternoon overwhelmed by street bands."[56] Perhaps with the growing presence of the brass from Variation 12 in the *Orchestral Variations* or the "explosions" in *School for Scandal* in mind, Copland's Uruguayan critic seeks to explain this phenomenon:

> One explanation for this metallic exuberance in American symphonism could lie in the education of U.S. musicians and musical amateurs who, from child-

hood, practice . . . in innumerable and multitudinous bands. Surely their aural sensibility adapts itself over the years to this sonic glitter, and surely the composer feels the need to write extensively and well for instruments so rooted in popular sentiment.[57]

Despite this musical manifestation of overweening power, orchestral works from the Colossus of the North were not without merit, however. With frequent canons, ample and singing phrases in the cellos, "ingenuous" lyricism, African American influences, and a hint of religious tradition via melodies redolent of Protestant hymnody, "American symphonism," as this critic calls it, is easily grasped. The result is a coherent, identifiable style that, on balance, is pleasantly effective—except for all that brass.[58]

On 31 July Copland lectured on "The Pleasures of Music" in an unheated room at the Universidad de la República to an audience of about sixty, which he later recorded for a SODRE broadcast.[59] He gave another lecture in Minas, a town about two hours from the capital, where he shared the stage with the critic-scholar Lauro Ayestarán, who had written so warmly of his music in 1947. By then Ayestarán had made many of his nearly four hundred recordings of folk music from the interior of Uruguay and also transcribed and analyzed indigenous and baroque musics of the Jesuit reductions (missions).[60] The setting for Copland's lecture was the Centro Democrático Lavalleja, where Ayestarán headed a series of guest presentations on a wide variety of topics. Copland spoke to a full house on "The Pleasures of Music" and days later, Norman Laird "Brownie" MacNeill, a song collector from south Texas, would demonstrate his knowledge of folk music from that region.[61]

As usual, Copland faced the media. On the afternoon of 30 July, after a particularly tiring rehearsal, he gave a press conference and then an interview. For the latter, the Uruguayan artist and writer Pablo Mañé Garzón visited Copland in his hotel room at the Montevideo Victoria Plaza. Garzón's caricature of Copland had appeared in the press a few days earlier, one of several drawings of Copland in the Latin American press that we might consider anti-Semitic today. Upon meeting Garzón, however, Copland grinned at the drawing of his "large . . . nose, myopic eyes, and pear-like head," as the artist described his own handiwork. "How come I'm always the ideal testing ground for caricaturists?" Copland wisecracked. In autographing the drawing, the composer wrote, "Cordially (in spite of everything), Aaron Copland."[62] Then the composer stretched out on the bed. "I'm tired!" he exclaimed, adding that few people realize how physically demanding conducting is. He also mentioned that he didn't really care for travel and all its complications. When Garzón asked him about the orientation of modern music, Copland readily offered a "living refutation to communist-inspired lies" about the United States. To be sure, he admitted that modern music lacked "a broad and enthusiastic public." "So you don't believe in an avant-garde for the masses then (una vanguardia de masas)?" Garzón inquired. "Oh, sure, I believe in it," Copland replied. But, he added,

> What's childish is an *a priori* attitude on the subject. What seems wrong to me on the part of the Russians . . . is the obedience to a decree that orders them to compose in a certain way. I prefer to follow my fantasy. An artist has to believe that art is free. Certainly I try to be understood by everyone. But if I fail here, I don't have to say that I went wrong. . . . There are genres that, due to their own nature, aren't destined for popularity. The Soviet government says to composers: you must write works that everyone can appreciate. This is fine in theory. . . . But the creative process is so complicated that to comply with one slogan or the other is difficult. To speak to the majority in a serious and profound way escapes the abilities [even] of authentically great musicians.[63]

Having once aimed to express himself in the "simplest possible terms," Copland now acknowledged that such an undertaking was often beyond the capacity of any composer. This reality, however, the Soviets had yet to recognize.

## Interim

On 5 August the SODRE directors gave Copland a small farewell party, at which he signed some ten record jackets. The next morning, he was up at 4:30 A.M. to catch the plane. After a layover in Caracas, he arrived in New York at 8:45 P.M. A few weeks later, he heard the premiere by the New York Philharmonic of *Connotations*, his most ambitious essay in twelve-tone writing to date, begun in 1961 on a commission to inaugurate Philharmonic Hall (now David Geffen Hall) at Lincoln Center. The title refers to the twelve-tone row and its manifold implications ("connotations") over the course of the work. Copland described the piece as "a succession of variations" suggesting "a free treatment of the . . . chaconne."[64] Whatever these traditional references, the work carries dissonance to a far greater extreme than the Piano Quartet or the Piano Fantasy. Having been criticized as a "purveyor of Americana," Copland now digested attacks the likes of which he had not heard since the premiere of *Symphonic Ode* back in 1932: "unnecessarily strident," "too long," or "dreary." (In fact, Copland explained that whereas other works on the inaugural program lent a bright and festive touch, *Connotations* expressed "something of the tensions, aspirations, and drama inherent in the world of today.")[65] To be sure, one critic recognized that *Connotations* represented "the ugly realities of industrialization, inflation, and cold war." Copland's gamble did not exactly pay off: another critic charged that the composer had succumbed to "the conformism of twelve-tone music," much the way Copland himself had criticized Brazilian "twelve-toners."[66]

In 1962 he had to be reminded to visit Washington, DC, for debriefing.[67] On 9 November, nearly three months after his return and ten days after the United States breathed a collective sigh of relief over the outcome of the Cuban missile crisis, Copland visited State Department officials. To judge from his single page of handwritten notes, he barely prepared for the meeting. He did mention that he occasionally found himself short of funds for day-to-day expenses.[68] Also, in a six-page report, he informed the State Department that his visit was a "comparatively isolated incident in the furtherance of the Cultural Exchange program," adding, as he had in 1941 and 1947, "I do not consider apposite the visits of American performing organizations in standard European repertory."[69]

As usual, Copland offered suggestions. "My first recommendation," he wrote, "would be that a *continuing* program be instituted, making it possible for two or three American composers (or critics) to go to Latin America each year. This sustained effort over a period of years would do much to give added meaning to the single visit from time to time, as is now customary." As always, however, radio was shortchanged. As Copland explained, "A fresh study should be made as to . . . what degree serious American music, available on discs, is being broadcast in the various Latin American countries. This outlet is still an important one in South America for contact with a broad audience. It would be worth our while to make up a set of possibly ten recordings, surveying the development of American music, with appropriate notes in Spanish and Portuguese, to be presented gratis to those radio stations who make a practice of broadcasting classical music. If successful, other surveys (symphonic music, progressive jazz, American opera) might follow."[70] In other words, Copland's recommendations for U.S. cultural diplomacy in Latin America remained essentially unchanged for twenty-plus years.

In planning his 1963 trip, Copland paid particular attention to finances. His expenses in Chile and Colombia were funded by the American Specialist program, but the visit to Argentina was covered by the CLAEM, the avant-garde center Ginastera now directed and where Copland would present a series of lectures for $3,000 plus travel expenses. His visit to Brazil was paid for by the Patronage Committee for the International Music Festival of Rio de Janeiro, on which he had been invited to serve.[71] At one point, he considered taking on conducting engagements and exchanged a few letters on the matter with Alfonso de Quesada, an agent he had met in Buenos Aires. Although the promised fees were attractive (in Caracas alone, he could have earned $1,000 per concert plus airfare), Copland decided against taking on additional commitments.[72]

More than in the past, Copland had to prod embassy personnel to coordinate his activities. Philip A. Turner, the cultural affairs officer in Santiago (whom Copland described in his diary as a "dumbbell"), proved especially vexing. As his lengthy, stream-of-consciousness missives reveal, Turner was unable to grasp the practical necessities for rehearsal and performance.[73] More than once Copland complained of lackadaisical orchestras, poor acoustics, and sloppy organization. And although his health seldom let him down, in his diary he refers more than once to his "tummy." In Chile, Copland developed a stomach ailment after a cocktail party of nearly three hundred at the ambassador's residence, where he "pumped hands until exhausted." The next day, he received prescriptions for Trilafon, an antinausea medication, and Miltown, the tranquilizer favored by dissatisfied housewives in the 1950s and 1960s.[74] We cannot be certain that he took either.

One little-appreciated dimension of Copland's travels—solitude—emerges in the 1963 trip. In Buenos Aires, the newspaper La Nación published in its Sunday supplement "Copland in the Quiet City," an interview "by two bright youngsters," as the composer noted in his diary.[75] The interview took place on a day when Buenos Aires was unusually empty. Several photos capture the composer in solitary, Hopper-esque settings: perched on the ledge of a stone wall with his knees drawn up or meditating in an empty amphitheater. The young journalists detected "a certain solitude" about Copland, a man "without wife or children," and observed that his "tall silhouette stands out against the deserted streets of Buenos Aires." A visual counterpart to the "bittersweet lyricism" of the opening of his clarinet concerto? Whatever loneliness Copland may have sometimes felt, his Latin American colleagues continued to lavish attention on him. During an hour-long layover in Lima (en route to Bogotá from Santiago) some of the Peruvian musicians he had met in 1941 showed up at the airport to greet him even though Peru was not on his itinerary. It was a gesture Copland truly appreciated.

## "It's been a long time since I felt so little needed"

On 7 September 1963 Copland left New York, again saying good-bye to Kraft, who saw him off for the all-night flight to Rio. When Copland arrived the next day, the month-long festival was in full swing. It was sponsored by the offices of the Secretary of Education and Culture, the Secretary of Tourism, and the director of the Teatro Municipal. First lady Jacqueline Kennedy and the Queen Mother Elisabeth of Belgium were among the guests, and performers included the Philadelphia Orchestra, the Philharmonic Orchestra of London, the Quinteto Chiggiano, pianists Claudio Arrau and Guiomar Novaes, singers William Warfield and Maria Lucia Godoy, and various Brazilian ensembles. The inaugural concert was devoted to Villa-Lobos, who had died four years earlier.[76]

The other members of the Patronage Committee were Stravinsky, Hans Werner Henze, Dallapiccola, Milhaud, Santa Cruz, and Chávez. Some participated in the festival, such as Stravinsky, then eighty-one, who visited Latin American only infrequently.[77] In 1963 he was traveling with his second wife, Vera, who decided that Rio de Janeiro was a "big bore" and complained of having to witness Afro-Brazilian religious rituals "and other boring events."[78] Well might Stravinsky have been invited to Rio's International Music Festival: his influence on Latin American composers is widely, if not always precisely, acknowledged. Just as critics dubbed Villa-Lobos's massively orchestrated *Choros* no. 8 the "*Sacre du printemps* of the Amazon," Revueltas's *Sensemayá*, with its ostinato and repeated melodic fragments, has impressed critics as Stravinskian.[79] One of the Russian composer's staunchest admirers in Latin America was Carpentier, who while living in Havana would habitually greet Amadeo Roldán and Alejandro García Caturla by whistling the *Rite*'s opening bassoon solo.[80] As noted in chapter 2, Buenos Aires admired Stravinsky's neoclassical style.

In Brazil, Copland heard Stravinsky conduct his mass at the Candelária church, a performance he found "very chaste."[81] The festival itself was "completely disorganized," at least for Copland. First, his reservation at the Hotel Gloria had to be changed: upon arriving, he slept there for three hours but was then obliged to move to the Copacabana Palace for reasons unclear. Also, his duties were ill-defined, suggesting that he had been invited merely to lend his name to the proceedings. He did attend a reception at the residence of Ambassador Gordon and shook hands in the receiving line with the U.S. tenor Richard Tucker. Copland also gave a lecture at the University of Guanabára, thanks to which—and to his surprise—he was awarded a certificate of *musicológo* (musicologist). "Muito simpatico," he noted in his diary, "but I doubt whether anyone in the audience of thirty-five knew a single note of my music!"[82] But he was often at loose ends. Sometimes he attended theater or ballet in the evenings with the Orams, still in Brazil to quell anti-U.S. sentiment.[83] He pursued some tourism, visiting the Botanical Gardens, and also looked in on acquaintances, such as José Vieira Brandão. He also met the conductor John

Neschling, Schoenberg's great-nephew. (Neschling's grandmother Malvine Bodanzky, née Goldschmiet, was Schoenberg's cousin.) Much of the time, however, Copland sequestered himself in his room at the Copacabana Palace, slogging away at his upcoming lectures for the CLAEM. "Not a very amusing life," he wrote in his diary on 13 September. The next day, he penned the melancholy words, "it was a lonely week," adding, "it's been a long time since I felt so little needed."

## Latin Americanism and the Avant-Garde

On 14 September Copland arrived in Buenos Aires. Ginastera met him at the airport along with Enrique Oteiza, director of the Fundación Di Tella, which oversaw the Instituto Torcuato Di Tella, the center for avant-garde art of which the CLAEM was part. Established in 1962 the CLAEM was funded by both the Instituto and the Rockefeller Foundation.[84] These were important years in Argentine cultural life. After Perón was ousted in 1955, pent-up intellectual and creative energy ensured that Sartre, Italian Neo-Realism, and French Nouvelle Vague were the common currency not only of intellectual elites but of Argentina's educated middle class.[85] Also—and with an enthusiasm perhaps unequalled elsewhere—Argentines were drawn to psychoanalysis, a phenomenon the historian Mariano Ben Plotkin playfully calls "Freud in the pampas."[86] Psychodrama was a staple of Argentine experimental theater, as in the works of the psychoanalyst-playwright Eduardo "Tato" Pavlovsky, which were presented in "happenings." (The English term was used.) Ginastera plumbed the depths of neurosis in his 1966 opera *Bomarzo*, a tale of lust and depravity that combines aleatory, atonality, serialism, microtones, clusters, and other resources of high modernism. Audiences for these works would not necessarily take to *Rodeo* or *Appalachian Spring*.

The CLAEM was more than a center for graduate study of avant-garde music. Its twelve *becarios* (scholarship grantees), who hailed from throughout Latin America, absorbed the principles of Latin Americanism, which Eduardo Herrera defines as "discourse by Latin Americans about themselves."[87] To be sure, Pan Americanism had been a friendly invitation for Latin Americans to rethink their relationship to Europe and, along with the United States, forge a hemispheric identity. But it was largely engineered by the United States; also, the failures of its geopolitical dimension had become all too obvious. Latin Americanism, on the other hand, stood up to *any* outside agenda.

Although under no obligation to do so, Copland met with several CLAEM students. (He may also have wanted to feel "needed.") Among them was

Gerardo Gandini of Argentina, who later received a Guggenheim Fellowship and taught for a time at the Juilliard School. Another, Marlos Nobre of Brazil, would receive the UNESCO prize and a Guggenheim Fellowship and serve as a visiting professor at Indiana University, Yale University, and the Juilliard School. Edgar Valcárcel of Peru later studied electroacoustic music at the Columbia-Princeton Center. Graciela Paraskevaídis, the first female becaria at the CLAEM, did not meet with Copland but remembered his visit and the reaction of her peers. As she recalled, they were respectful and greatly admired his orchestration. But as is the wont of young people, they also found Copland, then weeks away from his sixty-third birthday, "really old" (muy viejo).[88]

These talented students worked with the many international figures who visited the CLAEM for short residencies. Among them were composers (Dallapiccola, Sessions, Luigi Nono, Iannis Xenakis, Cristóbal Halffter, John Vincent, Earle Brown, Vladimir Ussachevsky, Eric Salzman) and musicologists (Robert M. Stevenson and Gilbert Chase). The CLAEM also maintained an electronic music studio and sponsored the Festival of Contemporary Music, balancing works by Latin American and international composers. It was a heady atmosphere: one CLAEM alumnus, Mariano Etkin, recalled the "feeling that one could do anything."[89] Two months before Copland's visit, Olivier Messiaen and his wife, Yvonne Loriod, arrived at the CLAEM. The week before Copland arrived, three concerts of contemporary music were given in a small festival, although none of his works was programmed.[90]

In Buenos Aires, Copland gave two concerts. His main activity, however, was his six lectures for the CLAEM. Initially, Ginastera had suggested that he present two or three a week on "something like Sociology of the Music of America ... the whole of America" (i.e., not just the United States).[91] When Copland pointed out, not unreasonably, that writing so many lectures in Spanish was "like writing a book," they agreed on six.[92] Copland also managed to spread out the talks over a slightly longer period, from 18 September to 1 October.[93] In addition, he narrowed his scope, addressing the present ("The Aesthetic Climate of Our Time" and "New Music in the Americas") but also the 1920s, neoclassicism, and the Second Viennese School.[94] Increasingly uncomfortable with Spanish, Copland tape-recorded some of these lectures in English to be translated and transcribed. Despite his intensive work in Rio, Copland fell behind. When already in Buenos Aires, he received at least one frantic missive from a "seriously concerned" secretary urging him to send the next batch of lectures for translation.[95] One afternoon he spent *"four hours,"* as he vented to his diary, with the Ecuadoran student-composer Mesías Maiguashca on a single script; the same day, Copland gave three interviews (one on the radio and two for newspapers).[96] He polished his remaining lectures in his hotel, near a well-traveled street in Buenos Aires known for its theaters, cafés, and bookshops. "It's *endless*," Copland complained. "A monk's life, with Lavalle St. around the corner."[97]

Copland's lectures were open both to the CLAEM community and the general public. As in the past, he drew a full house. From the outset, he managed to make an impression—although perhaps not one he desired. All is described in *El Mundo*, the newspaper that hastened to interview Copland on his first visit to Buenos Aires, when he encouraged hemispheric solidarity and the "democratization of music." Its principal music critic was now Jorge D'Urbano, who in 1947 had praised *Appalachian Spring* for so perfectly conveying the "naiveté, sentimentality, sweetness, and realism" of the United States. Now D'Urbano reflected on Copland's first lecture, "The Aesthetic Climate of Our Time." He observed that although the composer struck a "tone of a certain optimism," Copland also uttered a few words at the outset that betrayed his true feelings: "The panorama contemporary music presents is confused and alarming."[98] D'Urbano elaborated:

> That it's confusing everyone knows. . . . That it's alarming, not everyone knows or believes. That a composer of Copland's importance and [that] a scholar as astute as he should have resorted to this word to define what the music of our times awakens in his spirit, is cause for more than one reflection, and, certainly, for more than one concern. It struck me as a clarion call, as a red light briefly lit by the distinguished professor, without insisting on it so as to avoid fear, but without omitting it either, because therein . . . lies a good part of his attitude regarding the great crossroads in which little by little, albeit inexorably, today's art continues to situate contemporary man.[99]

To be sure, Copland concluded with an air of "equilibrium and prudence," carefully cultivated to "leave his audience in a calm state." D'Urbano, however, was not fooled. Even if Copland did not come out and say so directly, the "confused and alarming" panorama he now confronted amounted to a crisis.

## An "absolutely inoffensive cocktail"

Critics also reacted to Copland's music. One of his concerts was at the Facultad de Derecho (Law School) of the Universidad de Buenos Aires and recorded on Radio Nacional. It was an all-Copland program: *An Outdoor Overture*, the Third Symphony, the Suite from *The Tender Land*, *Statements*, and *El salón México*.[100]

Copland had asked Ginastera about the possibility of performing *Connotations*, despite the rehearsal time it would require.[101] In the end, that plan seemed impractical and Copland contented himself by playing it for some of the student composers at a party given by the Ginasteras. ("I couldn't tell what they thought," he noted in his diary.)[102] Had *Connotations* been performed at the Facultad, it would have been a disaster: according to Copland, the acoustics were "*ghastly* . . . like Notre Dame." He left each rehearsal with a sense of doom. Still, the concert attracted a "packed house of students, mostly, and like students, very enthusiastic," with many requests for autographs.[103] His other concert was at the Teatro Colón. He found the orchestra slower at "learning things" than he would have wished. "Sometimes I think I've 'had it' in these parts as far as orchestras go," he shrugged.[104] It hardly helped that days before the performance the parts for *Billy the Kid* and a piece by David Diamond (Copland does not mention which) had not yet arrived. Yet an ample audience showed up to hear him conduct *The Unanswered Question*, Overture to *Candide*, Harris's Third Symphony, and two works he had been performing in Latin America since 1941, *Billy the Kid* and *Quiet City*. He also tested his *Orchestral Variations*, hoping for a better experience than in Montevideo.

Critics took both concerts into account, with more than one relating Copland's music to the cultural environment of his native land. The composer and critic Silvano Picchi called Copland "without a doubt one of the dominant figures in the United States," an artist with a "typically North American accent."[105] D'Urbano too confirms Copland's roots in a review, "Authentically of the United States," thus identifying Copland's regional (rather than universal) perspective. D'Urbano also avails himself of Good Neighborly tropes, noting, for example, that Copland's music evokes "the original flavor of a new country."[106]

But in 1963 few listeners were interested in "freshness" or hemispheric unity. Picchi noted that although Copland "obeys the dictates of his temperament," he could not help but be influenced by "the imperatives of [his] environment," which in the United States "stimulates most [composers] to produce works that . . . do not always respond . . . to a transcendental reach or refined taste . . . [but] to paying the price of a [musical] language sometimes lowered so as to immediately reach the mass listener."[107] Another journalist, writing for the magazine *Panorama*, hinted at the image Carlos Suffern crafted in 1947 of the "good and inoffensive man" conflicted over modernism and buffeted by myriad perspectives: "During this past week, we have heard a quantity of Copland. . . . Various periods, various styles, various influences. But always Copland, with all the force . . . his personality possesses. It's certain that with all the influences he has received he doesn't overcome a single one but rather accumulates all. But the cocktail has working in its favor the fact that it's absolutely inoffensive."[108] Rather than synthesizing, Copland merely "accumulated," thus sealing his fate as a sincere but "all-absorbing" eclectic who despite his personality failed to surpass the merely inoffensive. This hardly secured him a place in the avant-garde.

While in Buenos Aires, Copland engaged in an animated conversation over the fate of contemporary music with Juan José Castro, back in Argentina after several years abroad, and Victoria Ocampo, now seventy-three, at her house in San Isidro, outside of Buenos Aires. He also dined with "Mrs. Di Tella" (Nelly Ruvira), whom he found "humane and sensible."[109] But at one party his "tummy" acted up again. On another occasion, he returned to his hotel exhausted after a late supper with the Ginasteras, Adela (Fuks) Bautista (widow of the Spanish expatriate composer Julián Bautista), Jacobo Ficher, and his wife, Ana Aronburg Ficher (whom Copland described as "quelle bloody bore"). Another dinner followed with many of the same people (now including Luis Gianneo and Riccardo Malipiero, nephew of composer Gian Francesco Malipiero and then teaching at the CLAEM). For Copland, the gathering "didn't come off." Enigmatically, he concluded, "They all know each other for too long and too well."[110] Perhaps, despite his many friends and professional associations, Copland *was* a loner at heart.

## "The State Must Not Direct the Artist"

On 3 October, after nonstop individual sessions with CLAEM students, Copland left on an evening flight for Chile. The country was then on cordial terms with the United States. In December 1962 the right-of-center president Jorge Alessandri traveled to Washington, DC, to visit Kennedy, and at the time of Copland's visit, the months' long exhibition "Image of Chile" (Imagen de Chile) was on display in the State Department Auditorium. At its inauguration, a black-tie affair, Bernstein's Chilean wife, Felicia Montealegre, recited Mistral and Pablo Neruda in Spanish and English (Neruda's communist affiliations notwithstanding), after which an early music group from the Pontifícia Universidad Católica of Santiago performed. Five nearby universities offered their facilities for poetry readings, roundtables on literature, folk dance demonstrations, and an all-Beethoven recital by Claudio Arrau, introduced by the U.S. Attorney General Robert F. Kennedy.[111]

## 11. The Sixties

Like many travelers flying over the Chilean-Argentine border, Copland had a splendid view of the Andes. Peering through the moonlight, he drank in the "snow-covered tops of mountains and deep black crevices between," one of few descriptions in his travel diaries that verges on the poetic.[112] His arrival, around 9:00 P.M., had been announced in the press.[113] The welcoming committee at the airport consisted of Santa Cruz, cultural affairs officer Turner, and two young composers, Celso Garrido-Lecca and León Schidlowsky. Garrido-Lecca (not to be confused with Pablo Garrido, the jazz enthusiast whom Copland met in 1941) was born in Peru and was now studying with Santa Cruz and Fré Focke, two teachers with radically different orientations. Another Focke student was the Chilean-born Schidlowsky, who attended the Hochschule für Musik in Detmold, Germany; Schidlowsky was also a member of the new music group Tonus.[114] Immediately after checking into the Hotel Carrera, Copland went off for Chinese food with several young composers, savoring "much excited talk about music, such as [he] hadn't heard for some time."[115]

The next day a press conference took place at Copland's hotel. The room was crowded, with some embassy staff claiming that Copland "pulled in" a bigger audience than President Josip Tito of Yugoslavia, who had visited a few weeks before.[116] One headline proclaimed, "Musician A. Copland Seeks Out Young Chilean Composers."[117] Another paper emphasized his interest in meeting "new generations of composers ... and to cooperate in musical interchange between his country and ours."[118] As Copland looked out over the ranks of microphones—at friends, colleagues, journalists, and "the curious," as one reporter put it—he acknowledged his longtime acquaintance with Santa Cruz, Alfonso Leng, Carlos Isamitt, and Próspero Bisquertt, making special mention of Orrego-Salas, then directing the Latin American Music Center in Indiana.[119] "Juan was born to compose," Copland observed.[120]

Copland referred to *Connotations*. One journalist reported that "the author of the popular work *El salón México*" described his approach to his latest work, stipulating that it would "not be performed during his visit because it required ... too much time."[121] When asked for his general impressions of Latin American classical music, Copland reverted to a Good Neighbor–era script. "I feel for Latin American music a sensation of greater proximity, greater intimacy," he remarked, adding, that it was "friendlier than European [music]."[122] Copland even brought up folklore, telling his Santiago public that "in each country there are musical differences, a fact, in my judgment, directly attributable to folklore."[123] To be sure, Copland acknowledged, "folk music isn't so appreciated by young composers." But it "will continue regardless," he predicted.[124] Again, Copland saw fit to "refute communist-inspired lies." As one reporter observed, when asked about artistic liberty, Copland "became quite serious [and] thought for a moment." Then he appealed to the individual personality. "The work of the artist must respond in all instances to the spirit of the individual," he stated. "It's fine if governments want to involve themselves in the arts but they shouldn't interfere in creative work," an implicit dig at the Soviet system.[125] The next day, a headline in *El Diario Ilustrado* read, "The State Must Not Direct the Artist, Copland Said." Other publications drove home the same point. *Las Últimas Noticias*, for example, quoted Copland directly on the role of government and the arts: "Music, like any other art, must be born of the spirit, and not from impositions of persons nor political parties."[126]

Pablo Garrido was still one of Copland's more fervent admirers. By then, he had visited the United States but was less active in jazz, instead dedicating his energies to Chilean folk music.[127] With his usual vigor, he wrote up Copland's visit in *La Nación*. "Artist, teacher, and human personality . . . [Copland] has understood [Latin Americans] better than anyone . . . and has done so for a good quarter century."[128] Copland was also "a combative defender of Latin American composers and, thanks to his powerful influence, the icy linguistic and sociopolitical barrier [between our two regions] is melting"; moreover, Copland possesses a "discernment and objectivity not normally found in blond-haired America" (i.e., Anglo-Saxon America).[129] Sometimes Garrido's effusions embarrassed Copland. One evening, Garrido took him out "to a *boite*," where he announced Copland's presence to the crowd—"idiotically," Copland felt.[130]

## Copland and Leftist Chilean Composers

Ambassador Charles W. Cole, a former president of Amherst College, was unusually attentive to Copland. He gave a small dinner and a gala cocktail party in Copland's honor, both at the ambassador's residence. Three hundred people were invited to the latter, and Copland heard "much undercover talk about the fact that a number of leftist musicians were present."[131] It is impossible to know who among the three hundred–plus invitees actually showed up but "leftist composers" were certainly on the guest list. Some would serve the government of Salvador Allende, the socialist president elected in 1970, such as Sergio Ortega, credited with composing the song much associated with Allende, "Venceremos" (We Will Prevail). Eduardo Maturana, a student of Focke and member of Tonus, and Fernando García, who had studied with

Orrego-Salas, were also invited.[132] A few days later, Copland listened to some of their works. Among them was García's cantata *América insurrecta* (Insurgent America) for orchestra, chorus, and speaker and dedicated to the Chilean communist party and its "forty years of struggle, 1922–1962," as inscribed in the score. The text, by Neruda, marvels at the bounty of the natural world and the struggle of the oppressed to access its quickly diminishing resources. García conceived of the work as one "great recitative," with the orchestra dominated by brass and percussion, including xylophone and wood blocks.[133] Dissonant fragments repeatedly surface, punctuated by conspicuous silences that offset the words of the speaker and the choral interjections, which are sometimes shouted. Although *América insurrecta* received prizes, Copland, who probably listened to a recording, was unimpressed.[134] He found the work "spotty in musical interest" and only "superficially effective," lacking "any real organization."[135] Sent to Latin America to "refute communist-inspired lies," Copland thus dismissed music inspired by communist principles.

As a "speaker piece," however, *América insurrecta* was part of a trend. César Bolaños of Peru drew on Che Guevara's diaries for his *Ñacahuasu, for Small Orchestra of 21 or More Instruments and Reciter*, and Schidlowsky composed nine such works, including *Caupolicán*, for speaker, mixed chorus, two pianos, and percussion, also on a text by Neruda. Harold Gramatges, a member of the Berkshire class of '46, composed *Muerte del guerrillero* (Death of a Guerrilla Fighter) for orchestra and speaker on a text by the Afro-Cuban poet Nicolás Guillén. Latin American composers thus bridged the gap between populism and the avant-garde through unambiguous spoken language that coexisted with dissonances and other contemporary strategies. It was an apt medium for Latin Americanism, as was the less avant-garde *cantata popular*. Chilean composers, such as Luis Advis, combined loosely adapted features of the baroque cantata with folklore: recitatives (*relatos*) were accompanied by cello or upright bass whereas arias (*canciones*) and choruses might be complemented by the *charango* (a ukulele-sized Andean lute), *bomba* (cylindrical drum), or *kena* (an Andean wooden vertical flute).[136] In fact, the rise of the *cantata popular* bore out Copland's prediction that the folk idiom would somehow carry on.

On 10 October Copland visited a composition class at the conservatory, taught by Gustavo Becerra, a former student of Santa Cruz. Becerra's music was performed at the Inter-American Festivals in Washington, DC: Symphony no. 1 in 1958 and his piano concerto in 1961. Later, while serving as a diplomat in West Germany, Becerra composed *Kinderkreuzzug* (Children's Crusade) for speaker and orchestra on a text by Bertolt Brecht.[137] At the conservatory, Copland observed "a sympathetic group, interested in the newest trends, but anxious to add a social purpose to their music."[138] In other words, they pursued goals not so different from Copland's during the 1930s. Seeking a "social purpose" with particular fervor was the young Ariel Dorfman, later a cultural adviser to Allende and a distinguished literary scholar. Born in Buenos Aires in 1942, Dorfman spent much of his childhood in the United States and moved to Chile in 1954, where he later worked as a journalist. In that capacity, he wrote for the weekly magazine *Ercilla*, which covered general news and cultural events. (Dorfman's most celebrated work was likely his book *How to Read Donald Duck*, a hard-hitting critique of U.S. capitalism as manifested in Disney cartoons.)[139] One morning, Dorfman came by Copland's hotel to interview the composer, who described him as a "twenty-one year-old journalist . . . very bright."[140] In his essay "Copland: Musician and Diplomat," Dorfman strikes a blow for Copland's reputation: despite the widespread tendency to link him with jazz or folklore, Dorfman notes, the composer preferred not to be "associated with these stages in his music and points out that afterwards he evolved in considerable measure." Copland made special mention of *Connotations*, recently premiered by Bernstein and "written with twelve-tone technique," as he told Dorfman.[141] Its intellectual depth would surely appeal to *Ercilla*'s educated readership.

As in 1941 Copland conducted the Orquesta Sinfónica de Chile, now in an all-Copland concert. He was delighted with the ensemble. "First rehearsal with the orchestra," he wrote in his diary on 7 October. "Lots of enthusiasm—we get on fine."[142] (Garrido-Lecca apparently attended each session.) The day of the dress rehearsal, Copland had to "dash away" to receive an honorary professorship from Rector (Dean) Eugenio González of the University of Chile, which all the principal Chilean composers attended with great solemnity and which culminated in a "touching speech" by Santa Cruz.[143] The concert itself was well received. One new work for the Chilean public was *Statements*. As in Mexico, it had a staunch advocate, the European-trained critic, composer, and conductor Federico Heinlein. Writing in *El Mercurio*, Heinlein praised its "six brief movements of uncommon attractiveness." He was so taken with "Jingo" (no. 5), with its "sober reserve of subjective and cerebral language" and "ironic humor," that he concluded that this lesser-known work surpassed "extroverted works such as *Billy the Kid* or the Third Symphony."[144] Several critics complimented Copland's conducting, calling him a "skillful interpreter" (un hábil intérprete) of his own music.[145] Another applauded his finesse with ballet scores, calling *Billy the Kid* "one of the glories of American theatrical dance" and "a rhapsody on the expansion toward the West of [the United States] in search of new frontiers."[146] They especially appreciated Copland's rapport with the players, from whom he elicited "affectionate respect and nearly consistent discipline."[147]

One irritant during Copland's visit was cultural affairs officer Turner. Copland learned that he was "not much liked by local musicians," mainly for complete lack of tact but also because he was inclined to meddle in local musical politics.[148] In attempting to ameliorate a conflict between Santiago's two orchestras, the Orquesta Sinfónica and the Filarmónica (the latter founded in 1955), Turner held a dinner at his house, presumably to entertain the "rival factions." At one point, the possibility that Copland would conduct both ensembles arose, although that plan was scrapped. Copland described a "ghastly evening," with dinner served at 11:00 P.M., and "the Turners full of apologies, which didn't help."

## "The cold truth"

Copland also presented three lectures. One, at the Instituto Chileno-Norteamericano on 7 October, was enlivened by the violinist Pedro D'Andurein who, with pianist Eliana Valle, performed Copland's Sonata for Violin and Piano; another lecture took place in what he described as "the gloomy lecture hall" of the Biblioteca Nacional. Again, the press showed the power of the headline: the day after Copland spoke on "The Current Situation in Contemporary Music," *La Nación* warned "Our Musical Era Is Confusing and Alarming." As the anonymous journalist reported, it was Copland himself who drew this remarkable conclusion, declaring to his public, "I say this as a composer and writer who has taken an active part and observed the development of new music for more than forty years. I repeat: we are living in a musical epoch that is confusing and alarming."[149] According to the same reporter, the "distinguished guest" then revealed the "cold truth" (la fría verdad): "the revolution fomented by Stravinsky and Schoenberg has reached its endpoint. A new situation, in many aspects unprecedented, has unfolded and no one can predict its future results."[150] In part, this state of uncertainty was due to mathematics and electronics, now encroaching on territory previously occupied by musical creation. "Composers are being threatened by eviction from their own houses," Copland asserted, "because a new type of individual, half engineer and half composer, has started to be attracted to musical composition."[151]

Heinlein, who also covered Copland's lectures, went deeper. Referring to Copland's best-known works in Chile—according to him, *Music for the Theatre*, *El salón México*, *Billy the Kid*, *Rodeo*, the Third Symphony, *Twelve Poems by Emily Dickinson*, and *Lincoln Portrait*—he situates Copland's turn toward simplicity. This he considers the central point in the composer's evolution, while acknowledging that analyzing Copland's past will likely not enlighten those trying to understand his current position.[152] In fact, Copland struck Heinlein as a speaker severed from his subject. Focusing on what he perceived as Copland's discomfort, Heinlein observes that, through fluent Spanish and convictions deriving from "great mental capacity and extraordinary human sympathy," Copland invited the public into the "anteroom" (vestíbulo) of new music. But in the interest of objectivity, Copland refused to illuminate this ill-defined "anteroom." Nor would he venture any judgment on contemporary techniques. More "softness of critical fibre?" For Heinlein, Copland's well-cultivated impartiality amounted to deliberate sabotage, which he described as "the Mephistophelian work of leading the listener astray, indirectly undermining [the listener's] faith in those new trends" that the composer himself had set out to explain.[153]

"Mephistophelian work" was no small undertaking. "With art and cunning [Copland] avoids presenting the audience with the best manifestations in the field of music that are the object of his talk," Heinlein charged, lamenting that "the examples [Copland] offers are almost entirely bereft of the magical poetry that is, precisely, the strength of the new sonorous process. What an impoverished idea the listener will take away . . . without Schaeffer, Stockhausen, Berio, Maderna or Bucurechliev [Boucourechliev], to name only a few!"[154] Instead, Copland played the ending of Varèse's *Arcana* of 1927 (to be sure, identifying the work as a "precursor") and one of Milton Babbitt's first totally synthesized works, which he identifies as *Ensemble*.[155] Apropos the Babbitt work, Heinlein commented tersely, "nomen est omen"—the name foretells. (It is unclear if Heinlein was alluding to Sinclair Lewis's timid Philistine.) Yet *Ensemble* struck Heinlein "at moments, like a giant Wurlitzer in whose keyboards and pedals a monkey with more or less intelligent hearing might improvise." Later, Copland asked the audience to sample various electronic sounds: "melodic fragments were heard to demonstrate the changes effected by attack and vibrato." The pièce de résistance was the first computer-generated melody, created in 1961 on the IBM 7094 and which Heinlein described as "an ineffable artifact that imitates, with exclusively electronic means, not only an instrument with melody and pianistic accompaniment but—'o brave new world, that has such people in it!'—an abdominal voice that modulates with perfect English phonetics the song 'Bicycle Built for Two.'"[156] Shakespeare and Huxley aside, Heinlein found this both "exceptionally tedious" and incapable of persuading listeners not already predisposed to the virtues of high modernism. Iannis Xenakis's

*Pithoprakta*, for forty-six–part string orchestra, two trombones, xylophone, and wood block, a recording of which Copland also played, reminded Heinlein of a visit to the dentist (evoca un aquelarre dentístico).

It would be easy to dismiss Heinlein as unsophisticated or intolerant. The fact that he studied with Boulanger and Schering, however, and introduced works by Dallapiccola and Schoenberg to the Chilean public puts this notion to rest.[157] Rather, like his Argentine counterparts, Heinlein feels for Copland, sensing the extent to which the composer was captive of the disconnect between his true self and musical developments for which he had no empathy and played little part in creating. Heinlein even finds an analogy in one of Copland's earliest works: "Throughout this ingenious talk, we remember that the first composition Copland published was a work for piano titled *The Cat and the Mouse*. With admirable hidden artifice, the presenter treated the modern trends that diminish his own aesthetic, just as 'the crafty cat plays with the miserable rat,' as the old tango says. Sleights of hand of a musician ostensibly open to the future, but an astute and subtle defender of a sound world—his own—who feels threatened by current trends."[158] The "old tango" to which Heinlein alludes is "Mano a Mano" (Hand to Hand), by Carlos Gardel and José Razzano. In it, the singer is an outcast emmeshed in a struggle as desperate as that of a cat tormenting a "miserable rat." Copland, a "crafty cat," now played with "miserable" music, unwittingly helping to seal its doom.

As far as the State Department was concerned, however, Copland's visit to Chile was an unqualified success. No longer a young radical himself, he could nonetheless converse amicably with "leftist composers" while winning the applause of listeners eager for a "rhapsody" on the U.S. frontier. At a supper party given by Santa Cruz, Ambassador Cole told Copland that in all his two-year posting in Santiago, he had never seen such a successful U.S. cultural event as Copland's concert with the Orquesta Sinfónica. "Nice to know!" the composer wrote in his diary.[159]

## "Today a Composer Doesn't Die of Hunger"

En route from Santiago to Bogotá, Copland had a layover in Quito and another in Lima. During the latter, he was delighted to see Enrique Iturriaga, whom he had met in Caracas at the 1954 festival, and Carlos Sánchez Málaga, an acquaintance from 1941, now the head of a local orchestra. Much as Copland regretted having to pass over Peru, he felt "the musical *ambiente* [was] too sickly to warrant a visit."[160] In Bogotá, embassy staff, along with the critic Otto de Greiff, whom

Copland had met in 1941, greeted him at the airport. A younger critic, Manuel Drezner, born in Costa Rica and trained as an engineer, also came along.

Walking around Bogotá, Copland had the unsettling feeling of recognizing very little from his previous stay. His former hotel had been burned to the ground, along with other parts of the capital, in 1948 after liberal leader Jorge Eliécer Gaitán was assassinated in broad daylight, unleashing a riot in which over two thousand people were killed. This was La Violencia, the "fratricidal" struggle between liberals and conservatives.[161] The U.S. military also made its presence felt, maintaining strong ties with its Colombian counterpart. (A Colombian battalion fought alongside U.S. troops in Korea, a gesture no other Latin American country made.) Consequently, Washington rewarded the authoritarian regime of Gustavo Rojas Pinilla with weapons and aircraft. In 1958 Rojas Pinilla was ousted by another military junta, however, and a pact ended La Violencia, albeit excluding several marginalized groups. In December 1961, when President Kennedy visited Colombia, the liberal presses cheered his arrival, many having supported U.S. conduct during the Bay of Pigs earlier that year. But they also covered numerous anti-U.S. demonstrations.[162]

Copland was relieved to have relatively few activities in Bogotá: two concerts and a handful of interviews, affording him "much needed" rest, as he put it. Still, he felt that with better planning his stay could have been more productive. On 13 October, the day after he arrived, he spoke with David Garth, the new cultural affairs officer, who, Copland reported, made "some lame excuses about the altitude and not wanting to overwork me." Following a social event at Ambassador Fulton Freeman's home, Copland wrote in his diary that Freeman was "a music-lover" and "proved it by turning on my Piano Quartet as background for cocktail pleasantries," a strange role for Copland's momentous foray into serialism.[163] Copland even enjoyed a few tourist activities. He visited the underground Salt Cathedral of Zipaquirá, built in 1932 and dedicated to Our Lady of the Rosary, the patron saint of miners of rock salt (halite) to whom miners could appeal before going off to work. (It is not, properly speaking, a cathedral but a church, and was shut down in 1990 due to safety concerns.) "Fantastic sight," Copland commented in his diary, "especially as a mass was being celebrated while we were there."[164] Copland also took in the Gold Museum, which displays many of the splendid accomplishments of Colombia's indigenous cultures. The attentive Luis Antonio Escobar, a composer, ensured that Copland ate few meals alone. Escobar also interviewed Copland on television, in Spanish. Another interview, also in Spanish, was for Radio Nacional.

For his concert with the Orquesta Sinfónica de Colombia, Copland was far from optimistic, however. Not only was the Teatro Colón Bogotá "ancient" but its stage was "tiny" and the orchestra "not as good as Chávez [had] reported," with an especially weak percussion section.[165] (Olaf Roots, the permanent conductor, attended each rehearsal and, according to Copland, enjoyed them more than Copland did.) As if this were not enough, one of the cellists died of a heart attack the afternoon of the concert, and because his wife played at the same stand, only four cellists remained for the performance. At the concert, the ensemble played the coda of *Appalachian Spring* as a tribute to their deceased colleague. Still, the theater was packed "and much enthusiasm engendered," Copland reported.[166] Student interest ran especially high. Colombia has a long tradition of student activism: for example, every 8 June, the Day of the Fallen Student (Día del Estudiante Caído) is observed to commemorate the 1929 death of a law student at the hands of law enforcement. In 1957 students were instrumental in bringing down Rojas Pinilla.[167]

As always, Copland was interested in young people. In a press conference, he offered practical advice to Colombian music students, often with a touch of humor. As Drezner reported in *El Espectador*,

> Copland presented himself with his broad smile and answered questions. . . . When asked how musicians nowadays can arrange their lives so that they don't have the fate, so often repeated in the annals of music history, of being unable to support themselves, Copland explained that today most serious composers find employment as university professors, or they have special commissions to write music for films or television. Chatting after the press conference, Copland said that the university environment was not necessarily the most appropriate for the creative musician. "Still," he joked, "a musician has the right to kick back a few drinks every now and then."[168]

Predictably, the next day one headline read, "Today a Composer Doesn't Die of Hunger, Says Aaron Copland." Copland also opined on aesthetic matters. Although he mentioned that folklore had "passed from the scene," he believed it possible that "the pendulum would swing again in the direction of national sentiment."[169] Copland also defended straightforward, accessible music that did not alienate an audience. Verdi, he affirmed, was "direct and sincere," although the Italian master was sometimes "taken as a whipping boy for those who feel compelled to express disdain to show off their knowledge."[170]

The symphony concert was repeated for students free of charge at the Teatro Colombia. One press announcement seems to have been written with that exacting and politically committed public in mind. It read: "At the Teatro Colombia this evening, Aaron Copland will repeat his concert from yesterday, free to students. . . . It's worth mentioning that when countries of the proletariat send such performances our way, they usually do so in such a fashion that only the 'oligarchs' can enjoy such offerings. Here, the duty of bringing culture to our people at no charge has been left to the U.S. capitalists."[171] The fact that all twenty-three hundred seats were full suggests that at least in this instance the U.S. capitalists got it right.

After a full day of rest, Copland left Bogotá on 20 October for New York. He could count Bogotá among his diplomatic triumphs, as a report from the U.S. embassy confirms:

> Mr. Copland's indefatigable spirit and unpretentious manner lent much to his very successful tour which, in the opinion of the Post, was singularly effective in fostering understanding and appreciation of American culture.... Copland's visit as an American Specialist is an excellent example of the very favorable and far-reaching impact which a leading American cultural personality can achieve. Furthermore, Mr. Copland's outstanding professional reputation is matched by his dynamic personality, a combination which ensures public recognition and clearly fulfills [our] objectives.[172]

Thus ended Copland's final State Department tour of Latin America. He does not seem to have written a report in 1963, perhaps on the premise that his six pages from 1962 would "count." Had he done so, he would likely have repeated his recommendations of the two prior decades.

\* \* \*

That cultural diplomacy is a process rather than a balance sheet with quantifiable results is keenly appreciated when relations disintegrate. Such was the case with the United States and Latin America after Copland's final tour of the region. Shortly after returning home, Copland was off to Munich, on another American Specialist grant. There he learned that President Kennedy had been assassinated, the emblem of a "brief shining moment" that brought hope to the nation and to the world. Copland was devastated. Yet Kennedy, for all his charisma, had worked to destabilize Latin American governments, a pattern his successor would follow. Under President Lyndon B. Johnson, Ambassador Gordon in Brazil requested covert resources from the CIA to overthrow Goulart. Ultimately these were not used. But in April 1964 a military dictatorship took power, and within hours, the United States recognized Humberto de Alencar Castelo Branco, the regime's first president.[173] For the next thirty years, civil liberties in Brazil were curtailed and political opponents dealt with, sometimes through torture. Musicians, including Caetano Veloso and Gilberto Gil, were arrested, imprisoned, and exiled.

## 11. The Sixties

The Johnson administration also determined that the Dominican Republic, precariously close to Castro's Cuba, was lurching toward communism. In April 1965 the U.S. Marines began occupying the country for the second time in the twentieth century. These events coincided with a tour by the University of Michigan Jazz Band, whose young members had been given pamphlets by the State Department, such as "Democracy vs. Dictators" and "Why We Treat Communists Differently."[174] They now felt a "sense of mystery and drama in being part of an event of worldwide political importance," as Danielle Fosler-Lussier suggests.[175] In Argentina, General Juan Carlos Onganía overthrew the weak but legally elected government of Arturo Illia; again, the United States promptly recognized the new regime. An early victim of the dictatorship was Ginastera, whose neurosis-laden *Bomarzo* was now banned.[176] As for the CLAEM, its avant-garde orientation was just the sort of project Onganía mistrusted. Since the center's Rockefeller money was due to run out, Ginastera had to seek support elsewhere. He succeeded only until 1971, when the CLAEM, along with the "feeling that one could do anything," closed its doors.[177] Ginastera relocated to Switzerland, where he remained the rest of his life, composing a cello concerto and a guitar sonata, among other works.

In 1967 Che Guevara was killed in Bolivia, a joint effort by the CIA and the Bolivian military and inspiring some of the "speaker pieces" just discussed. Surely the most spectacular intervention was the 1973 CIA-assisted coup in Chile. This time, however, a growing number of U.S. Americans took notice. Senator Frank Church of Idaho and journalist Seymour Hirsch brought to light the cover-ups and tactics of the administration of Richard M. Nixon, showing that elected U.S. leaders had given the nod to dictatorships that throttled civil liberties, practiced torture, and targeted housewives and students as enemies of the state to be "disappeared." Many in the United States were shocked at such conduct. One musical reaction to the coup is Frederic Rzewski's dazzling set of thirty-six variations for solo piano on the song "¡El pueblo unido jamás será vencido!" (The People United Will Never be Defeated) by Sergio Ortega, one of the "leftist composers" Copland may have met in Santiago in 1963.[178] Unlike the cheerful "rum and Coca-Cola" music or "tourist impressions" U.S. composers crafted in earlier times, Rzewski's variations invite us to dwell on the darker side of U.S.–Latin American relations.[179] Perhaps they also suggest that despite its errors and limitations, the Good Neighbor Policy had at least attempted to counteract political and cultural imperialism. Questions linger: How will it all be remembered? And did Copland have any role in shaping that memory?

# 12
# Latin American Classical Music and Memory

In 1971, well before sinking into the gray cloud of dementia, Copland looked back on one of his experiences in Latin America. In March 1957 he had returned to Venezuela for the Second Caracas Festival of Latin American music.[1] (As with his first visit to Caracas three years earlier, he traveled without government funding.) The 1957 festival featured a concert of music from the United States: Gail Kubik's *Thunderbolt Overture*, Harris's Third Symphony, Barber's Adagio for Strings, Ives's *Unanswered Question*, and Thomson's *Louisiana Story* (the orchestral work he fashioned from his Pulitzer Prize–winning film score). Copland conducted the final work on the program, *Lincoln Portrait*, with Juana Sujo as speaker. As in 1954 General Marcos Pérez Jiménez was still in power. But his regime was beginning to flounder amid rumors of his personal enrichment and the inequitable effects of the oil boom. As the historian Ramón J. Velásquez put it, the general mood of the country was "monotone, gray."[2]

In 1971 Copland described the all-U.S. concert to composer Philip Ramey. Evidently the memory of that performance had crossed Copland's mind more than once in the intervening years. "I was going to save that story for my memoirs!" he exclaimed to Ramey. He elaborated further:

> I myself was conducting. And to everyone's surprise, the reigning dictator who had rarely dared to be seen in public, arrived at the last possible moment. The speaker was a fiery young Venezuelan actress who narrated the text in Spanish. When she spoke the final words, "And that government of the people, by

# 12. Latin American Classical Music and Memory

the people, and for the people shall not perish from the earth" the audience of 6,000 rose to its feet as one and began shouting so loudly that I couldn't hear the end of the piece.

Here, Copland was referring to the triumphant, hymn-like restatement of "Springfield Mountain," marked *fortissimo* and swelling to triple *forte*. He added, "It was not long after that the dictator was deposed and fled from the country. I was later told by an American Foreign Service officer that the *Lincoln Portrait* was credited with having inspired the first public demonstration against him—that, in effect, it started a revolution."[3] Thus Copland lent credence to the notion that music can support—or even trigger—demonstrations of democracy.

## *Lincoln Portrait* and the "Sin of Suggestibility"

Copland's story is pure invention. Yet we learn a good deal from analyzing it, including the reasons why it cannot be true.[4] For example, at no point in his 1957 travel diary does Copland allude to any revolution-portending public commotion, an event so unlike any other in his Latin American travels (or in his career as a whole) that his omitting any mention of it strains credulity. He does register the audience's enthusiasm, writing "big smash for *Lincoln Portrait*" and "public received it with a massive 'bravo.' Quite exciting." He also noted the "many compliments in the green room on my conducting, everyone saying that for the first time the orchestra 'sounded.'"[5] Also in his diary, Copland described his visit to the studio of the sound engineer Gonzálo Plaza, who on 30 March played him a tape recording of the performance. The composer heard "several slips in the orchestra" but observed that Sujo was "quite moving in a rather hammy way."[6] That tape was then made into a recording by the Caracas-based organization Sociedad Amigos de la Música (Apartado 1052, issue date September 1957) and appears to be the only recording of the performance.[7]

However unlikely, it is at least possible that in his diary Copland simply forgot to mention the collective outburst. Yet several errors of fact mar his account of 1971. A minor one is the identity of the speaker, Juana Sujo, whom he described as a "fiery young Venezuelan actress." "Fiery" she may have been but she was not Venezuelan. Juana Sujo (née Sujovolsky) was born in Buenos Aires in 1918, the sister of the violinist Anita Sujovolsky, who performed there with Copland in 1941 and 1947 along with other members of the Jewish community.[8] Sujo (she shortened her surname for the stage) studied acting in Germany in the 1920s and was active in the Müncher Kammerspiele. When the Nazis came to power, she returned to Argentina and performed on radio, film, and live theater, specializing in the Spanish-language classics and contemporary Latin American plays. Increasingly at odds with Perón (she participated in at least one antigovernment demonstration), Sujo relocated to Caracas in 1949 and continued acting. She also established a drama school. In 1954 Pérez Jiménez withdrew funding from the school, however, on the premise that theater was an irrelevant art form. By 1957 Sujo was a beloved—and beleaguered—public figure.[9]

Another error of fact in Copland's narrative concerns Pérez Jiménez. It is not true that the dictator "rarely dared" appear in public: days earlier, he had attended the inaugural concert of the 1957 festival, as Copland himself reported in his diary. "The President of Venezuela came," he wrote on 20 March, "and his presence seemed to cow the audience."[10] Pérez Jiménez also appeared at a post-concert reception at the hilltop estate of Inocente Palacios, who again sponsored the festival.[11] Not surprisingly, the censored press congratulated Pérez Jiménez for supporting the event, with some reporters reminding readers that the enormous band shell in Colinas de Bello Monte where the festival concerts took place (in greater Caracas) was built on his watch.[12]

A third error lies in the foreign service officer's account—or Copland's memory of it. According to the composer, that individual stated that *Lincoln Portrait* "inspired the first public demonstration" against Pérez Jiménez. In fact, demonstrations had occurred prior to March 1957. Among these were protests by the Frente Universitario, a group of high school and university students opposed to the junta's closure of the national university, which ensured that they often found themselves under the surveillance of the hated police force, the Seguridad Nacional. In 1956, for example, a student strike at the Liceo Fermín Toro, a high school in downtown Caracas, coincided with carnival season. Police responded with such force that many were hurt and several killed.[13] In the United States, the press often blamed such demonstrations on communist infiltration.[14]

Certainly Copland is correct that "the dictator was deposed." In January 1958, when Pérez Jiménez had become an embarrassment to the military, a cabal of officers removed him. But civilians incensed at being excluded in the transfer of power took to the streets and eventually helped form a new government. Several hundred people died, and approximately fifteen hundred were wounded. Any relationship between these events and the performance of *Lincoln Portrait* ten months earlier is tenuous at best, however.

Further detail emerges in the recording by the Sociedad Amigos de la Música. Certainly it bears out many of Copland's observations. "Slips" in the orchestra include lack of balance in the woodwinds and various intonation problems, as in some of the unison statements of the "Camptown Races" fragments. Sujo is certainly "hammy," the quality Copland ordinarily discouraged in *Lincoln Portrait*. Yet it is not hard to see why she excited both Copland and her public, with her crisp diction, dramatic plosives, and registral shifts. Moments of feisty urgency (la reg-la ti-rán-ica!) alternate with calm exposition of facts (eso fué lo que dijo Abraham Lincoln), all leading to the final fire-and-brimstone exhortation, namely, the conclusion of the Gettysburg Address: "y que el gobierno del pueblo, por el pueblo y para el pueblo [audible breath] no desaparezca de la tierra!" Here, Sujo's voice becomes a strident trumpet call, urging listeners toward their better angels and soaring over the ensemble as she and Copland feed into one another's momentum to proclaim the sixteenth U.S. president's most celebrated words.[15]

Nonetheless, the recording contradicts the central point of Copland's narrative, that is, the behavior of the public. Audience members sat quietly throughout (with some coughing and shuffling) and listened attentively to Sujo's final utterance. They also sat quietly throughout the full twenty-second instrumental passage between it and the final cadence. Only at that point, by which time Copland had cut off the orchestra, did the public shout, "Bravo!" True, we might wonder if the recording was altered. (It is difficult to know where the microphones are placed.) But had the pandemonium Copland describes actually broken out—six thousand people shouting so fervently as to render the conclusion inaudible—there would have been no way to eliminate it without eliminating the music. Recording technology in 1957 was simply not up to the task.

Perhaps other witness corroborate Copland's version of events? Several international visitors attended the festival, including Spanish composer Joaquín Rodrigo and French composer, conductor, and theorist René Leibowitz. Three representatives of the United States were present as well: Thomson, who raised a stink when he declared that Latin American music was fifty years behind that of the United States; Chase, by then an academic but still reporting for *Musical America*; and Taubman, who published a multi-article series on the festival.[16] Of *Lincoln Portrait*'s final moments, Taubman recalled that, "When the closing words were reached—the famous ones from the Gettysburg Address, 'Government of the people, by the people, for the people'—there was a spontaneous burst of applause from the audience. Mr. Copland continued conducting and some in the audience tried to hush their compatriots so that the final chords could be heard. The applause did subside. But it broke out in earnest *at the end*. Though the crowd was hailing Mr. Copland for his achievement as a composer and conductor it was also deeply moved by one Abe Lincoln."[17] It is possible that Taubman heard pockets of noise at various intervals. Or, he may have been sitting near some of the more restless audience members. He observes, however, that the applause broke out "in earnest" only at the end, as confirmed by the recording. Having staunchly defended Copland during the HUAC debacle, Taubman now blended Copland's persona with that of "one Abe Lincoln," squelching any lingering doubts about the composer's patriotism.

Another press report is opaque. A reporter for the *Daily Journal*, the English-language paper in Caracas, states that the audience interrupted Sujo twice, first on the words "a government of the people, by the people, for the people," as Copland proposes. The second interruption occurred when Sujo declaimed, "No nation can exist half slave and half free," which the *Daily Journal* describes as "Lincoln's immortal words."[18] Certainly these words (from Lincoln's famous "house divided" speech, delivered in June 1858) are rightly described as immortal.[19] But they appear in neither the Spanish nor English text of *Lincoln Portrait*. Latin American critics, moreover, barely reacted to *Lincoln Portrait*. Of course, the censored Venezuelan press would hardly have reported on a prodemocracy demonstration. But Andrés Pardo Tovar, writing from Bogotá and under no such restrictions, mentioned *Lincoln Portrait* only in passing, calling it "exciting and very effective." Otto de Greiff, also in Bogotá, was less sanguine. *Lincoln Portrait* only corroborated his feeling that the entire program was "lacking in real novelty." (He called Barber's Adagio "almost popular" and Harris's symphony little more than "solid.")[20] Neither critic so much as hints at a massive demonstration.

It is possible that Copland knowingly fabricated this story, perhaps to refurbish his image. But a more plausible explanation for his discrepancy-riddled account lies in what psychologist Daniel L. Schacter calls "the sin of suggestibility," that is, being convinced of something that did not actually happen. ("Sin" for Schacter denotes the processes of memory error.) As he argues, "suggestibility in memory refers to an individual's tendency to incorporate misleading information from external sources—from other people, written materials or pictures, including the media—into personal recollections."[21]

Suggestibility often figures in eyewitness misidentifications, for example, where it can be reinforced with what Schacter calls "confirming feedback." In several studies, researchers provided such feedback to prospective witnesses by making encouraging comments ("good, you identified the actual suspect"), doing so even when study participants wrongly identified a perpetrator from a lineup.[22] Participants receiving confirming feedback then expressed confidence in their memories. Such certainty can go far in convincing a jury, although to be sure, witness confidence is no guarantee of guilt or innocence.

While Copland was conducting *Lincoln Portrait* in Caracas, he may well have heard isolated pockets of sound, which, as Taubman notes, were promptly hushed. A few days later, he listened to the recording and brought his travel diary up to date, mentioning neither random noises nor any commotion. He may also have read Taubman's review. Then, sometime between late January 1958 and June 1971, Copland talked to the foreign service officer who planted the suggestion that the performance "started a revolution" on behalf of democracy, an appealing thought to one whose loyalty to the United States had been so publicly challenged. "Confirming feedback" came in the actual overthrow of Pérez Jiménez. As Schacter points out, "suggestibility's pernicious effects highlight the idea that remembering the past is not merely a matter of activating or awakening a dormant trace or picture in the mind," but is rooted in "a far more complex interaction between the current environment . . . and what is retained from the past."[23] The patriotic message of *Lincoln Portrait*, Sujo's compelling reading, audience approbation, the courage of Venezuelan civilians in early 1958 who could have easily watched their country slide into another military regime—combined with Copland's desire to rehabilitate himself in the eyes of his compatriots, along with his faith in the power of music—all fuse into the "complex interaction" Schacter describes.

## Suggestibility and U.S.–Latin American Relations

More glaring than the flaws in Copland's memory is the collective "sin of suggestibility" by the United States. As we have seen, the principles that Lincoln so memorably articulated guided Latin American policy only incidentally during the Cold War. Just as the U.S. government had propped up other dictators, it supported Pérez Jiménez. In his case, however, support exceeded perfunctory diplomatic recognition. In February 1954 President Eisenhower awarded the Venezuelan dictator the Legion of Merit, which recognizes exceptional military leaders in allied countries, including those who opposed communism.[24] Pérez

Jiménez also won recognition in the United States for his business acumen. On 28 February 1955, at the height of the oil boom, he enjoyed the signal honor of appearing on the cover of *Time* magazine and, in the accompanying article, was dubbed "skipper of the dreamboat," that is, of the oil-rich Venezuelan economy. His comments therein dovetail neatly with existing conceptions of Latin America in the United States. Just as George Kennan described that "shadow of a tremendous helplessness and impotence," Pérez Jiménez disparaged his compatriots' capacity for self-government. "I make every effort to give Venezuelans the kind of government best adapted to them," he insisted to readers of *Time*. "People may call it a dictatorial regime, [but] my country is not ready for the kind of democracy that brings abuses of liberty. We are still in our infant years, and we still need halters."[25] Peréz Jiménez's likening of his fellow Venezuelans to animals (they evidently require "halters") echoes the words screenwriter John Huston put into the mouth of Napoleon III in the 1939 Good Neighbor film *Juárez*: "Democracy! The rule of the cattle by the cattle for the cattle!"

The United States offered Pérez Jiménez other tangible benefits. In January 1958, after agreeing to step down, the dictator and his chief of the Seguridad Nacional "fled the country," as Copland stated. Indeed, they flew straight to Miami where Pérez Jiménez lived for five years in a mansion on Pine Tree Drive complete with a staff of servants, bodyguards, and several cars.[26] Only extradition and a lengthy trial in Venezuela obliged him eventually to seek hospitality in Franco's Spain, where he lived out his remaining years.[27] All helped set the stage for an upsurge of anti-U.S. sentiment in Latin America that one reporter described as "the rudest surprise since Sputnik."[28] That "surprise" was Vice President Richard M. Nixon's goodwill visit in May 1958. Besides getting into a shouting match in Lima, Nixon had to be rescued by the Secret Service in Caracas when crowds shouted anti-U.S. slogans, stoned his motorcade, and nearly overturned his car. In reporting on this public relations disaster, the *New York Times* described a "supercharged atmosphere of extreme nationalism."[29] Nonetheless, the trip succeeded where Latin American diplomats had failed: now the demise of the Good Neighbor Policy was plain for all to see.

Copland's suggestibility is thus part of a broader, culturally ingrained "sin." The notion that Lincolnian ideals had informed U.S. policy toward Venezuela during the Cold War was comforting but wrong. It took hold not only in the mind of one foreign service officer but lodged itself in the narrative of one of Copland's best-known works. These interwoven threads of fact, music, memory, and forgetting all give new meaning to *Lincoln Portrait*'s opening declaration: "we cannot escape history."

## Memory, Music, and Latin America

Most studies of memory and Latin America, whether individual or collective, have focused on Cold War–era military dictatorships as experienced by Latin Americans.[30] Museums of memory, constructed in recent years in Buenos Aires, Santiago, Bogotá, and other cities, are visited by thousands, including relatives of those "disappeared" by military regimes.[31] Scholars have been far less preoccupied with U.S. consciousness of Latin America, even though U.S. Americans have habitually "forgotten" the region. Just as James Reston reportedly remarked in the 1940s that "the people of the United States would do anything for Latin America except read about it," the Cold War abetted this tendency.[32] Certainly when the damning conclusions of the *Church Report* brought to light U.S. conduct in Chile, many questioned their government's actions. Others, however, refused to believe that their elected officials were capable of overthrowing the government of a sovereign nation. This sense, that "it didn't happen," comes to life in the 1982 film *Missing* by Greek director Costa-Gavras, in which Jack Lemmon plays a staunch conservative, skeptical of U.S. intervention, who tries to track down his journalist son who went missing in Chile after the coup. (Ultimately the protagonist acknowledges CIA involvement.) Several decades later a significant portion of the U.S. voting population cheers the prospect of a border wall as if U.S. power grabs during the U.S.–Mexican War of the 1840s had never happened. Such erasure recalls the words of the German philologist and memory scholar Harald Weinrich: "one might paraphrase the meaning of 'forget' as 'to get rid (of something).'"[33]

Have we in the United States "gotten rid of" Latin American classical music, a repertory of such interest during the Good Neighbor period? After decades of advocacy by scholars, composers, and performers, several musical institutions are rising to the occasion, including university departments and publishers. Yet we can always expand our efforts. A Latin American–themed concert could honor the work of cultural diplomacy, kicking off with Cowell's *Fanfare for the Forces of Our Latin American Allies* followed by music of Latin American composers involved in Good Neighborly relations. Piano recitals could feature Guarnieri's *Ponteios* or Ginastera's *Doce preludios americanos*. Chamber musicians might try out Andrés Sas's *Cantos del Perú* or Villa-Lobos's Sixth String Quartet. What about an evening of Latin American *Concertos for Orchestra*? Besides those by José María Castro and Estévez, mentioned above, Washington Castro (Argentina), Ricardo Lorenz (Venezuela), Roberto Sierra (Puerto Rico), and Luis Ernesto Gómez (Venezuela) each wrote a *Concerto for Orchestra*. We also need to bring more repertory from manuscript to live performance. In

1947, when Copland heard Guarnieri's prize-winning Second String Quartet, he called it "a good, playable work." Today, it is available only in manuscript.

Another matter is image. Works such as Gershwin's *Cuban Overture* and Morton Gould's *Latin American Symphonette* evoke pleasant tourist experiences in part because their creators rejected modernism. Yet in doing so, they reinforce the notion that Latin American music is something other than "advanced." We in the United States could showcase more works by the Latin American avant-garde of the twentieth and twenty-first centuries, taking as a starting point composers Copland met in the 1960s, such as Edgar Valcárcel, the multinational Gustavo Becerra, Roque Cordero, or Juan Orrego-Salas, whose artful eightieth-birthday tribute for Copland, *Variations for a Quiet Man* for clarinet and piano, subtly quotes various gestures from *Appalachian Spring*. Works by living Latin American composers—Gabriela Ortiz, Jocy de Oliveira, Tania León, Paulo Chagas, Paul Desennes, Chañaral Ortega-Miranda, Pablo Ortiz, and many others—help correct this still-persistent representation of Latin America. The artistic merit of their music is equally deserving of our attention.

## Copland and History

Copland, too, rejected the notion of a modern or advanced Latin America. In 1971 he finished the *Three Latin-American Sketches*, adding the third movement, "Estribillo." Throughout, the musical ingredients are identical to those of *El salón México*: overwhelmingly triadic harmonies, long stretches of well-established key centers, and generally conventional orchestration. If in 1938 *El salón México* was not especially modern—its critics noted that the themes "fairly drip molasses" and that Copland did "not seek for strangeness"—*Three Latin-American Sketches* was far less so in 1971. One U.S. critic predicted "wide circulation" for the work, suggesting that it would "augment Copland's royalties if not his artistic stature."[34] In 1954 Copland complained that the music of his Latin American colleagues at the Caracas festival was "too Latin American." Yet his own music largely followed that same orientation.

In his writings, Copland sometimes reinforces this parochialism, even as he eventually recognized that asserting national identity was potentially "narrow and wrong." I have already discussed his essentialism, whether his contention that Brazilian composers are "uninhibited, abundant, non-critical, romantic" or that the "gray pallor" of Paz's music ran contrary to "the Latin temperament." In 1965 he addressed Latin American music in *Music in the Twenties*,

## 12. Latin American Classical Music and Memory 247

a series of twelve thirty-minute television programs, broadcast by WGBH Boston. Sporting a tuxedo, Copland balances formality and chattiness as he discusses neoclassicism, serialism, jazz, and twentieth-century opera. Program 8 of the series is dedicated to "Nationalism: New World Style" (a follow-up to "Nationalism: European Style," an earlier episode). Allowing that nationalism had lost much of its appeal, Copland speculates that "it may very well turn up in the years to come." Surprisingly, he focuses on Villa-Lobos, whose musical defects Copland had enumerated both privately and publicly for over two decades. On television, however, he announced that

> the first significant nationalist breakthrough in the writing of both Latin American and North American music came at the beginning of the twenties. If you want to date it you might say it began with the arrival in Paris in 1923 of Villa-Lobos, the Brazilian composer. I remember seeing him for the first time without knowing who he was at a soirée chez Nadia Boulanger and I remember what a striking figure he cut, in his forties, wielding his inevitable cigar, and being a rather voluble and forceful personality.[35]

"It was obvious," Copland adds, rather opaquely, "that [Villa-Lobos] came from Latin America." Recalling, perhaps, his own passion for Brazilian popular music, Copland urges his listeners to "take into account" Brazil, "Latin America's most fascinating country" today. The reason? "Think of those five different strains," Copland urges. "Negro, Spanish, Portuguese, Italian, and Indian and you'll see that a Brazilian composer, if he's trying to create a music peculiar to his own country, has a much richer source of material than is true of any of the other Latin American countries." Like Chávez and Revueltas, Villa-Lobos wrote music that "we connect both with him and his country of origin," as Copland told his television audience.

He concludes by assessing musical Pan Americanism:

> During the twenties, for the first time, we find the beginning of what has continued since that time—a tendency for North and South Americans to look toward one another with the idea of getting artistic sustenance from one another. The need to affirm national characteristics—it was uppermost in the minds of some of us (not all of us, but some of us at that time)—was the thing that united us both in our relationship to Europe and in the need to free ourselves from Europe.[36]

In 1976, however, Copland and Vivian Perlis of the Oral History of American Music project at Yale University began the composer's two-volume autobiography. There, he takes a different tack on Latin America. To be sure, by this time his memory may have begun to falter. (For example, he unthinkingly repeats his attacks on Brazilian "twelve-toners" and "dullards.")[37] But he also calls into question musical Pan Americanism. Recalling "the belief many of us in the arts had in those days—that the history of twentieth-century music was going to be written from both North and South America," he now adds, "Perhaps we were naïve."[38] Also in 1976 Copland gave an interview to the Mexican newspaper *Excelsior*, in which he revisited his rather implausible defense of "an avant-garde for the masses" even as his own music increasingly demonstrated the reality of two publics for "serious music."[39]

These twists and turns on Latin American music mirror Copland's uncertainty about the direction music as a whole had taken. In urging Latin American composers to avail themselves of folklore even into the 1960s, he projected nostalgia for the era when his own "brand" was well received largely *because* of folklore. Kimberly K. Smith's definition of nostalgia as "a key concept in the ... conflict over modernity" is apt here, as is Svetlana Boym's view on "modern nostalgia": the "longing for the loss of an enchanted world with clear borders and values."[40] For Copland, those borders were ample, embracing the U.S. West, a Mexican dance hall, rural Pennsylvania, and the sidewalks of New York. But they were nothing if not "clear," at least in comparison with the "flux and semiconfusion" that took their place.

The actual impact of Copland's words on Latin American music is debatable. Unlike Paz, he never devoted an entire book to the music of a "sister republic," and his writings on Latin American music appear in scattered essays, along with the occasional public statement. Still, some later scholars took a tone similar to Copland's. Compare, for example, unelaborated descriptions of "unmistakably Mexican" or "genuinely Peruvian" music or the notion that Latin American music is "filled with irresistible exotic color."[41] Even in recent textbooks, hollow qualifiers such as "unique," "distinctive," and "characteristic" discourage students from thinking critically about what they are hearing and what meanings it portends.[42] In striving to reject empty, essentialist language that exhausted itself decades ago, we in the United States can consider demographics: by 2050 Latinos are projected to make up 29 percent of the population.[43] Latin American classical music is as much a cultural reality as any other musical style or genre. In an interview with the U.S.-Cuban journalist and newscaster Ray Suarez, a Puerto Rican teenager named Ricardo Jiménez advocated for a Puerto Rican studies class in his overcrowded Chicago high school, exclaiming, "I found out that we [Puerto Ricans] have actors, that we have poets." He could have added the classical composers Roberto Sierra, Rafael

Aponte-Ledée, Luis M. Álvarez, Ernesto Cordero, Felipe Gutiérrez Espinosa, Juan Morel Campos, William Ortiz, Raymond Torres Santos, or Johnny Navarro Huertas.[44] Besides this repertory's aesthetic interest, the promise of intercultural understanding beckons. As Suarez declared to his U.S. readers, "you won't be able to understand the America [of the future] if you don't know Latino history. Latino history is your history. Latino history is *our* history."[45]

## Cultural Diplomacy Then and Now

In a 2020 book Robert M. Gates, Secretary of State under Presidents George W. Bush and Barack Obama, remembers the apogee of cultural diplomacy. In the chapter "Symphony of Power," he describes numerous accomplishments, among them the President's Special International Program for Cultural Presentations, the American Specialist Program, the People to People Program, and the United States Information Agency (USIA), established during the Eisenhower years to "tell America's story to the world."[46] Similarly, the Voice of America (VOA) launched its Jazz Hour for listeners behind the Iron Curtain.[47] Too often the United States has relied on military solutions and economic imperialism in international conflicts instead of diplomacy, however. Moreover, once the Cold War was seen to have ended, U.S. personnel, consulates, and missions worldwide were sharply reduced. In a 1996 congressional hearing, Secretary of State Warren Christopher reported on a dearth of basic amenities: to receive news in Sarajevo, diplomats had to "jerry-rig a satellite dish to the roof using a barbecue grill."[48]

Cultural diplomacy suffered accordingly. In 1999 the USIA was dismantled, its duties absorbed by the State Department. Cultural diplomats sensed not only the lack of an overarching strategy but of faith in the potential of artistic and cultural exchange (not to mention funding). As Cynthia P. Schneider, former ambassador to the Netherlands, argued, "Imagine trying to understand the U.S. in the 1950s–1960s purely through a political lens, with no knowledge of jazz, Arthur Miller, abstract expressionism, or *To Kill a Mockingbird*. Yet American policymakers, including sometimes even those in Embassies abroad, are rarely given the mandate or the time to understand the local cultural scene, and if they do, the knowledge rarely extends beyond the Cultural Affairs Department."[49] Such tensions surged under the administration of President Donald J. Trump, which sought additional budget cuts, threatened the Voice of America, abandoned the United Nations Educational, Scientific, and Cultural Organization (UNESCO), and sidelined or attacked individual diplomats.[50]

Yet one hopeful exception had arisen: in the aftermath of 9/11, when the wars in Iraq and Afghanistan had tarnished the reputation of the United States, the government again marshaled cultural diplomacy, now with hip hop as the tool of persuasion. Given the stinging critiques of systemic racism and income inequality in the United States that hip hop artists often express (not to mention glorifying sexism and violence), the genre was hardly an obvious choice. Yet just as freedom of speech figured in *The Cummington Story*, the fact that hip hop artists in the United States are able to articulate their grievances proved a selling point. These ideas began to develop during the administration of George W. Bush and culminated in the program Next Level, for hip-hop diplomacy. Formalized in 2013 under Obama, it relied on strategies developed in Eisenhower's People to People program, with citizen diplomats meeting aspiring hip hop artists worldwide. Support was increased under Trump and has continued under President Joe Biden.[51] Still, the immediate future of U.S. cultural diplomacy is unclear. In 1939 assistant secretary of state Adolph Berle asserted before the delegates of the first conference on Inter-American Relations in the Field of Music that we are all better off knowing "something about each other's art, and music, and books." Now, however, cultural horizons have shifted. Do we even have "our art," "our books," or "our music" when the Internet can confer an elusive sense of belonging at the same time that it foments division? As our very notions of time and space are reconceptualized, cultural exchange will be affected in ways we cannot at present foresee.

Certainly U.S.–Latin American cultural exchange is no longer "almost a forgotten aspect in the history of U.S. foreign relations," as J. Manuel Espinosa lamented in the 1970s. In 2012 Darlene J. Sadlier, one of the principal scholars of Good Neighbor cultural exchange, mused that the long history of tension in U.S.–Latin American relations "cannot help but make reasonable people feel a certain nostalgia for Good Neighbor policies."[52] Those policies were far from perfect. But we can summon up the positive aspects of Good Neighborliness and pay them more than lip service. Since 1931 U.S. presidents have marked Pan American Day, generally with a statement on Pan American amity. In April 2020 Trump referred to the "spirit of cooperation, hope, and progress" that has long united the Americas, words that undoubtedly surprise those who recall his oft-cited comments on Mexico's "criminals, drug dealers, rapists, etc."[53] Prior to Trump—and with less bombast—border walls were constructed in the absence of a coherent immigration policy. In reaction, some in the U.S. have begun practicing what we might call cultural diplomacy at home. Neither official practice nor oxymoron, cultural diplomacy at home rests on the same principles that guide cultural diplomacy in the international sphere. Robert Neustadt, a professor at Northern Arizona University, traveled with his students to the Arizona-Mexico border, where they sampled compositions by "sound-sculptor" Glenn Weyant, who plays the various border walls with a mallet or a cello bow. Young people also chatted and sang in a Red Cross–approved camp with people they might once have labeled "illegals" but now saw as human beings.[54] Grammy-winning jazz musician Arturo O'Farrill, whose project *Fandango at the Wall* sought to bring the United States and Mexico closer together through music, has reminisced over the heyday of cultural exchange and encourages such exchanges today, whether funded through the government or Kickstarter.[55] As in Copland's lifetime, different musical styles and genres vie for priority, with even those ignorant of classical music quick to defend its prestige. "We write symphonies," Trump thundered to a crowd in Warsaw in 2017 in a peroration on how "the West became great," as he put it.[56] It should be clear that Trump's much-maligned Mexicans have written plenty of symphonies. So, too, have Cubans, Peruvians, Nicaraguans, Brazilians, Argentines, and composers from elsewhere in Latin America.[57]

## "The only way to have a friend"

Many have written, often sympathetically, about the fading of Copland's star.[58] In 1970 Nicolas Slonimsky remarked that some "countries are offended when less advanced composers, such as Barber and Copland, are offered to them."[59] William Syndeman, a U.S. composer who received an American Specialist Grant, told the State Department that other countries "have heard the Barber and Copland Sonatas and the Gershwin Rhapsody and should not be led to believe that this is the only compositional activity occurring in America."[60] Clearly William Warfield's performances of "I Bought Me a Cat" would only go so far.[61]

In asking the question, "Who was Copland?" vis-à-vis his cultural diplomacy in Latin America, we have seen him change course, equivocate, and, as Theodor Chanler remarked early on, succumb to "half-diffident charitableness" and "softness of critical fibre" over musical matters. Perhaps like André Gide, one of his favorite authors, Copland believed he could "simultaneously embrace contradictory ideas."[62] We may find Copland's rhetorical half-measures irritating, or evidence of inner fragility. But his experience raises questions that remain unresolved today. Why do many in the United States express surprise when they learn that Latin Americans write twelve-tone music or electroacoustic music?

That Latin Americans have performed and composed jazz since the 1920s? How, exactly, do we distinguish accessible music, whether rooted in folklore of the Americas or the values of the Popular Front, from the products of the culture industry, also designed for accessibility? I hope that this book has brought forth—and perhaps illuminated—new perspectives on these questions.

One aspect of Copland's career on which we find near total unanimity is his generosity of spirit. If nowadays some argue that technology renders face-to-face meetings unnecessary, Copland's interpersonal rapport (People to People diplomacy before it was an official program) should give them pause. Three case studies affirm one of Copland's central convictions on cultural diplomacy, one, moreover, on which he emphatically did *not* waver. As noted, at the height of the red scare and at no small personal risk, he argued that "the only way to have a friend is to be one." He consistently put this idea into practice throughout his Latin American experience.

One "friend" was the late Mario Davidovsky of Argentina. Copland first became aware of Davidovsky in 1957, while serving on the jury for the Second Caracas Festival. Among the 107 scores submitted, one stood out. It was by the twenty-four-year-old Davidovsky, born of Lithuanian-Jewish parents and a student of the Jewish émigré composers Guillermo Graetzer, Erwin Leuchter, Teodoro Fuchs, and Ernesto Epstein. Davidovsky described his mentors as "close to Hindemith and the Second Viennese school"; as a student, moreover, he noticed "a rather 'cool and polite' demarcation between the Hochschule types" and the majority of Argentine composers, who were "more attuned to the thinking of the French Conservatory or Santa Cecilia in Rome."[63] Copland did not identify in his diary the work that caught his eye in 1957. But over fifty years later Davidovsky recalled that it was his *Suite sinfónica para el payaso* (Symphonic Suite for a Clown), composed in 1955 and also a ballet.[64] The jury, however, resisted. As Copland wrote in 1957, "The big fight was over a score by [Mario] Davidovsky, which I more or less forced the jury to look at. It looks remarkable on the page but the musical style is too closely Central European and there is obviously too much interest in the delight of a complex-looking page."[65] Still, Copland noted, "I am curious to meet the composer." Ultimately the other jurors were less flexible than he, and *Suite sinfónica para el payaso* was eliminated.

Yet Copland did meet Davidovsky, at the Berkshire Music Center in summer 1959. (He told Davidovsky he thought the *Suite sinfónica* deserved an honorable mention.)[66] During their lessons, Copland would listen attentively to the intense young man defending complexity and abstruseness. Surely Copland remembered what it was to be youthful and defiant. One day, guest lecturer Marc Blitzstein played for the students excerpts from some of his operas, or "light music," as Davidovsky called it.[67] Incensed by Blitzstein's simple musical language, Davidovsky walked out. Afterwards, Copland calmly took the young man aside and reminded him that tango, samba, and other popular genres were immensely important in Latin American classical music and that Blitzstein's approach to these materials was a principled one. Davidovsky, who later taught at Harvard and received several prestigious prizes, including a Pulitzer, later wrote that Copland helped him "more than any Argentinian."[68]

A second "friend" was the Argentine composer and former CLAEM student alcides lanza. In 1963, lanza attended Copland's lectures, "still vivid" in lanza's memory in 2015.[69] He recalls that Copland addressed "computer music, a subject rather new to me at the time. [Copland] spoke about and played examples of computer music from Illinois, by [Lejaren] Hiller and [Leonard] Isaacson, probably the *Illiac Suite*. Other lectures dealt with jazz and twelve-tone trends."[70] Whatever discomfort some Latin American critics detected on Copland's part regarding this repertory, he obviously spoke convincingly enough for lanza. Later, at a gathering at Ginastera's (possibly the one where Copland played the recording of *Connotations*), Copland asked, "Well, what do you plan to do after the CLAEM fellowship ends? A trip to Europe?" lanza recalled the conversation:

> I answered, "Maestro Copland, I would like to go to the United States, not to Europe."
> He asked me why so. . . .
> I answered, "Because I am interested in [the fact] that Varèse, Cage, Feldman, Partch are living there."
> Then Copland asked me, "Have you thought of the Guggenheim Fellowship?"
> "Yes, Maestro," I replied. "I have applied already twice but got negative answers."
> "Very well," Copland said. "You *must* apply again. But this time, you will put my name as a reference."[71]

In August 1965, now a Guggenheim fellow, lanza and his family moved to New York. He studied with Vladimir Ussachevsky at the Columbia-Princeton Electronic Music Center and, several prestigious grants later, began teaching composition at McGill University in Montreal, in 1971, where he directed the Electronic Music Studio. From time to time he would visit Copland in New York, where, lanza recalled, Copland was "always gracious, a gentleman, asking about my studies on electronic music, my compositions and other projects" and always willing to provide a letter of recommendation.[72]

Chilean composer León Schidlowsky offers an even more personal tribute. He and Copland first became acquainted in Santiago in 1963. (Copland noted in his diary Schidlowsky's "very Jewish personality." Of the young man's *Tríptico* for orchestra, from 1959, Copland concluded "not my dish.")[73] They met again in 1966, this time in New York when Schidlowsky was on tour with the Ballet Nacional Chileno. "Copland was a cultivated man," Schidlowsky wrote. "Open to all truths, honest and modest, which impressed me."[74] Copland invited him to "lunch at an exclusive club," where they discussed the cataclysmic changes in music during the twentieth century. Schidlowsky also recalled, "I knew various works by Copland, and among them, *Lincoln Portrait* impressed me," accounting, perhaps, for his own interest in "speaker pieces." He and Copland also explored their Jewish roots:

> [Copland] spoke to me about the trio *Vitebsk* . . . which he mentioned because it was based on Jewish materials. He then spoke to me about [his family's] real last name, Kaplan, and we exchanged opinions on our common Jewish origins. . . . I mentioned to him that I was thinking of writing a work, *New York*, in which I would use jazz elements. I don't think he ever heard it, but its premiere, which was scheduled for New York by the Symphonic Orchestra of Chile, only came about later in Caracas. . . . I told Copland that I was thinking of dedicating it to "my black brothers of Harlem," which I did, and Copland reacted encouragingly. With this, his progressive outlook on the equality of human beings became clear to me, such that skin color, religious belief, or origins were of no importance to him.[75]

"All these memories I have tried to relive amid the passing of time," Schidlowsky reflected. With these few words, he pinpoints the true nature of cultural diplomacy. Its benefits lie not so much in the *object*—the music, art, literature, theater, film being exchanged—but in what people feel, say, and remember. Many have disparaged Copland, both in his own time and today. Yet he is very much with us. I would wager that many sophisticated listeners, including those who populate the "solemn circles" of professional music, as the Brazilian critic Nogueira França put it, furtively admire certain fixtures of Copland's music. We might well crave a good tune (folkloric or not), a jazzy rhythm, "too much brass," or nostalgia for a past that never was. We might even welcome unsubtle calls to democracy, especially in an era when "government by the people" is threatened on a worldwide scale. Like Schidlowsky, we can strive to keep alive these ideals "amid the passing of time."

# Notes

## Chapter 1. Introduction

1. Aaron Copland, diary, 29 October 1947, "South American Journal 1947," box/folder 243/7, Aaron Copland Collection, Library of Congress, Washington, DC (hereafter CCLC).

2. Fosler-Lussier, *Music in America's Cold War Diplomacy*, 13–15.

3. Cummings, *Cultural Diplomacy and the United States Government*, 1. The term "public diplomacy" was coined in the 1960s, replacing "cultural diplomacy" in some circles. Arndt, *First Resort of Kings*, 480; Glade, "Issues in the Genesis and Organization Diplomacy." Because "cultural diplomacy" is current in musicology, I use it here.

4. Arndt, *First Resort of Kings*, 36–48.

5. Fagg, *Pan Americanism*; Sheinin, *Beyond the Ideal*; Vargas-Alzate, "Washington and Latin America."

6. Whitaker, *Western Hemisphere Idea*, 3.

7. Kenworthy, *America/Américas*, 18.

8. Tomlinson, *Singing of the New World*, 7.

9. Rosenberg, *Financial Missionaries*.

10. Pereira Salas, *Notes on the History*, esp. 17.

11. Espinosa, *Inter-American Beginnings*, 12–14.

12. Secretary of State Charles Evans Hughes, quoted in Espinosa, *Inter-American Beginnings*, 21.

13. Kahan, "Herbert Hoover's Diplomacy toward Latin America," 484–501.

14. Quoted in Espinosa, *Inter-American Beginnings*, 24.

15. Frye, *Nazi Germany and the American Hemisphere*, 131–51; Friedman, "There Goes the Neighborhood."

16. "The Presidency."

17. Holden and Zolov, *Latin America and the United States*, 142.

18. Raymont, *Troubled Neighbors*, 25–26.

19. Espinosa, *Inter-American Beginnings*, 79–87.

20. Abrams Ansari, "Aaron Copland"; Abrams Ansari, *Sound of a Superpower*, 143–45; Bartig, "Aaron Copland's Soviet Diary."

21. Among these studies are Crist, *Music for the Common Man*; DeLapp-Birkett, "Copland in the Fifties" and "Aaron Copland and the Politics"; Hubbs, *Queer Composition*; Levy, "From Orient to Occident" and *Frontier Figures*; Pollack, "Dean of Gay American Composers" and "Copland and the Prophetic Voice." See also Robertson and Armstrong, *Aaron Copland*.

22. Espinosa, *Inter-American Beginnings*, vii.

23. See, for example, Smith, *Improvised Continent*; Delgado and Camacho, *Diplomacia cultural y los derechos humanos*; Fox, *Making Art Panamerican*; Márquez Bravo, "Diplomacia Cultural y Propaganda"; Palomino, *Invention of Latin American Music*; Prutsch, *Creating Good Neighbors*; Sadlier, *Americans All*; Tota, *Seduction of Brazil*; Matallana, "Inventing Latin America."

24. Abrams Ansari, *Sound of a Superpower*; Beal, *New Music, New Allies*; Fosler-Lussier, *Music in America's Cold War Diplomacy*. Studies of other regions include Gienow-Hecht, *Sound Diplomacy*; Katz, *Build*.

25. Important exceptions include Campbell, "Creating Something Out of Nothing," and "Shaping Solidarity"; Herrera, *Elite Art Worlds*; Stallings, "Collective Difference"; Tacuchian, "Panamericanismo." "Classic" studies on music and Pan Americanism include Pereira Salas, *Notes* and *Los primeros contactos*.

26. See Pollack, *Aaron Copland*, 216–33; Abrams Ansari, "Aaron Copland," 340–42. Campbell situates Copland as a player in Latin American cultural diplomacy broadly conceived, in "Shaping Solidarity." See also Hess, "Copland in Argentina."

27. Saavedra, "Carlos Chávez's Polysemic Style"; Parker, "Copland and Chávez"; Pollack, "Aaron Copland, Carlos Chávez, and Silvestre Revueltas." See also Levin, "From the New York Avant-Garde."

28. Campos, *El folklore y la música Mexicana*; Copland, "Story behind My *El salón México*"; Crist, *Music for the Common Man*; Magrini, "Aaron Copland"; Murchison, *American Stravinsky*, 193–207; Toor, *Cancionero Mexicano*.

29. Fauser, "Aaron Copland, Nadia Boulanger," 543.

30. Pavuk, "No Immigrants or Radicals."

31. Hanke, *Do the Americas Have a Common History*, 20.

32. Hess, "Latin American Art Music."

33. For an insightful discussion of this point, see Fosler-Lussier, *Music in America's Cold War Diplomacy*, 207–25.

34. Sinor, "Reading the Ordinary Diary," 123.

35. Brody, "Founding Sons," 24; on nationalism and Pan Americanism, see Hess, *Representing the Good Neighbor*, 127–29.

36. Ramsey, "Pot Liquor Principle," 292.

37. Copland, Diary, 11 March 1957, "Venezuela Visit—Nov 26–Dec 9, 1954/Feb 21–Mar 31, 1957," box/folder 244/15 and 16, CCLC. He never finished the violin piece. See also Abrams Ansari, *Sound of a Superpower*, 136; Daniel, *Tanglewood*, 79.

38. Nye, "Soft Power and American Foreign Policy," 256.
39. Van Ham, *Social Power*, 68.
40. Purcell to Aaron Copland, 7 June 1962, box/folder 363/18, CCLC.
41. Pollack, *Aaron Copland*, 23, 26–27. Copland rarely attended synagogue as an adult and once claimed to have "resigned" from Judaism. He composed a handful of works related to Judaism. See Pollack, "Copland and the Prophetic Voice."
42. Pollack, "Dean of Gay American Composers."
43. Kostelanetz, *Aaron Copland*, 296. On the limits of Copland's affability, see Pollack, "Copland and the Prophetic Voice," 4.
44. Leonard, *Conservatoire Américain*, xvii–xviii.
45. Fauser discusses postwar strains in Franco-U.S. relations in "Aaron Copland, Nadia Boulanger," 527. See also Francis, *Teaching Stravinsky*.
46. Arndt, *First Resort of Kings*, 25; Kraske, *Missionaries of the Book*.
47. Copland, "What Europe Means," 15, 27.
48. Pollack, *Aaron Copland*, 92.
49. Copland, "Is the University Too Much with Us?"
50. Quoted in Ross, *Rest Is Noise*, 416.
51. Abrams Ansari lists Copland's travels from 1941, along with funding details, in *Sounds of a Superpower*, 143–45.
52. Quoted in Pollack, *Aaron Copland*, 232–33.

## Chapter 2. Copland and the Beginnings of U.S. Cultural Diplomacy

1. Bick, "In the Tradition of Dissent," 145–46.
2. On the *Ode*, see Perlis, "Aaron Copland and John Kirkpatrick," 62. Copland also programmed some unidentified songs.
3. On Leonard Bernstein's two-piano arrangement, see Perlis, "Dear Aaron, Dear Lenny," 163–64.
4. Several "second-string" critics worked under Olin Downes, the senior critic at the *Times*. See Robinson, "A Ping, Qualified by a Thud," 79.
5. "Copland Gives First of One-Man Concerts."
6. Ngai, *Impossible Subjects*, 49.
7. Pollack, *Aaron Copland*, 88–106.
8. Fauser, "Aaron Copland, Nadia Boulanger," 537.
9. Copland, *Music and Imagination*, 104.
10. Brody, "Founding Sons," 124.
11. The philosophical and political complexities of this viewpoint are elucidated in Dahlhaus, *Nineteenth-Century Music*, 37–41.
12. Saavedra, "Of Selves and Others," 5; Fojas, *Cosmopolitanism in the Americas*, 1–2; Attali, *Noise*, 14, 92.
13. Hess, *Representing the Good Neighbor*, 20–21.
14. Stearns, ed., *Civilization in the United States*, vii.
15. Discussed in Hess, *Representing the Good Neighbor*, 31.
16. Copland, *Copland on Music*, 203; Copland, *Music and Imagination*, 89.
17. Oja, "Copland-Sessions Concerts."

18. Delpar, *Enormous Vogue of Things Mexican*.
19. Kert, *Abby Aldrich Rockefeller*, 38; Hess, *Representing the Good Neighbor*, 32–33.
20. The concert is analyzed in Hess, *Representing the Good Neighbor*, 25–46.
21. Copland, "Carlos Chávez—Mexican Composer." Citations are from the reprint in Cowell, *American Composers on American Music*, 105.
22. Ibid.
23. Ibid., 102, 103.
24. Ibid. See also Crist, *Music for the Common Man*, 48.
25. Root, "Pan American Association of Composers"; Stallings, "Collective Difference"; on Chávez and the PAAC, see Taylor Gibson, "Music," 157–58.
26. Root, "Pan American Association," 52.
27. Critics cited in Hess, *Representing the Good Neighbor*, 27–28.
28. Cowell and Carl Ruggles were especially insulting, the latter calling it "a great mistake to have that filthy bunch of Juilliard Jews in the Pan American [Association]." Ruggles to Cowell, 21 June 1933; see also Cowell to Adolph Weiss, 28 October 1932, both cited in Bick, "In the Tradition of Dissent," 161.
29. On jazz and Copland historiography, see Fauser, "Aaron Copland, Nadia Boulanger," 530–34; see also Murchison, *American Stravinsky*, 58–62.
30. Pollack, "Dean of Gay American Composers," 41. See also Murchison, *American Stravinsky*, 106–7.
31. Faulkner, "Does Jazz Put the Sin in Syncopation?"
32. Savran, *Highbrow/Lowbrow*, 28–30.
33. Rosenfeld, *Hour with American Music*, 13.
34. Pollack, *Aaron Copland*, 43–44.
35. Murchison argues that Copland modeled *Cat and Mouse* on the second tableau of *Petrushka*. Murchison, *American Stravinsky*, 23–25.
36. Ibid., 65–68; Pollack, *Aaron Copland*, 43.
37. "Blues no. 2" was published in 1949 as the last movement of the set *Four Piano Blues*.
38. Metzer, "Spurned Love."
39. Copland, "Jazz Structure and Influence," 9, 13.
40. Cited in Levy, "From Orient to Occident," 311. See also Schiff, "Copland and the Jazz Boys."
41. Cited in Murchison, *American Stravinsky*, 48.
42. Pollack, *Aaron Copland*, 140.
43. Cited in Crist, "Compositional History," 266.
44. Parker, "Copland and Chávez," 435.
45. DeLapp-Birkett, "Speaking to Whom," 87–89.
46. Cited in ibid., 85.
47. Murchison, *American Stravinsky*, 130–31.
48. Pollack, *Aaron Copland*, 150n21.
49. Berger, *Aaron Copland*, 25. Chávez's music is also frequently described as "austere." Hess, *Representing the Good Neighbor*, 187–88.
50. Cited in Crist, *Music for the Common Man*, 31.

51. Fava, "Composers Collective of New York," 301.
52. Seeger, "On Proletarian Music," 125.
53. Gold, "Change the World," 5. See also Reuss and Reuss, *American Folk Music*, 44–47.
54. Oja, "Composer with a Conscience," 167.
55. Levy, "From Orient to Occident," 321–29.
56. Crist, *Music for the Common Man*, 82.
57. Ross, *Rest Is Noise*, 298.
58. Hess, "Last Great Cause."
59. Copland, "Workers Sing!" in Kostelanetz, *Aaron Copland*, 88–90.
60. Cited in Crist, *Common Man*, 28, emphasis original.
61. Copland, "Workers Sing!" 89.
62. Cited in Crist, *Music for the Common Man*, 29. See also Murchison, *American Stravinsky*, 174.
63. Pollack, *Aaron Copland*, 257–63, 330–32.
64. Other works for young people are *What Do We Plant, The Young Pioneers*, and *Sunday Afternoon Music*.
65. Carter, "Once Again Swing," 102–3; Rosenfeld, "Copland's Play Opera," 603–4.
66. Bick, "*Of Mice and Men*." Copland also considered showing *The City* in Latin America, the 1939 documentary on the problems of industrialized urban life and on which Pare Lorentz, Ralph Steiner, Lewis Mumford, and others collaborated. It was played during the 1939–40 World's Fair. Pollack, *Aaron Copland*, 337–39.
67. Cited in Levy, "From Orient to Occident," 316.
68. Cited in ibid., 315.
69. Cited in ibid., 313.
70. Copland and Perlis, *Copland, 1900 through 1942*, 160; Murchison, *American Stravinsky*, 140–46.
71. Thomson, "Aaron Copland," 67.
72. Levy, "From Orient to Occident," 314.
73. Saminsky, *Music of the Ghetto and the Bible*, 125.
74. Copland, "Jazz as Folk Music," 19. The essay relies to a degree on reports in the local press. Copland likely heard Arthur Briggs in Vienna. Pollack, *Aaron Copland*, 113.
75. Copland, "Jazz as Folk Music," 19.
76. Ibid.
77. Zuck, *History of Musical Americanism*; Fava, "Composers Collective," 331. See also Crist, *Music for the Common Man*, 42.
78. Gold, "Change the World," 5.
79. Levy, "From Orient to Occident," 339.
80. Baqueiro Fóster, "Aaron Copland." On jazz in Mexico, see this study, pp. 41–42.
81. Carmona, *Epistolario selecto*, 131.
82. For the program, see Copland and Perlis, *Copland, 1900 through 1942*, 215.
83. Brenner's *Your Mexican Holiday* went through five editions. See also Anita Brenner, *Idols behind Altars*.
84. Brenner, "Influence of Technique"; Glusker, *Anita Brenner*.

85. Saborit, "Masters Carlos Chávez and Miguel Covarrubias," 247–48; Taylor Gibson, "Chávez."

86. Brenner, *Your Mexican Holiday*, 141, 118.

87. Copland to Mary Lescaze, 13 January 1933, cited in Copland and Perlis, *Copland, 1900 through 1942*, 216.

88. "*El salón México* by Aaron Copland" (program booklet), 17. See also Copland, "Story behind My *El salón México*," 2–4. Copland's position is rather at odds with the dismantling of capitalism, a motive Elizabeth B. Crist attributes to the composer. See Crist, *Music for the Common Man*, 45, 54, 55. As noted, wealthy individuals embraced Mexico with enthusiasm equal to that of their left-wing compatriots. See Hess, *Representing the Good Neighbor*, 38.

89. Blitzstein, "Composers as Lecturers," 49.

90. On tourism and "personal property," see Jameson, "Reification and Utopia," 131.

91. "*El salón México* by Aaron Copland," 16.

92. P. S. [Pitts Sanborn], "Boston Orchestra Honors Composer"; Thompson, "Music of the Week End."

93. Downes, "Copland Novelty in Premiere Here"; see also Kolodin, "Music of the Week End: Boston Symphony Matinee"; Pakenham, "Recent Phonograph Recordings"; Perkins, "NBC Symphony Concert Led by Boult, of BBC."

94. Pollack, *Aaron Copland*, 300.

95. Cited in Farrow, *War on Peace*, 4.

96. Briggs, *Proud Servant*, 130; Stuart, "New Division."

97. Cited in Ninkovich, *Diplomacy of Ideas*, 30.

98. Briggs, *Proud Servant*, 130.

99. Sweet, *History of Latin America*.

100. Skidmore and Smith, *Modern Latin America*, 2. The survey dates from 1940.

101. Rodríguez, *Changing Race*, 106–8.

102. Wade, *Race and Ethnicity*, 13.

103. Wolf, *Styling Blackness*, 23–24.

104. Skidmore, *Black into White*; Hess, *Representing the Good Neighbor*, 88, 108, 189. Of course there is no such thing as "black" or "white" blood; further, "blackening" could—and did—occur just as easily. Wade, *Race and Ethnicity*, 31.

105. Never codified into federal law, the one-drop rule was observed in many states during much of the twentieth century. Lipsitz, *Possessive Investment*.

106. Katznelson, *Fear Itself*, 139–40.

107. Zack, *Race and Mixed Race*, 127–47.

108. Katznelson, *Fear Itself*, 141, 156–94. Only in 2022 did the Emmett Till Anti-Lynching Act make lynching a federal crime. On African American artists and the New Deal, see Wagner, *1934*.

109. Unsigned to Laurence Duggan and Richard F. Pattee, 8 August 1938, carbon copy, box 234/MC 468, folder 18, Manuscript Collection, Special Collections, University of Arkansas, Fayetteville, 2.

110. Decker, *Music Makes Me*, 171–77; Schwartz, *Flying Down to Rio*.

111. Hess, *Representing the Good Neighbor*, 96.

112. State Department Appropriation Bill, 6 December 1937, box 225/MC 468, folder 22, 37, Manuscript Collection, Special Collections, University of Arkansas, Fayetteville.

113. Arndt, *First Resort of Kings*, 60.

114. Cited in Ninkovich, *Diplomacy of Ideas*, 27.

115. Ibid., 27, 29–31.

116. Cited in ibid., 31; see also Skidmore and Smith, *Modern Latin America*, 45.

117. Hess, *Representing the Good Neighbor*, 19–20.

118. Ocampo, "Carta a Waldo Frank," 11; King, *Sur*, 8.

119. Corrado, "Stravinsky y la constelación," 96.

120. Ibid., 94. See also Caamaño, *La historia del Teatro Colón*, 643; Levitz, *Modernist Mysteries*.

121. Franco, *Modern Culture of Latin America*, 113–14; Béhague, *Music in Latin America*, 245–46; Hess, *Representing the Good Neighbor*, 128–29, 44–45. See also Tobin, *Neoclassical Music in America*.

122. Espinosa, "Cultural Heritage," 361.

123. "Brief History of the Project," 17 September 1940, unpublished notes, box 234/MC 468, folder 26, Manuscript Collection, Special Collections, University of Arkansas, Fayetteville, 1–9; Pernet, "For the Genuine Culture," 144–45; Fern, "Origins and Function."

124. Chase, "Musicological Congress," 8.

125. Lange, "Americanismo musical." See also Hess, *Representing the Good Neighbor*, 130; Castro Pantoja, "Antagonism, Europhilia, and Identity," 14.

126. Hess, "De aspecto inglés," 282; Pereira Salas, *Notes on the History*, 25; Hess, *Representing the Good Neighbor*, 81–85, 100–109.

127. On the bureaucratic entanglements regarding Copland's appointments, see Fauser, *Sounds of War*, 96.

128. Katz, Kuss, and Wolfe, *Libraries, History, Diplomacy*; Shepard, "Legacy of Carleton Sprague Smith."

129. "The Importance to Cultural Understanding of Folk and Popular Music," Digest of Proceedings (Address by Charles Seeger, Music Program Works Progress Administration), entry/box 24/30, RG 353, National Archives and Records Administration (hereafter NARA), College Park, Maryland, 4. Citations to the multisectional Digest are referred to as "Digest." See also Pernet, "For the Genuine Culture," 137–40; on folk music collection in the United States, see Chase, "Recorded Folk Music," 14; Bartis, "History of the Archive."

130. Digest (Wednesday Afternoon Session), 12.

131. Ibid. (Address by Dr. Francisco Curt Lange), 4.

132. Ibid. (Thursday Afternoon Session), 23.

133. Ibid. (Address of Dr. William Berrien), 2.

134. Ibid., 9.

135. Ibid. (Thursday Morning Session), 15–16.

136. Campbell, "Activist Diva."

137. Dett, "Negro Music," 1245.
138. Digest (Thursday Morning Session), 21.
139. Ibid.
140. Ibid. (Address of the Honorable A. A. Berle Jr., assistant secretary of state), 2.
141. Arndt, *First Resort of Kings*, 63–64.
142. Levy, *Frontier Figures*, 324.
143. de la Vega, "Latin American Composers," 164.
144. Copland, *Our New Music*, 212–30; Brody, "Founding Sons," 16.
145. Copland, *Our New Music*, 227.
146. Ibid., 229.
147. DeLapp-Birkett, "Speaking to Whom?" 90–91; Greenberg, "Avant-Garde and Kitsch."
148. Thomson, *State of Music*, 111–20. See also Chybowski, "Developing American Taste"; Katz, "Making America More Musical"; Adorno, "Analytical Study."
149. On this little-explored dimension of Copland's career, see Chowrimootoo, "Copland's Canons."
150. Copland, *Our New Music*, 236.
151. On this point, see Alfred Einstein, "National and Universal Music."
152. DeLapp-Birkett, "Dialogue without Words," 250.
153. Copland, "Playing It Safe at Zurich," 28–29.
154. Chanler, "New Romanticism," 66.
155. Ibid., 65.

## Chapter 3. Copland as Good Neighbor

1. Conchita Rexach to Copland, 23 July 1941, box/folder 355/11, CCLC.
2. Cramer, and Prutsch, "Nelson A. Rockefeller's Office." Originally called the Office for the Coordination of Commercial and Cultural Relations between the American Republics, the entity was renamed in March 1945 as the Office of Inter-American Affairs (OIAA), the abbreviation used in National Archives inventories.
3. Briggs, *Proud Servant*, 116.
4. Smith, "Musical Tour," xxi, 85, 157, 210, 85.
5. Rivas, *Missionary Capitalist*, 1.
6. Fauser, *Sounds of War*, 94–95. See also Tota, *Seduction of Brazil*, 49–50, and American "Amigo."
7. Rivas, *Missionary Capitalist*, 38.
8. Hess, *Representing the Good Neighbor*, 79.
9. Rivas, *Missionary Capitalist*, 46.
10. Minutes, OIAA Music Committee, 20 November 1940, box/folder 355/9, CCLC, 1. Unless otherwise indicated, "Minutes" refers to the minutes of the OIAA Music Committee.
11. Briggs, *Proud Servant*, 133, emphasis original.
12. Ninkovich, *Diplomacy of Ideas*, 39.
13. Ibid., 40.
14. Gellman, *Good Neighbor Diplomacy*, 1.

15. Hess, "Walt Disney's *Saludos Amigos*: Hollywood and the Propaganda of Authenticity," 111; see also Lavine and Wechsler, *War Propaganda and the United States*.
16. Ninkovitch, *Diplomacy of Ideas*, 42.
17. Santa Cruz, *Mi vida en la música*, 608.
18. The name of committee changed several times. I refer here to the "OIAA Music Committee."
19. Minutes, 23 January 1941, box/folder 355/10, CCLC, 1.
20. Mount, "Chile: An Effort at Neutrality," 162–65.
21. Etchepare and Stewart, "Nazism in Chile"; Cassigoli, "Sobre la presencia nazi en Chile."
22. Edward G. Trueblood, "Chilean-U.S. Cultural Relations: The Early Years 1938–1940," unpublished memoir, box 235/MC 468, folder 235–11, Manuscript Collection, Special Collections, University of Arkansas, Fayetteville, 9a.
23. Smith, "Musical Tour," 46.
24. "Candide," "Only Human," *Sunday Mirror*, 17 November 1940, 27. A typewritten copy is found in box/folder 355/9, CCLC.
25. Hess, "De aspecto inglés," 279–80.
26. Smith to OIAA Music Committee, 17 December 1940, box/folder 355/9, CCLC.
27. Bartholomew to Smith, 7 January 1941, box/folder 355/10, CCLC.
28. Clark, "A Proposal for Latin American Popular Music Broadcasts," 1 November 1940, box/folder 355/9, CCLC, 2.
29. Minutes, 8 January 1941, box/folder 344/10, CCLC, 1.
30. Cited in Levy, "From Orient to Occident," 317.
31. Hess, "Anti-Fascism by Another Name."
32. Minutes, 23 and 25 January 1941, box/folder 355/10, CCLC.
33. Novaes did support North-South musical exchange, establishing a scholarship fund for Brazilian musicians to study in the United States. Smith, "Musical Tour," 98.
34. Minutes, 8 January 1941, box/folder 355/10, CCLC, 2.
35. Loesser to Smith, carbon copy sent to the Music Committee by Smith on 14 April 1941, box/folder 355/10, CCLC, 2.
36. Ibid.
37. Whittall, "Individualism and Accessibility, 1945–75."
38. Smith reports Rodziński's reaction to the committee in his communication of 14 April 1941, found in box/folder 355/10, CCLC, 1. See also Goossens to Barbour, 16 May 1941; John S. Edwards, manager, Saint Louis Symphony; Paul Lemay, music director, Duluth Symphony Orchestra; Howard Hanson, Eastman School of Music; Burnet C. Tuthill, music director, Memphis Symphony Society, all in box/folder 355/11, CCLC.
39. Smith to Copland, 21 July 1941, box/folder 355/11, CCLC.
40. "Fairbanks Jr. to Go to South America"; Smoodin, *Animating Culture*, 138–43; Hess, "Walt Disney's *Saludos Amigos*."
41. Meyer, "Toscanini and the Good Neighbor Policy," 240.
42. Cited in Hess, "Leopold Stokowski," 398.

43. Faber, "Learning from the Latins," 280.
44. Cited in Cowie, *Emergence of Alternative Views*, 23.
45. Faber, "Learning from the Latins," 280–81.
46. "Argentine Rioters End U.S. Movie." See also O'Neil, "Demands of Authenticity," 360.
47. Analyzed in Campbell, "Shaping Solidarity," 98–112.
48. In a memo to the committee of 6 July 1941, Smith excerpted a paragraph from an undated letter from Sá Pereira and added his own reflections. Box/folder 355/11, CCLC.
49. Campbell, "Shaping Solidarity," 91.
50. Oja, *Making Music Modern*, 26.
51. Project authorization, 15 May 1941, box/folder 355/10, CCLC, 1.
52. Ibid., 2. Campbell covers the tour in "Shaping Solidarity," 113–22.
53. Minutes, 6 February 1941, box/folder 355/10, CCLC, 8.
54. Hess, "Anti-Fascism by Another Name," 376, 378–80.
55. See, for example, Campbell, "Shaping Solidarity," 74–85.
56. Report, n.d., box/folder 355/9, CCLC, 10–11. Numerous surveys were undertaken during the Good Neighbor period. See Sadlier, *Americans All*, 84–118; Smith, "Musical Tour," 64.
57. Stallings, "Pan/American Modernisms," 38; Vaughan and Cohen, "Brown, Black, and Blues."
58. Chávez also flirted with *estridentismo*, a modernist movement similar in some ways to futurism. See Hess, *Representing the Good Neighbor*, 53.
59. Cited in Corrado, "Victoria Ocampo y la música," 59.
60. Menanteau, *Historia del jazz en Chile*, 22–28.
61. Derbez, *Datos para una historia*, 23.
62. Moore, "Commercial Rumba," 179.
63. Lange, "Americanismo musical," 119.
64. Derbez, *Datos para una historia*, 24. Another Mexican critic gendered jazz, remarking that "new all-female jazz orchestras were comprised of hysterical women." Cited in ibid., 23.
65. Averill, "Haitian Dance Bands."
66. Cited in Derbez, *Datos para una historia*, 28.
67. Campbell, "Shaping Solidarity," 82.
68. Roosevelt, "Announcing Unlimited National Emergency."
69. Minutes, 10 April 1941, box/folder 355/10, CCLC, 2.
70. Untitled, undated report (pages missing) in box/folder 355/9, CCLC, 17.
71. Minutes, 10 July 1941, box/folder 355/11, CCLC, 1.
72. Smith, *William Grant Still*, 64.
73. "Leopoldo Stokowski Dio"; "With the Orchestras."
74. Smith, "Musical Tour," 55. Josetti visited Hitler's Germany and wrote of it in *Intercâmbio*, a German-Brazilian propaganda magazine. See Musser, "German-Brazilian Cultural Exchange," 129.
75. Campbell, "Shaping Solidarity," 82.

76. Hess, "'Old Man River' at the Front?"

77. Beattie and Curtis, "South American Music Pilgrimage," 19.

78. See Stam, *Tropical Multiculturalism*, 107–32. In 1993 the documentary *It's All True: Based on an Unfinished Film by Orson Welles*, directed by Bill Krohn was released, with original footage.

79. Hess, *Representing the Good Neighbor*, 97, 114.

80. Minutes, 10 July 1941, box/folder 355/11, CCLC, 1.

81. Schulman and Ascoli, eds., *Force for Change*.

82. Leon Robbin Gallery, guest list, exhibition item 5, "*And They Lynched Him on a Tree*: William Grant Still (1895–1978) and Katherine [Chapin] Biddle (1890–1977)," Booth Family Center for Special Collections, *Georgetown University Library*, 1 April–31 August 2006, https://www.library.georgetown.edu/exhibition/and-they-lynched-him-to-a-tree, accessed 15 July 2020.

83. Cited in Shirley, "William Grant Still's Choral Ballad," 431.

84. Ibid., 449.

85. On Faulkner and *Sur*, see King, *Sur*, 75–76.

86. Stallings, "Collective Difference," 153–66.

87. Ibid., 164.

88. Stallings, "Pan/American Modernisms," 41.

89. Minutes, 12 December 1940, box/folder 355/9, CCLC, 2.

90. McPhee to Smith, 3 April 1941, box/folder 355/10, CCLC, 1.

91. McPhee to Copland, dated "Friday" [4 April 1941], box/folder 355/10, CCLC.

92. Taylor to OIAA Music Committee, memo, n.d., box/folder 355/9, CCLC, 2.

93. Young, "Brazilian Institute," 242.

94. Bartholomew to Smith, 2 April 1941, box/folder 355/10, CCLC, 2.

95. Ninkovich, *Diplomacy of Ideas*, 37.

96. Duberman, *Worlds of Lincoln Kirstein*, 359. On the lineage of the American Ballet Caravan, see Garafola, "Lincoln Kirstein," 26–29.

97. Campbell discusses the tour at length in "Shaping Solidarity," 123–224; on *Billy the Kid* and the company, see Steichen, *Balanchine*, 202, 213–14.

98. "Pan American Festival Lists"; see also Goudy, "Coolidge Fiesta in Mexico."

99. Galván, "ABCs," 519.

100. Ros-Fábregas, "Nicolas Slonimsky"; Slonimsky, *Music of Latin America*.

101. The catalogue can be found at https://libwww.freelibrary.org/assets/pdf/fleisher/Latin-American-works.pdf.

102. Minutes, 6 February 1941, box/folder 355/10, CCLC, 5–6.

103. The non–Latin American works included a sonata for violin and piano by Edward T. Cone, three songs by Russell G. Harris, and a sonata for cello and piano by Paul Nordoff. "Contemporary Festival"; Downes, "American Music Heard at Museum."

104. Corrado, "Viena en Buenos Aires," 8–11; Slonimsky, *Music of Latin America*, 97.

105. Fuller, "I.S.C.M.—Dated Model," 34. See also Hess, "Copland in Argentina," 206.

106. Thomson, "Music."

107. Project Analysis, "Representative Library of American Orchestral Compositions in Recordings," 12 February 1941, box/folder 355/11, CCLC, 1.

108. Minutes, advisory committee on music to the Department of State, 13 June 1941, entry/box 24/30, RG 353, NARA, 10.

109. "Music Committee Objectives, Methods and Projects Needing Funds as of January 23, 1941," box/folder 355/10, CCLC, 3.

110. Minutes, 23 January 1941, box/folder 355/10, CCLC, 4–5.

111. Minutes, 29 May 1941, box/folder 355/10, CCLC, 1.

112. Cited in Pincus, "At Tanglewood." See also Hudde, "Negotiating Politics and Aesthetics," 142–47, 183–201.

113. Grant refers to Copland's request in a letter to Smith, 19 December 1940, box/folder 355/9, CCLC.

114. Minutes, 8 January 1941, box/folder 355/10, CCLC, 2.

115. Ibid.

116. Copland to Antônio Sá Pereira, 5 March 1941, box/folder 355/19, CCLC.

117. Campbell, "Shaping Solidarity," 94.

118. "Memorandum on the Scholarships for Latin-American Students," Margaret Grant to the OIAA Music Committee, 20 June 1941, box/folder 355/11, CCLC, 1–2.

119. Taubman, "Koussevitzky Leads Army Band."

120. Oja, Bernstein Meets Broadway, 48.

121. Ibid., 48–49.

122. Crist, *Music for the Common Man*, 64.

123. Moe, cited in Copland, "Report of South American Trip, August 19–December 13, 1941," box/folder 358/28, CCLC, 2. Copland's stay was extended. See appendix 8.

124. Moe to Copland, 6 June 1941, box/folder 358/25, CCLC, 1.

125. Moe to Copland, 14 August 1941, box/folder 358/25, CCLC.

126. Moe to Copland, 6 June 1941, box/folder 358/25, CCLC; Walter C. Rundle to Moe, 14 July 1941, memorandum, and Moe to Copland, 11 August 1941, both in box/folder 355/11, CCLC.

127. Sumner Welles to Copland, 4 April 1941, box/folder 358/25, CCLC. Edward G. Trueblood, now the acting chief of the Division of Cultural Relations, confirmed the appointment. Trueblood to Copland, 17 April 1941, box/folder 358/28, CCLC.

128. Minutes, Advisory Committee on Music to the Department of State, 13 June 1941, entry/box 24/30, RG 353, NARA, 15.

129. See Fauser, *Sounds of War*, 97. Hull to Copland, 8 September 1941, box/folder 355/12, CCLC.

130. Taylor to Smith, 2 July 1941, and Smith to Copland, 15 July 1941, both in box/folder 355/11, CCLC.

131. "To Latin America."

132. Parmenter, "Portrait of an American Composer."

133. Moe to Copland, 14 August 1941, box/folder 358/25, CCLC.

134. María de Freitas to Adolfo Salazar (Spanish music critic resident in Mexico City), 6 August 1941, box/folder 358/25, CCLC.

135. Moe to Freitas, 15 August 1941, box/folder 355/11, CCLC.

136. Corrado, *Vanguardias al Sur*, 43–61.
137. Maranca, *Cartas a Juan Carlos Paz*, 25–37.
138. Paz, "Bach y la música de hoy," 80.
139. Saminsky, "In the Argentine," 32.
140. Buch, "L'avant-garde musicale," 18–21.
141. Paz to Copland, 10 June 1941, box/folder 260/15, CCLC.
142. Paz to Copland, 3 August 1941, box/folder 260/15, CCLC. Paz is referring to Copland's recording of April 1935 (Columbia, 68320/1-D).
143. Paz to Copland, 3 September 1941 and 15 September 1941, both in box/folder 260/15, CCLC.
144. Kirstein to Smith (copy to Copland), 10 July 1941, box/folder 355/11, CCLC, 1.
145. Ibid., 2. See also Duberman, *Worlds of Lincoln Kirstein*, 363–64.
146. Rexach to Copland 8 July 1941, box/folder 355/11, CCLC.
147. Smith to Copland, 18 July 1941, ibid.
148. Gustavo Durán to Copland, 31 July 1941, ibid.
149. Smith to Copland, 1 August 1941, ibid.

## Chapter 4. Diplomat "in the Field"

1. Report, carbon copy, box 226/MC 468, folder 13, Manuscript Collection, Special Collections, University of Arkansas Libraries, Fayetteville, 1.
2. Cherrington, "Division of Cultural Relations," 138.
3. Sadlier, *Americans All*, 95–96.
4. Lauderbaugh, "Bolivarian Nations," 119–23. See also C. S. Smith, "Musical Tour," 18.
5. Walter C. Rundle to Henry Allen Moe, 9 July 1941, memo, box/folder 355/11, CCLC.
6. Brady, "War Plan Juan," 24–26.
7. Schwartz, *Flying Down to Rio*.
8. "Interview with Aguirre of Aguirre Guest Tours" and "Short Term Undertakings," both in box 657, OIAA Records Relating to Tourism (E-40), RG 229, NARA; *Travel Trade: The Business Paper of the Travel Industry* 33. no. 3, October 1945, 42.
9. Thorp, "Latin American Economies," 45.
10. Copland does not mention seeing Chávez in 1941 but used his address, Isabel la Católica 30, for receiving mail (instead of the American Consulate). Revueltas had died in 1940. See "Itinerary for Aaron Copland," box/folder 358/26, CCLC.
11. Navarro, *Hacer música*, 31.
12. "WPA Plans New Concerts."
13. Diary (Mexico), 20–28 August 1941, "South American Diary, August–December 1941," box/folder 243/15, CCLC. All diary entries in this chapter are from this source.
14. Galindo Dimas, "Compositores de mi generación."
15. Diary, 20–28 August.
16. Ibid.
17. Arvey, "For Modern Mayans."

18. Weinstock, *Mexican Music*, 11; Saavedra, "Of Selves and Others," 322; Hess, *Representing the Good Neighbor*, 80; Matallana, "Inventing Latin America."

19. Taubman, "Records: Youth Group." The album is *A Program of Mexican Music: Sponsored by the Museum of Modern Art* (Columbia M-414).

20. Diary, 20–28 August.

21. Ibid.

22. "Mexican Composers."

23. "With Some Orchestras." See also "With the Orchestras."

24. Diary, 20–28 August. See also Zepeda, *Vida y Obra de José Pablo Moncayo*.

25. Alcaraz, *La obra de José Pablo Moncayo*, 10.

26. Baqueiro Foster, "El Huapango." Some of these arrangements can be heard on the Columbia recording *A Program of Mexican Music* (see note 19).

27. Powell, *Mexico and the Spanish Civil War*; Mateos, "Los repúblicanos españoles."

28. Carredano, *Adolfo Salazar*; Trujillo, "Adolfo Salazar as Composer"; López Cobo, "Jesús Bal y Gay"; Alonso, "From the People to the People."

29. Diary, 20–28 August.

30. "Concerts the Microphone Will Present this Week."

31. Arndt, *First Resort of Kings*, xix.

32. Bushnell, *Eduardo Santos and the Good Neighbor*.

33. Diary (Colombia), 31 August.

34. Uribe Holguín, *Vida de un músico colombiano*. See also Castro Pantoja, "Antagonism, Europhilia, and Identity," 11–48; Bermúdez, "Toward a History of Colombian Musics"; Ospina Romero, "Los estudios sobre la historia de la música en Colombia."

35. Uribe Holguín, *Vida de un músico colombiano*, 127–41. See also Uribe Holguín, "¿Cómo piensan los artistas colombianos," 352; Bermúdez, "Un siglo de música en Colombia."

36. Varney, "Introduction."

37. Copland also tagged as merely "pleasant" the music of Uribe Holguín's compatriot Adolfo Mejía, then thirty-four and a student of Boulanger and Charles Koechlin. He gave Mejía's *Pequeña Suite* for orchestra an asterisk, however.

38. Chase, "Guillermo Uribe Holguín."

39. Slonimsky, *Music of Latin America*, 172.

40. "Microphone Presents."

41. "Fair Tops 200,000 Second Day in Row."

42. Diary, 2 September. See also Castro Pantoja, "Antagonism, Europhilia, and Identity," 33–34.

43. Diary, 2 September.

44. Pollack, *Aaron Copland*, 183.

45. Bowles, "On Mexico's Popular Music," 225.

46. "El Bejuco" and "Caminata" were available on New Music Quarterly Recordings, no. 1414 B, and Art of This Century, 803B, respectively. See Glanville-Hicks, "Paul Bowles," 95–96.

47. Diary, 3 September.

48. Smith, "Musical Tour," 253.

49. Diary (Ecuador), 5–6 September.
50. Barreda Laos, *Hispano-América en guerra.*
51. Sakuda, *El futuro era el Perú.*
52. "Célebre compositor norteamericano."
53. Diary (Peru), 11 September.
54. Holzmann, "De la trifonía a la heptafonía" and "Cuatro ejemplos."
55. Sas, "Ensayo sobre la música nazca" and *La música de la catedral.*
56. Diary, 6 September.
57. Ritter, "Peru and the Andes," 363.
58. Diary, 11 September.
59. Straus, "Emanu-el Begins 3-Choir Festival."
60. Both titles appear in the press with some variation. See Copland, Report of South American Trip, August 19–December 13, 1941, 7. It is not clear who translated his lectures into Spanish, but Conchita Rexach is a likely candidate.
61. Diary, 9 September.
62. See "En el Instituto [Cultural] Peruano Norteamericano." The other papers were *La Prensa, El Comercio,* and *Universal.*
63. "La conferencia del compositor Aaron Copland."
64. Ibid.
65. Ibid.
66. Ibid. See also Levy, "White Hope."
67. "La conferencia del compositor Aaron Copland." Copland makes essentially the same case in *Our New Music,* 166.
68. "La conferencia del compositor Aaron Copland."
69. Copland also worked informally with Bernstein. Pollack, *Aaron Copland,* 532–40. Chávez, widely respected for his conducting, was a possible model as well. Hess, *Representing the Good Neighbor,* 77.
70. Diary, 6 September.
71. Campbell, "Shaping Solidarity," 257.
72. Cited in ibid., 182.
73. Cited in ibid., 185–86.
74. Cited in ibid., 182.
75. [Raygada?], "Teatros y Artistas."
76. "Guido d'Arezzo," "De Música."
77. [Raygada?], "Teatros y artistas."
78. "Guido d'Arezzo," "De Música."
79. Ibid.
80. Ibid.
81. "De Arte"; [Raygada?], "Teatros y artistas."
82. Diary, 13 September.
83. Diary, 15 September.
84. In recent years, Afro-Uruguayans have challenged Uruguay's long-held status as one of Latin America's "white republics." Hess, *Experiencing Latin American Music,* 145–49.

85. Meyer, "Toscanini and the Good Neighbor Policy," 236–37.
86. González, *Creative Destruction*, 75; López-Alves, "Why Not Corporatism?"
87. "Graf Spee Incident Gives Latins Unity."
88. Lange, "Compositor Norteamericano en Montevideo."
89. Ibid.
90. Chase, "Recent Books," 214.
91. Diary (Uruguay), 12 October.
92. Diary, 8 October.
93. Diary, 11 October.
94. "Conferencias."
95. Ibid.
96. Diary, 11 October.
97. Copland refers in his diary to a concerto for piano by Tosar, but that title is incorrect.
98. Diary, 11 October.
99. Diary, 12 October.
100. "La personalidad de Aaron Copland."
101. "La Buena Vecindad."

## Chapter 5. Copland in Argentina

1. Tota, *Seduction of Brazil*, 33.
2. Rapoport, *¿Aliados o Neutrales?*
3. Hull, *Memoirs of Cordell Hull*, 2:1396; Braden, "Germans in Argentina," 43.
4. Newton, *"Nazi Menace" in Argentina*, xiv–xv, emphasis original.
5. Frank, "Nazis in Argentina," 17, 67.
6. Newton, "Nazi Menace" in Argentina, 175–76.
7. Glocer, *Melodías del destierro*; Rein, *Argentine Jews or Jewish Argentines?*
8. Glocer, "Guillermo Graetzer."
9. Glocer, *Melodías del destierro*, 86–77.
10. Ibid., 80–81.
11. Tulchin, *Argentina and the United States*, 75.
12. Manso, *Juan José Castro*, 83.
13. Sheinin, *Argentina and the United States*, 80.
14. Fernández Moreno, "Cinematográfico," 218.
15. "Aaron Copland propicia."
16. Ibid.
17. Ibid.
18. Copland, *Our New Music*, 233–42; radio address cited in Levy, "From Orient to Occident," 317.
19. "Aaron Copland, el Célebre Compositor."
20. Ibid.
21. Ibid.
22. Hurtado, "En defensa de la atonalidad." See also his *Estética de la música contemporánea*.

23. Hurtado, "Virgil Thomson," 55.
24. Hurtado, "Aaron Copland habla."
25. Ibid.
26. Ibid.
27. "Aarón Copland Habló Ayer Sobre."
28. Cited in Scarabino, *El Grupo Renovación*, 75.
29. Ibid., 69.
30. Borges, "El escritor argentino y la tradición."
31. Cited in García Muñoz, "Juan José Castro," 21.
32. Diary (Argentina), 30 September, South American Diary, August–December 1941, box/folder 243/15, CCLC. All diary entries in this chapter are from this source.
33. "Festival in Warsaw."
34. Saminsky, "In the Argentine," 36; Straus, "Emanu-el Begins 3-Choir Festival."
35. Diary, 3 October.
36. Diary, 17 October.
37. In Buenos Aires, Copland saw *Los Afincaos*, a film about the indigenous populations of Northern Argentina, directed by Leónidas Barletta and with Ficher's score.
38. "Jacobo Ficher Wins $500 Coolidge Prize."
39. Downes, "Young Composers Heard at Concert." On Downes and neoclassicism, see Hess, *Representing the Good Neighbor*, 27. Ficher's Prelude to *Melchor*, a "choral ballet," which Straus found "sturdy and competent," was performed at a choral concert in New York, and his song "Palabras a Mama" was featured on the album *South American Chamber Music* and broadcast on WQXR in May 1941. Straus, "Emanu-el Begins 3-Choir Concert"; "Concerts the Microphone Will Present This Week"; Slonimsky, *Music of Latin America*, 89.
40. Saminsky, "In the Argentine," 33; Slonimsky, *Music of Latin America*, 89.
41. Diary, 2 October.
42. Diary, 6 October.
43. Corrado, *Vanguardias al sur*, 82.
44. Diary, 22 October, emphasis original.
45. Manso, *Juan José Castro*, 23–42.
46. Slim, "Stravinsky Holograph in 1936."
47. Saminsky, "In the Argentine," 33; Hess, *Representing the Good Neighbor*, 120–21.
48. D'Urbano, *Música en Buenos Aires*, 38–39.
49. Diary, 16 October.
50. Diary, 6 October.
51. Diary, 21 October.
52. Ibid.
53. Slonimsky, *Music of Latin America*, 84.
54. Copland, "Fauré, a Neglected Master," 580.
55. Diary, 22 October.
56. Schwartz-Kates, *Alberto Ginastera*, 44. See also Ginastera's *Impresiones de la puna* for flute and string quartet of 1934.
57. Diary, 18 October.

58. Around 2000, the pianist Barbara Nissman persuaded Ginastera's second wife, Aurora Nátola-Ginastera, to allow her to perform and record the concerto. Schwartz-Kates, *Alberto Ginastera*, 128.

59. Copland does not mention *Estancia* in his diary, but Ginastera recalls showing it to him. Copland and Perlis, *Copland since 1943*, 112.

60. Kirstein, "Latin American Music for Ballet," 333–34; Campbell, "Shaping Solidarity," 218n61; Garafola, "Lincoln Kirstein," 28–29.

61. The Ballet Caravan never performed *Estancia*. A choreographed version had to wait until August 1952 for a performance, when Juan Emilio Martini conducted it at the Colón (choreography by Michel Borowski, decor by Dante Ortolani). See Plesch, "Resisting the Malambo."

62. Quoted in Suárez Urtubey, *Alberto Ginastera*, 72.

63. Diary, 14 October.

64. I.G.A., "Aplaudióse una página de Copland"; Talamón, "Se Realizó Anoche Un Concierto"; J. M., "Symphoniekonzert Juan José Castro." See also reviews in *Crítica*, *Le Théâtre*, *La Razón*, *Hora*, and *Il Mattino d'Italia (CCLC)*.

65. [Roberto García Morillo?], "Música sinfónica en el Colón."

66. J., "Se Aplaudió en el Colón." The right-wing paper *El Crisol* did not review the concert but simply announced *An Outdoor Overture* on 12 October, describing the work as "clear, direct, optimistic, and its orchestration, clean, full, and brilliant." *El Crisol*, 4.

67. Chiesa, "Música sinfónica se ofrece."

68. Glocer, *Melodías del destierro*, 35. The name of the paper refers to the *Fronde*, a series of rebellions in seventeenth-century France.

69. "Concierto sinfónico con la dirección de Juan José Castro."

70. Ibid.

71. "La Semana Cultural del Reich"; "Rabel," "Arte Degenerado," both in *El Pampero*.

72. "Otra insidia Yanqui-Judía."

73. Ibid.

74. Copland also played the work informally in Chile. Diary, 25 September. See also Pollack, *Aaron Copland*, 351–56; Starr, "War Drums, Tolling Bells."

75. Glocer, *Melodías del destierro*, 215–16, 221–22.

76. Ibid., 185–86, 166–67.

77. Ibid., 181, 180.

78. Nicholls, "Henry Cowell's 'United' Quartet."

79. "Copland-Slonimsky."

80. Roberto García Morillo [?], "Anoche se dio"; "En el Teatro del Pueblo se ofreció"; "Música americana en el Teatro del Pueblo."

81. "Música Americana."

82. García Morillo [?], "Anoche se dio."

83. Paz, "Aaron Copland Entre Nosotros."

84. Ibid.

85. Ibid.

86. Ibid.

87. García Morillo [?], "Anoche se dio."

## Chapter 6. Copland in Brazil

1. Marx also guest-conducted the Detroit Symphony, the Cleveland Orchestra, the National Symphony, the New York Philharmonic-Society Orchestra, and the New York–based chorus the Schola Cantorum. Cohen, "Rediscovering Walter Burle Marx." See also "Brazil's Marx Brothers."

2. Hess, *Representing the Good Neighbor*, 81–85, 90–95. Livingston-Isenhour and Caracas García, *Choro*.

3. Rosenfeld, "Current Chronicle," 516; O'Gorman, "Philharmonic in Brazilian Program," 17.

4. Thompson, "Burle Marx Conducts."

5. Hess, *Representing the Good Neighbor*, 81–110.

6. Copland, *Copland on Music*, 203. Copland briefly mentions Villa-Lobos in *Our New Music*, 202.

7. From 1934 to 1937 Vargas served as president under constitutional rule. Williams, *Culture Wars in Brazil*, 6–9; Levine, *Father of the Poor*.

8. Musser, "German-Brazilian Cultural Exchange," 124.

9. McCann, *Brazilian-American Alliance*, 151.

10. Kazanjian to Division of Cultural Relations, 19 December 1942, memorandum, box 234/MC 468, folder 3, 3, Manuscript Collection, Special Collections, University of Arkansas, Fayetteville.

11. Davila, "Myth and Memory," 262–63.

12. Cavalcanti, *When Brazil Was Modern*, 13.

13. Hess, *Representing the Good Neighbor*, 100.

14. Magaldi, *Music in Imperial Rio de Janeiro*, 3–4, 83, 137–38; Cristina Magaldi, "Cosmopolitanism and World Music."

15. Béhague, *Heitor Villa-Lobos*, 8–9.

16. Wisnik, *O coro dos contrários*, 72.

17. Appleby, *Heitor Villa-Lobos*, 85–86.

18. Williams, *Culture Wars in Brazil*, 15, 69–82.

19. Paixão Cearense, "Villa-Lobos e o estado novo," 150.

20. Translated in Wright, *Heitor Villa-Lobos*, 108. See also Vassberg, "Villa-Lobos"; Villa-Lobos, *O ensino popular de música no Brasil*.

21. Wright, *Villa-Lobos*, 107.

22. Villa-Lobos, *Sua Obra*, 143. See also Hess, *Representing the Good Neighbor*, 98–99.

23. Beattie and Curtis, "South American Music Pilgrimage," 18.

24. Beattie communicated these impressions privately to Seeger, who passed them on to Copland and others. See Seeger to Moe, 8 September 1941, box/folder 355/11, CCLC.

25. Diary (Brazil), South American Diary, August–December 1941, 8 November, box/folder 243/15, CCLC. All diary entries in this chapter are from this source.

26. Wright, *Villa-Lobos*, 68–69. The work should not be confused with the earlier *Rudepoema*, which Villa-Lobos also dedicated to Rubinstein and which Copland may have heard in New York in 1940. Hess, *Representing the Good Neighbor*, 125–26.

27. Diary, 13 November.

28. Diary, 10 November.

29. Diary, 9 November.
30. Anderson, "José Vieira Brandão."
31. Diary, 25 November.
32. Slonimsky, *Music of Latin America*, 124.
33. Ibid., 139.
34. Diary, 22 November.
35. Diary, 20 November.
36. Guerra-Peixe, *Maracatus do Recife*.
37. See Campbell, "Shaping Solidarity," 215–23.
38. Diary, 11 November.
39. Bohm, "Philharmonic Is Heard under Brazil Auspices"; Kolodin, "Marx Leads Music by Brazilians"; Thompson, "Burle Marx Conducts."
40. McPhee, "South American Once More," 245.
41. Diary, 26 November.
42. Koellreutter composed two flute sonatas, one in 1937 and the other in 1939.
43. Diary, 18 November.
44. Quoted in Verhaalen, *Camargo Guarnieri*, 2.
45. Galván, "ABCs of the WPA Music Copying Project," 522.
46. Cited in Verhaalen, *Camargo Guarnieri*, 105.
47. Diary, 17 November.
48. Salema, "Música."
49. R. B., "Música."
50. J. I. C., "Correio Musical." See also "Música: Escola Nacional."
51. "Música: Escola Nacional."
52. Ibid.
53. "Correio Musical."
54. Ibid.
55. R. B., "Música."
56. "No Rio um grande musicista norte-americano."
57. Ibid.
58. Magaldi, "Two Musical Representations of Brazil: Carlos Gomes and Villa-Lobos," 205.
59. Smith, *Musical Tour*, 48.
60. Diary, 7 November.
61. Clark, "Doing the Samba," 265. See also Roberts, "Lady in the Tutti-Frutti Hat"; Shaw, *Social History*, 26–43.
62. Bakota, "Getúlio Vargas and the Estado Novo," 209.
63. Campos Hazan, "Raça, Nação e Jose Mauricio Nunes Garcia."
64. Smith, *Musical Tour*, 44, 78.
65. Barbosa, "Mister Copland Caíu No Samba."
66. Ibid.
67. Ibid.
68. Diary, 22 November.
69. Slonimsky, *Music of Latin America*, 3.

70. Silva, "Camargo Guarnieri e Mário de Andrade."
71. Béhague, "Ecuadorian, Peruvian, and Brazilian Ethnomusicology." A source contemporaneous with Copland's era is Luper, "Musical Thought."
72. Smith, *Musical Tour*, 37, 39.
73. Diary, 18 November.
74. Diary, 17 November.
75. Bruce, Negro Problem.
76. Salter, *Negro Problem*, 165.
77. Du Bois, "Strivings of the Negro People." See also Washington, *Negro Problem*; Wilkerson, *Warmth of Other Suns*, 542–54.
78. Oliveira, "Toward a Phenomenology," 213.

## Chapter 7. Copland in Chile

1. Fergusson, *Chile*, 308–9.
2. Mount, "Chile," 163–65.
3. "Chile and the Nazis."
4. "Toda Sudamérica debe repeler a los nazis, dice *El Mundo*."
5. "Después de la Guerra Habrá que Desintoxicar al Pueblo Alemán."
6. Pereira Salas, *Notes on the History*, 8, 17.
7. Romera, "La pintura norteamericana."
8. *La Nación*, 14 September 1941.
9. *La Nación*, 15 September 1941.
10. "Un Gran Concurso de 'Rumbas y Congas.'"
11. Diary (Chile), 15 September, South American Diary, August–December 1941, box/folder 243/15, CCLC. All diary entries in this chapter are from this source.
12. Diary, 17 September.
13. Santa Cruz, *Mi vida en la música*, 654.
14. Slonimsky, *Music of Latin America*, 163. See also Stevenson, "Chilean Music"; *Revista Musical Chilena,* special issue.
15. Kirstein, "Latin American Music," 334–35.
16. Diary, 19 September.
17. Ibid.
18. Chase, "Domingo Santa Cruz"; Smith, "Composers of Chile," 28.
19. Diary, 25 September.
20. Diary, 19 September.
21. Diary, 22 September.
22. Diary, 24 September.
23. Merino, "Nuevas luces sobre Acario Cotapos"; Stallings, "Collective Difference," 68–69.
24. "Programs of the Week," 21 April 1918; Oja, *Making Music Modern*, 375. Cotapos incorrectly claimed that he and Varèse founded the guild. Aharonián, "Un extraño señor llamado Acario Cotapos," 116.
25. Downes, "Music."
26. Hall, "Novelties in Madrid."

27. Diary, 24 September.
28. Slonimsky, *Music of Latin America*, 157.
29. Barros and Dannemann, "Carlos Isamitt."
30. I thank Juan Eduardo Wolf for this clarification.
31. Wolf, *Styling Blackness in Chile*, 17–49. Wolf details musical ramifications of this erasure.
32. Isamitt, "Araucanian Art," 362–64.
33. Salas Viu, "Creación musical y música aborígen," 17.
34. Diary, 19 September.
35. Allende, "Chilean Folk Music," (ed. note). Allende's songs were performed on two PAAC concerts. Stallings, "Collective Difference," 177, 179.
36. González, "Making of a Social History."
37. Bonastre Bertrán, *Felipe Pedrell*.
38. Quiroga, "Las *Doce Tonadas* para piano," 27.
39. Allende, "Chilean Folk Music," 917.
40. Ibid., 920.
41. Talamón, "P. H. Allende," 58.
42. Allende, "Chilean Folk Music," 917. Here, Allende is quoting an unnamed "Spanish professor."
43. Varas and González, *En busca de la música chilena*, 185.
44. Wolf, *Styling Blackness*, 30.
45. Ibid., 32.
46. "4 Here to Chant the Songs of Chile."
47. Mistral, cited in Varas and González, *En busca de la música chilena*, 211. See also 19 of the same study.
48. "4 Here to Chant."
49. "City Celebration Will Usher in Fair." Ambassador Claude Bowers translated the address.
50. Varas and González, *En busca de la música chilena*, 185.
51. Diary, 17 September.
52. Menanteau, *Historia del Jazz*, 23–24; "El jazz en Chile."
53. Sabella, "El Violín Cubista."
54. Menanteau, *Historia del Jazz*, 24.
55. Radano, *Lying Up a Nation*, 168.
56. Pereira Salas, "La llegada de los 'Negro Spirituals'"; see also Menanteau, *Historia del Jazz*, 26.
57. Rondón, "Música y negritud en Chile"; Domingo Gómez, "Los cantores africanos."
58. "El concurso de Swing Despierta."
59. Ibid.
60. Wolf, *Styling Blackness*, 33; Mistral cited in Borge, *Tropical Riffs*, 41.
61. Menanteau, *Historia del Jazz*, 62. See Sun Eidsheim, *Race of Sound*.
62. Garrido, "Crónicas de Pablo Garrido." On Justa, see Sampson, *Blacks in Blackface*, 422, 517.

63. Garrido, "Crónicas de Pablo Garrido."
64. He was probably also aware of race-based restrictions in the United States on jazz performers the stature of Count Basie. Monson, "Problem with White Hipness," 408–9.
65. Baldwin, *Price of the Ticket*, 292.
66. Diary, 25 September.
67. Garrido, "Aaron Copland."
68. Ibid.
69. Ibid.
70. Ibid.
71. Ibid.
72. Ibid.
73. Ibid.
74. "La música es uno de los medios."
75. Smith, *Musical Tour*, 190.
76. Isamitt, "Música sinfónica y de cámara," 32.
77. Diary, 27 October.
78. Salas Viu, "El público y la creación musical (III)," 48. See also Correa, "Domingo Santa Cruz," 316.
79. "Critic and the Lady," 34.
80. Goldschmidt, "Concierto sinfónico."
81. Ibid.
82. Ibid.
83. Ibid.
84. Ibid.
85. "Música: El sinfónico de ayer." The critic omits the horn player, John Barrows.
86. Ibid.
87. *Hoy*, 6 November 1941, n.p., box/folder 358/24, CCLC. The same newspaper reprinted Copland's essay on Chávez from *Our New Music* in Spanish translation for its issue of 29 October 1941.
88. "La música es uno de los medios."
89. Santa Cruz, *Mi vida en la música*, 623–24.

## Chapter 8. The Americas at War

1. Frank, *Arturo Toscanini*, 326. See also Manso, *Juan José Castro*, 142.
2. Manso, *Juan José Castro*, 143.
3. Frank, *Arturo Toscanini*, 326–27.
4. Taubman, "Program Honors Juan José Castro."
5. Castro's first biographer, Rodolfo Arizaga, cites an interview the conductor gave in 1947 to the Havana-based magazine *Bohemia*, in which this story appears but which I have been unable to obtain. Manso repeats the anecdote.
6. Schoultz, "Benevolent Domination," 13.
7. Rankin, "Mexico," 23.

8. Ocampo, "La guerra en América."

9. Diary (Cuba), 12 December, South American Diary, August–December 1941, box/folder 243/15, CCLC. All diary entries in this chapter are from this source.

10. Diary, 8 December.

11. Stallings, "Collective Difference," 12, 26–31; Root, "Pan American Association," 61. Both composers are well represented in the Fleisher Collection (see appendix 5).

12. Roldán, "Artistic Position," 175. See also Cowell, "Roldán and Caturla of Cuba."

13. Ardévol, *Introducción a Cuba*, 91–92, and "El Grupo Renovación de La Habana," 18.

14. Diary, 7 December. Cowell published one of Ardévol's piano sonatinas in *New Music* 7, no. 4 (July 1934): 3–5.

15. Benítez, "Música y músicos."

16. Ibid.

17. Program in Copland, "Report of South American Trip (1941)."

18. *Crónica social.*

19. He appends three lists: points to cover in his report, an outline for a forthcoming article, and scores he lent some Latin American colleagues.

20. Cited in this study, p. 35.

21. Copland, "Report of South American Trip," 43. He listed several radio stations on which he did not appear, suggesting that he kept a separate log for radio-related matters.

22. Ibid., 42.

23. Copland, "Composers of South America," 75.

24. Ibid., 75.

25. Ibid., 76.

26. Neither was "development" a neutral term in Latin America, even if it did not become a buzzword until the Cold War. See Rosenberg, *Spreading the American Dream*, 7–13.

27. Copland, "Composers of South America," 80–81.

28. See, for example, Vera, *Sweet Penance of Music*.

29. Copland, "Composers of South America," 78.

30. Ibid., 78–79. Copland allows that in miniatures, such as the art song or short piano pieces, one can detect "the distinctive Brazilian note most easily—the sinuous melodies, the Negroid background rhythms, the peppery repeated notes, and the peculiar brand of nostalgia they called *saudade*."

31. Ibid., 79.

32. Ibid.

33. Ibid., 81–82.

34. Ibid., 76.

35. Ibid., 77.

36. Ibid., 77–78.

37. Hurtado, "Below the Equator," 122.

38. Cited in Buch, "L'avant-garde musicale," 18.

39. Ibid., 18, 20.

40. Francis, "United States at Rio, 1942," 77–95.

41. Rankin, "Mexico," 26.

42. McCann, *Brazilian-American Alliance*, 240–58.

43. Tota, *Seduction of Brazil*, 85.

44. The film became controversial during the Cold War and later. See Hess, "Walt Disney's *Saludos Amigos*."

45. Hess, "Jean Berger," 43.

46. Hess, "From 'Greater America' to *America's Music*."

47. Over the three-year life of *Music of the New World*, Chase broadcast Copland only once: *Quiet City* on 29 June 1944. See box/folder 11/19, JPB 04-32, Gilbert Chase Papers, New York Public Library for the Performing Arts, New York.

48. As for Copland's draft status, he was ultimately reclassified as 3-A, that is, deferred due to hardship to dependents. Copland financially helped his parents, now in their eighties, and occasionally his brother Leon. See Fauser, *Sounds of War*, 21–22; Pollack, *Aaron Copland*, 18–20.

49. Frankenstein, "West Coast Hears Festival." Frankenstein mistakenly counted seven Latin Americans.

50. Ibid.

51. Copland and Taylor, "Recorded Libraries of American Music for Latin American Radio Stations," memo, 16 January 1942, box/folder 355/11, CCLC, 1.

52. Sadlier, *Americans All*, 84.

53. Radio Reaction Reports (E-82), OIAA Radio Division, box 968, RG 229, NARA.

54. Brown, "Balzo Appears in Goodwill Piano Series."

55. "Programs of the Week" (1942).

56. Minutes, 12 June 1941, box/folder 355/10, CCLC, 2; Labonville, *Juan Bautista Plaza*, 188–89. See also 224–25.

57. Published as Plaza, "Music in Caracas."

58. Campbell, "Shaping Solidarity," 222.

59. Downes, "South Americans Heard at Concert."

60. Santa Cruz, *Mi vida en la música*, 650–62.

61. "Address of Sr. Don Domingo Santa Cruz," 5; see also *Toledo Blade* (Ohio), 24 March 1942 and 3 April 1942; and *Dallas Texas News*, 18 March 1942, all in box/folder 9/1, Toledo Museum of Art Archives, Toledo, Ohio.

62. "Music Educators National Conference"; Lawler, "Latin Americans See Our Musical Life." See also Izdebski and Mark, "Vanett Lawler."

63. Britton, "Music Education."

64. Santa Cruz, "On Hemispherical Unity," 13.

65. Verhaalen covers the trip in *Camargo Guarnieri*, 22–24.

66. Quoted in ibid., 23. See also R. L., "Guarnieri Concert Here."

67. Quoted in Verhaalen, *Camargo Guarnieri*, 23. Compare Thomson's earlier remarks on Brazilian music, discussed in Hess, *Representing the Good Neighbor*, 122–24.

68. "Carlos Chávez Leads National Symphony."

69. Boston Symphony Orchestra Concert Program (1942–43).

70. Quoted in Verhaalen, *Camargo Guarnieri*, 223–24.

71. Crist, *Music for the Common Man*, 151.

72. See ibid., 155–58, for line-by-line references.

73. As Crist points out, echoes of the Hebrew Bible lend weight to such locutions: "And God said, saying." Ibid., 160.

74. Boston Symphony Orchestra Concert Program, 906.

75. Crist, *Music for the Common Man*, 155. As discussed below, leftist Latin American composers wrote "speaker pieces" during the 1960s and 1970s.

76. Pisani, *Music for the Melodramatic Theatre*.

77. Walter Simmons, for example, found "no real depth" in Lincoln Portrait but believed that "as a picturesque filmscore in symphonic form it [was] quite delightful." Cited in Pollack, *Aaron Copland*, 417–18.

78. William Shuman to Copland, 31 March 1943, cited in Crist, *Music for the Common Man*, 162.

79. Silber, "Abraham Lincoln," 356.

80. May, *Slavery, Race, and Conquest*, 3.

81. Holden and Zolov, *Latin America and the United States*, 30; Sarmiento, *Vida de Abraham Lincoln*.

82. Santovenia, *Lincoln*, 89–103.

83. Smoodin, *Animating Culture*, 139.

84. Hogan, *Abraham Lincoln and Mexico*.

85. Downs, *Second American Revolution*.

86. O'Neil, "Demands of Authenticity," 363–64. See also Woll, *Latin Image*, 61.

87. Juárez is hardly problem free. Paul Muni, who plays Juárez, hailed from the Austro-Hungarian Empire; also, the production team's research on the film was shamelessly hyped. O'Neil, "Demands of Authenticity," 364.

88. Nugent, "Hollywood Adopts a Point of View"; "'Juarez' Sensational Hit."

89. Woll, *Latin Image*, 61. See also "Confidential: Copy of Report, Received from the Local Censor Board, in the Territory Named," received by Joseph Breen of the Production Code Association and dated 15 September 1939, correspondence file, Special Collections, Margaret Herrick Library, Academy of Motion Picture Arts and Sciences, Los Angeles, California.

90. Later, the Spanish translation was slightly modified. *Lincoln Portrait*, box/folder 69/46.4, CCLC.

91. Also reflecting Copland's growing interest in the Spanish-speaking world was the chorus "Las agachadas" (loosely translated as "The Shake-Down Song"), based on a dance-song from Burgos province (Spain) in honor of Kurt Schindler. See Katz and Armistead, "In the Footsteps of Kurt Schindler: Ballad Collecting in Soria."

92. Levy, *Frontier Figures*, 340–50.

93. Pollack, *Aaron Copland*, 377; Crist, *Music for the Common Man*, 64–68.

94. Madrid and Moore, *Danzón*, 225.

95. Hess, *Representing the Good Neighbor*, 68–69.

96. Taubman, "Town Hall Host to the Composers."

97. McPhee, "Scores and Records," 58. See also Mellers, "Aaron Copland and the American Idiom," 17.

98. DeLapp, ed., *Appalachian Spring*.

99. Fauser, *Aaron Copland's* Appalachian Spring.

100. Quoted in Crist, "Critical Politics," 254. See also Crist, "Aaron Copland's Third Symphony."

101. Cited in Crist, "Critical Politics," 235.

102. Cited in ibid., 246–47, 237.

103. Ibid., 237. Copland discusses his admiration for Shostakovich in Aaron Copland, "From the '20s to the '40s and Beyond," 82. When Shostakovich himself heard the Third Symphony in 1947, he heard echoes of "Rimsky-Korsakov, Tchaikovsky, Mahler, Stravinsky" but not himself. Cited in Crist, "Critical Politics," 236.

104. Lerner, "Aaron Copland."

105. Investigation of Un-American Propaganda Activities, 1542.

106. Thomson, quoted in Copland and Perlis, *Copland, 1900 through 1942*, 236–37. See also Taubman, "Greek Conductor Starts Last Week."

107. Stevenson, "Heitor Villa-Lobos's Los Angeles Connection," 2.

108. Stevenson, "Brazilian Report." See also Hess, *Representing the Good Neighbor*, 129–36.

109. Downes, "Hector Villa-Lobos."

110. Reginald S. Kazanjian to Charles Thompson, 19 December 1942, box 234/MC 468, folder 3, Manuscript Collection, Special Collections, University of Arkansas, Fayetteville, 9–10.

111. Answers: (1) three times; (2) possible answers include Montevideo, 1933; Buenos Aires, 1936; Lima, 1938; Panama City, 1939; Havana, 1940.

112. Lyons, "Youth Quiz Program."

113. Funds for the meeting itself were covered by the National Committee on International Intellectual Cooperation. Minutes, 11 February 1944, "Sub-Committee on Musical Interchange with the U.S.S.R," box/folder 355/12, CCLC, 1.

114. Ibid., 1. The committee met a few times and made several recommendations but disbanded early on. I thank Kevin Bartig for this information.

115. Rankin, "Mexico," 32.

116. Mount, "Chile," 168–69.

## Chapter 9. The Early Cold War

1. Lôbo, "Samba para Mr. Copland!" Copland did not record the Palácio Quitandinha event in his diary.

2. Hilton, *Brazil and the Soviet Challenge*, 208. See also Sadlier, *Americans All*, 196.

3. Donoghue, "Harry S. Truman's Latin American Policy."

4. Raymont, *Troubled Neighbors*, 82.

5. Gil, *Latin American–United States Relations*, 284; Raymont, *Troubled Neighbors*, 69–90.

6. Rowland, *History of the Office*, 271–78.

7. Earl J. McGrath to Robert M. Stevenson, 11 October 1949, box 235/MC 468, folder 46, Manuscript Collection, Special Collections, University of Arkansas, Fayetteville, 1.

8. Colligan, "Visiting Professor," 332.

9. I thank Kevin Bartig for this information. See also Bartig, "Aaron Copland's Soviet Diary," 576.

10. Abrams Ansari, *Sound of a Superpower*, 142–45. Also given are trips taken without government support.

11. Hurtado, Introducción, 10. See appendix 6.

12. Daniel, *Tanglewood*, 69.

13. Hawkes, "Festival at Tanglewood," 16.

14. On an all-Latin American chamber music concert on 4 August, see Hudde, "Negotiating Politics and Aesthetics," 282.

15. See Parmenter, "News and Sidelights"; Seeger to Orrego-Salas, 10 January 1946, Juan Orrego-Salas Legacy Collection, Latin American Music Center (LAMC), Cook Music Library Digital Exhibitions, Indiana University, Bloomington, http://collections.libraries.indiana.edu/cookmusiclibrary/items/show/80. Also in 1945 José Vieira Brandão enrolled as a scholarship student at the University of Southern California and gave recitals in various U.S. cities. Brandão was active in music education circles. Borges de Oliveira Santos, "Biografia documentada."

16. Tosar presented a concert of his own music at the Pan American Union on 4 May 1947. "Concerts at the Pan American Union," 681.

17. Ginastera to Copland, 2 September 1944, in Schwartz-Kates, "Correspondence of Alberto Ginastera," 291.

18. Schwartz-Kates, *Alberto Ginastera*, 6. On Ginastera in the United States, see Hess, *Representing the Good Neighbor*, 147–58.

19. Ginastera to Copland, 30 November 1945, in Schwartz-Kates, "Correspondence of Alberto Ginastera," 291.

20. Yedra, *Julián Orbón*, 19–20.

21. Orrego-Salas, "Becerra y los del 1925"; Peles and Spies, "Conversation with Claudio Spies."

22. Hudde, "Negotiating Politics and Aesthetics," 284.

23. Cordero, "Vigencia de la música culta," 161–62.

24. Copland and Perlis, *Copland since 1943*, 112.

25. Schwartz-Kates, *Alberto Ginastera*, 7.

26. Plotkin, *El día que se inventó*.

27. Ginastera's tangles with Perón are incompletely documented. Biographers generally refer to two dismissals, one from 1945, which Ginastera described to his principal biographer, Pola Suárez Urtubey. Suárez Urtubey, personal communication with author, 9 June 2008. In 1952 Ginastera's duties as head of the conservatory at La Plata were suspended. Schwartz-Kates, *Alberto Ginastera*, 8.

28. Ginastera, "Inter-American Review: Political Shadow."

29. The petition and list of signatories are given in Manso, *Juan José Castro*, 179.

30. See Ginastera, "Los conciertos," 96–99. I thank Silvia Glocer for information on Aguirre.

31. Dezillio, "Entre la nación y la emancipación."

32. Schwartz-Kates, *Alberto Ginastera*, 55. Ginastera eventually withdrew the work. Melanie Plesch has edited one of the two surviving manuscripts of the symphony for performance.

33. Copland and Perlis, *Copland since 1943*, 78.
34. "Young Latin Americans."
35. "South Americans Vie in a New Music Test."
36. Green and Goodman Esman, "Cultural Centers," 3.
37. The others (three historians, one humanist, and one architect) are listed in Espinosa, *Inter-American Beginnings*, 309.
38. Colligan to Copland, 28 October 1946, box/folder 355/13, CCLC.
39. Copland to Gropp, 23 August 1947, box/folder 359/11, CCLC.
40. Colligan to Copland, 27 November 1946, box/folder 355/13, CCLC.
41. Colligan to Copland, 3 January 1947, box/folder 355/13, CCLC.
42. "Information for a Visiting Professor," box/folder 359/11, CCLC, 1.
43. López-Alves, "Why Not Corporatism?" 199–200.
44. Not Juana Sujo, as stated in Copland and Perlis, *Copland since 1943*, 82.
45. Copland is referring to the RCA Victor Red Seal (M/DM 1088) recording, the tempi of which he deemed "screwy."
46. Diary (Uruguay), 29 October, South American Journal 1947, box/folder 243/7, CCLC. All diary entries in this chapter are from this source.
47. Pollack, *Aaron Copland*, 19.
48. Diary, 11 September. On Copland's conducting, see Pollack, *Aaron Copland*, 532–40.
49. Diary, 31 October and 1 November.
50. Abrams Ansari, *Sound of a Superpower*, 136. By the end of his career, Copland was earning $2,000 or more for a single concert. Pollack, *Aaron Copland*, 92.
51. Diary, 1 November.
52. "Buen concierto se ofreció."
53. Ibid.; "Joven y vigorosa música."
54. "Buen concierto se ofreció"; "Aaron Copland nos dio."
55. "Buen concierto se ofreció."
56. "En torno a las tres obras."
57. "Buen concierto se ofreció"; "Se realizó en el auditorio."
58. Ayestarán, "Aaron Copland."
59. "Buen concierto se ofreció."
60. Diary, 30 October. Of Balzo's "pals," Copland identifies only Tosar.
61. Copland to Robert F. Barry (of Barry and Co., South American Division of Boosey & Hawkes), 23 August 1947, box/folder 359/11, CCLC.
62. Martínez Estrada, *¿Qué es esto?* See also Fiorucci, "Los marginados de la Revolución"; Plotkin, *Mañana es San Perón*; Shumway, *Invention of Argentina*; Albino, "La revolución abrió."
63. King, *Sur*, 100.
64. Diary (Argentina), 22 October.
65. Schwartz-Kates, *Alberto Ginastera*, 194n18.
66. Diary, 9 November.
67. In 1946 Erich Kleiber conducted her orchestral suite *Estampas* at the Colón, and Juan José Castro premiered her *Coral, Fuga y Final* with the Asociación Filarmónica. Program note, *Seminario de Jóvenes Músicos Argentinos*, 7 October 1946, box/folder 359/12, CCLC. See also Caamaño, *La historia del Teatro Colón*, 642.

68. Azzi and Collier, *Le Grand Tango*, 15–16.
69. Diary, 10 November.
70. Diary, 12 November.
71. Diary, 10 November. See also "Mr. Copland Feted by Publishers."
72. Diary, 10 November.
73. Diary, 8 November.
74. *Sociedad Hebraica Argentina* (newsletter).
75. "Anti-Revolutionary Trend."
76. Franklin to Copland, 26 September 1947, box/folder 359/11, CCLC.
77. Diary, 15 November.
78. Jorge D'Urbano, "Aaron Copland dirigió un concierto." D'Urbano's books include *Cómo escuchar un concierto* (1955) and *Música en Buenos Aires* (1966). He translated Paul Henry Lang's *Music in Western Civilization* into Spanish.
79. "Concierto de jerarquía"; Plotkin, *El día*, 184–85. The critic for *El Laborista* merely commented that Copland's performance was "well executed." See "Un interesante recital."
80. "Concierto de Aaron Copland"; "Páginas de Copland."
81. Ginastera, "Aarón Copland," 83.
82. Ibid., 80.
83. [García Morillo?], "Copland dirigió un concierto"; "Brillante concierto." See also "Aaron Copland Dio"; "Obras de Copland."
84. D'Urbano, "Aaron Copland dirigió."
85. Ibid.
86. "Un concierto en honor."
87. R. A. G., "Importantes Fueron los Actos," 1.
88. Suffern, "Conciertos," 6.
89. Ibid. See also "Un concierto en honor de Copland"; "Dedicóse un Concierto a Obras de A. Copland."
90. Suffern, "Conciertos," 6.
91. Ibid., 7.
92. Ibid.
93. Ibid. On Copland's youthful admiration for Tchaikovsky, see Pollack, *Aaron Copland*, 36.
94. Ibid.
95. Ibid.
96. Valenti Ferro, "Formuló Declaraciones Aaron Copland."
97. Tacuchian, "Panamericanismo, propaganda," 135–41.
98. They took this step despite tensions in their relationship. In 1951 Kraft married and subsequently became involved with various women. Copland and Kraft remained lifelong friends. Pollack, *Aaron Copland*, 242–45.
99. Two other individuals, "Eduardo" and "Nilson," sometimes accompanied Copland and "H."
100. Diary (Brazil), 10 September.
101. Copland to Bernstein, 24 September 1947, in Crist and Shirley, *Selected Correspondence*, 184.

102. Script for radio broadcast, Radio Roquete Pinto, 9 September 1947; Radio Ministerio de Educação, 14 September 1947, box/folder 216/13, CCLC.

103. Butterworth, *Music of Aaron Copland*, 120.

104. Charles Del Rosso, who interviewed Copland, claimed that the composer contradicted himself by identifying a different passage as Brazilian, specifically, the short, scalar motive immediately following the fermata about one-third of the way through the cadenza. It is not, however, in F major. Del Rosso, "Study of Selected Solo Clarinet Literature," 30.

105. Koidin, "Benedito Lacerda and the Golden Age of Choro."

106. Other parts of Brazil lay claim to the samba, including Rio de Janeiro. See Shaw, *Social History of Brazilian Samba*, 3–25.

107. In his diary entry of 12 September, Copland gave the title incorrectly.

108. Diary, 12 September.

109. At Goodman's request, Copland was obliged to alter several passages that the famous clarinetist found too difficult. Adelson, "Too Difficult for Benny Goodman."

110. Quoted in Pollack, *Aaron Copland*, 525.

111. Abrams Ansari, "Masters of the President's Music," 141.

112. Pollack, *Aaron Copland*, 437, 480. See, for example, Clement Greenberg, "Art," 241.

113. Lymes, "Highbrow, Lowbrow, Middlebrow," 151; Macdonald, "Ernest Hemingway," 105, 95.

114. "A Música e o Cinema."

115. Diary, 6 October.

116. Diary, 3 September.

117. Diary, 9 September.

118. Nogueira França, "Música: As Conferencias de Aaron Copland," part I. Some of these lectures were translated. See "A Música Americana e a Cena Americana" and "A Música Norte Americana."

119. Nogueira França, "Música: As Conferencias de Aaron Copland," part 1.

120. Nogueira França wrote for various papers and published several books.

121. Diary, 10 October.

122. Ibid.

123. Diary, 23 August.

124. "A retumbante vitória de uma vocação de artista"; Tavares de Sá, "Brasil–Estados Unidos."

125. Diary, 11 September.

126. Copland to Bernstein, 24 September 1947, in Crist and Shirley, *Selected Correspondence*, 184.

127. Berkowitz, "Concert of North American Music."

128. Ibid.

129. Nóbrega, "Diário Musical." See also (Ayres) de Andrade, "Música"; Cabral, "Música"; Bevilacqua, "Orquestra Sinfônica Brasileira."

130. Muricy, "Eleazar de Carvalho e a Música Norte-Americana"; Novais, "Música"; D'Or, "Música."

131. Nogueira França, "Música: Obras Sinfônicas Norte-Americanas."

132. "Oberon," "Música: Ainda A Volta da Eleazar."

133. Nogueira França, "Música: Concerto de Obras Contemporâneas."

134. Berkowitz, "Aaron Copland." See also Bevilacqua, "Sociedade Brasileira"; Nóbrega, "Diário Musical: Sociedade Brasileira."

135. Script and notes for radio broadcast, 29 September 1947, Ministerio de Educação, box/folder 216/16, CCLC.

136. Script for radio broadcast, 9 September 1947, Radio Roquete Pinto, box/folder 216/8, CCLC.

137. Notes for talk on Radio Gazeta, 18 September 1947, box/folder 216/11, CCLC.

138. Script for radio broadcast, 12 September 1947, Radio Nacional, box/folder 216/15, CCLC, 2–3.

139. In October 1946 Bernstein recorded the work for RCA Victor, with Robert Shaw as the Monitor, the recording Copland would have played. On the *Airborne Symphony*, see Fauser, *Sounds of War*, 261–64.

140. Script for radio broadcasts, 9 September 1947, Radio Roquete Pinto, box/folder 216/8, CCLC. See also radio script, Radio Nacional, 16 September 1947, box/folder 216/10, CCLC.

141. Mariz, *Figuras da música brasileira*, 65–67.

142. Neves, *Música contemporânea brasileira*, 95.

143. Ibid.

144. Santoro seems to have withdrawn this work, which is scored for cello and piano.

145. Paraskevaídis, "Música dodecafónica." Música Viva also attracted critics and scholars, such as Otavio Bevilacqua and Luiz-Heitor Côrrea de Azevedo. See Egg, "O Grupo Música Viva."

146. Diary, 27 August.

147. Diary, 1 September.

148. Diary, 5 October.

149. Diary, 19 October.

150. Program, Koellreutter's composition students, 5 October 1947, box/folder 359/12, CCLC. Katunda gave knuckle-twisting recitals consisting of Bach's "Goldberg" Variations and Chopin's Etudes, opp. 10 and 25. Henahan, "Eunice Katunda in Demanding Recital"; Strongin, "Miss Katunda Plays Recital."

151. Gradenwitz, "Contemporary Music Festival."

152. In 1942, two years before he began working with Koellreutter, Guerra-Peixe composed a march for band, *Fibra de herói* (Hero's Valor), a souvenir of Brazil's entry into World War II that is still heard today.

153. Mariz, *Cláudio Santoro*.

154. Diary, 27 August.

155. Diary, 5 October.

156. Diary, 22 September.

157. In 1941 Copland met Fernândez in Santiago.

158. Diary, 25 and 28 August. See Igayara, "Oscar Lorenzo Fernândez"; Bruno Kiefer, "Oscar Lorenzo Fernândez."

159. Diary, 2 September.
160. Diary, 23 August.
161. Lewis de Mattos, "Estética e Música."
162. Diary, 13 October.
163. "As Coisas Mais Impressionantes."
164. "Artes e artistas."
165. Diary, 19 October. See also Verhaalen, *Camargo Guarnieri*, 196.
166. Diary, 21 October.
167. Veríssimo, *Brazilian Literature*, 2.
168. Diary, 22 October.
169. Díaz, *Africanness in Action*.
170. Diary, 18 November.
171. "Aaron Copland na Bahia"; "É famoso compositor norte-americano."
172. Jatobá, "Música: Aaron Copland."
173. The program was produced by the broadcaster Antonio Maria of Radio Sociedade de Bahia. See "É famoso compositor norte-americano."
174. Díaz, "Between Repetition and Variation"; Lewis, *Ring of Liberation*.
175. The origins of the Brazilian berimbau are debated. Some argue for direct origins in Kongo-Angolan musical bows but most agree that the berimbau was modified in Brazil. See Díaz, "Between Repetition and Variation," 54; see also Röhrig Asunção, *Capoeira*.
176. Diary, 19 November.
177. Diary, 20 November.
178. Starkloff, *Theology of the In-Between*.
179. Diary, 20 November.
180. The extended description is from Copland's diary, 21 November.
181. Crook, *Music of Northeast Brazil*, 107, 110–48.
182. Cited in ibid., 26. See also Guerra-Peixe, *Maracatus do Recife*.
183. Diary, 23 November.
184. Diary, 24 November.
185. Diary, 25 November.
186. "Information for a Visiting Professor," box/folder 359/11, CCLC.
187. While in Washington, Copland also gave a verbal statement, later confirmed in Edmund R. Murphy, acting head, Cultural Centers Section, Division of Libraries and Institutes, to Copland, 3 February 1934, box/folder 359/11, CCLC.
188. Copland, "Report of South American Trip as Visiting Professor," 7.
189. Ibid., 14–15.
190. See especially untitled article in the *Record*, 4, no. 1 (1948): 32–34.
191. Copland, "Composer's Report."
192. Azzi and Collier, *Le Grand Tango*, 48. See "South American Contest."
193. Connolly and McLaughlin, "Music Pours."
194. Among his works are *Te Deum puerorum Brasiliae*, written for Pope John Paul II's visit to Rio de Janeiro in 1997, and *Terras Brasilis*, commissioned by the Ministry

of Culture to mark the five-hundredth anniversary of the arrival of the Portuguese in Brazil.

195. Machado de Paula, "A Escrita de Cláudio Santoro," 38–39. Nearly all sources on Santoro mention this episode. Visa applications from that period are not retained in U.S. government records.

196. The staff organization for the OAS was the Pan American Union. Holden and Zolov, *Latin America and the United States*, 190.

197. Rabe, *Eisenhower and Latin America*, 13.

198. Holden and Zolov, *Latin America and the United States*, 196–97.

## Chapter 10. Shifting Ground and the Crisis of Modernism

1. Copland, aware that Santoro had been unsuccessful, wrote in his travel diary, "What a shame about the Guggenheim fiasco!" Diary (Brazil), 27 August 1947, "South American Journal 1947," box/folder 243/7, CCLC.

2. Carroll, *Music and Ideology*, 37–49. Santoro briefly experimented with what has been called "nationalist dodecaphony" in his *Música para cordas* and a handful of other works, in which he attempted to incorporate Brazilian idioms into serial structures ("dodecafonismo brasileiro"). See Mariz, *Figuras*, 73. See also Machado de Paula, "A Escrita de Cláudio Santoro," 73–99; Hartmann, "Cláudio Santoro e o II Congreso" and "Paulistana no 1."

3. Santoro's address, "Le problème du Compositeur Contemporain Dans sa Position Sociale," is discussed in Hartmann, "Cláudio Santoro e o II Congreso," 464.

4. Ibid.

5. See Shreffler, "Ideologies of Serialism" and "Myth of Empirical Historiography"; Straus, "Myth of Serial 'Tyranny'"; "A Response to Anne C. Shreffler" and "A Revisionist History of Twelve-Tone Serialism in American Music." Other paths to high modernism at mid-century, such as aleatory, were labeled "experimental," involving neither neoclassicism nor serialism. Beal, *New Music, New Allies*, 3.

6. Hess, *Representing the Good Neighbor*, 144.

7. Latham, *Modernization as Ideology*, 70.

8. LaFeber, "Latin American Policy," 64–65.

9. Matthews, "Latin American Unrest."

10. Hess, *Representing the Good Neighbor*, 144.

11. See Wellens, *Music on the Frontline*.

12. Paul, "From American Ethnographer to Cold War Icon," 446.

13. Babbitt, "Who Cares If You Listen?" An editor provided the title, not Babbitt, who proposed "The Composer as Specialist." See Brody, "Music for the Masses," 162–63.

14. Salzman, "*Modern Music* in Retrospect," 19, 18.

15. Warshow, *Immediate Experience*, 3.

16. Mason, "Paris Festival," 19.

17. Shreffler, "Ideologies of Serialism," 222, 225.

18. Copland arranged the work so that the speaker could be omitted. In 2020 the German-born British composer Max Richter took the Universal Declaration of Hu-

man Rights as a point of departure for his album *Voices*, which features recordings of the voices of Eleanor Roosevelt and U.S. actor Kiki Layne.

19. Theoharis, *Seeds of Repression*.

20. Shibusawa, "Lavender Scare and Empire," 727. Hubbs addresses similar binaries in relation to Copland. See Hubbs, *Queer Composition*, 154–59.

21. Quoted in Shibusawa, "Lavender Scare and Empire," 727. See also Johnson, *Lavender Scare*, 69–70; Dean, *Imperial Brotherhood*; Sherry, *Gay Artists*.

22. A purge of ninety-one suspected homosexuals at the State Department became a topic on Capitol Hill in February 1950. See Shibusawa, "Lavender Scare and Empire," 723–24.

23. Johnson, *Lavender Scare*, 66–67. See also Gellman, *Secret Affairs*.

24. See Arndt, *First Resort of Kings*, 64–65; Briggs, *Proud Servant*, 405.

25. Griffith, *Politics of Fear*, 38–39; Hess, "Anti-Fascism by Another Name," 381.

26. Crist summarizes the grievances eventually brought against Copland. Crist, *Music for the Common Man*, 197. See also this study, pp. 18–20.

27. On Blitzstein, who, as noted, served in World War II, see Fava, "L'ombra del maccartismo." Left-wing causes with which Bernstein was associated are given in Oja, *Bernstein Meets Broadway*, 180, 184; see also Gentry, "Leonard Bernstein's 'The Age of Anxiety.'" On Downes, see Hess, "'If that be treason, let them make the most of it.'"

28. "Final Program," Cultural and Scientific Conference for World Peace, National Council of Arts, Sciences, and Professions, series 22, W. E. B. Du Bois Papers, Special Collections, University of Massachusetts, Amherst. https://credo.library.umass.edu/view/pageturn/mums312-b283-i001/#page/1/mode/1up.

29. "Effect of the Cold War on the Artist in the United States," TS, box/folder 211/23, CCLC. Abrams Ansari discusses Copland's remarks in "Aaron Copland," 344–45.

30. Copland's speech is reprinted in Kostelanetz, *Aaron Copland*, 128–31 although without the references to Roosevelt.

31. Abrams Ansari, "Aaron Copland," 344.

32. See DeLapp-Birkett, "Dialogue without Words," 249. See also Schoenberg, "How One Becomes Lonely" and Feisst, "How Arnold Schoenberg Became Lonely."

33. Cited in DeLapp-Birkett, "Dialogue without Words," 249.

34. Copland and Perlis, *Copland since 1943*, 152–54.

35. *Red Channels*, 39–41.

36. DeLapp-Birkett, "Dialogue without Words," 249.

37. Copland, *Music and Imagination*, 75, emphasis original.

38. Ibid., 79.

39. Ibid., 104.

40. Ibid., 95.

41. Ibid., 91. Copland overlooks the fact that scarcely any of Revueltas's music concerns "the Amerindian man." In his 1937 essay on Revueltas, Copland praised his Mexican colleague's evocation of "the bustling life of the Mexican fiesta," in works such as *Esquinas*, *Ventanas*, and *Caminos*. See Copland, "Mexican Composer."

42. Brody, "Founding Sons," 23.

43. Silva, *Camargo Guarnieri*, 144.
44. Chávez, "El dodecafonismo," 69.
45. Silva, *Camargo Guarnieri*, 146.
46. The paper was the *Tribuna da Imprensa* of Rio de Janeiro. Cited in Silva, *Camargo Guarnieri*, 148.
47. See Paraskevaídis, "Música dodecafónica."
48. Cordero, "¿Nacionalismo versus dodecafonismo?" 28.
49. Ibid., 29.
50. Becerra Schmidt, "Los años cincuenta," 45. See also Paraskevaídis, "Eduardo Maturana."
51. Tabor, "Juan Carlos Paz"; Viñao, "Old Tradition We Have Just Invented"; Heile, *Music of Mauricio Kagel*.
52. Herrera, *Elite Art Worlds*.
53. Salazar, *Music in Our Time*, 328–31.
54. Paz, *La música en los Estados Unidos*, 111, 114.
55. Ibid., 173, 109.
56. Ibid., 111. Parallels with Kirkpatrick's comments on Copland are striking: in 1942 he suspected "more concession than conviction" in works such as *El salón México*. Kirkpatrick, "Aaron Copland's Piano Sonata," 246–47.
57. Paz, *La música en los Estados Unidos*, 45.
58. The Argentine composer Daniel Devoto concurred. In a 1959 review essay, he registers Copland's praise for Chávez in *Our New Music* but snipes that, perhaps in doing so, Copland wished "to atone for having composed *El salón México*." Devoto, "Panorama de la musicología latinoamericana," 92.
59. Pollack, *Aaron Copland*, 439–45.
60. Baker, "Aaron Copland's *Twelve Poems*," 2.
61. The first scholar to connect Copland's embrace of serialism with the red scare was Jennifer DeLapp (now DeLapp-Birkett), "Copland in the Fifties." For a nuanced account of scholarly approaches to this issue, see Abrams Ansari, *Sound of a Superpower*, 128–34; Pollack, *Aaron Copland*, 451–59; and Crist, *Music for the Common Man*, 193–201.
62. Pollack, *Aaron Copland*, 445–50.
63. DeLapp-Birkett, "Dialogue without Words," 249.
64. DeLapp-Birkett identifies a folk-like atonal tune in the third movement (mm. 23–33 and mm. 98–117). DeLapp-Birkett, "Dialogue without Words," 260–61.
65. In 1967 Copland told Edward T. Cone of his earlier suspicions of German music but added that from around 1950, he realized that "the younger fellows, Boulez and such made it clear that you could keep the [serial] method while throwing away the [Teutonic] esthetic." Cone and Copland, "Conversation with Aaron Copland," 140–41. As Abrams Ansari points out, we tend to "overlook the possibility that Copland might have found aesthetic satisfaction in experimenting with the serial method." *Sound of a Superpower*, 136.
66. Crist, *Music for the Common Man*, 196–97.
67. Ross, *Rest Is Noise*, 412.

68. One of the Hollywood 10, Bessie had joined and then left the party but not before his career as a screenwriter was ruined.
69. Hearings before the Select Committee, 605.
70. Ibid.
71. Ibid., 605.
72. Ibid., 610.
73. Ibid., 606.
74. Ibid., 617.
75. Ibid., 617. Moe incorrectly states that Copland studied with Boulanger during the grant period.
76. Ibid., 617.
77. Ibid., 618.
78. Ibid., 620.
79. Busbey went after Haldore E. Hanson, a State Department official and former war correspondent, who published a book on the Sino-Japanese War of 1930; William Benton, assistant secretary of state; Esther Calukin Brunauer, a career diplomat active in establishing UNESCO; and the Office of International Information and Cultural Affairs (OIC). Griffith, *Politics of Fear*, 39.
80. Quoted in Pollack, *Aaron Copland*, 453.
81. Taubman, "Copland on Lincoln." See also Pollack, *Aaron Copland*, 453–54.
82. "Week's Radio Concerts." WABF was based in Mobile, Alabama, but licensed to serve New York. In 1953 the call letters were changed to WBAI.
83. Cooke, "State as Impresario," 218. See also Milton Bracker, "Books of 40 Authors Banned."
84. Bracker, "Books of 40 Authors Banned."
85. "Mark Twain Is Cleared by U.S." The piece notes that it was not clear to "what tests the Missouri-born author has been submitted."
86. Two summaries of the hearing are Pollack, *Aaron Copland*, 451–60; Copland and Perlis, *Copland since 1943*, 185–203.
87. Copland and Perlis, 195.
88. Also cited in ibid., 195, is a "stenographic transcript" of *Hearing*, vol. 88, which includes "Testimony of Aaron Copland," *Proceedings of the Committee on Government Operations*, U.S. Senate, 47–98.
89. Pollack, *Aaron Copland*, 456–57.
90. "All Red Ties Denied."
91. Ibid.
92. Abrams Ansari, *Sound of a Superpower*, 128–29. This document is in a folder in the Copland Collection, along with other notes on his experience with the HUAC.
93. Thomson and Laves, *Cultural Relations*, 59–62.
94. Marder, "McCarthy."
95. On the aftermath of the hearing, see Pollack, *Aaron Copland*, 459–60.
96. Abrams Ansari, "Shaping the Policies," 41.
97. Cited in ibid.
98. The author was Swedish economist Gunnar Myrdal, commissioned by the corporation on the premise that an outsider would be more objective.

99. Fosler-Lussier, *Music*, 101–22. See also Davenport, *Jazz Diplomacy*.

100. Pollack, *Aaron Copland*, 455. See also Santa Cruz's essay on music and communism, "Las normas musicales."

101. Several of Carpentier's literary works have been translated into English, including *Los pasos perdidos* (The Lost Steps), one of few novels in which the protagonist is a musicologist.

102. Calzavara, *Trayectoria cincuentenaria*.

103. Carpentier, *Ese músico*, 1:434.

104. "The Hemisphere"; diary, "Venezuela Visit—November 26–December 9, 1954," box/folder 244/15 and 16, CCLC. Copland wrote a continuous entry for his 1954 visit.

105. A military junta, of which Pérez Jiménez was a part, seized power in 1948, positioning him to step into the presidency in 1952.

106. "Meet . . . Aaron Copland."

107. Parker, "Clare Boothe Luce" and "Recurring Melodic Cell."

108. Diary, "Venezuela Visit."

109. Copland, "Festival in Caracas."

110. Copland, "Fantasy for Piano."

111. Ibid. See also Berger, *Aaron Copland*, 96.

## Chapter 11. The Sixties

1. For once, Canada was included in the Pan Americanist project, with works by Violet Archer, Harry Somers, François Morel, Harry Freedman, John Weinzweig, and Neil McKay. See Hess, *Representing the Good Neighbor*, companion website. On Latin American *Concertos for Orchestra*, see this study p. 245.

2. Hess, *Representing the Good Neighbor*, 147–58. See also Hess, "Avant-garde Music."

3. Salzman and Des Marais, "Aaron Copland's Nonet."

4. Cardoza y Aragón, "Interview." See also Schlesinger, *Bitter Fruit*; Grandin, "Your Americanism and Mine."

5. J. F. Kennedy, "Address at a White House." See also Raymont, *Troubled Neighbors*, 127–30.

6. Hershberg, "United States, Brazil," 6–7.

7. An excellent database of various tours is in Fosler-Lussier, *Music in America's Cold War Diplomacy* at https://musicdiplomacy.org/database.html.

8. Monod, "Disguise, Containment,."

9. Fosler-Lussier, *Music in America's Cold War Diplomacy*, 29.

10. Gillespie, *To Be, or Not . . . to Bop*, 421. See also Carletta, "Those White Guys Are Working for Me."

11. Abrams Ansari, "Masters of the President's Music," 60–61. See also Fosler-Lussier, *Music in America's Cold War Cultural Diplomacy*, 47–48.

12. Sánchez to Copland, 12 December 1961, box/folder 363/18, CCLC.

13. Copland to Sánchez, 27 December 1961, ibid.

14. Purcell to Copland, 7 June 1962, ibid.

15. Borup to Copland, 7 June 1962, ibid.

16. Diary (Mexico), 15 July 1962, "Notes on Trip to Mexico-Brazil-Uruguay: July August 1962," box/folder 245/5, CCLC. All diary entries on the 1962 trip in this chapter are from this source.

17. Diary, 16 July.
18. Diary, 19 July.
19. Muller, "Estrenará en México."
20. This tidbit was reported apropos critical reaction to an upcoming performance of Chávez's *H.P.* "It did not fail to surprise us that Carlos Chávez should unearth his concert suite *H.P.* two days after a press conference in which he qualified all Soviet composers as 'incredibly bad' and Khachaturian as 'vulgar on a grand scale'; because his *H.P.* is conspicuous . . . for a total lack of distinction, which only confirms the wisdom of the Evangelist's phrase 'It's easier to see the mote in your neighbor's eye than the beam in your own.'" *Audiomúsica*.
21. Muller, "Estrenará en México."
22. Alonso-Minutti, "Composer as Intellectual," 276. I thank Ana Alonso-Minutti for her valuable assistance on the Ives concert and Chávez's essay, discussed below.
23. Chávez, *La Cultura Musical*.
24. Chase, *America's Music*, 678. See also Hess, "From 'Greater America to America's Music.'"
25. Chávez, "La Cultura Musical." See also Chávez, "Copland."
26. Pérez Patino, "Carlos Chávez Presentó."
27. At no point in his Latin American diaries does Copland mention Julián Carrillo, who practiced microtonalism as early as the 1920s and whose music was performed by the League of Composers in New York. See Madrid, *In Search of Julián Carrillo*, and Taylor Gibson, "Music of Manuel M. Ponce."
28. The talk was organized by the embassy and the Avalon Foundation of New York, later the Andrew W. Mellon Foundation. *News*.
29. Askinazy, "Copland Lecture Well Received."
30. Copland's statement is a matter of debate. See Agawu, *Representing African Music*.
31. Pérez Patino, "Carlos Chávez Presentó." Copland made the same point in *What to Listen For in Music*, 33.
32. "La música dodecafónica para el gusto actual."
33. "Música: Haydn Resultó Monótono."
34. Fraga, "Acierto y Talento."
35. "Música: Haydn Resultó Monótono."
36. Crespo, "El comunismo mexicano."
37. *Política*.
38. Ibid.
39. *La Prensa*.
40. *Diario de la Tarde*.
41. *Excelsior*. Despite its hyperbolic ring, the statement is true in light of *El salón México*, *Three Latin-American Sketches*, and the "Mexican Dance" from *Billy the Kid*.
42. Muller, "Estrenará en México."
43. Fraga, "Acierto y Talento." On cosmopolitanism among Mexican composers, see Alonso-Minutti, "Forging a Cosmopolitan Ideal."
44. Dueñas, "Con Aaron Copland."
45. Hershberg, "United States, Brazil," 9.

46. In 2014 the National Security Archive posted tape recordings of these meetings, which historian Peter Kornbluh transcribed. They are available at http://www2.gwu.edu/~nsarchiv/NSAEBB/NSAEBB465/, accessed 29 August 2020.

47. Diary (Brazil), 24 July.

48. Diary, 28 July.

49. Nogueira França, "Aaron Copland, compositor."

50. Nogueira França, "Aaron Copland: Músico do quotidiano."

51. Abrams Ansari, "Copland on Television."

52. Embassy memo, 24 July 1962, box/folder 363/19, CCLC.

53. Katz, Kuss, and Wolfe, *Libraries, History, Diplomacy*, 422.

54. Diary (Uruguay), 3 August.

55. Diary, 2 August.

56. W. R., "Demasiados metales," emphasis original.

57. Ibid.

58. Ibid.

59. This talk was drawn from Copland's eponymous article, which appeared in the 4 July 1959 issue of the *Saturday Evening Post*, and but for a few modifications, is the same talk he gave at the University of New Hampshire on 16 April 1959.

60. These materials are in the Lauro Ayestarán Collection in the Library of Congress.

61. Diary, 2 August.

62. Mañé Garzón, "Copland."

63. Ibid.

64. Kostelanetz, *Aaron Copland*, 275.

65. Ibid., 274.

66. Critics cited in Pollack, *Aaron Copland*, 499–501.

67. George T. Moody, acting chief, American Specialist Branch, Office of Cultural Exchange, to Copland, 9 October 1962, box/folder 363/18, CCLC.

68. See exchange of letters between Copland and Elizabeth Braunstein, program officer of the Division for Americans Abroad of the Bureau of Educational and Cultural Exchange, box/folder 364/11, CCLC.

69. Copland, "Report of Latin American Trip: July 5 to August 6, 1962," 4.

70. Ibid., 5.

71. Oscar H. Alcanzar, general coordinator, Festival Internacional de Musica do Rio de Janeiro, to Copland, 5 June 1963, box/folder 364/11, CCLC.

72. Quesada to Copland, 9 May and 12 July 1963, box/folder 364/11, CCLC.

73. Diary entry, 9 October, "Latin American Diary Sept–Oct 1963," box/folder 245/9, CCLC, all diary entries on the 1963 trip in this chapter are from this source; Turner to Copland, 15 August 1963, box/folder 364/11, CCLC.

74. Prescription (undated), box/folder 364/12, CCLC.

75. Diary, 21 September. "Copland en la ciudad silenciosa."

76. "Brazil Festival Honors Villa-Lobos."

77. Besides his trip of 1936, Stravinsky toured in August–September 1960, with projected conducting engagements in Mexico City, Bogotá, Lima, Santiago, Buenos Aires, Rio de Janeiro, and Caracas, although he canceled the two final engagements. See Levitz, "Igor the Angeleno," and Saavedra, "Stravinsky Speaks."

78. Walsh, *Stravinsky*, 481; see also 430–31.

79. Béhague, *Music in Latin America*, 145. See also Kuss, *Music in Latin America*, 1:135.

80. Much the way Victoria Ocampo heard parallels between *The Rite* and Duke Ellington's music, Carpentier compared the rhythmic structures and enhanced percussion of Stravinsky's Russian-period works to the music of the Cuban *rumbero* "Papá Montero." Carpentier, *Ese músico que llevo dentro*, 2:18–24.

81. Diary (Brazil), 8 September.

82. Diary, 12 September.

83. Diary, 9 September.

84. Herrera, *Elite Art Worlds*.

85. See King, *El Di Tella*, 31, 81–100, 158–59; Giunta, *Vanguardia*; Neiburg and Plotkin, *Intelectuales y expertos*.

86. Plotkin, *Freud in the Pampas*.

87. Herrera, *Elite Art Worlds*, 131. See also Vázquez, *Conversaciones*.

88. Graciela Paraskevaídis, in-person interview with author, 27 June 2009, Buenos Aires. Several CLAEM personalities are discussed in Alonso-Minutti, Herrera, and Madrid, *Experimentalisms in Practice*.

89. Etkin, "Riesgo, dinero y heterodoxia," 53.

90. Novoa, "Aaron Copland en el Centro Latinoamericano," 11. I thank Ms. Novoa for sharing her unpublished work with me.

91. Ginastera to Copland, 24 August 1962, box 11, Instituto Di Tella Archives, Buenos Aires, Argentina.

92. Copland to Ginastera, 19 September 1962, ibid.

93. Ginastera to Copland, 7 October 1962; Copland to Ginastera, February 26, 1963, ibid.

94. *Noticias Gráficas*, 16 September 1963, box 9, Instituto Di Tella Archives, Buenos Aires, Argentina.

95. Josefina Schröder to Copland, undated, box/folder 364/11, CCLC.

96. Diary (Argentina), 17 September, emphasis original. One of these newspaper interviews was the photo-essay "Copland in the Quiet City," mentioned above. The other I have been unable to track down.

97. Diary, 19 September, emphasis original.

98. D'Urbano, "Música: claridad y sabiduría."

99. Ibid.

100. D'Urbano, "Composiciones de Copland."

101. Copland to Ginastera, 19 September 1962, box 11, Instituto Di Tella Archives, Buenos Aires.

102. Diary, 1 October.

103. Diary, 26 September, emphasis original.

104. Diary, 24 September.

105. Picchi, "Con obras propias dirigió"; see also D'Urbano, "Composiciones de Copland."

106. D'Urbano, "Auténticamente norteamericano."

107. Picchi, "Con obras propias dirigió."

108. "Música: Copland por Copland."
109. Diary, 27 September.
110. Diary, 2 October.
111. "Imagen de Chile en USA." "Image of Chile" was inaugurated after a conference of cultural directors from fifteen Latin American countries. "Chile Introduces Its Arts to U.S."
112. Diary (Chile), 3 October.
113. "Esta noche llega."
114. Fugielle Videla, "León Schidlowsky."
115. Diary, 3 October.
116. Diary, 4 October.
117. "Busca a Jóvenes Compositores."
118. "Conferencia de prensa."
119. Ibid.
120. "El Estado no debe dirigir."
121. "Conferencia de prensa de A. Copland."
122. Ibid.
123. Ibid. See also "Busca a Jóvenes Compositores."
124. "Conferencia de prensa de A. Copland."
125. "El Estado no debe dirigir."
126. "Busca a Jóvenes Compositores."
127. Garrido, *Biografía de la cueca*.
128. Garrido, "Aaron Copland: Músico Universal."
129. Ibid.
130. Diary, 5 October.
131. Diary, 4 October.
132. The guest list is found in box/folder 364/12, CCLC.
133. Cited in González, "Guia auditiva," n.p.
134. *América insurrecta* received the Premio Municipalidad de Santiago and the Taller del 60 prize for "the best Chilean composition" of 1962. It also figures in the list of *Cuarenta principales* (Top Forty) of Chilean twentieth-century classical works, a register crafted by the musicologist Juan Pablo González, *Pensar la música*, 295. See also Riesco, "Octavo Festival."
135. Diary, 9 October.
136. González, *Música popular chilena*, 21–23. See also Carrasco, *La nueva canción*.
137. During Allende's administration, Becerra served as a cultural attaché to the Chilean Embassy in Bonn. When Pinochet came to power, Becerra remained in Germany.
138. Diary, 10 October.
139. *Para leer el Pato Donald* was published in 1971 and the English translation in 1975.
140. Diary, 6 October. Because articles in *Ercilla* were unsigned at this time, we cannot know with absolute certainty that Dorfman is the author of "Copland: Músico y Diplomático," which appeared in the issue of 9 October 1963. The dates, however,

align with Copland's account of the interview, his description of Dorfman, and Dorfman's biography. For several years, Dorfman has not answered email inquiries.

141. Dorfman, "Copland: Músico y Diplomático."
142. Diary, 7 October.
143. "Copland, Miembro Honorario"; diary, 11 October.
144. Heinlein, "Música en la Semana."
145. Ibid.
146. Robilant, "Aaron Copland."
147. Heinlein, "Música en la Semana."
148. Diary, 4 October.
149. "'Nuestra época musical es confusa.'"
150. Ibid.
151. Ibid.
152. Heinlein, "Aaron Copland."
153. Ibid.
154. Ibid.
155. Babbitt began *Ensembles for Synthesizer* in 1962 but completed the work in 1964. It is possible that Babbitt, who sometimes coincided with Copland at Tanglewood, gave him the recording of an early version. I thank Eric Chasalow for this suggestion.
156. Heinlein, "Aaron Copland."
157. Merino, "Federico Heinlein."
158. Heinlein, "Aaron Copland."
159. Diary, 11 October.
160. Diary, 12 October. Copland's judgment is unduly harsh. By the 1960s Peru boasted several composers in symphonic music alone: José Malsio (1924–2007), Francisco Bernardo Pulgar Vidal (1929–2012), and Enrique Iturriaga (1918–2019).
161. Lindsay-Poland, *Plan Colombia*, 27.
162. Mount and Randall, "Colombian Press," 22.
163. Diary (Colombia), 13 October.
164. Ibid.
165. Diary, 14 October. Escobar reported Chávez's opinion to Copland by letter. See Escobar to Copland, 20 December 1962, box/folder 364/11, CCLC.
166. Diary, 17 October.
167. Safford and Palacios, *Colombia*, 327.
168. Drezner, "Hoy un Compositor." See also Copland, "Is the University Too Much with Us?"
169. Drezner, "Hoy un Compositor."
170. Ibid.
171. "Copland," *El Espectador*.
172. Abrams Ansari, "Aaron Copland," 352.
173. Later that year, the United States recognized a military government in Peru. LaFeber, "Latin American Policy," 71–73.
174. Fosler-Lussier, "Cultural Diplomacy," 73.

175. Ibid., 82.
176. Buch, *Bomarzo Affair*; Hess, "Ginastera's *Bomarzo*."
177. Herrera, *Elite Art Worlds*, 162–75.
178. Hess, *Representing the Good Neighbor*, 171–86.
179. Paraskevaídis, "Algunas reflexiones."

## Chapter 12. Latin American Classical Music and Memory

1. Carpentier, "El Segundo Festival."
2. Velásquez, *Venezuela moderna*, 181.
3. Ramey, *Copland Conducts Copland*.
4. It surfaces in various sources. See Crist, *Music for the Common Man*, 163; Cuomo and Holzer, eds., *Lincoln on Democracy*. César Muñoz, the Venezuelan host of *La Cata Musical* (A Peek at Music), also reinforces Copland's story. See "La canción que derribó a la dictadura en venezuela," *youtube.com*, 22 April 2019, accessed 8 September 2020. See also "1958 Venezuelan coup d'état," *wikipedia.org*, 19 April 2022, accessed 7 September 2020. The anecdote does not appear in Copland and Perlis, *Copland since 1943*, although Copland did relate the story to Perlis, a fact for which I thank Mather Pfeiffenberger, who kindly provided me a recording of the conversation.
5. Diary, 26 March 1957, "Venezuela Visit—Nov 26–Dec 9, 1954/Feb 21–Mar 31 1957," box/folder 244/15 and 16, CCLC. Unless otherwise noted, all diary entries on the 1957 trip are from this source.
6. Diary, 26 March 1957. In 1951 she had performed *Lincoln Portrait* with Estévez in a joint celebration of U.S. and Venezuelan independence, the latter observed on 5 July.
7. The recording is at the Library for the Performing Arts of the New York Public Library (LZR 42840). My thanks to Danielle Cordovez, who made a copy available to me. The jacket reads, "The recording presented by SAM [Sociedad de Amigos de la Música] in this disc was realized during the execution of the fifth concert of the Second Festival of Latin American Music in Caracas, made in [Caracas] on 28 March 1957."
8. I thank Silvia Glocer for this information.
9. Dembo, *Juana Sujo*. See also Kennedy, *Oxford Encyclopedia*, 2:1310.
10. Diary, 20 March 1957.
11. "El Presidente Marcos Pérez Jiménez." See also Taubman, "Lavish Festival."
12. "Venezuela está orgullosa."
13. See Taylor, *Venezuelan Golpe*, 48–52.
14. See, for example, "Venezuelan Rioting Laid to Communists."
15. Sujo and Copland's *Lincoln Portrait* is relatively brisk, clocking in at 13:32. Compare Maya Angelou with Louis Langree and the Cincinnati Symphony (15:12) or Gregory Peck, with Zubin Mehta and the Los Angeles Philharmonic (15:01).
16. I have been unable to find the exact source of Thomson's remark, although Copland mentions in his diary on 26 March 1957 that it provoked a "big scandal." Among those who bristled at it was Guarnieri. According to a reporter for *El Nacional*, Guarnieri gave a talk on 29 March in which he "subtly departed from . . . the position

established by Virgil Thomson" by discoursing on freedom from the constraints of the ego and "personal vanity" (untitled clipping, 31 March 1957). Thomson backtracked, lamely proposing that he meant only that whereas Latin America had not had time to develop a musical culture, it could look forward to "a great future." "Virgil Thomson Thinks Caracas Has Nicest Rich." See also Chase, "Caracas Host."

17. Taubman, "Music," emphasis added.
18. "Standing Ovation for U.S. Music."
19. Lincoln's text reads, "I believe this government cannot endure, permanently half slave and half free."
20. Pardo Tovar, *Intermedio*; de Greiff, "Los Festivales de Caracas."
21. Schacter, *Seven Sins of Memory*, 113.
22. Ibid., 114–16.
23. Ibid., 129.
24. Ewell, "Extradition of Marcos Pérez Jiménez," 306. Actually, the United States miscalculated here: Pérez Jiménez treated communists more kindly than some of his civilian predecessors, employing known communists in his government to appease some of his opponents. Taylor, *Venezuelan Golpe*, 50.
25. "Hemisphere: Venezuela," 24.
26. Elwell, "Extradition," 292.
27. Cardoza Uzcátegui, "La imagen de Venezuela."
28. Raymont, *Troubled Neighbors*, 107.
29. Szulc, "Beneath the Boiling-Up," 19.
30. See, for example, the special issue in *Memory Studies* 8, no. 1 (2015); Mercado, *In a State of Memory*.
31. Douglass and Vogler, *Witness and Memory*; Hite, *Politics and the Art of Commemoration*. See also Neustadt, "Music as Memory and Torture"; O'Connell, "Narrating History through Memory."
32. Cited in Wiarda, *Soul of Latin America*, vii.
33. Weinrich, *Lethe*, 1.
34. Ericson, "Lilit Gampel."
35. *Aaron Copland: Music in the 20's.*
36. In statements that were not broadcast, Copland discusses serialism's role in persuading composers to reject nationalism. Abrams Ansari, "Copland on Television," 422.
37. Copland and Perlis, *Copland since 1943*, 79–80.
38. Ibid., 78.
39. Copland, "Lo popular y el rigor."
40. K. K. Smith, "Mere Nostalgia," 507; Boym, *Future of Nostalgia*, 8.
41. Béhague, *Music in Latin America*, 126, 168. Valuable in many ways, this book was for decades the only single-volume textbook on Latin American music. See also Blackwood, *Music of the World*, 99, and Hess, *Representing the Good Neighbor*, 4–5.
42. Salvatore, *Imágenes de un imperio*, 4.
43. Current debates over the competing terms "Latino," "Latino/a," and "Latinx" have yet to be resolved.
44. Hess, "Latin American Art Music," 77.

45. Suarez, *Latino Americans*, xi.

46. Gates, *Exercise of Power*, 35–37.

47. Katz, *Build*, 30.

48. Farrow, *War on Peace*, xxii.

49. Schneider, "Unrealized Potential of Cultural Diplomacy," 262. See also Grincheva, "U.S. Arts and Cultural Diplomacy."

50. Burns, "Demolition of U.S. Diplomacy." See also Burns, *Back Channel*.

51. Katz, *Build*, 33–53. On hip hop's worldwide reach, see, for example, Aidi, *Rebel Music*; Rollefson, *Flip the Script*; on hip hop in Latin America, see, for example, Ramsdell, "Cuban Hip Hop Goes Global."

52. Sadlier, *Americans All*, 195.

53. Proclamation No. 10,009; Philips, "They're Rapists."

54. Neustadt, "Border Songs."

55. O'Farrill, *Fandango at the Wall*, 16–17. See also Hess, "From 'Greater America.'"

56. Ross, "Toscanini, Trump, and Classical Music."

57. Hess, "Symphony in Latin America."

58. Fauser, *Aaron Copland's* Appalachian Spring, 99–100; Crist, *Music for the Common Man*, 195.

59. Fosler-Lussier, *Music in America's Cold War Diplomacy*, 25

60. Beal, "Negotiating Cultural Allies," 119.

61. Fosler-Lussier, *Music in America's Cold War Diplomacy*, 129.

62. Anderson, "'To Become as Human as Possible,'" 60.

63. Mario Davidovsky and author, email communication, 14 April 2014.

64. Ibid.

65. Diary, 21 February 1957. In this entry, Copland reports on activities that took place over several days.

66. Mario Davidovsky and author, email communication, 14 April 2014.

67. Copland and Perlis, *Copland since 1943*, 281–82.

68. Ibid., 281.

69. alcides lanza and author, email communication, 17 August 2015.

70. Copland discussed these works in the Soviet Union. See Bartig, "Aaron Copland's Soviet Diary," 582.

71. Jones, *alcides lanza: Portrait of a Composer*, 50.

72. alcides lanza and author, email communication, 17 August 2015.

73. Diary entry, 7 October 1963, "Latin American Diary Sept–Oct 1963," box/folder 245/9, CCLC.

74. León Schidlowsky and author, communication, 16 August 2014. I contacted Schidlowsky in August 2014. His son David Schidlowsky kindly wrote down his father's recollections, which he sent me from Tel Aviv, where both reside. They are reproduced here. I was unable to interview Juan Orrego-Salas, who died in 2019. But see his "Aaron Copland, Un Músico de Nueva York."

75. Ibid.

# Recommended Reading

Abrams Ansari, Emily. "Aaron Copland and the Politics of Cultural Diplomacy." *Journal of the Society for American Music* 5, no. 3 (2011): 334–69.
———. *The Sound of a Superpower: Musical Americanism and the Cold War.* New York: Oxford University Press, 2018.
Arndt, Richard T. *The First Resort of Kings: American Cultural Diplomacy in the Twentieth Century.* Washington, DC: Potomac, 2005.
Azzi, Susanna, and Simon Collier. *Le Grand Tango: The Life and Music of Astor Piazzolla.* New York: Oxford University Press, 2000.
Béhague, Gerard. *Heitor Villa-Lobos: The Search for Brazil's Musical Soul.* Austin: Institute of Latin American Studies, University of Texas at Austin, 1994.
Bermúdez, Egberto. "Toward a History of Colombian Musics." In *The Colombia Reader: History, Culture, Politics,* edited by Ann Farnsworth-Alvear, Ana María Gómez López, and Marco Palacios, 75–87. Durham, NC: Duke University Press, 2017.
Borge, Jason. *Tropical Riffs: Latin America and the Politics of Jazz.* Durham, NC: Duke University Press, 2018.
Briggs, O. Ellis. *Proud Servant: The Memoirs of a Career Ambassador.* Kent, OH: Kent State University Press, 1998.
Burns, William J. *The Back Channel: A Memoir of American Diplomacy and the Case for Its Renewal.* New York: Random, 2019.
Butterworth, Neil. *The Music of Aaron Copland.* London: Toccata, 1985.
Campbell, Jennifer L. "Creating Something Out of Nothing: The Office of Inter-American Affairs Music Committee (1940–1941) and the Inception of a Policy for Musical Diplomacy." *Diplomatic History* 26, no. 1 (2012): 29–39.
Cándida Smith, Richard. *Improvised Continent: Pan Americanism and Cultural Exchange.* Philadelphia: University of Pennsylvania Press, 2017.

Carroll, Mark. *Music and Ideology in Cold War Europe*. Cambridge: Cambridge University Press, 2003.

Copland, Aaron. *Our New Music: Leading Composers in Europe and America*. New York: McGraw-Hill, 1941.

Copland, Aaron, and Vivian Perlis. *Copland, 1900–1942*. New York: St. Martin's, 1984.

———. *Copland since 1943*. New York: St. Martin's, 1989.

Crist, Elizabeth B. *Music for the Common Man: Aaron Copland during the Depression and War*. Oxford: Oxford University Press, 2005.

Crist, Elizabeth B., and Wayne D. Shirley. *The Selected Correspondence of Aaron Copland*. New Haven, CT: Yale University Press, 2006.

Davenport, Lisa. *Jazz Diplomacy: Promoting America in the Cold War*. Jackson: Mississippi University Press, 2009.

DeLapp-Birkett, Jennifer. "Aaron Copland and the Politics of Twelve-Tone Composition in the Early Cold War United States." *Journal of Musicological Research* 27, no. 1 (2008): 31–62.

Delpar, Helen. *The Enormous Vogue of Things Mexican: Cultural Relations between the United States and Mexico, 1920–1935*. Tuscaloosa: University of Alabama Press, 1992.

Dickinson, Peter, ed. *Copland Connotations: Studies and Interviews*. Rochester, NY: Boydell and Brewer, 2002.

Espinosa, José Manuel. *Inter-American Beginnings of U.S. Cultural Diplomacy, 1936–1948*. Washington, DC: U.S. Department of State, 1976.

Fagg, John Edwin. *Pan Americanism*. Malabar, FL: Krieger, 1982.

Fauser, Annegret. *Aaron Copland's Appalachian Spring*. New York: Oxford University Press, 2017.

———. *Sounds of War: Music in the United States during World War II*. New York: Oxford University Press, 2013.

Fosler-Lussier, Danielle. *Music in America's Cold War Diplomacy*. Oakland: University of California Press, 2015.

Gellman, Irwin F. *Good Neighbor Diplomacy: United States Policies in Latin America, 1933–1945*. Baltimore, MD: Johns Hopkins University Press, 1979.

Gienow-Hecht, Jessica C. E. *Sound Diplomacy: Music and Emotions in Transatlantic Relations, 1850–1920*. Chicago: University of Chicago Press, 2009.

Griffith, Robert. *The Politics of Fear: Joseph McCarthy and the Senate*. 2nd ed. Amherst: University of Massachusetts Press, 1987.

Hanke, Lewis, ed. *Do the Americas Have a Common History? A Critique of the Bolton Theory*. New York: Knopf, 1964.

Herrera, Eduardo. *Elite Art Worlds: Philanthropy, Latin Americanism, and Avant-Garde Music*. New York: Oxford University Press, 2020.

Hess, Carol A. *Representing the Good Neighbor: Music, Difference, and the Pan American Dream*. New York: Oxford University Press, 2013.

Holden, Robert H., and Eric Zolov, eds. *Latin America and the United States: A Documentary History*. New York: Oxford University Press, 2000.

Hubbs, Nadine. *The Queer Composition of America's Sound*. Berkeley: University of California Press, 2004.

Katz, Mark. *Build: Hip Hop Diplomacy in a Divided World.* New York: Oxford University Press, 2020.
Kenworthy, Eldon. *America/Américas: Myth in the Making of U.S. Policy toward Latin America.* University Park: Pennsylvania State University Press, 1995.
Kostelanetz, Richard, ed. *Aaron Copland, A Reader: Selected Writings 1923–1972.* New York: Routledge, 2004.
Kuss, Malena, ed. *Music in Latin America and the Caribbean: An Encyclopedic History.* Austin: University of Texas Press, 2004.
Labonville, Marie Elizabeth. *Juan Bautista Plaza and Musical Nationalism in Venezuela.* Bloomington: Indiana University Press, 2007.
Leonard, Thomas M., and John F. Bratzel, eds. *Latin America during World War II.* Lanham, MD: Rowman and Littlefield, 2007.
Levy, Beth E. *Frontier Figures: American Music and the Mythology of the American West.* Berkeley: University of California Press, 2012.
Madrid, Alejandro L. *In Search of Julián Carrillo & Sonido 13.* New York: Oxford University Press, 2015.
Magaldi, Cristina. *Music in Imperial Rio de Janeiro: European Culture in a Tropical Milieu.* Lanham, MD: Scarecrow, 2004.
Murchison, Gayle. *The American Stravinsky: The Style and Aesthetics of Copland's New American Music, the Early Works, 1921–1938.* Ann Arbor: University of Michigan Press, 2012.
Ninkovich, Frank A. *The Diplomacy of Ideas: U.S. Foreign Policy and Cultural Relations, 1938–1950.* Cambridge: Cambridge University Press, 1981.
Oja, Carol J. *Bernstein Meets Broadway: Collaborative Art in a Time of War.* New York: Oxford University Press, 2014.
Oja, Carol J., and Judith Tick, eds. *Aaron Copland and His World.* Princeton, NJ: Princeton University Press, 2005.
Parker, Robert L. "Copland and Chávez: Brothers-in-Arms." *American Music* 5, no. 4 (1987): 433–44.
Pollack, Howard. *Aaron Copland: The Life and Work of an Uncommon Man.* New York: Holt, 1999.
Raymont, Henry. *Troubled Neighbors: The Story of U.S.–Latin American Relations from FDR to the Present.* Boulder, CO: Westview, 2005.
Reuss, Richard A., and JoAnne C. Reuss. *American Folk Music and Left-Wing Politics, 1927–1957.* Lanham, MD: Scarecrow, 2000.
Rivas, Darlene. *Missionary Capitalist: Nelson Rockefeller in Venezuela.* Chapel Hill: University of North Carolina Press, 2002.
Rosenberg, Emily S. *Financial Missionaries to the World: The Politics and Culture of Dollar Diplomacy, 1900–1930.* Cambridge, MA: Harvard University Press, 1999.
Ross, Alex. *The Rest Is Noise: Listening to the Twentieth Century.* New York: Farrar, Straus, and Giroux, 2007.
Saavedra, Leonora, ed. *Carlos Chávez and His World.* Princeton, NJ: Princeton University Press, 2015.

Sadlier, Darlene J. *Americans All: Good Neighbor Cultural Diplomacy in World War II.* Austin: University of Texas, 2012.

Skidmore, Thomas E., and Peter H. Smith. *Modern Latin America.* 6th ed. New York: Oxford University Press, 2005.

Slonimsky, Nicolas. *Music of Latin America.* New York: Crowell, 1945.

Steichen, James. *Balanchine and Kirstein's American Enterprise.* New York: Oxford University Press, 2019.

Stevenson, Robert M. *Music of Mexico: A Historical Survey.* New York: Crowell, 1952.

Suarez, Ray. *Latino Americans: The 500-Year Legacy That Shaped a Nation.* New York: Penguin, 2013.

Tota, Antonio Pedro. *Seduction of Brazil: The Americanization of Brazil during World War II.* Austin: University of Texas Press, 2009.

Wade, Peter. *Race and Ethnicity in Latin America.* London: Pluto, 1997.

Woll, Allen L. *The Latin Image in American Film.* Rev. ed. Los Angeles: UCLA Latin American Center, 1997.

# Index

*Admiral Graf Spee*, 71
Adomian, Lan, 212
Advis, Luis, 229
Agea, Francisco, 212
Agee, James, 199
Agrella, Neftalí, 114
Aguirre Cerda, Pedro, 114
*A Hora do Brasil. See Hora do Brasil, A*
Alessandri, Jorge, 226
Alimonda, Altéia, 49, 177, 179
Alimonda, Heitor, 177
All-American Youth Orchestra, 39
Allende, Pedro Humberto, 112–14, 118; *Doce tonadas de carácter chileno popular*, 112–13; *Escenas campesinas*, 118
Allende, Salvador, 228, 230, 296n137
Alliance for Progress (AFP), 188, 208
Almanac Singers, 130–31
Amado, Jorge, 95
Ameche, Don, 108
Amengual, René, 111, 125, 129, 138–39
American Ballet Caravan, 47, 53, 58, 68–69, 87, 98, 109. *See also* Kirstein, Lincoln
American Composers Alliance, 31
American Conservatory. *See* Conservatoire Américain
American Musicological Society, 27, 131

American-Soviet Friendship Committee, 155, 192
American Specialists Program, 209, 219, 236, 249, 251. *See also* State Department
Anderson, Marian, 43, 204
Andrews Sisters, 40
Andrade, Ayres de, 102
Andrade, Mário de, 104–5, 106, 125
Ansermet, Ernest, 84
anti-Semitism, 8, 16, 20–21, 76, 77, 83, 88–89, 217
Arbenz, Jacobo, 208
Archer, Violet, 292n1
Ardévol, José, 122–23, 131, 156, 205
Armour, Norman, 78
Armstrong, Louis, 116, 204
Arrau, Claudio, 221, 226
Arvey, Verna, 60
Auden, W. H., 27
Ávila Camacho, Manuel, 58, 140
Axis, 4–5, 25, 58, 62, 64, 71, 77, 93, 128, 140, 154
Ayala, Daniel, 59, 60, 129
Ayarza, Rosa Mercedes, 65
Ayestarán, Lauro, 161, 217

Babbitt, Milton, 189, 232, 297n155

## Index

Bach, Johann Sebastian, 41, 77, 87, 88, 92, 95, 108, 126, 129, 286n150. See also *Bachianas brasileiras*
Backhaus, Wilhelm, 179
Baker, Josephine, 115
Balanchine, George, 47, 53, 69, 98–99
Baldomir, Alfredo, 71
Baldwin, James, 115
Bal y Gay, Jesús, 61
Balzo, Hugo, 71, 73, 74, 86, 130–31, 161
Baqueiro Fóster, Gerónimo, 61
Barber, Samuel, 40, 175, 183, 184, 194, 216, 238, 242, 251
Barbour, Philip L., 28, 37, 70, 131
Barrows, John, 41, 277n85
Bartholomew, Marshall, 28, 36, 37, 46, 162
Bartók, Béla, 38, 86, 167
Basie, William James (Count), 115, 277n64
Batista, Fulgencio, 208
Batlle Berres, Luis, 159
Bautista, Julián, 163, 226
Beattie, John W., 44, 95–96, 97
Becerra, Gustavo, 229, 246, 296n137
Belton, William, 179
Beltroy, Manuel, 66, 67
Benítez, Nena, 123
Bennett, Robert Russell, 40, 98
Berkeley, Lennox, 185
Berkshire Music Center, 31, 32, 44, 53; and Latin America, 49, 59, 155–58, 173, 177, 185, 196, 205, 215, 229, 252. See also Tanglewood
Berle, Adolph, 29, 250
Bernstein, Leonard, 31, 136, 160, 169, 176, 189, 191, 230; and Latin America, 50, 132, 173, 175, 178, 184, 211
Berrien, William, 28, 36
Bessie, Alvah C., 199–200, 201, 291n68
Biden, Joseph R., 250
Billings, William, 172, 175
Bisquertt, Próspero, 110, 227
Bliss, Mildred Barnes, 27, 207
Bliss, Robert Woods, 27, 207
Blitzstein, Marc, 23, 67, 79, 191, 252–53; *Airborne Symphony*, 175, 176
Bloch, Ernest, 79
Bolaños, César, 229
Bolognini, Remo, 121
Borges, Jorge Luis, 81

Borup, Edgar, 210
Boston Symphony Orchestra, 17, 18, 23, 50, 86, 133, 137, 159; and Latin America, 49
Boulanger, Nadia, 12, 14, 18, 207, 215, 247; and Latin America, 65, 93, 187, 204, 233
Boult, Adrian, 23
Bowles, Paul, 47, 64, 123
Braden, Spruille, 37, 162
Braga, Antônio Francisco, 28
Brandão, José Vieira, 96, 97–98, 125, 221, 282n15
*branqueamento*, 24
Brenner, Anita, 22, 213
Bressols, Narciso, 154
Briggs, Arthur, 259n74
Briggs, O. Ellis, 3, 24, 160, 161
Bristow, George, 175
Brown, Earle, 223
Bruce, William Cabell, 105
Buchwald, Theo, 66
Buckley, William F., 190
Buenos Aires Convention for the Promotion of Inter-American Cultural Relations, 5, 155
Burns, Robert, 73
Busch, Fritz, 77, 128
Bush, George W., 249, 250
Büsser, Henri, 73

Calloway, Cabell (Cab), 115
Calmon, Pedro, 44
Calvo, Esther de, 132
Camargo Guarnieri, Mozart. See Guarnieri, Mozart Camargo
Campo, Conrado del, 109
Canal Zone, 62, 131
Caracas Festival of Latin American Music, First, 204–6, 233
Caracas Festival of Latin American Music, Second, 238, 240, 252
Cárdenas, Lázaro, 136
Cardoza y Aragón, Luis, 208
Carnegie Corporation, 46, 49, 204
Carpenter, John Alden, 42
Carpentier, Alejo, 7, 204, 221, 292n101, 295n80
Carpio Valdés, Roberto, 65
Carrillo, Julián, 212, 293n27
Carter, Elliott, 20

Carvajal, Armando, 118
Carvalho, Eleazar de, 156, 169, 173, 210
Casal Chapí, Enrique, 161
Casella, Alfredo, 82
Castañeda, Jorge, 132
Castelo Branco, Humberto de Alencar, 236
Castro, Fidel, 208
Castro, José María, 6, 91, 99, 100, 124, 125, 128, 129, 162, 183, 185; *Concerto for Orchestra*, 86, 245; Concerto Grosso, 85; *Piezas breves*, 129; *Sonata de primavera*, 85–86, 130
Castro, Juan José, 6, 80, 86, 128, 156, 226; as composer, 84, 88; and folklore, 81; and Perón, 157, 162, 164; in United States, 77–78, 121–22, 131
Castro, Juan José, Sr., 84
Castro, Washington, 85; *Concerto for Orchestra*, 245
Castro, Sergio de, 74, 125, 162
Castronuovo, Orestes, 87
Caturla, Alejandro García, 16, 122, 127, 221
Caymmi, Dorival, 170, 179, 184
Central Intelligence Agency (CIA), 154, 188, 199, 208, 237; Congress for Cultural Freedom, 188
Centro Latinoamericano de Altos Estudios Musicales. *See* CLAEM
Chagas, Paulo, 246
Chanler, Theodor, 31, 68, 251
Chapin, Katherine (Biddle), 44
Chase, Gilbert, 27, 41, 59, 63, 110, 131, 158, 212, 223, 241; *Music of the New World*, 129
Chávez, Carlos, 6, 59, 60, 61, 82, 127, 129, 130, 195, 196, 211, 213, 221, 235, 247; Copland on, 15–16; and Copland's music, 18, 22, 23; in United States, 15–16, 22, 42, 133
Chávez, Carlos, Ives and Copland on, 212; "North Carolina Blues," 45; Piano Sonata no. 3, 15–16; Sonatinas (for solo piano, cello and piano, violin and piano), 15–16; Symphony no. 3, 205
Cherrington, Ben, 26, 139
Cincinnati Symphony Orchestra, 39, 130, 133, 159, 298n15
Citkowitz, Israel, 79, 162
CLAEM (Centro Latinoamericano de Altos Estudios Musicales), 197, 219, 222–24, 226, 237, 253

Clark, Evans, 28, 36, 37, 41, 47
Cleveland Institute of Music, 38
Cleveland Orchestra, 39, 273n1
Club de Jazz de Chile, 115
Cluzeau Mortet, Luis, 73
Cohen, Ethel, 158
Cohn, Roy M., 202
Cold War, 5–6, 153–55, 185–86, 204, 243–45, 249; and music, 188–89, 191–93, 212
Cole, Charles W., 228, 233
Colligan, Francis J., 158
Columbia Broadcasting Service (CBS), 19, 28, 37, 48, 130, 131, 132
communism, 5, 18–19, 29, 58, 135, 190, 237, 299n24; and cultural diplomacy, 208–9; and homosexuality, 190; in Latin America, 154, 186, 214, 237, 240; and U.S. culture, 188–89, 194, 200–201, 218, 228, 229. *See also* Copland, Aaron; political activities
Composers Collective, 18–19, 21, 212
Conciertos de la Nueva Música, 52, 89, 91
Cone, Edward T., 265n105, 290n65
Conference on Inter-American Relations in the Field of Music, First, 27–29, 36, 43, 44, 207
Conjunto Vacarno, 70, 123
Conservatoire Américain, 11
Contreras, Salvador, 48, 59, 60; *Pieza*, 48
Convention for the Promotion of Inter-American Cultural Relations, 5, 155
Coolidge, Elizabeth Sprague, 47
Copland, Aaron: and anti-Semitism, 16, 20–21, 88–89, 217; awards, 137, 203; Brazilian popular music, 102, 103–4, 153, 170, 180, 181–83, 184, 253; as conductor, 12, 68–69, 159–60; communism, 211, 228 (*see also* Copland, Aaron, and McCarthyism); Cuban music, 50, 104, 122; dementia, 12, 238; eclecticism, 6, 13, 21, 22, 52, 89, 137, 167–68, 174, 197, 226; essentialism, 9, 126, 127, 246; family, 11, 159, 279n48; folklore, 9, 21–22, 31, 79, 80, 123, 126, 137, 168, 194, 199, 206, 227–28; homosexuality, 6, 11, 87, 171, 190, 230; jazz, 13, 16–17, 20, 21–22, 30, 80, 117, 123, 125, 171; Jewishness, 6, 11, 20, 21, 79, 87, 88–89, 254; libraries, 10, 12, 40, 48, 125, 130, 172–73, 202; and McCarthyism, 6, 190–93, 199–204, 205;

Copland, Aaron (*continued*): and modernism, 6, 14, 18, 23, 40, 53, 88, 91, 166, 168, 174, 194–95, 210, 213, 224, 225, 231–33; and Music Advisory Committee, 27, 44, 51; and nationalism, 14, 30, 247; and Office of Inter-American Affairs (OIAA), 32, 35–38, 45, 47–49, 51–52, 75, 87, 91, 117, 124; and Pan Americanism, 15–16, 57, 71, 106, 120, 208, 248; political activities, 6, 18–20, 138, 191–93;and radio, 8, 10, 19, 23, 30, 37, 40, 48, 63–64, 66–67, 72, 78–79, 80, 102, 120, 125, 130, 159, 161–62, 169, 170, 175–76, 183, 219; and State Department, 8, 10, 11, 51, 93, 125, 140, 153, 155, 158, 159, 183–84, 190, 193, 203, 219; and twelve-tone music, 9, 31, 127, 176–77, 181, 193, 194, 198, 206, 212, 218–19; universalism, 9, 14, 15, 30–31, 154, 159–61, 168, 194–95, 210–13

—works: *Appalachian Spring*, 137, 155, 159, 160, 164, 165, 166, 167, 197, 210, 222, 224, 235, 246; *As It Fell upon a Day*, 13, 36, 101; Ballad Concerto (unfinished), 9; *Billy the Kid*, 29–30, 40, 47, 53, 58, 66, 68–70, 75, 79, 91, 133, 137, 225, 230, 231; Blues no. 1, 17, 72; Blues no. 2, 17, 181; *The City*, 54, 259n66; Clarinet Concerto, 169–71, 220, 285n109; *Connotations*, 218–19, 225, 227, 230, 253; *The Cummington Story*, 138, 163–64, 172, 179, 250; *Danzón cubano*, 136, 166, 167, 197, 208; *El salón México*, orchestral version, 6, 23, 29, 38, 40, 53, 63, 73, 79, 118, 119, 123, 136, 197, 208, 210, 213–14, 215, 224, 227, 231, 248; *El salón México*, two-piano version, 13; *Fanfare for the Common Man*, 133, 137; *The Heiress*, 193; "The House on the Hill," 22; *Humoristic Scherzo: The Cat and the Mouse Day*, 17, 175, 233, 258n35; "An Immortality," 22; "Into the Streets May First!," 19, 116, 138; *Lincoln Portrait*, 133–36, 157, 159, 160, 164–65, 167, 201–2, 214–15, 231, 238–44; *Music for Radio: Saga of the Prairie*, 19, 37; *Music for the Theatre*, 3, 16, 17, 22, 42, 47, 63, 68, 123, 215; Nonet, 207–8; *The North Star*, 137; *Of Mice and Men*, 20, 53, 73, 101, 137; *Orchestral Variations*, 216, 225; Organ Symphony (First Symphony), 14, 17; *Our Town*, 20, 53, 73, 172, 179; *An Outdoor Overture*, 20, 80, 87–89, 90, 91, 118–19, 159, 161, 164, 165, 197, 215, 224; Piano Concerto, 17, 117–19; Piano Fantasy, 9, 206, 212; Piano Quartet, 198, 206, 218, 234; Piano Sonata, 90, 91, 101, 106, 123, 124, 173, 197; Piano Variations, 13, 18, 20, 22, 23, 52, 53, 91, 166, 167, 179, 179, 216; *Preamble for a Solemn Occasion*, 189, 198; *Quiet City*, 20, 68, 73, 118, 119, 123, 225, 279n47; *Rodeo*, 136, 181, 197, 222, 231; *The Second Hurricane*, 19; Short Symphony (Second Symphony), 18, 22; Sonata for Violin and Piano, 137, 166–67, 174, 175, 179, 231; *Statements*, 20, 138, 211, 213, 215, 224, 230; *Sunday Afternoon Music*, 259n64; *Symphonic Ode*, orchestral version, 18, 22, 218; *Symphonic Ode*, two-piano version, 13; *The Tender Land*, 199; *The Tender Land*, suite, 199, 211, 213, 216, 224; Third Symphony, 137, 138, 156, 165, 167, 173–74, 206, 210, 224, 230, 231; *Three Latin-American Sketches*, 206, 208, 246, 293n41; *Three Moods*, 17; *Time Table*. See *Music for the Theatre*; *Twelve Poems of Emily Dickinson*, 198, 231; *Two Pieces* (for string quartet), 18, 22, 166, 174, 179; *Two Pieces* (for violin and piano), 17; *Vitebsk*, 13, 20, 79, 174, 254; *What Do We Plant?*, 259n64; *The Young Pioneers*, 259n64

—writings and public statements: "Carlos Chávez—Mexican Composer," 15–16; "Composer From Brooklyn: An Autobiographical Sketch," 30; "The Composers of South America," 126–28; "Composer's Report on Music in South America," 184; "Effect of the Cold War on the Artist in the U.S.," 191–93; "Fauré, A Neglected Master," 85–86; "Jazz Structure and Influence," 17; *Music and Imagination*, 194–95; *Music in the Twenties*, 246–47; *Our New Music*, 30–31, 50, 67, 79, 117, 155; "The Pleasures of Music," 217; *What to Listen for in Music*, 30, 293n31; "Workers Sing!" 19

Copland-Sessions Concerts, 15
Cordero, Roque, 156, 196, 246
Cosme, Luiz, 178
Costa, Lucio, 94

Cotapos, Acario, 111; *Voces de Gesta*, 111
Covarrubias, Miguel, 42
Cowell, Henry, 16, 20, 52, 90, 122, 133, 158, 188, 207, 245; *Fanfare to the Forces of Our Latin American Allies*, 133, 245; "United" String Quartet, 90
Cowell, Sidney, 188
Creel, George, 8
Crosby, Bing, 36
Cuatro Huasos, Los, 113–14
Cultural and Scientific Conference for World Peace, 191–93, 194, 200
cultural diplomacy, 3, 4–9, 23–26; and Axis, 33, 43, 57, 89, 94, 130, 135; as defense, 25, 34, 37; and folk music, 28, 29, 37; and jazz, 34–35, 37, 41–42, 204, 209; and music, general, 10, 26–29; and race, 25, 29, 44–46, 119; vs. public diplomacy, 255n3
Curtis, Louis Woodson, 44, 95, 96, 97

Dallapiccola, Luigi, 198, 221, 233
Dallas Symphony Orchestra, 60
Damrosch, Walter, 17–18
Dantón, Jorge, 164
Davidovsky, Mario, 6, 8, 252–53
Dawson, William, 72
Dawson, William L., 29
Declaration of Lima, 26
Defauw, Désiré, 129
Department of State, U.S. *See* State Department
Desennes, Paul, 246
Dett, R. (Robert) Nathaniel, 29, 119
Devoto, Daniel, 6, 290n58
Diamond, David, 79, 225
Dies, Martin, 29
Disney, Walt, 39, 75, 141, 230; *Saludos amigos!* 34, 128–29; *The Three Caballeros*, 180
Division of Cultural Relations, 5, 27, 29, 32, 34, 36, 51, 57, 140, 190; and Latin America, 25, 94, 139
Division of the American Republics, 24, 25, 34, 190
Dominican Republic, 4, 5, 237
Dorfman, Ariel, 230, 297n140
Douglas, Stephen, 135
Downes, Olin, 23, 48, 82, 111, 140, 191, 192, 257n4; and Villa-Lobos, 131, 139

Drezner, Manuel, 234, 235
Dualde, Hugo, 159
Duarte de Perón, María Eva (Evita), 162
Du Bois, William Edward Burghardt (W. E. B.), 43, 105
Duggan, Laurence, 25, 29, 34, 190
Dumbarton Oaks Research Library and Collection, 207
Durán, Gustavo, 37, 41, 44, 53–54, 131, 190
Durán, Sixto, 64
Dushkin, Samuel, 61, 132
Dutra, Eurico, 140

Eastman School of Music, 28, 133
Eisenhower, Dwight D., 188, 201, 204, 243, 249, 250
Eitler, Esteban, 90
Eitler, Stefan (Esteban), 196
Elkus, Albert, 129
Ellington, Edward Kennedy (Duke), 42, 115, 116, 117, 295n80
Escobar, Luis Antonio, 234, 297n165
Espinosa, Guillermo, 62, 63, 207
Espinosa, J. Manuel, 6, 26, 250
Estévez, Antonio, 156, 205; *Concerto for Orchestra*, 207, 245
Estrada, Carlos, 73–74
Etkin, Mariano, 223
Etler, Alvin, 41, 119
Evans, Walker, 199
Evanti, Lillian (Annie Lillian Evans), 29, 43
Evergood, Philip, 108

Fabini, Eduardo, 73
Fairbanks, Douglas, Jr., 39
Faulkner, William, 45
Fauré, Gabriel, 85, 86, 214
Federal Bureau of Investigation (FBI), 193, 199
Fels, Samuel Simeon, 100
Fergusson, Erna, 107
Fernández, Oscar Lorenzo, 36, 92, 178, 193; *Batuque*, 92, 178
Fernández Moreno, César, 78
Festival of Pan-American Chamber Music, 47, 60, 82
Ficher, Jacobo, 82–83, 86, 129, 162, 163, 226, 271n37

Fiene, Ernest, 108
Fitelberg, Grzegorz, 129
Fleisher, Edwin Adler, 47, 100
Focke, Fré, 196, 227, 228
Foster, Stephen, 197
Franck, César, 63
Frank, Waldo, 15, 39–40, 77, 126, 195
Franklin, Albert B., 164
Freedman, Harry, 292n1
Free Library of Philadelphia, 47
Freeman, Fulton, 234
Freitas, María de, 37, 52
Freitas e Castro, Ênio, 179
Fromm Foundation, 185
Fuchs, Joseph, 208
Fuchs, Teodoro, 252
Fulbright, J. William, 203
Fuller, Donald, 48

Gaitán, Jorge Eliécer, 235
Galindo Dimas, Blas, 49, 50, 59–60, 129, 156; *Sones mariachi*, 60
Gandini, Gerardo, 223
García, Fernando, 228–29
García Morillo, Roberto, 82, 86, 88, 129, 156
Gardel, Carlos, 163, 233
Garrido, Pablo, 114–17, 118, 125, 227, 228
Garrido-Lecca, Celso, 227, 230
Gates, Robert M., 249
Gershwin, George, 40, 122, 179, 184, 197, 246, and cultural diplomacy, 208, 251
Gianneo, Luis, 87, 124, 129, 131, 162, 183, 185, 226
Gide, André, 26, 82, 251
Gielen, Michael, 163
Gilbert, Henry F., 40
Gillespie, Dizzy, 209
Ginastera, Alberto, 6, 32, 86–87, 124, 125, 129, 130, 185, 198, 219, 226, 253; and the Centro Latinoamericano de Altos Estudios Musicales (CLAEM), 222–23, 237; Copland on, 87, 127–28; on Copland, 165, 167; and Perón, 157, 162, 164; in United States, 156, 157, 207
—works: *Doce preludios americanos*, 156, 245; *Estancia*, 87, 272n59; *Hieremiae prophetae lamentationes*, 157; *Panambí*, 86; *Sinfonía porteña*, 86, 128, 167
Gnattali, Radames, 36, 98, 125

Gold, Mike, 19
Goldschmidt, Albert (Alberto), 118–19
Gomes, Antônio Carlos, 92
Gómez, Luis Ernesto, 245
Goodman, Benny, 169, 285n109
Good Neighbor policy, 4–5, 7, 12, 23–26, 32, 40, 71, 74, 75, 89, 133, 168, 173–74, 192, 204, 237; and advertising, 76, 129; and aviation, 58; demise of, 154, 185–86, 244; and Hollywood, 25, 58, 40, 41, 73, 78, 108, 135–36; musical values of, 4, 5, 15, 16, 35, 39, 69–71, 86, 88, 110, 116, 124, 179, 225, 227; nostalgia for, 250; popularity of, 34, 47, 129, 130; and tourism, 58
goodwill tours, 39–41, 51, 124, 178, 204, 209
Goossens, Eugene, 39, 133, 159, 263n38
Gordon, Lincoln, 214, 221, 236
Gorrell, Juan, 64
Goulart, João, 214, 236
Gould, Morton, 98, 246
Graetzer, Wilhelm (Guillermo), 77, 163, 252
Graham, Martha, 137
Gramatges, Harold, 123, 156, 229
Grant, Margaret, 49
Great Depression, 4, 18, 20, 73, 80
Greiff, Otto de, 62, 63, 233, 242
Griffes, Charles, 175
Gropp, Arthur E., 158
Group Theatre, 20, 171
Gruenberg, Louis, 79
Grupo de los Cuatro, 59
Grupo Renovación (Argentina), 52, 81, 85, 157
Guarnieri, Mozart Camargo, 6, 36, 106, 124, 125, 131, 179, 185, 198, 245, 289n16; Copland on, 99–101, 127, 129; on twelve-tone music, 195–96; in the United States, 132–33, 207
—works: *Abertura concertante*, 132–33; *Dança brasileira*, 133; *Encantamento*, 100, 133; Second String Quartet, 179, 246; Violin Concerto, 100
Guatemala, 5, 41, 62, 132, 208, 214
Guerra-Peixe, César, 174, 177, 183, 286n152
Guevara, Ernesto (Che), 208, 229, 237
Guggenheim Foundation, 14, 34, 49, 51, 52, 70, 78, 84, 156, 185, 223, 253, 288n1; and McCarthyism, 199–201
Guillén, Nicolás, 229

# Index

Haiti, 4, 42
Halffter, Cristóbal, 223
Halffter, Rodolfo, 61, 196, 212
Hanson, Howard, 28, 100, 133
Harris, Roy, 16, 17, 36, 67, 68, 101, 184; Piano Trio, 72, 90, 123; Third Symphony, 40, 63–64, 67, 175, 216, 225, 238, 242
Hawkes, Ralph, 156
Hawkins, Coleman, 116
Hayes, Alfred, 19, 116
Hayes, Roland, 43
Heinlein, Federico, 7, 230–33
Hemingway, Ernest, 37, 171
Henze, Hans Werner, 221
Herzog, George, 41
Hiller, Lejaren, 253
Hindemith, Paul, 38, 41, 77, 109, 252
Hitler, Adolf, 4, 27, 43, 62, 77, 83, 89, 93, 121, 130, 264n74
Holiday, Billie, 115
Holzmann, Rudolf (Rodolfo), 65, 66, 87, 196
Hoover, Herbert, 4, 33
Hoover, J. Edgar, 199
Hopkinson, Francis, 175
Hopper, Edward, 108, 220
*Hora do Brasil, A*, 102
Horwitz, Leonard B., 140
House Un-American Activities Committee (HUAC), 6, 29, 189–90, 193, 204, 213, 242
Houston, Elsie, 27, 121
Howard University Choir, 209
Hoyen, George, 28, 35
Hughes, Langston, 19, 45, 200, 201
Hull, Cordell, 5, 33, 77, 141
Hume, Paul, 201–2
Hurtado, Leopoldo, 6, 79–80, 90, 127–28, 155, 183
Huston, John, 244

Ianelli, Alfredo, 49
d'Indy, Vincent, 62, 84
Institute of International Education (IEE), 156, 190
Instituto Interamericano de Musicología (Montevideo), 27, 72, 161
Inter-American Conference for the Maintenance of Continental Peace and Security, 153
Inter-American Conferences, 4, 5
Inter-American Music Festivals, 207. *See also* Conference on Inter-American Relations in the Field of Music, First
International Society for Contemporary Music (ISCM), 47, 48, 52, 59, 82, 129, 177
Isaacson, Leonard, 253
Isamitt, Carlos, 111, 112, 124, 125, 227
Iturriaga, Enrique, 66, 233, 297n160
Ives, Charles, 16, 40, 101, 172, 188; and Copland, 197–98, 210–13; *The Unanswered Question*, 211, 213, 216, 225, 238; as universal, 210–13

Jacob, Paul Walter, 77
Jacobi, Frederick, 49
Jatobá, Paulo, 180
jazz: in Latin America, 22, 41–52, 59, 72, 113–17, 227, 228; and racism, 16, 20, 41, 113–14, 120; and reputation of U.S. culture, 26, 34, 37, 78, 161, 171. *See also* Copland, Aaron: jazz; cultural diplomacy: jazz
Jewish musicians in Latin America, 77, 163, 173, 252
Jijena Sánchez, Rafael, 86
Johnson, Lyndon B., 236, 237
Josetti, Rodolpho, 43, 264n74
Juárez, Benito, 135
*Juárez. See* Good Neighbor policy; Hollywood
Justa, Helen, 115

Kagel, Mauricio, 207
Kahn, Erminie, 157–58
Katunda, Eunice, 177, 286n150
Kazanjian, Reginald S., 94, 139
Keele, Harold, 199–201
Keller, Kerry, 115
Kennan, George, 185–86, 244
Kennedy, Jacqueline, 221
Kennedy, John F., 188, 208, 214, 226, 234, 236
Kennedy, Robert F., 226
Keppel, Frederick, 46
Kern, Jerome, 133
Kinsky, Robert (Roberto), 77
Kirby, John, 117
Kirkpatrick, John, 13, 48, 290n56
Kirstein, Lincoln, 29, 47, 53, 58, 68, 69, 75, 131; and Latin American music, 87, 98–99, 109, 272n61

Knoll, Sofía, 90
Knott, Sarah Gertrude, 41
Koechlin, Charles, 100, 268n37
Koellreutter, Hans Joachim, 99, 174, 176–77, 179, 184, 195–96, 198, 272n42
Kondrashin, Kyril, 210
Korngold, Erich, 136
Kostelanetz, André, 133
Koussevitzky, Sergey, 17, 31, 50, 68, 97, 117, 155, 159; and Latin America, 49, 100, 156, 173
Koussevitzky Foundation, 185
Kraft, Victor, 169, 183, 210, 220, 284n98
Krenek, Ernst, 5, 77
Krieger, Edino, 177, 185, 215
Krombholc, Jaroslav, 173
Kröpfl, Francisco, 196–97
Krueger, Karl, 48
Kubik, Gail, 238

Lacerda, Benedito, 170, 179
Lange, Francisco Curt, 7, 27, 28, 42, 72, 74, 129, 161; "Americanismo musical," 27, 71; *Boletín latino-americano de música*, 72
lanza, alcides, 8, 253
Latin Americanism (in music), 222
Latin American Music Center (LAMC), Indiana University, 110
League of Composers (Liga de Compositores, Argentina), 162, 184
League of Composers (United States), 14, 31, 41, 121, 131, 201, 293n27
League of Composers Woodwind Quintet, 41, 47, 53, 54, 119
Leibowitz, René, 241
Leng, Alfonso, 110, 227
León, Tania, 246
Letelier, Alfonso, 110
Leuchter, Erwin, 77, 163, 252
Levant, Oscar, 42, 48
Limantour, José Yves, 61
Lincoln, Abraham, 133–35, 243; in Latin America, 135–36
Lippman, Walter, 78
Lôbo, Fernando, 153, 170
Loesser, Arthur, 38, 64, 189
Loesser, Frank, 38
Lomax, Alan, 41

Lombado, Guy, 50
López Contreras, Eleazar, 33
Lorentz, Pare, 25, 259n66
Lorenz, Ricardo, 245
Loring, Eugene, 69
Loriod, Yvonne, 223
Luce, Clare Boothe, 205
Luening, Otto, 205
Lunceford, Jimmie, 115
Lymes, Russell, 171
lynching, 25, 44–45, 115, 209, 260n108

Macdonald, Dwight, 171
MacDowell, Edward, 40
MacLeish, Archibald, 27, 44
Maiguashca, Mesías, 8, 223
Malipiero, Gian Francesco, 81, 82
Malipiero, Riccardo, 226
Mañé Garzón, Pablo, 7, 217–18
Maristany, Christina, 101
Martínez King, Isidora, 108
Marx, Burle, 27, 92, 178, 273n1
Mason, Daniel Gregory, 20
Masselos, William, 211–12
Maturana, Eduardo, 196, 228
Mayer Serra, Otto, 61
Maynor, Dorothy, 43
McBride, Robert, 40, 41, 53, 119
McCarthy, Joseph, 6, 190, 193, 199, 202–5. See also Copland, Aaron: McCarthyism; State Department: McCarthyism
McClellan, John, 202
McKay, Neil, 292n1
McPhee, Colin, 45–46, 99, 137
Mejía, Adolfo, 62, 87, 268n37
Mendel, Arthur, 18
Menin, Peter, 173, 174, 185
Merman, Ethel, 36
Mesquita, Esther, 132
Messiaen, Olivier, 223
*mestizaje*, 24, 112
Mexican-U.S. War, 4
Mignone, Francisco, 33, 36, 41, 92, 99, 124, 178; *Fantasia Brasileira* no. 4, 92–93; *Maractú de Chico-Rei*, 92, 99, 182
Milhaud, Darius, 17, 60, 61, 79, 129, 134, 185, 221; *Saudades do Brasil*, 167
Miranda, Carmen, 103, 108

# Index

Mistral, Gabriela, 110, 113, 115, 226
Mitchell, Howard, 210
Mitropoulos, Dimitri, 156
Moe, Henry Allen, 34, 44, 46, 50, 51, 52; and McCarthyism, 199–201
Moncayo, José Pablo, 59, 124, 125; *Huapango*, 60–61, 133
Montealegre, Felicia, 226
Montecino, Marcelo, 49
Morales, Gustavo, 122
Morel, François, 292n1
Mozart, Wolfgang Amadeus, 41, 138
Muller, Angela, 211
Mumford, Lewis, 259n66
Munch, Charles, 48
Mundt, Karl, 202
Museum of Modern Art (MoMA), 60, 121, 132
Música Viva, 176, 177, 196
Music Educators National Conference (MENC), 132
Mussolini, Benito, 93, 95, 121
Myrdal, Gunnar, 292n98

National Broadcasting Company (NBC), 28, 37, 129, 130. *See also* Chase, Gilbert: *Music of the New World*
National Council on American-Soviet Friendship, 155
NBC Symphony Orchestra, 23, 57, 121, 178
Negrete, Samuel, 110–11
neoclassicism (in music), 26, 81, 82, 84, 85, 91, 109, 122, 174, 221, 223, 224. *See also* Ardévol, José; Castro, José María; Castro, Juan José; Santa Cruz, Domingo
Neruda, Pablo, 226, 229
Neschling, John, 221–23
New Deal, 5, 25, 134
New School for Social Research, 13, 15, 30
New York Philharmonic, 185, 209, 218
New York Public Library, 27, 82, 131
Nicholson, Carlos, 70
Niemeyer, Oscar, 94
Nin-Culmell, Joaquín, 27, 61
Nixon, Richard M., 237, 244
Nobre, Marlos, 223
Nogueira França, Eurico, 7, 100, 172, 174, 197, 254; on musical "totalitarianism," 215

Nono, Luigi, 223
Norweb, R. Henry, 70
Novaes, Guiomar, 38, 221, 263n33

Obama, Barack, 249, 250
Ocampo, Victoria, 26, 45, 226; on jazz, 42, 295n80
Occidental College, 139
O'Farrill, Arturo, 251
Office of Inter-American Affairs (OIAA), 32–35, 46, 70, 75, 76, 89, 140, 154, 200, 204, 262n2; OIAA Committee on Art, 131; OIAA Motion Picture Division, 34, 128; OIAA Music Committee, 35–38, 40–43, 45, 47–49, 51, 52, 58, 87, 94, 105, 117, 124, 130, 189, 216; OIAA Radio Division, 130, 131. *See also* Copland, Aaron; Office of Inter-American Affairs (OIAA) and
Oliver, María Rosa, 163
Olivier, Sir Laurence, 189
Onganía, Juan Carlos, 237
Oram, Frank H., 214, 221
Oram, Mary, 214, 221
Orbón, Julián, 156, 157, 211; *Homenaje a la tonadilla*, 205
Organization of American States (OAS), 185; music division, 207
Orquestra Sinfônica Brasileira (OSB), 169, 210
Orquesta Sinfónica de Chile, 117, 230, 231, 233
Orquesta Sinfónica del Servicio Oficial de Difusión Radioeléctrica (OSSODRE, Uruguay), 71, 73, 74, 210
Orquesta Sinfónica de México (OSM), 18, 45, 59, 211
Orquesta Sinfónica de Venezuela, 204
Orquesta Sinfónica de Yucatán, 43
Orquesta Sinfónica Nacional de Colombia, 62, 234–35
Orquesta Sinfónica Nacional del Perú, 66
Orrego-Salas, Juan, 7, 12, 124, 125, 227, 229; in the United States, 110, 156; *Variations for a Quiet Man*, 246
Ortega, Sergio, 228, 237
Ortega-Miranda, Chañaral, 246
Ortiz, Gabriela, 246
Ortiz, Pablo, 246

Oteiza, Enrique, 222
O'Toole, Donald Lawrence, 199
Ovalle, Jayme, 98

Padua, Newton, 98
Palacios, Inocente, 204, 206, 240
Pan American Airways (System), 58
Pan American Association of Composers (PAAC), 16, 38, 111, 122; and anti-Semitism, 16
Pan American Day, 4, 38, 250
Pan American Festival of Chamber Music, 47, 60, 82
Pan Americanism, 3–4, 7, 33, 138–41; and music, 5–6, 49, 102, 118–19, 128–33
Pan American Union, 4, 5, 34, 43, 185; and music, 26, 28, 33, 44, 46, 100, 112, 130–32, 133, 156
Panassié, Hugh, 115
Paraskevaídis, Graciela, 8, 223
Pardo Tovar, Andrés, 242
Parker, H. T. (Henry Taylor), 18
Parmenter, Ross, 51
Pattee, Richard, 25–26
Pawley, William D., 154
Paz, Juan Carlos, 6, 32, 42, 81, 86, 89, 129, 162, 196, 199, 211, 215; Copland on, 83–84, 124, 127–28, 246; on Copland, 52–53, 90–91, 197–98; on Ginastera, 167; *Música para trío*, 48; *Passacaglia*, 48; *Tres movimientos de jazz*, 42
Pearl Harbor, attack, 57, 65, 121, 128
Pedrell, Carlos, 73
Pedrell, Felipe, 73, 112
People to People Program. *See* State Department
Pérez Jiménez, Marcos, 205, 238, 240, 243, 244, 292n105
Perle, George, 52
Perlis, Vivian, 247
Perón, Juan Domingo, 140, 157, 162, 165, 222, 240, 282n27. *See also* Castro, Juan José: and Perón; Ginastera, Alberto: and Perón
Pershing, General John, 11
Piazzolla, Astor, 163, 185
Picchi, Silvano, 225

Pierre Degeyter Club, 18
Pisk, Paul, 52, 79
Piston, Walter, 40, 67, 81, 101, 174, 175, 183, 184; *Carnival Song*, 64, 123; and universalism, 194–95
Pixinguinha (Alfredo da Rocha Viana Filho), 170, 179
Pizzetti, Idelbrando, 82
Plaza, Gonzálo, 239
Plaza, Juan Bautista, 129; in the United States, 131, 132
Ponce, Manuel, 72, 129
Popular Front, 18, 252
Porter, Quincy, 36
Portinari, Cândido, 178
Posada Amador, Carlos, 62
Posselt, Ruth, 48
Prado, Manuel, 65, 70, 136
Prado, Pedro, 110
President's Special International Program for Cultural Presentations. *See* State Department
propaganda, 4, 8, 33, 34, 43, 44–45, 57, 58, 77, 102, 138, 209
Purcell, Edward, T., 10, 209–10, 216

racism, 9, 19, 24–25, 105, 106, 119, 130, 185, 250. *See also* jazz; racism
radio, 4, 33, 57, 63, 65, 71, 80, 85, 87, 89, 98, 114, 121, 122, 129, 130, 202; and Office of Inter-American Affairs (OIAA), 41, 131. *See also* Copland, Aaron: radio
Ramey, Phillip, 171, 238
Raygada, Carlos, 65, 69
*Reader's Digest*, 76, 78, 80, 168
Reichold, Henry Helmut, 155, 156
Revueltas, Silvestre, 16, 59, 195, 247, 289n41; "Canto de una muchacha negra," 45; *Sensemayá*, 221; String quartets nos. 3 and 4, 47–48
Rexach, Conchita, 32, 37, 53, 269n60
Ricordi (Buenos Aires), 33, 34
Riegger, Wallingford, 16
Rietti, Vittorio, 82
Rivadavia, Bernardino, 38
Rivera, Diego, 15
Robeson, Paul, 43

# Index

Rockefeller, Abby Aldrich, 15
Rockefeller, Nelson A., 33, 34, 36, 49, 51, 57, 60, 76, 79, 89, 91, 102. *See also* Office of Inter-American Affairs (OIAA)
Rockefeller Foundation, 46, 110, 132, 156, 222, 237. *See also* CLAEM (Centro Latinoamericano de Altos Estudios Musicales)
Rodrigo, Joaquín, 241
Rodziński, Artur, 38
Rogers, Bernard, 79
Roig, Gonzalo, 27
Rojas Pinilla, Gustavo, 234, 235
Roldán, Amadeo, 16, 122, 123, 127, 221
Roosevelt, Eleanor, 189
Roosevelt, Franklin D., 3, 4–5, 19, 23–24, 25, 33, 34, 58, 121, 138, 141, 153, 154, 204; and Abraham Lincoln, 133, 135; and concept of Good Neighbor, 5, 193; and McCarthyism, 190, 192
Roots, Olaf, 235
Rosas, Juan Manuel, 135
Rosay, Lily, 66
Rosenfeld, Paul, 15, 16, 17, 20, 92, 114, 171
Rubinstein, Artur, 73, 96, 273n26
Rubirosa, María Isabel, 123
Ruggles, Carl, 258n28
Rzewski, Frederic, 237

Saenz, Moisés, 70
Saint Maló, Alfredo de, 27
Salas Pereira, Eugenio, 35, 108, 115, 256n25
Salas Viu, Vicente, 112
Salazar, Adolfo, 7, 61, 197
Salazar, Antônio de Oliveira, 93
Salter, William Mackintire, 105
Salzman, Eric, 223
Samaroff, Olga, 44
samba, 25, 44, 103–4, 153, 170, 253. *See also* Copland, Aaron: Brazilian popular music
Saminsky, Lazare, 21, 79, 88; on Latin American music, 52, 82, 83, 84
Sanborn, Pitts, 23
Sánchez, Manuel, 209
Sánchez de Fuentes, Eduardo, 27
Sánchez Málaga, Carlos, 65, 70, 233
Sandburg, Carl, 133
Sandi, Luis, 132, 212

San Francisco Ballet, 209
Sangree, Carl, 138, 164
Sanjuan, Pedro, 129
Sanromá, Jesús María, 48
Santa Cruz, Domingo, 6, 107, 108, 126, 128, 198, 204, 221, 227, 229, 230, 233; *Five Pieces* (for string orchestra), 109–10; and "occidentalism," 34, 107, 109, 120; in United States, 34, 131–32, 207
Santoro, Cláudio, 99, 124, 125, 174, 176, 177, 286n144; and communism, 185, 187
Santórsola, Guido, 159, 160, 161
Santos, Eduardo, 62, 63
Santos, Gustavo, 63
Santos, Paulo, 215
Santovenia, Emeterio, 135
Sá Pereira, Antônio, 49, 96, 98, 132
Sarmiento, Domingo Faustino, 135
Sas, Andrés, 65, 66, 70, 127; *Cantos del Perú*, 66, 245; *Quenas*, 59
Satie, Erik, 62, 160
Sayao, Bidu, 92
Scherchen, Hermann, 177, 178
Schidlowsky, León, 8, 227, 229, 254, 300n74
Schine, David, 202
Schoenberg, Arnold, 19, 38, 77, 79, 134, 163, 185, 191, 193, 194, 198, 222, 231, 233; Woodwind Quintet, op. 26, 31
Schola Cantorum, 62, 81, 84
Schuman, William, 173, 174, 184, 216
Scottsboro Boys, 19, 45
Sebastiani, Pía, 162, 185
Second Workers Music Olympiad, 19, 116, 138
Seeger, Charles, 18, 19, 28, 43, 45, 46, 96, 131
Segovia, Andrés, 72
Servicio Oficial de Difusión Radio Eléctrica (SODRE), 71, 72, 216, 217, 218
Sessions, Roger, 15, 67, 81, 126, 223; *Chorale-Preludes*, 72, 90; and jazz, 17; and universalism, 194–95
Sevareid, Eric, 178
Shaw, Irwin, 20
Shostakovich, Dmitry, 137, 167, 191, 197–98, 281n103
Siccardi, Honorio, 81, 82, 85, 86, 124
Siegmeister, Elie, 19

Sierra, Roberto, 245, 248
Simon and Garfunkel, duo, 66
Simpson, Sid, 199, 200
Singer, Jacques, 60
Slonimsky, Nicolas, 16, 47, 63, 66, 82, 83, 85, 90, 98, 104, 109, 111, 133, 251
Smith, Carleton Sprague, 27, 28–29, 33, 57, 110, 118, 131, 158; and Brazil, 36, 102, 103, 104–5, 216; and Office of Inter-American Affairs (OIAA) 35, 38, 39, 40, 42, 43, 44, 46, 53, 54, 94
Smith, Warren Storey, 18, 137
Sociedade de Cultura Artistica, 43
Somers, Harry, 292n1
Southern Music, 66
Spanish-American War, 4
Spanish Civil War, 19, 37, 135, 161, 190, 199, 213; Mexico and, 61. *See also* Copland; political activities
Spies, Claudio, 156
Spiller, Ljerko, 166
Spivak, Raúl, 166
Stalin, Josef, 121, 193
State Department, 3, 8, 10, 11, 12, 39, 54, 162, 183, 184, 219, 233, 237; American Specialists Program, 209, 249; Cultural Centers, 158, 173, 184, 202; and Good Neighbor Policy, 5, 25, 29, 34, 46, 51, 57, 58, 79, 108, 131; and McCarthyism, 190, 199, 201, 202–3, 204; People to People Program, 204, 249; President's Special International Program for Cultural Presentations, 204, 249; Sub-Committee on Musical Interchange with the U.S.S.R., 140, 155; Visiting Professor Program, 153, 158, 159, 183. *See also* Copland, Aaron: and State Department
Stearns, Harold, 15, 20
Steinbeck, John, 20, 73
Steiner, Ralph, 259n56
Stevens, David H., 46
Stevenson, Robert M., 155, 223
Stieglitz, Alfred, 171
Still, William Grant, 40, 43; *Afro-American Symphony*, 40, 43; *And They Lynched Him On a Tree*, 44–45, 46, 105, 200; *From the Black Belt*, 43; *Song of a City*, 43; "Y lo colgaron de un árbol," 45

Stokowski, Leopold, 39, 43
Strang, Gerald, 52, 90
Straus, Noel, 66, 271n39
Strauss, Richard, 73, 110, 137
Stravinsky, Igor, 17, 19, 22, 27, 61, 86, 90, 134, 166, 181, 205, 221, 231; and Juan José Castro, 84; and Latin America, 26, 38, 68, 77, 88, 89, 128, 167
Stravinsky, Vera, 221
Suarez, Ray, 248–49
Sub-Committee on Musical Interchange with the U.S.S.R. *See* State Department
Suffern, Carlos, 6, 82, 129, 166–68, 174, 197, 225
Sujovolsky, Anita, 90, 239
Sujovolsky (Sujo), Juana, 238, 239, 240–43, 283n44
*Sur*, 26, 45, 122, 165
Syndeman, William, 251
Szenkar, Eugen (Jenö Szenkár), 173

Talamón, Gastón, 113
Tanglewood, 31, 49, 59, 155, 297n155. *See also* Berkshire Music Center
Taruskin, Richard, 26
Tatum, Art, 42
Taubman, Howard, 60, 121, 136, 138, 201–2, 241–42, 243
Taylor, Davidson, 28, 37, 44, 46, 48, 130
Teatro Colón (Bogotá), 234–35
Teatro Colón (Buenos Aires), 26, 77, 80, 86, 87, 157, 162, 164, 167, 225
Teatro del Pueblo, 83, 89
Teatro Solís, 71
Thompson, Charles, 139
Thompson, Oscar, 23, 92
Thompson, Randall, 40
Thomson, Virgil, 21, 30, 47, 67, 68, 80, 101, 133, 138, 193, 238; on Latin American music, 48, 132, 241, 279n67, 298n16
Toledo Museum of Art, 131
Toro, Mercedes de, 162
Tosar, Héctor, 74, 124, 125, 127, 131, 156, 157, 159, 160, 161, 185, 282n16, 283n60; Concertino, 74, 159, 205
Toscanini, Arturo, 39, 71, 178, 202
Tourel, Jennie, 132
Town Hall, 20, 130

Trueblood, Edward G., 35, 266n127
Truman, Harry S., 153, 154
Trump, Donald, 249, 250, 251
Tucker, Richard, 221
Turina, Joaquín, 62
Turner, Philip A., 220, 227, 231

United States Information Agency (USIA), 249
universalism in music, 9, 10, 14, 23, 86, 95–95, 100, 113, 122, 139, 154, 161, 194–95, 211–12; and cultural diplomacy, 25–26, 30–32, 34, 38, 168
University of Michigan Jazz Band, 237
D'Urbano, Jorge, 7, 84, 164–66, 167, 197, 224, 225
Uribe Holguín, Guillermo, 62, 63, 87, 125, 127; *Suite típica*, 63; *Trozos en el sentimiento popular*, 63
Ussachevksy, Vladimir, 223, 253

Valcárcel, Edgar, 223, 246
Valdés, Gilberto, 122
Valle-Inclán, Ramón del, 111
Valencia, Antonio, 62
Valenti Ferro, Enrique, 168
Van Vactor, David, 41, 119
Varèse, Edgard, 16, 232, 253; *Amériques*, 40
Vargas, Getúlio, 93–95, 102, 103, 104, 139, 140; and *brasilidade*, 94
Velasco Maidana, José María, 33
Veríssimo, Érico, 139, 179
Verlaine, Paul, 74
Verneuil, Raoul de, 65
Viana Filho, Afredo da Rocha. *See* Pixinguinha
Vianna, Fructuosa, 129
Viñes, Ricardo, 112
Villa-Lobos, Heitor, 15, 36, 41, 92–94, 103–4, 156, 172, 178, 221; Copland on, 100, 125, 127, 205, 247; in United States, 92, 94, 96–97, 129, 131, 133, 139; Vargas government and, 94–95
—works: *Bachianas brasileiras*, 92, 95; *Choros 11*, 96; *Choros no. 8*, 92, 94; String Quartet no. 6, 96–97, 245
Villaurrutia, Xavier, 45
Vincent, John, 223
Visiting Professor Program. *See* State Department

Warfield, William, 221, 251
Webb, James H., 211
Webern, Anton, 77, 196
Weil, Germán, 90
Weill, Kurt, 77, 79
Weingartner, Felix, 62
Weinzweig, John, 292n1
Weiss, Adolph, 41, 119
Welles, Orson, 25, 44, 103, 176, 180
Welles, Sumner, 24, 34, 51, 190
whitening. *See branqueamento*
Wilder, Alec, 47, 68
Wilder, Thornton, 20, 39
Williams, Alberto, 28
Winchell, Walter, 36, 37
Wolff, Albert, 68, 162–63
Works Progress Administration (WPA), 28, 47, 59, 199
World's Fair, 1939–40, 27, 43, 92, 94, 99, 113

Xancó, Ernesto, 176
Xenakis, Iannis, 223, 232

Yaddo Festival, 18, 31
Yale Glee Club, 28, 40, 47, 96

Zagarra, Alejandro, 49
Zhdanov, Andrei, *zhdanovismo*, 187, 192, 215

Carol A. Hess is a professor of musicology at the University of California, Davis. She is the author of *Experiencing Latin American Music* and *Representing the Good Neighbor: Music, Difference, and the Pan American Dream*.

# Music in American Life

Only a Miner: Studies in Recorded Coal-Mining Songs   *Archie Green*
Great Day Coming: Folk Music and the American Left   *R. Serge Denisoff*
John Philip Sousa: A Descriptive Catalog of His Works   *Paul E. Bierley*
The Hell-Bound Train: A Cowboy Songbook   *Glenn Ohrlin*
Oh, Didn't He Ramble: The Life Story of Lee Collins, as Told to Mary Collins
   *Edited by Frank J. Gillis and John W. Miner*
American Labor Songs of the Nineteenth Century   *Philip S. Foner*
Stars of Country Music: Uncle Dave Macon to Johnny Rodriguez
   *Edited by Bill C. Malone and Judith McCulloh*
Git Along, Little Dogies: Songs and Songmakers of the American West   *John I. White*
A Texas-Mexican *Cancionero*: Folksongs of the Lower Border   *Américo Paredes*
San Antonio Rose: The Life and Music of Bob Wills   *Charles R. Townsend*
Early Downhome Blues: A Musical and Cultural Analysis   *Jeff Todd Titon*
An Ives Celebration: Papers and Panels of the Charles Ives Centennial Festival-
   Conference   *Edited by H. Wiley Hitchcock and Vivian Perlis*
Sinful Tunes and Spirituals: Black Folk Music to the Civil War   *Dena J. Epstein*
Joe Scott, the Woodsman-Songmaker   *Edward D. Ives*
Jimmie Rodgers: The Life and Times of America's Blue Yodeler   *Nolan Porterfield*
Early American Music Engraving and Printing: A History of Music Publishing in
   America from 1787 to 1825, with Commentary on Earlier and Later Practices
   *Richard J. Wolfe*
Sing a Sad Song: The Life of Hank Williams   *Roger M. Williams*
Long Steel Rail: The Railroad in American Folksong   *Norm Cohen*
Resources of American Music History: A Directory of Source Materials from Colonial
   Times to World War II   *D. W. Krummel, Jean Geil, Doris J. Dyen, and Deane L. Root*
Tenement Songs: The Popular Music of the Jewish Immigrants   *Mark Slobin*
Ozark Folksongs   *Vance Randolph; edited and abridged by Norm Cohen*
Oscar Sonneck and American Music   *Edited by William Lichtenwanger*
Bluegrass Breakdown: The Making of the Old Southern Sound   *Robert Cantwell*
Bluegrass: A History   *Neil V. Rosenberg*
Music at the White House: A History of the American Spirit   *Elise K. Kirk*
Red River Blues: The Blues Tradition in the Southeast   *Bruce Bastin*
Good Friends and Bad Enemies: Robert Winslow Gordon and the Study of American
   Folksong   *Debora Kodish*
Fiddlin' Georgia Crazy: Fiddlin' John Carson, His Real World, and the World of His
   Songs   *Gene Wiggins*
America's Music: From the Pilgrims to the Present (rev. 3d ed.)   *Gilbert Chase*
Secular Music in Colonial Annapolis: The Tuesday Club, 1745–56   *John Barry Talley*
Bibliographical Handbook of American Music   *D. W. Krummel*
Goin' to Kansas City   *Nathan W. Pearson Jr.*
"Susanna," "Jeanie," and "The Old Folks at Home": The Songs of Stephen C. Foster
   from His Time to Ours (2d ed.)   *William W. Austin*
Songprints: The Musical Experience of Five Shoshone Women   *Judith Vander*

"Happy in the Service of the Lord": Afro-American Gospel Quartets in Memphis
 *Kip Lornell*
Paul Hindemith in the United States   *Luther Noss*
"My Song Is My Weapon": People's Songs, American Communism, and the Politics of
 Culture, 1930–50   *Robbie Lieberman*
Chosen Voices: The Story of the American Cantorate   *Mark Slobin*
Theodore Thomas: America's Conductor and Builder of Orchestras, 1835–1905
 *Ezra Schabas*
"The Whorehouse Bells Were Ringing" and Other Songs Cowboys Sing
 *Collected and Edited by Guy Logsdon*
Crazeology: The Autobiography of a Chicago Jazzman   *Bud Freeman,
 as Told to Robert Wolf*
Discoursing Sweet Music: Brass Bands and Community Life in Turn-of-the-Century
 Pennsylvania   *Kenneth Kreitner*
Mormonism and Music: A History   *Michael Hicks*
Voices of the Jazz Age: Profiles of Eight Vintage Jazzmen   *Chip Deffaa*
Pickin' on Peachtree: A History of Country Music in Atlanta, Georgia
 *Wayne W. Daniel*
Bitter Music: Collected Journals, Essays, Introductions, and Librettos   *Harry Partch;
 edited by Thomas McGeary*
Ethnic Music on Records: A Discography of Ethnic Recordings Produced in the United
 States, 1893 to 1942   *Richard K. Spottswood*
Downhome Blues Lyrics: An Anthology from the Post–World War II Era
 *Jeff Todd Titon*
Ellington: The Early Years   *Mark Tucker*
Chicago Soul   *Robert Pruter*
That Half-Barbaric Twang: The Banjo in American Popular Culture   *Karen Linn*
Hot Man: The Life of Art Hodes   *Art Hodes and Chadwick Hansen*
The Erotic Muse: American Bawdy Songs (2d ed.)   *Ed Cray*
Barrio Rhythm: Mexican American Music in Los Angeles   *Steven Loza*
The Creation of Jazz: Music, Race, and Culture in Urban America   *Burton W. Peretti*
Charles Martin Loeffler: A Life Apart in Music   *Ellen Knight*
Club Date Musicians: Playing the New York Party Circuit   *Bruce A. MacLeod*
Opera on the Road: Traveling Opera Troupes in the United States, 1825–60
 *Katherine K. Preston*
The Stonemans: An Appalachian Family and the Music That Shaped Their Lives
 *Ivan M. Tribe*
Transforming Tradition: Folk Music Revivals Examined   *Edited by Neil V. Rosenberg*
The Crooked Stovepipe: Athapaskan Fiddle Music and Square Dancing in Northeast
 Alaska and Northwest Canada   *Craig Mishler*
Traveling the High Way Home: Ralph Stanley and the World of Traditional Bluegrass
 Music   *John Wright*
Carl Ruggles: Composer, Painter, and Storyteller   *Marilyn Ziffrin*
Never without a Song: The Years and Songs of Jennie Devlin, 1865–1952
 *Katharine D. Newman*

The Hank Snow Story   *Hank Snow, with Jack Ownbey and Bob Burris*
Milton Brown and the Founding of Western Swing   *Cary Ginell,
    with special assistance from Roy Lee Brown*
Santiago de Murcia's "Códice Saldívar No. 4": A Treasury of Secular Guitar Music from
    Baroque Mexico   *Craig H. Russell*
The Sound of the Dove: Singing in Appalachian Primitive Baptist Churches
    *Beverly Bush Patterson*
Heartland Excursions: Ethnomusicological Reflections on Schools of Music
    *Bruno Nettl*
Doowop: The Chicago Scene   *Robert Pruter*
Blue Rhythms: Six Lives in Rhythm and Blues   *Chip Deffaa*
Shoshone Ghost Dance Religion: Poetry Songs and Great Basin Context
    *Judith Vander*
Go Cat Go! Rockabilly Music and Its Makers   *Craig Morrison*
'Twas Only an Irishman's Dream: The Image of Ireland and the Irish in American
    Popular Song Lyrics, 1800–1920   *William H. A. Williams*
Democracy at the Opera: Music, Theater, and Culture in New York City, 1815–60
    *Karen Ahlquist*
Fred Waring and the Pennsylvanians   *Virginia Waring*
Woody, Cisco, and Me: Seamen Three in the Merchant Marine   *Jim Longhi*
Behind the Burnt Cork Mask: Early Blackface Minstrelsy and Antebellum American
    Popular Culture   *William J. Mahar*
Going to Cincinnati: A History of the Blues in the Queen City   *Steven C. Tracy*
Pistol Packin' Mama: Aunt Molly Jackson and the Politics of Folksong   *Shelly Romalis*
Sixties Rock: Garage, Psychedelic, and Other Satisfactions   *Michael Hicks*
The Late Great Johnny Ace and the Transition from R&B to Rock 'n' Roll
    *James M. Salem*
Tito Puente and the Making of Latin Music   *Steven Loza*
Juilliard: A History   *Andrea Olmstead*
Understanding Charles Seeger, Pioneer in American Musicology   *Edited by Bell Yung
    and Helen Rees*
Mountains of Music: West Virginia Traditional Music from *Goldenseal*
    *Edited by John Lilly*
Alice Tully: An Intimate Portrait   *Albert Fuller*
A Blues Life   *Henry Townsend, as told to Bill Greensmith*
Long Steel Rail: The Railroad in American Folksong (2d ed.)   *Norm Cohen*
The Golden Age of Gospel   *Text by Horace Clarence Boyer; photography by Lloyd Yearwood*
Aaron Copland: The Life and Work of an Uncommon Man   *Howard Pollack*
Louis Moreau Gottschalk   *S. Frederick Starr*
Race, Rock, and Elvis   *Michael T. Bertrand*
Theremin: Ether Music and Espionage   *Albert Glinsky*
Poetry and Violence: The Ballad Tradition of Mexico's Costa Chica   *John H. McDowell*
The Bill Monroe Reader   *Edited by Tom Ewing*
Music in Lubavitcher Life   *Ellen Koskoff*
Zarzuela: Spanish Operetta, American Stage   *Janet L. Sturman*

Bluegrass Odyssey: A Documentary in Pictures and Words, 1966–86   *Carl Fleischhauer and Neil V. Rosenberg*
That Old-Time Rock & Roll: A Chronicle of an Era, 1954–63   *Richard Aquila*
Labor's Troubadour   *Joe Glazer*
American Opera   *Elise K. Kirk*
Don't Get above Your Raisin': Country Music and the Southern Working Class   *Bill C. Malone*
John Alden Carpenter: A Chicago Composer   *Howard Pollack*
Heartbeat of the People: Music and Dance of the Northern Pow-wow   *Tara Browner*
My Lord, What a Morning: An Autobiography   *Marian Anderson*
Marian Anderson: A Singer's Journey   *Allan Keiler*
Charles Ives Remembered: An Oral History   *Vivian Perlis*
Henry Cowell, Bohemian   *Michael Hicks*
Rap Music and Street Consciousness   *Cheryl L. Keyes*
Louis Prima   *Garry Boulard*
Marian McPartland's Jazz World: All in Good Time   *Marian McPartland*
Robert Johnson: Lost and Found   *Barry Lee Pearson and Bill McCulloch*
Bound for America: Three British Composers   *Nicholas Temperley*
Lost Sounds: Blacks and the Birth of the Recording Industry, 1890–1919   *Tim Brooks*
Burn, Baby! BURN! The Autobiography of Magnificent Montague   *Magnificent Montague with Bob Baker*
Way Up North in Dixie: A Black Family's Claim to the Confederate Anthem   *Howard L. Sacks and Judith Rose Sacks*
The Bluegrass Reader   *Edited by Thomas Goldsmith*
Colin McPhee: Composer in Two Worlds   *Carol J. Oja*
Robert Johnson, Mythmaking, and Contemporary American Culture   *Patricia R. Schroeder*
Composing a World: Lou Harrison, Musical Wayfarer   *Leta E. Miller and Fredric Lieberman*
Fritz Reiner, Maestro and Martinet   *Kenneth Morgan*
That Toddlin' Town: Chicago's White Dance Bands and Orchestras, 1900–1950   *Charles A. Sengstock Jr.*
Dewey and Elvis: The Life and Times of a Rock 'n' Roll Deejay   *Louis Cantor*
Come Hither to Go Yonder: Playing Bluegrass with Bill Monroe   *Bob Black*
Chicago Blues: Portraits and Stories   *David Whiteis*
The Incredible Band of John Philip Sousa   *Paul E. Bierley*
"Maximum Clarity" and Other Writings on Music   *Ben Johnston, edited by Bob Gilmore*
Staging Tradition: John Lair and Sarah Gertrude Knott   *Michael Ann Williams*
Homegrown Music: Discovering Bluegrass   *Stephanie P. Ledgin*
Tales of a Theatrical Guru   *Danny Newman*
The Music of Bill Monroe   *Neil V. Rosenberg and Charles K. Wolfe*
Pressing On: The Roni Stoneman Story   *Roni Stoneman, as told to Ellen Wright*
Together Let Us Sweetly Live   *Jonathan C. David, with photographs by Richard Holloway*
Live Fast, Love Hard: The Faron Young Story   *Diane Diekman*
Air Castle of the South: WSM Radio and the Making of Music City   *Craig P. Havighurst*

Traveling Home: Sacred Harp Singing and American Pluralism   *Kiri Miller*
Where Did Our Love Go? The Rise and Fall of the Motown Sound   *Nelson George*
Lonesome Cowgirls and Honky-Tonk Angels: The Women of Barn Dance
    Radio   *Kristine M. McCusker*
California Polyphony: Ethnic Voices, Musical Crossroads   *Mina Yang*
The Never-Ending Revival: Rounder Records and the Folk Alliance   *Michael F. Scully*
Sing It Pretty: A Memoir   *Bess Lomax Hawes*
Working Girl Blues: The Life and Music of Hazel Dickens   *Hazel Dickens
    and Bill C. Malone*
Charles Ives Reconsidered   *Gayle Sherwood Magee*
The Hayloft Gang: The Story of the National Barn Dance   *Edited by Chad Berry*
Country Music Humorists and Comedians   *Loyal Jones*
Record Makers and Breakers: Voices of the Independent Rock 'n' Roll Pioneers
    *John Broven*
Music of the First Nations: Tradition and Innovation in Native North America
    *Edited by Tara Browner*
Cafe Society: The Wrong Place for the Right People   *Barney Josephson,
    with Terry Trilling-Josephson*
George Gershwin: An Intimate Portrait   *Walter Rimler*
Life Flows On in Endless Song: Folk Songs and American History   *Robert V. Wells*
I Feel a Song Coming On: The Life of Jimmy McHugh   *Alyn Shipton*
King of the Queen City: The Story of King Records   *Jon Hartley Fox*
Long Lost Blues: Popular Blues in America, 1850–1920   *Peter C. Muir*
Hard Luck Blues: Roots Music Photographs from the Great Depression
    *Rich Remsberg*
Restless Giant: The Life and Times of Jean Aberbach and Hill and Range Songs
    *Bar Biszick-Lockwood*
Champagne Charlie and Pretty Jemima: Variety Theater in the Nineteenth
    Century   *Gillian M. Rodger*
Sacred Steel: Inside an African American Steel Guitar Tradition   *Robert L. Stone*
Gone to the Country: The New Lost City Ramblers and the Folk Music Revival
    *Ray Allen*
The Makers of the Sacred Harp   *David Warren Steel with Richard H. Hulan*
Woody Guthrie, American Radical   *Will Kaufman*
George Szell: A Life of Music   *Michael Charry*
Bean Blossom: The Brown County Jamboree and Bill Monroe's Bluegrass
    Festivals   *Thomas A. Adler*
Crowe on the Banjo: The Music Life of J. D. Crowe   *Marty Godbey*
Twentieth Century Drifter: The Life of Marty Robbins   *Diane Diekman*
Henry Mancini: Reinventing Film Music   *John Caps*
The Beautiful Music All Around Us: Field Recordings and the American
    Experience   *Stephen Wade*
Then Sings My Soul: The Culture of Southern Gospel Music   *Douglas Harrison*
The Accordion in the Americas: Klezmer, Polka, Tango, Zydeco, and More!
    *Edited by Helena Simonett*
Bluegrass Bluesman: A Memoir   *Josh Graves, edited by Fred Bartenstein*

One Woman in a Hundred: Edna Phillips and the Philadelphia Orchestra
   *Mary Sue Welsh*
The Great Orchestrator: Arthur Judson and American Arts Management
   *James M. Doering*
Charles Ives in the Mirror: American Histories of an Iconic Composer   *David C. Paul*
Southern Soul-Blues   *David Whiteis*
Sweet Air: Modernism, Regionalism, and American Popular Song
   *Edward P. Comentale*
Pretty Good for a Girl: Women in Bluegrass   *Murphy Hicks Henry*
Sweet Dreams: The World of Patsy Cline   *Warren R. Hofstra*
William Sidney Mount and the Creolization of American Culture   *Christopher J. Smith*
Bird: The Life and Music of Charlie Parker   *Chuck Haddix*
Making the March King: John Philip Sousa's Washington Years, 1854–1893
   *Patrick Warfield*
In It for the Long Run   *Jim Rooney*
Pioneers of the Blues Revival   *Steve Cushing*
Roots of the Revival: American and British Folk Music in the 1950s   *Ronald D. Cohen
   and Rachel Clare Donaldson*
Blues All Day Long: The Jimmy Rogers Story   *Wayne Everett Goins*
Yankee Twang: Country and Western Music in New England   *Clifford R. Murphy*
The Music of the Stanley Brothers   *Gary B. Reid*
Hawaiian Music in Motion: Mariners, Missionaries, and Minstrels   *James Revell Carr*
Sounds of the New Deal: The Federal Music Project in the West   *Peter Gough*
The Mormon Tabernacle Choir: A Biography   *Michael Hicks*
The Man That Got Away: The Life and Songs of Harold Arlen   *Walter Rimler*
A City Called Heaven: Chicago and the Birth of Gospel Music   *Robert M. Marovich*
Blues Unlimited: Essential Interviews from the Original Blues Magazine
   *Edited by Bill Greensmith, Mike Rowe, and Mark Camarigg*
Hoedowns, Reels, and Frolics: Roots and Branches of Southern Appalachian Dance
   *Phil Jamison*
Fannie Bloomfield-Zeisler: The Life and Times of a Piano Virtuoso
   *Beth Abelson Macleod*
Cybersonic Arts: Adventures in American New Music   *Gordon Mumma,
   edited with commentary by Michelle Fillion*
The Magic of Beverly Sills   *Nancy Guy*
Waiting for Buddy Guy   *Alan Harper*
Harry T. Burleigh: From the Spiritual to the Harlem Renaissance   *Jean E. Snyder*
Music in the Age of Anxiety: American Music in the Fifties   *James Wierzbicki*
Jazzing: New York City's Unseen Scene   *Thomas H. Greenland*
A Cole Porter Companion   *Edited by Don M. Randel, Matthew Shaftel,
   and Susan Forscher Weiss*
Foggy Mountain Troubadour: The Life and Music of Curly Seckler   *Penny Parsons*
Blue Rhythm Fantasy: Big Band Jazz Arranging in the Swing Era   *John Wriggle*
Bill Clifton: America's Bluegrass Ambassador to the World   *Bill C. Malone*
Chinatown Opera Theater in North America   *Nancy Yunhwa Rao*
The Elocutionists: Women, Music, and the Spoken Word   *Marian Wilson Kimber*

May Irwin: Singing, Shouting, and the Shadow of Minstrelsy   *Sharon Ammen*
Peggy Seeger: A Life of Music, Love, and Politics   *Jean R. Freedman*
Charles Ives's *Concord*: Essays after a Sonata   *Kyle Gann*
Don't Give Your Heart to a Rambler: My Life with Jimmy Martin, the King of Bluegrass
    *Barbara Martin Stephens*
Libby Larsen: Composing an American Life   *Denise Von Glahn*
George Szell's Reign: Behind the Scenes with the Cleveland Orchestra
    *Marcia Hansen Kraus*
Just One of the Boys: Female-to-Male Cross-Dressing on the American Variety Stage
    *Gillian M. Rodger*
Spirituals and the Birth of a Black Entertainment Industry   *Sandra Jean Graham*
Right to the Juke Joint: A Personal History of American Music   *Patrick B. Mullen*
Bluegrass Generation: A Memoir   *Neil V. Rosenberg*
Pioneers of the Blues Revival, Expanded Second Edition   *Steve Cushing*
Banjo Roots and Branches   *Edited by Robert Winans*
Bill Monroe: The Life and Music of the Blue Grass Man   *Tom Ewing*
Dixie Dewdrop: The Uncle Dave Macon Story   *Michael D. Doubler*
Los Romeros: Royal Family of the Spanish Guitar   *Walter Aaron Clark*
Transforming Women's Education: Liberal Arts and Music in Female Seminaries
    *Jewel A. Smith*
Rethinking American Music   *Edited by Tara Browner and Thomas L. Riis*
Leonard Bernstein and the Language of Jazz   *Katherine Baber*
Dancing Revolution: Bodies, Space, and Sound in American Cultural History
    *Christopher J. Smith*
Peggy Glanville-Hicks: Composer and Critic   *Suzanne Robinson*
Mormons, Musical Theater, and Belonging in America   *Jake Johnson*
Blues Legacy: Tradition and Innovation in Chicago   *David Whiteis*
Blues Before Sunrise 2: Interviews from the Chicago Scene   *Steve Cushing*
The Cashaway Psalmody: Transatlantic Religion and Music in Colonial Carolina
    *Stephen A. Marini*
Earl Scruggs and Foggy Mountain Breakdown: The Making of an American Classic
    *Thomas Goldsmith*
A Guru's Journey: Pandit Chitresh Das and Indian Classical Dance in Diaspora
    *Sarah Morelli*
Unsettled Scores: Politics, Hollywood, and the Film Music of Aaron Copland and
    Hanns Eisler   *Sally Bick*
Hillbilly Maidens, Okies, and Cowgirls: Women's Country Music, 1930–1960
    *Stephanie Vander Wel*
Always the Queen: The Denise LaSalle Story   *Denise LaSalle with David Whiteis*
Artful Noise: Percussion Literature in the Twentieth Century   *Thomas Siwe*
The Heart of a Woman: The Life and Music of Florence B. Price   *Rae Linda Brown,*
    *edited by Guthrie P. Ramsey Jr.*
When Sunday Comes: Gospel Music in the Soul and Hip-Hop Eras
    *Claudrena N. Harold*
The Lady Swings: Memoirs of a Jazz Drummer   *Dottie Dodgion and Wayne Enstice*

Industrial Strength Bluegrass: Southwestern Ohio's Musical Legacy
    *Edited by Fred Bartenstein and Curtis W. Ellison*
Soul on Soul: The Life and Music of Mary Lou Williams    *Tammy L. Kernodle*
Unbinding Gentility: Women Making Music in the Nineteenth-Century
    South    *Candace Bailey*
Punks in Peoria: Making a Scene in the American Heartland    *Jonathan Wright
    and Dawson Barrett*
Homer Rodeheaver and the Rise of the Gospel Music Industry    *Kevin Mungons
    and Douglas Yeo*
Americanaland: Where Country & Western Met Rock 'n' Roll    *John Milward,
    with Portraits by Margie Greve*
Listening to Bob Dylan    *Larry Starr*
Lying in the Middle: Musical Theater and Belief at the Heart of America    *Jake Johnson*
The Sounds of Place: Music and the American Cultural Landscape    *Denise Von Glahn*
Peace Be Still: How James Cleveland and the Angelic Choir Created a Gospel
    Classic    *Robert M. Marovich*
Politics as Sound: The Washington, DC, Hardcore Scene, 1978–1983    *Shayna L. Maskell*
Tania León's Stride: A Polyrhythmic Life    *Alejandro L. Madrid*
Elliott Carter Speaks: Unpublished Lectures    *Edited by Laura Emmery*
Interviews with American Composers: Barney Childs in Conversation
    *Edited by Virginia Anderson*
Queer Country    *Shana Goldin-Perschbacher*
On the Bus with Bill Monroe: My Five-Year Ride with the Father of Blue Grass
    *Mark Hembree*
Mandolin Man: The Bluegrass Life of Roland White    *Bob Black*
Music and Mystique in Muscle Shoals    *Christopher M. Reali*
Buddy Emmons: Steel Guitar Jazzman    *Steve Fishell*
Music in Black American Life, 1600–1945: A University of Illinois Press
    Anthology    *Compiled by Laurie Matheson*
Music in Black American Life, 1945–2020: A University of Illinois Press
    Anthology    *Compiled by Laurie Matheson*
Ballad Hunting with Max Hunter: Stories of an Ozark Folksong Collector
    *Sarah Jane Nelson*
Play Like a Man: My Life in Poster Children    *Rose Marshack*
Samuel Barber: His Life and Legacy    *Howard Pollack*
Aaron Copland in Latin America: Music and Cultural Politics    *Carol A. Hess*

The University of Illinois Press
is a founding member of the
Association of University Presses.

―――――――――――

University of Illinois Press
1325 South Oak Street
Champaign, IL 61820-6903
www.press.uillinois.edu